P9-CEL-680

NOW I CAN DIE IN PEACE

NOW I CAN DIE IN PEACE

How ESPN's Sports Guy Found Salvation, With a Little Help From Nomar, Pedro, Shawshank and the 2004 Red Sox

BILL SIMMONS

"Blood Feud" originally appeared in the April 2002 issue of *Boston* magazine.

For information address ESPN Books, 19 East 34th Street, New York, New York 10016.

ISBN 1-933060-05-0

ESPN Books are available for special promotions and premiums. For details contact Michael Rentas, Assistant Director, Inventory Operations, Hyperion, 77 West 66th Street, 11th floor, New York, New York 10023, or call 212-456-0133.

10 9 8 7 6 5 4 3

For my mom (the writing gene)
and my dad (the Red Sox gene)

CONTENTS

REJUVENATION

October 1998–December 2000

THE ABYSS

March 2001–December 2003

HOPE IS A GOOD THING

February 2004–October 2004

THE GREAT ESCAPE

October 2004–April 2005

PROLOGUE

My editors had to dissuade me from naming this book *Love Child of the Impossible Dream*. The more I thought about it, they were probably right—it sounds like the title of a John Mayer album, or maybe a crappy civil rights epic starring Reese Witherspoon and Omar Epps. And we wouldn't want that. But as the unassuming opening of a prologue about a budding Red Sox fan, it definitely works. You could call me a love child of the Impossible Dream. You really could.

The Impossible Dream happened in 1967, the year the Beatles released *Sgt. Pepper's Lonely Hearts Club Band* and Muhammad Ali uttered the words, "I ain't got no quarrel with those Vietcong." Both of my parents were attending college in Massachusetts that year: my mother at Boston College (in Chestnut Hill), my father at Holy Cross (in Worcester, a 45-minute drive from Fenway Park). Since the Cross was an all-male school at the time[1], Dad would hitchhike on weekends to any town or city with females, fleeing the campus so frequently, one of his old roommates still calls him Suitcase to this day. His most frequent destination was Boston College, where he crashed with an old high school friend named Jay Breslin. Well, you know who else was friends with Jay Breslin? My mother. Known for wearing the shortest miniskirts on campus, she ended up falling for my father, a wannabe hippie from a rival school. And the rest was history.[2]

They didn't pick just any year to fall in love. Before the Impossible Dream season, the Red Sox hadn't captured a World Series in 48 years, an agonizing span featuring one measly pennant and nine consecutive losing seasons since 1958. They were

1 Imagine being stuck at an all-male school in 20-degree weather? Yikes. If you're scoring at home, Holy Cross finally started admitting women in 1972, although they didn't start admitting women who put out until 1999.

2 By the late '70s, hitchhiking was discouraged because serial killers and serial rapists quickly realized that this was an easy way to find potential victims—just cruise around and search for hotties with their thumbs sticking out. In fact, you could call it the **Golden Age of Serial Killing**, with Ted Bundy being the era's Michael Jordan. Then the media went to work. When I was nine years old, I watched a TV movie called *Diary of a Teenage Hitchhiker* (starring Charlene Tilton), which put the fear of God in me and everyone else under 15—all I remember is some creepy dude in a brown van picking up cute hitchhikers as scary synthesizer music played in the background. After that, I wouldn't have hitchhiked at gunpoint. But in the late '60s, everyone hitched rides with no repercussions. And thank God, because my dad didn't have enough money to afford a car and you wouldn't be reading this book right now otherwise.

the morons who sold Babe Ruth, the star-crossed franchise that always fell short, the borderline racists who earned Last Major League Team to Sign a Black Ballplayer status in 1959. With Bill Russell's Celtics infinitely more successful, with Bobby Orr's Bruins infinitely more exciting, the Red Sox had become the Fredo Corleone of the Boston sports scene. So when they emerged from nowhere to contend for the 1967 pennant, everyone in New England rallied around them—a ragtag blend of unproven players, castoffs, and unknown stars who ended up becoming the most famous Boston team of that generation. Carl Yastrzemski won the Triple Crown in his breakout season (nobody has done it since). Jim Lonborg won 22 games and the Cy Young Award (the first in team history). Popular slugger Tony Conigliaro took a beanball from Angels pitcher Jack Hamilton, a sickening moment that everyone in New England would remember like the JFK assassination (Tony C's career was never the same). Despite winning just 92 games, the Sox clinched the American League pennant at a sold-out Fenway Park on the last possible day, and only after about 82 other things fell into place to make it happen. Even when a powerful Cardinals team held them off in the seventh game of the World Series, nobody could complain. The Red Sox were relevant again. And since he was hitching into Boston every weekend, like countless other college students in the area, my father jumped on the Red Sox bandwagon and never looked back.

Now...

There's nothing worse than a bandwagon jumper. If sports were a giant prison and fans were the convicts, bandwagon jumpers would be like child molesters—the lowlifes who crossed the line and deserved to be ridiculed/tortured/humiliated/defiled by everyone else. When they name me Commissioner of Sports some day, I'm passing legislation that enforces the following rules for sports fans.

Rule No. 1: No sports bigamy—you have to select one team in each sport. Unless you live in Utah, you *cannot* root for two teams at once to hedge your bets, and you *cannot* unconditionally love two teams at the same time when there's a remote chance that they might go head-to-head someday.[3]

Rule No. 2: If your city has fielded a professional team since your formative years, you *have* to support that team. None of

3 The best example: The 2000 World Series, when tens of thousands of fair-weather New Yorkers were forced to choose between the Mets and Yankees—almost like the mom in *The Good Son* choosing whether to drop Macaulay Culkin or Elijah Wood off the cliff. Of course, a small percentage decided to play the "Either way, I'm a winner" card, which was just like admitting, "I suck as a person and I have no soul."

this, "The Bengals weren't very good when I was growing up in Cincy, so I became a Niners fan" crap. Local teams are like family—you have to stick with them through thick and thin. Even if they're living on welfare and making occasional appearances on Jerry Springer.

Rule No. 3: You can't root for a team, back off during a down cycle, then renew the relationship once the team starts winning again. Those Cowboys fans who jumped off the bandwagon in the late '80s, jumped back on during the Emmitt/Aikman Era, jumped back off in the late '90s, then made another jump when Parcells came aboard—you know who you are.[4]

Rule No. 4: If you're between the ages of 20 and 40 and root for the Yankees, Cowboys, Braves, Raiders, Steelers, Celtics, Lakers, Bulls, Canadiens and/or Oilers without hailing from their respective regions...well, you better have a reason that goes beyond, "When I was picking a favorite team as a kid, they were the best so I picked them." And if that *was* your reason, be honest about it. Don't make up stuff like "I really liked the Yankee hats!" and "I just remember thinking that Kareem's goggles were the coolest things ever!" Bullshit. You liked them because they were winning and you wanted to feel good about yourself. Just admit it.

Rule No. 5: If you marry someone who roots for another team, you can't be bullied into switching allegiances. You'd be amazed how often this happens; the power of women to whip men never ceases to amaze me. I enjoy when the guy starts making excuses: "Well, once I moved to Boston from New York, I got caught up in this whole Red Sox thing and the American League, so I stopped following the Mets," or "I never liked the Browns as much as she liked the Bengals, so I'm taking one for the team," or even my personal favorite, "We wanted our kids to root for the same team as their parents." Don't you love when "the sake of the kids" becomes a reason? What is this, like a Jewish-Catholic thing?[5]

Rule No. 6: Once you choose a team, you're stuck with that team for the rest of your life, unless one of the following conditions applies:

a) You grew up in a city without a team for that specific

4 I was in college when the Emmitt/Aikman Era came together—you have never seen so many Cowboys hats and T-shirts come out of the woodwork, with an astonishing correlation between people who jumped on **the Cowboys bandwagon** and people who rowed crew. These were also the same people who **a)** hit on your girlfriend when you were away for the weekend, **b)** drank Bud Dry, and **c)** enjoyed Jim Nantz.

5 By the way, I have to question any Red Sox fan who would marry a Yankee fan. Unless you have never been laid before and this is legitimately your only chance to have regular sex, it's simply unacceptable. Would you marry someone from Al-Qaeda?

sport, so you picked a random team to fill that void... and then your city landed a team (like everyone in D.C. who switched from the Orioles to the Nationals this season).

b) One of your immediate family members or best friends ends up playing professionally or taking a relevant management/coaching/front office position with a certain team.

c) You followed your favorite college star (and this has to be a once-in-a-generation favorite college star) to the pros and supported his team du jour—like any UNC fan who adopted the Bulls because of Michael Jordan, or even any Santa Clara grad who rooted for the Mavericks and Suns because of Steve Nash. As long as you're not turning your back on a local franchise, this is acceptable.

d) The owner of your favorite team treated his fans so egregiously that you couldn't take it anymore, so you decided to stop following them until the team was sold. Let the record show that I reached this point with the Boston Bruins 10 years ago. When it happens, you have two options: Either renounce that team and pick another one, or pretend they're dead and you're a grieving widow. That's what I did. For years, I was an NHL widow. I didn't even want to date another team.

e) Your team moves to another city. All bets are off when that happens. In fact, if you decided to turn off that sport entirely, nobody would blame you.

Anyway, my father qualified for a Red Sox bandwagon jump under Rule 6e, growing up in Brooklyn as a Dodgers fan until their shocking move to Los Angeles in 1958. Heartbroken, he refused to support the Yankees and couldn't rally the proper enthusiasm for the Mets, spending nine full seasons without a favorite team. Right up until 1967. So his jump to the Red Sox was justified. Others made the leap for similar reasons, still others to join the crowd. The fact remains, the Boston Red Sox evolved into something beyond a mere baseball franchise in 1967. Already blessed with a massive fan base in New England, the growing influx of visiting students pushed that number to another level.[6] More and more kids were attending college and graduate school in the '60s, partly because higher education was becoming a nationwide priority, partly to avoid Vietnam. Those were the kids who inevitably fell for the Sox, either settling in New England or continuing to support them from afar. Those were the kids who ended up raising tiny Sox fans one day.

6 No major city has as many high-quality colleges and universities within a 150-mile radius of its baseball stadium: Harvard, BC, BU, Northeastern, Suffolk, Tufts, Wesleyan, UNH, Yale, Brown, Holy Cross, Amherst, Williams, UMass, Trinity, Brandeis, Bryant, UConn, URI, and Providence College, to name 20. And that's not even counting Bowdoin, UVM, UMaine, and Dartmouth—all of which are in Red Sox Country.

And if you're wondering why Red Sox fans seem to be multiplying across the country like pods in *Invasion of the Body Snatchers*—well, that's why. It's the only fan base in sports that consistently regenerates itself. Maybe you didn't come to New England intending to fall in love with the Red Sox, it's just that you couldn't help it.

In my father's case, not only did he fall in love with the Red Sox, he fell for my mother and they ended up having me. Nine years later, they ended up getting divorced.

But he still had the Red Sox. And he still had me.

I can't remember a single day of my life that didn't involve the Boston teams. By the time I was eight months old, my parents already had me wearing a Red Sox hat. At two, I was perusing the *Boston Globe*'s sports section every morning.[7] At three, I owned my first baseball glove. When I was four, my father purchased a single season ticket for the Celtics and started carrying me into games—just our luck, we caught two championships in the first three years, including the famous triple-OT game against Phoenix in the 1976 NBA Finals. At five, I owned an extensive collection of baseball and hockey cards, rattled off statistics like a young Bill James, even performed a dead-on impersonation of Carl Yastrzemski's swing.

After my sixth birthday, my parents were summoned to see my first-grade teacher twice: Once because I was refusing to start my 8:00 a.m. class until I finished the sports section of the *Globe*; once because I was coloring my face black in self-portraits and referring to myself as Jabaal Abdul-Simmons. Even then, I knew the odds were against me—I wanted to play point guard for the Celtics so badly, I decided that changing my skin color and having a Muslim name was my only real chance. So I started signing my homework assignments "JABAAL" and refusing to answer unless my teacher used my Muslim name. You know, just like Ali refusing to answer to "Cassius Clay," only imagine he was a six-year-old white kid. If this happened now, they would have loaded me with Ritalin and diagnosed me with EATD (Ethnic Attention Transformation Disorder) or something equally ludicrous. Back then, they called your parents in, made you spend second period with "your own personal teacher" and hoped you grew out of it.

Well, I grew out of it. Somewhat. Equally obsessed with the

7 That's not a lie: I could read by the time I was two. When I was six, I started reading **the Hardy Boys** series, which were written for "boys 10 to 14" (that's what it said on the back of each book). I took this as a personal affront and finished the entire 58-book series before I turned nine. These are the things that happen when you're an only child in the mid-'70s and you get only five TV stations.

four local teams, the vast majority of my nights started revolving around them. My first Red Sox memories come from the 1974 season—I have a hazy memory of Jim Rice and Fred Lynn getting called up for the final month, and of taking an immediate liking to Freddie. Everything about him was cool—his looping lefty swing, the red 19 on his back, those reckless diving catches,[8] the way he hauled in a third out and jogged back to the dugout with his glove tucked to his chest. Immediately, he became My Guy. I practiced running around the backyard with my glove tucked to my chest. My knees were skinned from throwing myself popups and diving headfirst after them. I even dressed up as No. 19 for two straight Halloweens.

And since Freddie was My Guy, the '75 Sox became My Team. I watched as many games as possible, including Lynn's three-homer game at Tiger Stadium (probably the most exciting moment of my life to that point). My first few Fenway trips happened that year as well, including an A's game where Oakland manager Alvin Dark picked up the third-base bag and stomped back to the dugout with it, as well as a Brewers game featuring the great Hank Aaron running on fumes.[9] It couldn't have been a better year to fall for the Sox. Look at the players on that team: Lynn, Yaz, Jim Rice, Luis Tiant, Carlton Fisk, Bill Lee, Dewey Evans, Cecil Cooper (my other favorite), Bernie Carbo, Rico Petrocelli—even that year's inaugural Saturday Night Live cast wasn't as loaded. If the '67 season was like catching lightning in a bottle, this '75 season felt like the beginning of something more substantial. Nobody in baseball had a better nucleus of young players.

In the playoffs against Oakland, with Rice sidelined by a broken wrist in the ALCS, Yaz replaced him in left and turned back the clock with some clutch hits and sparkling defensive plays.[10] The defending champs never knew what hit them. One month before, my grandfather had bought me a television for my sixth birthday, and since my parents trusted me for some reason, they allowed me to keep the TV in my room under an unbelievable "You can't watch it after bedtime" policy, which was right up there on the Shortsighted Scale with Neville Chamberlain signing the Munich pact with Hitler.[11] And that's how I watched them clinch a sweep in Oakland on a school night, with Yaz going 2-for-4 and gunning down Reggie Jackson at second base on a pivotal throw.

8 *This Week In Baseball* (hosted by Mel Allen) ended every show with a riveting montage of slow-motion moments accompanied by inspiring symphonic music, capped by one of Lynn's diving catches and **a Pete Rose headfirst dive** into third base. You can't believe how cool this was compared to everything else happening on TV at the time—it felt like the endings to *The Natural*, *Hoosiers*, and *The Longest Yard* all rolled into one. Strangely enough, they used the same music to end the *ABC Nightly News* in the mid-'70s (a song called "Gathering Crowds").

9 I just remember my dad saying, "That's Hank Aaron, the greatest home run hitter of all time" and being totally unimpressed because Freddie Lynn and I were in the same ballpark—literally—so Hank Aaron could have been Aaron Spelling for all I cared.

10 I remember thinking at the time, "How is Yaz doing this? He's 35! That's like eight years older than my Dad!" Nowadays, Yaz would be on **his fifth Balco cycle** and just entering his prime.

11 This was the most underrated historical

We were headed to the World Series. Tiant pitched a gem against the Big Red Machine in Game One (I still remember him haphazardly running the bases with that goofy warmup jacket), followed by the Series turning on a bizarre interference play in Game Three,[12] with the Sox eventually falling behind three games to two. That was followed by a surreal three-day rain delay, allowing Tiant to pitch Game Six at Fenway—the famous game that Carbo saved with a heroic three-run dinger into the bleachers (my vote for Most Underrated Boston Sports Moment), Fisk won in the 12th (with the homer off the leftfield foul pole) and Matt Damon and Robin Williams immortalized in *Good Will Hunting* (in the "gotta see about a girl" scene). Sadly, I wasn't awake for the last five innings. After all, I had just turned six. But I did stay up for Game Seven, and only because my father wanted me awake when the Red Sox won their first World Series in 57 years.

Didn't happen. They lost.

I just assumed they would be back every year. Why the hell not? Then I started reading a 1973 book by Al Hirshberg called *What's the Matter With the Red Sox?*, which surfaced in our first grade classroom for some reason, along with an *Impossible Dream* record album that my teacher eventually removed because I wouldn't stop listening to it. She was fine with the Hirshberg book—at least I was reading *something* constructive, separating me from just about every other weirdo in the class, including The Kid Who Threw Chairs, The Kid Who Always Smelled Like Poop and The Kid Who Made Weird Bird Noises.[13] In retrospect, they should have taken Hirshberg's book away from me. I was too young. I didn't need to know these things yet. I could have been saved.

Here were the first two sentences of the book: "What's the matter with the Red Sox? In Boston, in all of New England except Southern Connecticut, in the Maritime Provinces—wherever baseball is discussed in these areas—this was first a plaintive cry, then a chronic complaint, and finally, a way of life."

Here was my reaction: "Um ... what? There's something wrong with the Red Sox? Whaddya mean?"

Although I didn't know what the words *plaintive* or *chronic* meant, I kept reading. And my life was never the same. In a scant 230 pages, I learned the barbaric history of my favorite baseball team. Here was the timeline:

moment of the 20th century, Chamberlain basically saying, "Okay, Adolf, you can have Czechoslovakia, but that's it" and Hitler saying, "Yeah, yeah, I already told you, I'm done after that." Even **Isiah Thomas** wouldn't have made that deal.

12 In the 10th inning, Cincy's Ed Armbrister laid down a sacrifice bunt right over home plate, then "accidentally" lurched into Fisk, who was pouncing on the ball and ended up launching an off-balance throw into centerfield (leading to the eventual winning run). For whatever reason, no interference was called. Sox fans did *not* handle this well. There have been prison riots that had safer conditions than the city of Boston that night.

13 Then again, the other kids probably remember me as The Kid Who Gave Himself a Muslim Name—which probably trumped all of them. Well, except for The Kid Who Always Smelled Like Poop.

1919: They sell Babe Ruth to the Yankees for $125,000, where he breaks every offensive record in the book, wins seven championships, and gets a candy bar named after him.

1933: After a series of last-place finishes, millionaire Tom Yawkey buys the Sox and immediately starts pouring money into them. Somehow, this doesn't do any good.[14]

1938–1942: Blessed with a young Ted Williams and a slew of high-priced veterans plucked from other teams, the Sox finish second four times in five years. Even during the year when Lou Gehrig died from a disease so debilitating they named it after him, the Yankees are still able to hold off the Red Sox.

1943–1945: Williams misses three straight seasons in his absolute prime so he can serve in World War II.[15]

1946–1951: Williams returns as the team wins 104 games and loses the '46 World Series to the Cards in seven. Even though they're favored to win the pennant every year during this stretch, that ends up being the only World Series appearance—in 1948, they lose a playoff game to the Indians, and in 1949, they blow a do-or-die series at Fenway against the Yanks. Something is clearly wrong at this point, although nobody can put their finger on it. *What's the matter with the Red Sox?*

1952–1966: The wheels come off—five winning seasons in 15 years.

1967: The Impossible Dream.

1968–1972: More misery.

1973–????: Probably more misery.

That's not all I learned. There were chapters about myriad boneheaded front-office decisions over the years, how the team was perennially seduced by the Green Monster[16] (so they kept building around sluggers instead of pitching). There was a chapter about the team's reluctance to sign black players; not only did they squander chances to sign Jackie Robinson and Willie Mays, but manager Mike Higgins once told Hirshberg, "There'll be no niggers on this ball club as long as I have anything to say about it." There was a chapter about the tempestuous history between Boston reporters and players, with a whopping 10 newspapers causing all kinds of trouble in the '40s

14 Yawkey was like a chain-smoking, post-Depression version of **Mark Cuban**—he loved throwing money around and hanging out with his own players. In Hirshberg's book, there's a story about Yawkey being wounded because Williams never came to Fenway for one of the '67 World Series games—choosing to send a congratulatory telegram instead—which sounded so Cuban-esque that I kept waiting to read that a forlorn Yawkey was wearing a Red Sox football jersey when he received the telegram. It's also tough to measure Yawkey historically because he made such an enormous charitable impact with The Jimmy Fund, but at the same time, there's hard-to-ignore evidence that he was racist and operated his team accordingly—in fact, *Boston Herald* columnist Howard Bryant wrote an entire book called *Shut Out* examining the team's shaky history with black players, which extended beyond Yawkey's death. For instance, in 1980, Rice was the only black player other than Chico Walker (who played a whopping 19 games). Until 1993, the Red Sox never signed a black free agent. How is that even possible?

and '50s. There was a chapter about the shocking amount of bad luck over the years: Conigliaro's beanball; Jim Lonborg blowing out a knee on a skiing trip; Luis Aparicio falling down as the tying run in a crucial game in '72; Johnny Pesky holding the ball for a split second too long in the '46 World Series; Joe McCarthy pitching journeyman Denny Galehouse over ace Mel Parnell in the '48 playoff game.

Maybe I was only six, but this book had a profound effect on me. *Was my team doomed?* Sure seemed like it. Just one year earlier, I figured out that Santa Claus was a sham because he couldn't possibly hit everyone's house in one night, although I peeked downstairs to see my parents sticking gifts under the tree to make sure. So I was a realist (the Santa Claus theory), but also a little kid (peeking on Christmas Eve to make sure). And that's how I approached the Sox over the next few years: I knew things were probably going to end badly, but that didn't stop me from watching as many games as possible and hoping I was wrong. When they jumped to a seemingly insurmountable fourteen-game lead over the Yankees in July of 1978, it seemed like our fortunes had changed. Then the Yanks started creeping back into the race—to the abject horror of everyone in New England—as the lead dwindled and eventually disappeared during the demoralizing Boston Massacre.[17] But just when it looked like the Sox were finished, they battled back with their own little streak, winning 12 of their last 14 (including their last eight) to force a one-game playoff.

You can't possibly imagine how big that game was. We didn't have cable TV. We didn't have video games. We didn't have the Internet, cell phones, DVD players or iPods. Honestly, there wasn't much happening in 1978.[18] And when you don't have a ton of distractions, the distractions that *do* exist take on epic proportions. You know, like the Red Sox. This wasn't just the most important game of my entire life, it remains the biggest Boston game ever and will never be topped. We *had* to beat the Yankees. When you combine the circumstances of that season with the Shakespearean relationship between those two teams, as well as the ghoulish setting of Fenway Park in the late afternoon and a petrified crowd ... seriously, has there ever been another baseball game quite like that? Even when ESPN Classic shows the old broadcast, there's an eerie vibe from the fans: deafening silences, urgent cheers, a palpable nervous energy,

15 We can all agree that Williams was one of the 25 greatest athletes of all time, right? With the exception of Ali, name someone else in that top 25 who missed three years of their prime because of outside circumstances. You can't. These things only happened to the Red Sox.

16 Originally built in 1912, Fenway was renovated by Yawkey in 1934, who gave it **that famous left field wall**, which was 37 feet high and sat just 310 feet from home plate (an inviting target for righthanded power hitters who were always advertised as being "perfect for Fenway"). From 1934 to 1946, the wall was covered in advertisements until Yawkey painted it green before the 1947 season—hence, the nickname Green Monster. Contrary to urban legend, **Jim Henson** had nothing to do with it.

17 On September 7, the Yankees rolled into Fenway trailing by just four games, then pulled into a dead heat by outscoring the Sox 42-9 in four games. That was the Massacre. The definitive moment: A haunting photo of Yaz slumping against the Green Monster during the umpteenth pitching change—it was like that famous photo of

almost like 35,000 people were warned that they would be collectively slaughtered if the Red Sox lost.

My parents kept me home from school that day, like thousands of other kids in the Boston area. It felt like we were preparing for a nuclear attack; I'm not even sure if I was excited or scared. We watched the game in the basement of our new house in Brookline, the same basement where I would watch USA 4–USSR 3 just 16 months later (from one extreme to the other). Nursing a 2–0 lead in the seventh, Mike Torrez yielded the infamous three-run homer to light-hitting shortstop Bucky Dent, a pop fly that somehow drifed over the Monster and spawned Bucky's lifelong nickname in Boston: Bucky Fucking Dent.[19] The Yanks padded the lead with two more runs, followed by the Sox answering with two in the bottom of the eighth. Yankees 5, Red Sox 4. With one out in the ninth, Rick Burleson walked against a tiring Goose Gossage (pitching into a third inning). Jerry Remy followed[20] with a line drive to rightfield, where a flustered Lou Piniella—completely blinded by the setting sun—thrust his glove out and somehow snared the ball, almost like a guy defensively swatting at a bee and miraculously connecting. Burleson held at second. Unbelievable.

Now Rice was up. Remember, this was his famous "46 HR/139 RBI/406 total bases" MVP season during an era when sluggers didn't have oversize heads, extended jaws, and back acne (or as I like to call it, "bacne"). If you put Rice on an HGH program back then, he would have belted the first 700-foot homer.[21] Believe me, there was nobody more imposing in 1978. You wouldn't have wanted anyone else up in this spot. Anyway, Rice ended up *creaming* a ball to right-center that looked like the game-winning double, only it veered right to Piniella (playing him perfectly in right-center), so the crowd ended up making one of those combination shriek/groans that became a Fenway trademark over the years. With Burleson advancing to third, the tying run was just 90 feet from home plate. And Yaz was coming up.

Understand this about Yaz: Nobody personified the Red Sox quite like him. A surly chain-smoker with a thick Boston accent, poor Yaz wore every harrowing Boston defeat on his face; he always looked 10 years older than he actually was, like a famous actor who seems too old to be starring in a baseball movie.[22] Of course, no Red Sox player came through more

the naked little girl running in Vietnam.

18 During that same year, there was a blizzard that came out of nowhere on a Friday afternoon, dumping three feet of snow and stranding thousands of people on the Mass Pike. We were so blindsided and underprepared that my school actually canceled classes for three straight weeks. **I don't think I've ever been so bored** in my whole life. I'm telling you, there was nothing to do in 1978.

19 You could make a very good case that this was the most traumatic moment in the history of Fenway Park—roughly equivalent to losing your softball league's title after the token girl on the opposing team knocked a pop fly over the leftfielder's head, only your life depended on the game.

20 Quirkiest fact about a shaky '78 Red Sox team that somehow won 99 games: Burleson batted leadoff (on-base percentage that year: .295), followed by Remy (OBP: .321). If a team tried this now, the writers at the *Baseball Prospectus* would have a collective conniption.

21 My favorite "Jim Ed Rice was really fucking strong" fact: More than

times when it mattered, and few Boston athletes ever had a better sense of The Moment. Seeing him stride to the plate against the fireballing Gossage, well, other than Kirk Gibson's famous homer off Dennis Eckersley, has there ever been an at-bat that felt more like a movie scene? There was grizzled old Yaz trying to save the season, his lungs filled with nicotine residue, the sun setting behind him, needing a single to save the season. If this were a movie, William Devane would have played him, and Yaz would have ripped a Gossage fastball into the rightfield bullpen, and everyone would have happily skipped out of the dugout in slow motion, and the fans would have charged the field, and Yaz would have been swarmed as he hopped on home plate, and then the credits would have rolled. The end.

Here's the thing that killed me (and everyone else): Right as we were entertaining these magical thoughts, Yaz swung late on a Gossage heater and abruptly popped up to third. What sports movie would ever end like that? I remember the ball slicing up in the air, Yaz grimacing in disgust and slamming his bat like a shovel, the crowd shrieking in horror, Graig Nettles settling underneath it, the Yankees celebrating, everything going quiet, Yaz limping back to the dugout, the finality of it all.

I started crying. I cried and cried. My mom rubbed my head. I kept crying. Life wasn't fair. I kept crying.

I had just turned nine years old.

Rooting for the Red Sox wasn't much fun after that. With Yawkey passing away in 1976, his widow ended up selling much of her stake at a discount to a syndicated group with cash flow problems, leading to a never-ending array of lawsuits and counterlawsuits that didn't get fully settled until 1981. Suddenly the Red Sox stopped spending money on free agents and pushed five popular stars out of town—Lee and Tiant in the winter of '78, then Fisk, Burleson and Lynn two winters later.[23] Just like that, The Best Young Team in Baseball had been dismantled. The 1981 season started with Fisk returning to Fenway in a White Sox uniform and vindictively crushing a pivotal home run on Opening Day—a morbidly upsetting moment to anyone who cared about the team—launching a five-year stretch where the team was kind of competitive, but not really. All I remember were these six things:

once he broke his bat just by checking his swing. Seriously.

22 Three quintessential examples: Robert Redford in *The Natural*; Roy Scheider in *Tiger Town*; and that guy who played Eddie Harris in *Major League* (the same guy who tried to steal Norman Dale's job in *Hoosiers*). One of the all-time great That Guys. I'll even give you his name, since you just spent $25 for this book—Chelcie Ross.

23 Fisk and Lynn ended up leaving on a contract technicality—the team "forgot" to mail them contracts in time, making them free agents, although everyone knew they did it purposely to cut costs. In Fisk's case, he signed with the White Sox without the Red Sox receiving any compensation, which was fantastic because Fisk turned out to be one of the five best catchers of all time. Lynn and Steve Renko fetched the putrid package of a washed-up Joe Rudi, no-name Jim Dorsey and noodle-armed Frank Tanana. At the time, ABC could have traded **Gabe Kaplan, Henry Winkler and Ricardo Montalban** to NBC for Skip Stevenson and Claude Akins and I wouldn't have been as bitter.

1) The unforgivable 1981 strike, which spawned the most boring summer in the history of mankind.

2) Rice being the team's only consistent All-Star representative even though he was a mortal lock for a 6–4–3 with a runner on first and one out.

3) Yaz finally reaching the landmarks of 3,000 hits, 400 home runs, and 500,000 Marlboro Reds.

4) Watching Fisk and Lynn return every year in the wrong uniforms, knowing there was no valid reason they weren't on the team anymore.

5) The young Wade Boggs unveiling a classic swing and an even more classic porn mustache, quickly emerging as a legitimate threat either to hit .400 or end up with a mistress who posed in *Penthouse*.[24]

6) Reading Peter Gammons' 1985 book, *Beyond the Sixth Game*, a recap of 1975–1984, when free agency ruined baseball as we knew it (with Boston used as the model, allowing Gammons to earn Most Scarring Red Sox Book honors for that decade).

Looking back, it was a profoundly unhappy time to support the Boston Red Sox. You couldn't shake the nagging sense that a window had closed, that the current ownership wasn't fully committed to fielding a contending team. Stuck living in southern Connecticut after my parents divorced, I found myself watching more and more of the Mets, if only because they rarely showed Sox games on cable and I needed a baseball fix. In the summer of 1985, with the Sox headed for another .500 finish, I watched enough Dwight Gooden starts on Channel 9 to make me wonder, "Wait, am I crossing the line here?" Here was a team that cared about its fans and here was a player who *mattered*. That's a pretty enticing package, especially for a Boston transplant whose favorite team gave away his childhood hero. If I didn't care about the Red Sox so much, that '85 Mets team could have turned me into a sports bigamist. Which would have been terrible.[25]

And I wasn't alone. Everyone forgets this now, but the Sox turned off a large percentage of their fan base with the Fisk-Lynn-Tiant moves. In 1978 and 1979, more than 2.3 million fans passed through Fenway each season for an average of 29,000

24 Only one of those things ended up happening: the *Penthouse* pictorial. I'm not sure what was worse—that Boggs' mistress, Margo Adams, made the cover, that she glowingly raved about his oral sex skills, or that my college roommates and I actually paid four bucks to see her naked. There wasn't enough airbrushing on the planet to make Margo Adams attractive—she was like a poor man's Linda Lovelace. Then again, when she called him a "connoisseur" of oral sex, that led to one of my favorite jokes in college: Imitating Red Sox PA announcer Sherm Feller every time Boggs came to the plate with, "Now batting … No. 26 … the connoisseur of cunnilingus … Wade Boggs … connoisseur of cunnilingus, Boggs …"

25 In retrospect, it was more of a harmless flirtation than anything. If this were a TV movie on Lifetime, Gooden would have been the smoking-hot au pair (played by **Elisha Cuthbert**) who caused me to stray from my uncaring wife (played by Kim Delaney). And then Kim and I would have worked it out in the end.

fans per home game. By 1984, that number had dipped to 1.66 million and 20,000 per game. On April 29, 1986, when Roger Clemens struck out 20 Seattle batters and turned the franchise's fortunes around—in fact, everything that led to the 2004 World Series started that day—there were fewer than 14,000 spectators at Fenway that night. People were just more interested in the Celtics and Patriots...until Clemens' remarkable performance changed everything. By 1988, the team was averaging more than 30,000 fans per game, a mark it topped 11 times over the next 16 years as the children of the Impossible Dream generation finally had enough money to purchase tickets.[26] By 2004, that number had climbed to 36,298, which was also the capacity of the ballpark. In other words, every home game sold out.

26 Following the 1994 strike, guess who was the only team whose attendance actually increased in the '95 season? That's right, Boston.

Following Clemens's 20K game, the next eight years featured everything you could want from a baseball team—three playoff appearances ('86, '88, '90), likable stars (Clemens, Boggs, Rice, Evans, Mike Greenwell, Mo Vaughn), likable veterans (Don Baylor, Bruce Hurst, Mike Boddicker, Jeff Reardon, Lee Smith), and a front office that wasn't afraid to throw money around (even if it was usually at the wrong guys). That stretch also featured the most scarring moment in franchise history (Game Six of the '86 World Series), as well as Dan Shaughnessy's release of *The Curse of the Bambino* (a smarter, more diabolical rehashing of Hirshberg's book) and the subsequent brainwashing by curse-related rhetoric of every national magazine and TV network (don't worry, we're covering this later in bloody, laborious detail). Complicating things, the first generation of post-Babe Red Sox fans was passing away without seeing the team win a World Series. The symbolism was clear to everyone: *Someday, that could be me.*

Around this same time, I was pursuing a writing career that started with a weekly column for my college newspaper at Holy Cross—yes, Dad's old school—eventually deciding to write about sports for a living. I earned my master's from Boston University in 1993 and spent the next three years as a high school sports reporter and editorial assistant for the *Boston Herald*. And here's where my life and the Red Sox intersected again. In 1994, the indefensible strike wiped away the World Series, a loss of innocence for anyone who'd ever cared about sports. I found myself stuck with all these baseball memories that suddenly seemed insignificant. If they didn't care about me, why should I care about them? When baseball returned for the '95 season, I remained bitter until the Sox started winning again—right until the playoffs, when veteran closer Rick Aguilera gave up a game-tying homer to Cleveland's Albert Belle in Game One, followed by Red Sox castoff Tony Peña belting the game-winner in the 13th. After getting kicked in the teeth for three decades by this team, giving up on baseball during the strike, then getting sucked back in the following season, this particular collapse seemed especially cruel. They ended up getting swept, extending their postseason losing streak to a whopping 11 games. The more things changed, the more they stayed the same.

Meanwhile, things were going miserably with my writing career. Stuck at a newspaper where nobody ever retired, where people waited until their mid-30s for the chance to become the backup beat writer for the Boston Bruins, I was slowly realizing two things.

First, newspapers weren't saying, "Hey, let's hire a white male columnist in his 20s!"[27]

And second, I wouldn't be making decent money until the new millennium, if ever.

When I glanced around and realized how many mediocre writers were blocking my way—with no chance of anyone leaving, since they were protected by the union—I grew increasingly bitter and it affected my enthusiasm for the job. Ten years later, I would have been one of those vindictive wannabes who posted anonymously on message boards for "sports journalists" (translation: unhappy copy editors and unsuccessful writers slamming everyone who is successful). You know, just to make myself feel better. But the Internet hadn't really taken shape yet—I had nowhere to turn.

Frustrated to the point of insanity, disenchanted with my newspaper experience beyond despair, I finally ended up leaving the paper and launching an ill-fated freelance career.[28] You have to understand, I always dreamed of writing a column for one of the Boston papers, and every move I made after college was made with that goal in mind: *I'm gonna be the next Ray Fitzgerald, I'm gonna be the next Leigh Montville, I'm gonna be the next Gerry Callahan.* And you have this romantic ideal in your head about the way life works, and then you find out that life doesn't work that way—and it's just about the most discouraging thing you can imagine.

27 This turned out to be my smartest move: At the *Globe*, where I always dreamed of ending up, Shaughnessy and Bob Ryan have been the featured columnists since 1989—that's 16 years and counting.

28 In retrospect, this would have been the perfect time to break out the Jabaal Abdul-Simmons gimmick again.

So I wrote a couple of freelance pieces for the *Boston Phoenix* over the next three months, but my heart wasn't in it and as fate would have it, they hired a new news editor who improbably told me, "Um, we're going to shift away from the sports thing."[29] Now it was the beginning of June. I had no contacts, no leads and no idea what I was doing with my life. Every night I was sitting home writing episodes for a made-up TV series about people in college, despite the fact that I had no contacts in Hollywood and no idea how to write a screenplay.[30] I was making $0.00 per week and living off peanut butter and cereal. I was lost. Totally, completely lost.

And then a pretty neat thing happened: I started bartending.

I ended up doing the restaurant/bar routine all summer—woke up at noon, worked past midnight, stayed out partying until 3 a.m. five nights a week, spent cash like Monopoly money—and it was the best thing that could have happened to me. Everyone was lost, everyone just wanted to have fun, everyone was interesting and every night was more interesting than the last. The inherent danger of the restaurant business is that you could look up from a drunken, smoky haze one morning and realize that three years just passed, that the *carpe diem* mentality just sidetracked the course of your life. Fortunately for me, that never happened. Within a few months, I started thinking to myself, "I need to give writing one more shot." I just didn't know how. Or where. In May of 1997, I launched my own web page called "Boston's Sports Guy," which could only be found through Digital City Boston if you had an AOL account. Since they were paying me peanuts, I kept the bartending gig and worked at a breakneck pace over the next 18 months, not really knowing where I was headed, just knowing that it felt like the right direction. Like with the Red Sox, sometimes you just have to believe.

It took time to find my voice as a columnist, mainly because the Boston sports scene had been so depressing over the previous decade. Eventually I learned to write from a fan's perspective, but that wasn't clicking at first because I needed to learn to love sports again. My angriest column was written in October of 1997, after yet another rebuilding year in Boston that featured an unprecedented double whammy—Clemens rolling off one of the great pitching seasons in recent years in Toronto, followed by Florida winning the World Series. The Marlins thing

29 Good move for a weekly paper in Boston, only the most rabid sports city in the country.

30 One of my 10 biggest fears in life is that copies of these episodes will somehow turn up on the Internet. They couldn't have been worse. It's not possible.

damn near killed me. Here were the Red Sox slogging through their 79th straight season without a championship, and here were the Marlins, who had just formed a team about three weeks ago. And they were the ones celebrating? How was that fair? Fortunately, I was able to vent about these things in a cathartic piece called "Why I'm Really Starting to Hate Baseball." I didn't really know what I was doing as a columnist, but I knew this was what I wanted to do. Even if barely anyone was reading.[31]

When the Red Sox acquired Pedro Martinez from the Expos that winter, my life as a sports fan (as well as my writing career) was never the same. In a good way. Over the next seven years, thanks to Pedro, Nomar Garciaparra and everyone else, I fell in love with the Red Sox all over again. The journey was captured in the columns you're about to read from 1998 to 2005—some of which were written for that old BSG site, some of which were written for ESPN.com—as I finally fulfilled two lifelong dreams:

1) Writing sports columns for a living.

2) Seeing my favorite team win the World Series.

Since this book combined those two dreams, I jumped at the opportunity to tinker with many of these columns, partly for space reasons, partly because some material overlapped, partly because I never took enough time with them in the first place. All of the rewriting was done for stylistic reasons, not for content—I was painstakingly careful to avoid messing with the opinions, feelings and emotions in every piece. The ultimate goal was to make them better and crisper, that's all. If the original columns were like unpublished entries in a journal, this is the final polished version of that journal—how I found salvation as a Red Sox fan, with some additional material thrown in when necessary (as long as that material didn't change the original point). Think of it as the director's cut of a DVD, with the footnotes serving as the commentary.

One more note: When the Sox won the 2004 World Series, the resulting overexposure would have embarrassed both Hilton sisters and possibly even Nicole Richie. Between the documentaries, the DVDs, *Fever Pitch*, all the magazine covers, the 200 quickie books, and everything else, the country soon tired of reading about the Sox and their fans. And you know

31 I ended up pulling double duty with bartending and the column through the summer of 1998, when I sucked it up and threw everything I had into the website for $500 a week from the portal that was hosting it. By the spring of 2001, just on word of mouth, I was up to about 9,000–10,000 readers per day and the site had earned official "cult" status (a nice way of saying that something was creative and well-done without actually being successful). Strangely, when I moved to ESPN.com in 2001 and increased my readership by a hundred times in a matter of months, a small number of those original readers accused me of selling out. The lesson, as always: You can't win.

what? I couldn't really blame them. I actually wanted to write this book after the 2003 season, only I was juggling two jobs at the time and couldn't swing it.[32]

Just know that this book isn't about the Red Sox as much as a kid who fell out of love with baseball, slowly found himself sucked back in, then battled the demons that came with supporting a star-crossed franchise. Maybe last October's events gave me a better title than *Love Child of the Impossible Dream*, as well as a much happier ending (well, unless you're a Yankee fan). But this book would have happened whether they won the World Series or not. As Manny Ramirez would say, it was destination.

Bill Simmons
June 2005

32 In November 2002, I started writing for Jimmy Kimmel's new late-night show on ABC, cutting back to three columns a month for ESPN.com and *ESPN The Magazine*. In April 2004, ESPN lured me back full-time and **I had to break up with Jimmy**, although we remained on good terms and agreed to share custody of our three children.

October 1998–December 2000

REJUVENATION

DUQUETTE'S BIG MOVE

On November 18, 1997, the Red Sox acquired Pedro Martinez only weeks after he won the Cy Young Award for Montreal. It would become the most important trade in franchise history, and not just because of how Pedro pitched in Boston. Finally—finally!—the Sox were targeting young stars entering their primes over proven stars who had already peaked.

Sounds pretty simple, right? Not for the Red Sox. During my first three decades as a Boston fan, they trotted out more has-beens and overrated names than Sly Stallone during the entire first season of *The Contender*.[33] This isn't always a bad thing. For instance, in *The Contender* it's fun to see random crowd shots of James Woods and Don Johnson, or a barely recognizable Carl Weathers high-fiving Sly after an exciting round. But when the year-to-year fate of your baseball team is involved, it becomes a bit of a problem. In the '80s and '90s, Boston became a way station of sorts for recognizable veterans wrapping up good careers: Jeff Reardon, Frank Viola, Andre Dawson, Tom Seaver, Don Baylor, Tony Perez, Tony Pena, Jeff Reardon, Jack Clark, Danny Darwin, Frank Viola, Mike Boddicker, Tom Brunansky, Otis Nixon, Jose Canseco, and Steve Avery. Not all of those players failed in Boston (there's no way the 1986 team would have made the World Series without Baylor), but most of them did, and the general pattern was more disturbing than anything.

There was a bigger problem, of course. Seduced by those high-scoring games at Fenway, the franchise had a curious weakness for power hitting over quality pitching, whether it

33 If you're reading this in 2050, *The Contender* was NBC's boxing reality-TV show that never quite resonated with viewers. Since it was hosted by **Sylvester Stallone and Sugar Ray Leonard** (a combined 195 out of 200 on the Unintentional Comedy Scale), I did my best to get people watching, even writing, "Since Sly Stallone single-handedly ended the Cold War for us, the least you could do is give his reality show a whirl." Didn't work.

was through trades, free agency or even the minor league draft. In a 1991 feature for the *Boston Globe*, Peter Gammons pointed out this mindset hadn't changed even though every successful Boston season from the previous 50 years (1946, 1948, 1949, 1967, 1975, 1978, 1986, 1988, and 1990) was fueled by dominant aces like Tex Hughson, Mel Parnell, Lonborg, Tiant, Dennis Eckersley and Roger Clemens—and even second-tier horses like Dave Ferriss, Ellis Kinder, Bill Lee, Torrez, Rick Wise, Bruce Hurst, Oil Can Boyd, and Mike Boddicker. As Gammons wrote, "If one looks through Red Sox history, one finds that while they have prized and worshipped the Sacred Righthanded Power Hitters, their success has been dominated not by homers but by hitters, period, and their best won-lost records have come when they have had pitching."

Enter Dan Duquette. The Amherst College grad made a name for himself in Montreal, where he assembled a loaded Expos squad that eventually cruised to a 74–40 record in 1994 before the strike intervened. A diehard Red Sox fan who relied on then-unconventional devices like statistical analysis and foreign scouting, Duquette quickly became a favorite of Gammons, who wrote a laudatory profile in 1992 and pimped him for Boston's vacant GM job after the 1993 season.[34] Understand something about Gammons at the time: Before message boards, DirecTV's baseball package, webcasts and everything else, his word carried an enormous amount of weight with Sox fans, many of whom devoured his weekly "Sunday Notes" column and implicitly trusted his every word. If Gammons liked someone, that was good enough—we needed to get him.[35] Throw in the fact that Duquette (a Dalton native) always dreamed of running the Red Sox, as well as the inevitable PR boost from hiring a local guy, and no other candidate had a chance.

Upon landing the job, Duquette unveiled his plan: Overhaul Boston's feeble minor league system, strengthen its scouting departments (especially overseas), avoid damaging long-term deals for veterans who had already peaked, and gamble on low-risk, high-reward players who had proven themselves in the past (like Erik Hanson) or shown flashes at the major league level (like Tim Wakefield and Reggie Jefferson).[36] Hoping to remain competitive while building something more substantial for the long haul, Duquette understood that big-market teams were better off stockpiling prospects who could eventually be moved

34 GM Lou Gorman was fired right after the 1993 season, thanks to a series of screw-ups that included the calamitous Larry Andersen/Jeff Bagwell trade; the Lee Smith/Tom Brunansky trade; the Jack Clark/Andre Dawson/Frank Viola/Matt Young signings; and a non-trade for Willie McGee in 1990 coupled with his famous quote, "What would we do with Willie McGee?" He will always be remembered as a lovable, quotable guy who responded to critics with beauties like "The sun will rise, the sun will set, and I will have lunch."

35 The most famous examples: Clark ("makes everyone better") and Dawson ("the finest person I have met in more than 20 years covering baseball"), both of whom were spectacular flops.

36 In a 1998 column, I joked that "With some luck, maybe we'll look back at Duquette and his revamped minor league system the same way Egyptians look back at **Abdul Nasser** and his development and nurturing of the Liberation party." See, I knew that poly sci degree would pay off some day.

for proven commodities. Without revenue sharing or a salary cap, small-market teams couldn't afford talented players headed for free agency, so they were forced to build a young nucleus, hope everything crested for one season (like with the Expos in 1994), then exchange those studs for prospects (in trades) and draft picks (compensation from free agency). Lather, rinse, repeat. By contrast, big market teams could allow everyone else to develop young talent, then pluck the blue-chippers like a prime-time show plucking rising stars off a soap opera.

As long as the Red Sox kept producing desirable prospects for trade bait, with their payroll, they would be unstoppable. That was Duquette's logic, and when many of his patchwork moves helped the team make the playoffs in 1995, New England rallied behind him. Throw in the well-received selection of Georgia Tech star Nomar Garciapparra in the 1995 draft and the Duke couldn't miss.

Things quickly turned, however, during a frustrating 1996 season, when the Sox underachieved for four months and made a belated run near the end, followed by Clemens' bitter departure and a pitiful 1997 season (when I skewered Duquette in a column called "Who Ruined Our Baseball Summer?"[37]). Media members were openly mocking the Duke's secretive style; there was something creepy and distant about him, like he was evolving into the baseball version of *The Manchurian Candidate*. Even Gammons turned on him in a September column called "Time to Make a New Plan, Dan,"[38] which included barbs like, "It seems as if nothing has changed since Tom Yawkey died" and "Duquette is not pulseless, although he has allowed himself to be so portrayed."

Only one thing saved him. Thanks to Duquette's original plan, Boston's revamped farm system was deep enough that they could dangle two prized pitching prospects (Carl Pavano and Tony Armas Jr.) for Martinez, a package that Montreal ended up accepting over a similar overture from the Yankees. For a franchise that desperately needed to make a splash after the Clemens fiasco, this was the boldest statement Boston could make. But since it was unclear whether the team would re-sign Pedro after the 1998 season, writers and fans were cautiously excited at best.[39] In our wildest dreams, nobody imagined that he would stick around and evolve into the most dominant pitcher in 30 years.

37 I gave Duquette a 95 out of 100 on the "Ruined the Summer" Scale for reasons including "Pushed Clemens away to Toronto and spent his money on Steve Avery, Robinson Checo, and Shane Mack" and "Has same haircut as my elementary school shop teacher."

38 Considering that Gammons basically hired the guy, it was a shocking double-cross along the lines of Nina Myers with Jack Bauer in the first season of *24*, or even **Shawn Michaels super-kicking Marty Janetty** through a plate-glass window. The column almost seemed like an intervention, as Gammons pleaded with the Duke to hire a major league advisor and a public relations guru. My favorite excerpt: "Scrap the Iron Curtain, cultivate and enjoy the media. You always wanted this job, now you don't seem as if you enjoy it, and your family and friends shouldn't have to agonize every time they pick up the paper or turn on the radio."

39 Here's what I wrote: "After a summer of watching the Aaron Seles and Tim Wakefields of the world, management realized that you can't win without a stopper—someone who stomps out to the mound every five days and makes you feel like you can't lose on that given day. Whether it's for a year or ten years, at least we have some hope again. Every time Pedro Martinez is pitching for Boston next season, I'll remember to myself that *Pedro Martinez is pitching for Boston that day*. How can you kill your team for getting a guy like that?"

40 In my defense, this was probably the most depressing season in Boston sports history—a year that included an ugly Bill Parcells-Bob Kraft divorce, followed by Year One of the unhappy Pete Carroll Era for the Patriots; the Celtics losing out on Tim Duncan in the 1997 lottery, followed by Year One of **the ruinous Rick Pitino Era**; the Bruins *and* Celts finishing last in their respective leagues; Aaron Sele starting Opening Day at Fenway; and a sub-500 Red Sox season featuring 435 blown saves by Heathcliff Slocumb, a domestic violence incident involving Wil Cordero, and Clemens winning the Cy Young in Toronto.

As the foundation for that ascension was built during the '98 season—a solid first season for Pedro (19–7, 2.89 ERA), coupled with a six-year extension from the Sox—my columns remained cartoonishly hostile at times, with angles like "Why I'm Resigning as a Boston Sports Fan" and "Ten Reasons I Hate the Bruins."**40** Eventually I learned to tailor my style towards the fan's perspective, writing stuff like "The Best 30 Sports Movies Ever" and "Why Girls Can't Understand the Sports Thing," as I tried to distinguish myself from the generic angles in every newspaper and magazine. I answered reader questions in something called "Sports Guy Feedback," kept running diaries of the NBA draft, even wrote a two-part remake of *The Godfather* starring Rick Pitino. Basically, anything that my friends and I were discussing—whether it was "Who are the ugliest players in the NBA?", "Who's the best looking Wimbledon babe?", or "How was the cast of *Seinfeld* like MJ and the Bulls?"—ended up becoming a column. And since nobody else was writing about this stuff, I started building a small but loyal readership. Even though I didn't really know what I was doing.

More important, I found myself enjoying sports again, with many of those moments being captured in my Red Sox columns. And as the team began reconnecting with its fans through two likable stars (Pedro and Nomar), the region's hopes for a World Series title ballooned throughout the season. In one of the stranger outcomes in franchise history, Duquette became drunk with power over that time—seriously, it was like a bad action movie, right down to the comical crewcut that made him look like Michael Douglas in *Falling Down*—pushing Clemens and Mo Vaughn out of town and turning into a celebrated control freak. By the 2000 season, the team had scaled back its scouting, deemphasized the "Let's beef up our minor leagues!" plan and settled on merely outspending everyone else, culminating in Manny Ramirez's whopping $160 million deal during the winter of 2000. Complicating matters, Duquette's bizarre behavior had become increasingly hard to fathom, between his celebrated failure to return phone calls from other general managers, his callous treatment of team employees, and his condescending attitude towards writers, players, and even his own manager.

Quite simply, nobody liked him. Once Gammons started

pushing for his departure, it was only a matter of time. Dan Duquette ended up getting canned right before the 2002 season, 31 months before the Red Sox won their first World Series in 86 years. Fifty years from now, I will remember him as the guy who drafted Nomar, signed Manny, and traded for Pedro, as well as the monosyllabic eccentric who allowed his dream job to eventually get the best of him. But starting with the 1998 season, Duquette was one of the people who gave Red Sox fans hope again. And that's where our story begins.

June 2005

WHY NO-MAH IS A KEEP-AH

October 5, 1998

As we regroup from another playoff collapse and brace for Mo Vaughn's inevitable departure, only one player will keep Boston fans smiling throughout the winter: Our shortstop.

Forget how the Indians-Red Sox series turned out.[41] We'll always remember Nomar Garciaparra clapping in the dugout during the final inning, trying anything to keep his team alive, never giving up hope... and when it was over, stepping out of the dugout and applauding the Fenway Faithful. After everything he gave us this year—the clutch hits, the breathtaking plays in the field, the smiles, and the hope—the last thing we would have expected was for *him* to applaud *us*. But he did.

Listen, I remember every person in sports who ever let me down. I remember supporting Roger Clemens through thick and thin for 12 years, then watching him sign with Toronto and barely mention Red Sox fans on his way out. I remember the players and owners shutting down the 1994 baseball season and canceling the World Series—maybe the worst decision in the history of professional sports. I remember the appalling lack of emotion Jack Tatum displayed after paralyzing Darryl Stingley in 1978. I remember the thankless way the Sox pushed Fisk, Lynn, and Evans out of town. I remember Harry Sinden and Jeremy Jacobs refusing to spend enough money to secure a Stanley Cup from 1988 to 1993, squandering the primes of two superstars (Ray Bourque and Cam Neely) in the process.[42] I remember Irving Fryar fumbling and snorting his way though eight horrible years in New England before moving to Miami, finding God and becoming an All-Pro.

I remember M.L. Carr, John Y. Brown, and Victor Kiam destroying my favorite teams; Lenny Bias costing the Celtics a dynasty because he wanted to get high; Glen Wesley missing the open net in the triple OT game. I remember Cedric Maxwell killing the '85 Celts because he didn't work hard enough to return from knee surgery. I remember John McNamara keeping Bill Buckner in over Dave Stapleton; KC Jones burying Reggie Lewis as a rookie; Raymond Berry picking Tony Eason over Steve Grogan before Super Bowl XX; and Don Zimmer man-

41 The Indians took the series in four games. In Game Four, Tom Gordon gave up the go-ahead double after Jimy Williams brought him in one inning early for the first time all year, leading to Flash's second blown save of the season. These were the types of things that happened to the Red Sox. All the time.

42 This is a reference to a now-defunct professional league called the **National Hockey League** (NHL for short). The league featured teams of hockey players based in different cities—every spring, the champion was awarded a trophy called The Stanley Cup.

gling the final two months of the '78 season by refusing to use his bench. I remember Dan Duquette humiliating and embarrassing Mo Vaughn before showing him the door. In other words, I remember everything. Hell, I even remember how Larry Bird sucked in the '85 Finals after injuring his shooting hand in a bar fight...but since he's Larry Legend, we'll let that one slide.[43]

If you remember every slight, like me—which you probably do—then that's the biggest ongoing hurdle we face as fans: Forgetting why we like sports in the first place. We enter into "the fan thing" with good intentions, but as athletes continue to disappoint, as ticket prices continue to climb, as teams embrace luxury boxes and corporate sponsors, it's become a chore to enjoy sports heading into the 21st century. And I haven't even mentioned cynical newspaper columns and negative sports radio blather yet. Look at Boston fans. How can we root for Antoine Walker when he acts so immature at times? How can we root for the Bruins when they skimp on payroll and keep raising ticket prices? How can we support the Sox after the way they treated Mo Vaughn? How can we root for the Patriots when their owner has as much business making football decisions as you or me? And how can anyone follow these teams unconditionally when they can't afford to take their kids to more than a few games a year?

Sometimes they can push us too far. When they junked the '94 World Series, some baseball fans vowed never to watch another game. Why? Because it was impossible for them to lend their support and emotion for a group of people who obviously don't care about anyone but themselves. Although the strike didn't change the sport's financial infrastructure—players make too much money, ticket prices are too high, and there's an enormous disparity between the haves and the have-nots—it had one crucial repercussion: Players and owners realized that they needed to actually give something back. Hence, all the autographs, all the smiles, all the waving and everything else we've been lapping up. Maybe it's not enough, but it's a start.[44]

Regardless, it's become more and more difficult to focus on The Good Things in sports, the main reason why everyone relished the Mark McGwire/Sammy Sosa race so much. Two athletes were in the limelight that we actually *liked*. When does that ever happen?[45] It's the same reason we loved MJ's overdue

43 Somehow, I didn't get struck by lightning when I originally wrote that.

44 You can sense how much the strike traumatized me—even four years later, I was still bitching about it. Also, there's a Bob Ley-like tone to this column, which started back when I was writing editorials for the Op-Ed page of the *Boston Herald* in the mid-'90s and took me a few years to shake. Looking back, I probably wasn't getting enough sex.

45 As it turned out, the "actually liked" part had a seven-year shelf life. Although the homerun chase did lead to the McGwire-Sosa botched high-five/hug, which rivaled **Apollo and Rocky's beach hug** in *Rocky III* on the Awkward Scale.

comeback—we missed the ferocious way he competed, how he derived a certain charge from vanquishing opponents, how he would play for free (give or take $30 million). And it's why we appreciated Nomar's gesture so much last week. He didn't have to come out of the dugout and applaud the Fenway fans after Game Four. But he did. And he left everyone in Fenway and everyone watching on TV with the same feeling: There's a guy who cares about us.

Here's my theory: Fans are like dogs. Feed us, walk us, fill our bowls with water every few hours, give us those little rawhide treats... just remember to rub our heads and bellies every once in a while. That's what Nomar did on Saturday night. You can have A-Rod, Jeter, Griffey and Sosa; I'll take Nomar, and not just because he's the most talented Red Sox player I've ever seen (what other right-handed hitter homers into the freaking bullpen at Fenway?), or because he competes as hard as anyone who ever wore a Boston uniform. The guy says and does all the right things. Sadly, that counts as an asset in today's sports world.

Best of all, we have him for the forseeable future, making him the lone bright spot in a winter that looks bleaker than most. Vaughn and Clemens will be long gone. Jimy Williams will still be around, which scares me even as I'm typing it. Duquette will still be in charge, running his neo-Nazi Red Sox regime into the 21st century and extinguishing anyone who dares to cross his path. But none of that matters right now. Maybe it took us a few years, but we finally found a new candidate for The Pantheon—the rarefied Boston Sports Holy Ground that houses Larry Bird, Bobby Orr, Ted Williams, Bill Russell, John Havlicek, Bob Cousy and Red Auerbach. Clemens never quite made it. Neither did Kevin McHale. Bourque was never in the ballpark. Drew Bledsoe is a long way away, and that's an understatement.

Nomar? He looks poised to make a genuine Pantheon Run if he can stay healthy.[46] After these first two season, he gives me the same feeling that Bird gave me with the Celtics during the Bill Fitch Era. Even though I was only 10 years old, I knew something was different about him. He stood out. Same with Nomar. And given that he understands the connection between the Sox and their fans, he has a legitimate chance to own this city for the next decade. With one simple gesture, Nomar

46 This could have happened if he hadn't injured his wrist. When you read the rest of these other Nomar-related columns over the rest of the book, this one feels more poignant than it did at the time. It's hard to believe how this played out. Even now.

Garciaparra remembered one crucial fact that just about every other athlete always forgets: Every fan loves to have their belly rubbed sometimes. Even Red Sox fans.

(In fact, my tail is wagging right now. When does spring training start?)

PUTTING ON A HAPPY FACE

March 5, 1999

The Red Sox left me with a queasy feeling all winter, almost like when that "It's been six months since your last teeth cleaning" notice comes in the mail. Like many Sox fans, I was disgusted by everything that transpired—the indefensible departure of Mo Vaughn (with nobody to replace him), an inexplicable $26 million contract gift-wrapped for Jose Offerman, Band-aid pitching solutions like Mark Portugal and Pat Rapp, no major trades to get everyone buzzing about the season. They finished 22 games behind the Yankees, barely made the playoffs and got smoked by Cleveland. A winter passed... and the team didn't just fail to improve, it probably got worse. I mean, Bob Hamelin started at DH in yesterday's spring training game? Bob Hamelin! What time did they have to drive him back to Dunkin' Donuts so he could make his Thursday night shift?

The question remains: Is there any reason to get excited about the upcoming season? I took my no-sarcasm pills and tried to come up with 20 legitimate reasons why we should be excited about this 1999 Red Sox team.

1) No-mahhhhhhhh!

Time to find out if he can become a franchise hitter with Mo on the West Coast. Fortunately, he's entering his third full season, and any diehard roto geek knows what that means—that's usually the year hitters make The Leap. Unfortunately, he'll probably see 15 good pitches to hit all season. Fortunately, he's one of those hitters who could make contact on a pitchout. I think we're fine here.

2) Rich Garces

Only Oprah and Chris Farley have struggled more with their weight than Garces... and Farley's dead. Also, no baseball player in the history of the sport has suffered more visa problems—for whatever reason, Garces is harder to smuggle into this country than six tons of heroin. But isn't it impossible *not* to root for a fat guy with the nickname El Guapo? He's like Bosley in *Charlie's Angels*—you don't really need him, but he's fun to have around.[47]

47 Which reminds me, was Bosley his first name or his last name? Even when I was seven, I was wondering about this stuff. Was his name something like Bob Bosley or was it something like Bosley Jones? And was he gay or not? Why didn't he ever **take a drunken crack at Jaclyn Smith** one night? I mean, was it just me or was Jackie practically ASKING FOR IT from Bosley every episode??? She loved Bosley! Or did she just love him in that "I love my gay male friend because he's safe to be around" sense, so she was extra-affectionate? I need to know these things.

3) John Valentin's potential comeback year

After signing his big contract extension, he proceeded to stink up the joint in '98 and looked like he was following Jim Rice's diet from the 1989 season.[48] But with Johnny V entering his prime, there's no reason to think he won't bounce back in '99. As an aside, I love how Valentin plans on wearing the "Mo's going going gone" under his T-shirt all year. Knowing Duquette, he'll probably have Valentin poisoned during a pregame meal this month.

[48] When I went to San Francisco to visit friends in 1994, after a week of boozing, cigarette smoking and 2 a.m. meals, I came back to Boston a good eight pounds heavier and looking like **Elvis during his final Vegas tour**. Sure, I lost the weight, but ever since then, whenever my dad sees someone who gained weight in a short amount of time, he always jokes, "They look like you when you came back from San Francisco." Anyway, the 1998 version of John Valentin was in Dad's Hall of Fame for the "They look like you when you came back from San Francisco" joke. Some others: Antoine Walker after the 1999 NBA Lockout ended; Kirstie Alley; the guy who played Detective James Martinez on *NYPD Blue*; Kathleen Turner; every other John Travolta movie from 1996 on; Dennis Johnson; Tom Hanks; Carl Everett in 2001; and the MVP, Jason Alexander.

4) Flash Gordon

Sure, he choked in his biggest appearance last year, giving up the go-ahead double to Cleveland in Game Four that killed the season. But he's still one of the best *regular season* closers in baseball. For 162 games, you're in good hands.

(I know, I know… I'm trying to behave…)

5) Speed and defense!

Are you ready to see a Red Sox team hit balls into the gap, steal bases and take the extra base on long flyballs? Me neither. Just reading these preseason stories feels like getting the Holy Cross alumni magazine and reading an "Administration tells female coeds: 'Stop dressing like sluts!'" feature. But at least it's a different way of thinking, and "different" is perfectly acceptable when you haven't won a World Series in 80 years. Whether it plays out like Eddie Murphy's decision to record the *Party All the Time* album remains to be seen.

6) Derek Lowe

Maybe the most underrated Duquette move, swapping floundering closer Heathcliff Slocumb for Lowe (an up-and-coming set-up man in the bullpen) and Jason Varitek (who won a spot in the catching platoon last year) when a bag of baseballs and a couple of bats would have sufficed. Lowe may have been Boston's best bullpen guy in the playoffs. That's a fact. Say what you want about Duquette, but that was the single greatest deal since Andy Dufresne bought the rock hammer from Red for $10.

7) Sabes

Not only did Bret Saberhagen come back from a rotator cuff injury to pitch effectively last season, poor Sabes went through a divorce so acrimonious that he nearly retired from baseball, just because he didn't want to turn part of his paycheck over to his ex-wife every week. The lesson, as always: Women are purely and simply evil. But as my buddy Gus said last summer, "It's always good to have a guy named 'Sabes' on your team, isn't it?"

8) Roger and Mo coming to town in different uniforms

When in doubt, remember: Cheer Mo, boo Roger. It's like knowing that your bread plate is on the left and your water is on the right. Cheer Mo, boo Roger. Cheermobooroger.

9) Tim Wakefield

Does Wakefield look back at his 14–1 start in '95 the same way Alicia Silverstone looks back at those five or six weeks after *Clueless* came out? Of course he does. Still, Wake goes somewhat unappreciated in Boston—you can pencil him in for 12–15 wins and 220–240 innings every season. Granted, he threw 23 pitches in Game Two of the playoffs before the Indians sent him packing, but we'll let that slide since it's a new season. He eats up those innings. You need guys like that on a pitching staff.[49]

10) Pedro

When Pedro's pitching, I'm watching. Although I'm worried they catered to him too much this winter—after the signings of Ramon Martinez (his brother) and Jose Offerman (his buddy), I'm ready to be asked to stand for the Dominican national anthem before home games this season.

11) Darren Lewis and Damon Buford

As a longtime Sox fan accustomed to the sight of Tony Armas stumbling around the outfield like the town drunk, or Ellis Burks and Mike Greenwell colliding like a receiver and a strong safety every three innings, it was a pleasure to watch Lewis and Buford chase down flyballs into the deep recesses of the triangle at Fenway. They can even steal a few bases for you. One potential bad omen: Lewis looked so shot by the end of August that the Fenway groundskeeper accidentally drew a big chalk outline of Lewis' body in centerfield after a night game. But we'll see.

12) Dan Duquette is still one of the brightest young execs in baseball

I mean, he did trade for Pedro and Lowe and rescue Wakefield from the scrap heap. Maybe it wouldn't kill us to overlook some of his mistakes. Like offering $6 million more

49 I didn't always feel this way about Wakefield, who sucked over the next two years: a 5.08 ERA in 1999 and a 5.48 ERA in 2000. During that rocky stretch, I wrote one of my favorite jokes in the history of my old website: "Saying Tim Wakefield eats up innings for the Red Sox is like saying that Michael Gee eats up newspaper pages for the *Boston Herald*."

for Offerman than any other team, especially when he already had three other second basemen on the 40-man roster. Or signing Reggie Jefferson and Troy O'Leary to long-term deals and making them completely un-tradeable. Or botching the Vaughn and Clemens contracts. Or signing Darren Lewis to a three-year contract to play center field and then offering Bernie Williams $90 million two weeks later. Or getting Damon Buford and Jim Leyritz for Aaron Sele (who somehow won 18 games last year), then giving away Leyritz for three guys who aren't even on the 40-man roster anymore. Or signing Robinson Checo and Steve Avery for anything more than $10 an hour. Or giving up a 15-game winner (Jamie Moyer) for Darren Bragg. (You know what? Let's just stop here.)

12) Kip Gross and Pat Rapp

Journeyman pitchers who may or may not make the roster. I've just always wanted the Red Sox to have a guy named Gross. You might know his brother, Really. Also, if Pat Rapp stinks, we can always call him Pat Crapp.[50]

13) No more Dennis Eckersley!

And while we're here, no more Jim Corsi! He was built like Bob Stanley, pitched like Stanley, looked like Stanley, even wore the Steamer's same number. I mean, did they have to give Jim Corsi no. 46?[51] That's like the new camp counselors at Crystal Lake handing out Jason's old hockey mask to the most psychotic kid in camp on Friday the 13th. Can't they just skip 46 and go from 45 to 47 on the roster, like how some hotels refuse to have a 13th floor? Would anyone be against this?

14) Jose Offerman

Forget that Boston overpaid for him or that he was an obvious panic signing to make up for Mo Vaughn's departure. Forget that the Sox don't have the balls to play him at first base—where he belongs, by the way—because they don't want to deal with the "Offerman replaces Mo" media fuss that would accompany such a move. Bottom line? Offerman is a .300 hitter who steals bases and hits lots of doubles and triples—as long as he doesn't have a nervous breakdown from all the attention he'll be getting in Beantown. At the very least, it will be interesting.

(You don't know how hard it was to write that last paragraph. If you'll excuse me for on second, I just need to slam my head against my desk a few times. I'll be right back.)

50 And you wonder why nobody would hire me.

51 Our researchers swear that Corsi wore no. 41 that season, but I distinctly remember him wearing 46 in spring training and switching to 41 right before the season. We agreed to split the difference and run the section with this disclaimer—until someone creates the website www.numbersthatguysworeinspringtraining.com, we may never have an answer.

52 Interesting comment here: Expectations just weren't that high for this team. Then again, we had no idea Pedro would become the next Sandy Koufax.

53 As it turned out, I ended up going that July. Some highlights: Being in the same ballpark with every Living Baseball Legend from the 20th century (well, except for Pete Rose and **Rusty Kuntz**); when they wheeled out Ted Williams, it was like they were wheeling out God to throw out the first pitch; when they introduced Clemens, I was booing so vehemently, I think a tonsil actually flew out of my mouth and landed in centerfield; before the first pitch, four *Top Gun* planes came zooming over the top of the

(WHAM!)
(POW!)
(CRACK!)
(KABAAM!)

15) Ramon Martinez

A potentially no. 3 starter and dugout buddy for Pedro, even if he can't pitch until August (which doesn't really matter because this team is obviously gearing toward 2000, anyway).[52] And even if Ramon gets hurt again, who cares? It's not our money. I think the Sox should go the whole nine yards and sign 25 Dominican players.

16) Trot Nixon

Honestly, the Trot Nixon Era is one of the only reasons I'm truly excited about the '99 Sox. I really like this guy. Can't explain it. Then again, since Dwight Evans was pushed out of town in 1990, rightfield has been a bigger disaster spot in Boston than Spinal Tap's drummer vacancy

17) The 1999 All-Star Game at Fenway

Count me in.[53]

18) Newspaper articles about grizzled vets in the Sox clubhouse

I always enjoy spring training articles[54] about veterans like Sabes, Mark Portugal, Mike Stanley, and so on, where they talk about their long careers and all the things they've seen and all the lessons they've learned. I'm a sucker for those. This team is more grizzled than Jack Palance, Robert Loggia, and Strom Thurmond combined.

19) John Wasdin

Sit back and enjoy the fun as Wasdin attempts to set the team record for "Most appearances in a season when the Sox are winning or losing by six runs or more." In June, he'll pass Sammy Stewart on the all-time list. In July, he'll pass Mark Clear. In August, he'll pass Tom House. Then in September, the biggie: The Steamer, Bob Stanley. Should be a mesmerizing ride.

20) The "If" Factor

With the Red Sox, there's always the "If" Factor, no matter how bad the team is. For instance, if you wanted to spin something along the lines of "This team might surprise people in

park, out of nowhere, and gave everyone a collective heart attack ("Goddamit Maverick!"); Pedro was magnificent—two hitless innings with five K's (in the height of the Steroid Era, as it turned out); after Robbie Alomar messed up Pedro's perfect performance by botching that grounder in the second, some guy behind me screamed out, "SCREW YOU, YOU SPITTER!" Highest of high comedy. Summed up everyone's feelings.

One lowlight: Not only was it a terrible game after the first two innings, but **the crowd was so clueless** (tons of phonies and pseudos) that Pedro had two K's before everyone in the crowd stood up and started cheering on every pitch. When Pedro walked off the mound after the second inning, he didn't receive get a full-fledged standing O; it was almost like the fans thought he was pitching the whole game or something. The crowd should have been chanting "Peh-dro! Peh-dro!" all through the second inning, only none of these nitwits knew what to do. It was like seeing U2 in concert and nobody knowing the words to "Sunday Bloody Sunday."

54 Some of my other favorite generic spring training angles: "The New

1999," you could do it the following way (and Peter Gammons probably will):[55]

"Remember, a team is only as good as its stars, and the Sox have three of the best players in baseball in Nomar, Pedro and Flash. Now, if Valentin can rebound this year, if Stanley and O'Leary can consistently knock in runs, if Lewis and Buford can get on base, and if Offerman can have a season like he did with Kansas City last year, the Sox will score some runs. And if Saberhagen and Wakefield can match their production from last season, the Sox could get 50–55 wins from their top three starters. In addition, if Portugal, Rapp and/or Brian Rose can solidify the 4–5 spots in the pitching rotation and the Sox can get some middle relief help from Jim Corsi, Wasdin, Gross, etc, the pitching staff will be in superb shape, especially with the Lowe/Gordon combo in the eighth and ninth innings. And if Duquette can swing a trade for a power hitter in July, these guys might actually make some noise in the playoffs!"

(Looks good on paper, doesn't it? In the words of the great Joaquin Andujar, "youneverknow.")[56]

Guy," "The Position Change," "The Reclamation Project," "The Guy Who's Unhappy With His Contract," "The Guy Who Always Wanted to Play Here," and, of course, "The Foreign Guy With the Visa Problem."

55 One of my favorite Gammons quirks: Every spring training, he assesses different teams and goes into his "If…" routine. I wish he reviewed upcoming movies as well. "If Cuba Gooding Jr. can get back to his *Jerry Maguire* form, if Horatio Sanz can finally become the next John Belushi, and if **Mischa Barton finally gets naked** in the movie, I think *Boat Trip 2* could be the comedy smash of the summer!" With some prodding, Gammons could be the next Earl Dittman.

56 So what happened? Somehow the team ended up winning 94 games and the wildcard, even with Sabes missing half the season, Flash throwing 17 innings, and Wakefield going in the tank. On the flip side, Nomar and Pedro had Hall of Fame seasons; Lowe, O'Leary, Offerman and Stanley came up big; and they received unexpected contributions from Garces and Brian Daubach. Likable team, fun season.

SEE YA, FENWAY

May 17, 1999

When I was 15 years old, I grew seven inches in three months, shooting from 5-foot-3 to 5-foot-10 right after my ninth grade graduation. Looking back, it was of the most important events of the summer of 1984, right up there with MJ's coming-out party in the Olympics, NBC greenlighting *Miami Vice* and Apollonia's nude scene in *Purple Rain*. I remember being ecstatic about three things: **a)** I was finally as tall as the tallest girls in my grade; **b)** I could come THISCLOSE to touching a regulation-size basketball rim; and **c)** I was finally taller than my Uncle Bob.[57] Those were unbelievable developments, right up there with seeing my first armpit hair.

The one negative? I would never fully enjoy a baseball game at Fenway Park ever again.

Let's be honest: If you're taller than 5-foot-3 and weigh more than 130 pounds, you won't be comfortable at Fenway. The park was built in 1912; everybody was short in 1912. Even seen a bathtub or a shower from a house back then? It was like the land of the midgets. When they built Fenway, they probably never imagined that the park would still be kicking around ninety years later. And that's fine. Unfortunately, unless you're built like John Harrington, Bob Costas or Sarah Michelle Gellar, you can't sit through a nine-inning game at Fenway without needing to see a chiropractor afterward. Take me, for instance: At 6-foot-1 and around 180 pounds, every trip to Fenway makes me feel like I'm stuck in the middle seat on a cross-country flight.

So that's one reason Fenway needs to go. I could think of a hundred more reasons—for instance, the place is haunted; the concession stands stink; the place is haunted; there are only 15,000 decent seats in the whole place; the place is haunted; the park is falling apart; the place is haunted; there's a 3 percent chance you could be stuck behind a beam for nine innings; and, of course, THE PLACE IS FUCKING HAUNTED!—but it all goes back to that basic premise: Fenway isn't a comfortable place to watch baseball unless you're short. I mean, it's pretty sad when a Red Sox fan has more fun attending baseball games at Yankee Stadium.[58]

57 My **Uncle Bob is the Tom Cruise of the Simmons family**—he's listed at 5-10, but there's no way he's taller than 5-7. In the mid-'70s, he once sent my father a postcard from Fort Lauderdale that included a section about his new girlfriend with "36-24-36!" in parentheses; somehow I ended up reading it, forcing my father to explain what those numbers meant. I was, like, seven. Needless to say, Uncle Bob has been my favorite member of the Simmons family ever since.

58 I didn't mean this—I was just lashing out.

None of this matters to the Save Fenway defenders. They love Fenway because of the "tradition." Sure, it's a tradition of heartbreak, but it's a tradition. Williams played there. Fisk hit his home run there. DiMaggio and Ruth played there. So did Yaz and Rice. Clemens and Bob Feller pitched there. So did Tom Seaver and Nolan Ryan. They love the Wall and Pesky's Pole. They love the Citgo sign. They love seeing Boston's skyline in the distance. They love the fact that their parents took them to Fenway when they were kids. They fondly remember the first time someone puked on them in the bleachers.

All of that stuff is pretty cool, I admit. But it still doesn't make up for the fact that Fenway Park was built in NINETEEN TWELVE!

Come on people! Work with me![59] There's a thin line between tradition and sadomasochism. Anyone who has visited Camden Yards will tell you how superior the experience is, whether you're discussing the concession stands, the immaculate condition of the park, the food/drink options, the roomy seats, the luxury of walking around and still seeing the game, and best of all, a never-ending supply of available good seats.[60] With Fenway, you need connections just to get tickets inside the third/first bags; the average fan gets stuck in right field, sitting in a seat facing second base, wishing they were Tattoo from *Fantasy Island* for the next three hours.

Well, there's hope for us. Last weekend, the Red Sox announced their intentions to build a new baseball park adjacent to the old one on Yawkey Way, hoping to complete the project in time for the 2003 season. Of course, in classic Boston tradition, the team doesn't even own the land adjacent to Fenway, which means the project will probably drag along for years in a "Big Dig" kind of way.[61] And that's fine. At least it's a start. I don't care that our team needs a new stadium to "compete ecomomically in the 21st century"; I want a stadium that belongs in the 21st century. And Fenway Park doesn't belong anymore. Sad but true.

Since the Sox promised to keep "crucial" characteristics of the old ballpark alive—the Wall, the Triangle, Pesky's Pole, Williams' red seat and so on—the announcement lacked that "OH MY GOD! THEY'RE TEARING DOWN FENWAY!" element that seemed so inevitable. Fans actually seem okay with this—I didn't receive more than 10 e-mails about it all weekend.

59 Telltale sign of a writer who hasn't quite figured out his style yet: Too many exclamation points.

60 Within two to three years, even Camden was dated, blown out of the water by state-of-the-art ballparks like Safeco Field, Pac Bell and Minute Maid Park. In the early '90s? It was like going from black-and-white to HDTV. Also, the greatest, most random play I've ever seen happened in Camden, when Mark McLemore hit an inside-the-park homer but got **knocked unconscious** by the throw from the outfield as he slid across home plate. I attended that game with my old college roomie John "Jack-O" O'Connell, as well as our buddy Joe House and his brother, Tim. Two nights before, we met a female friend for drinks who brought a girlfriend with her who wasn't wearing any underwear. Jack-O realized this because we were sitting in one of those giant booths and the girl was sitting across from him, spread-eagle, so he elbowed Tim for confirmation. Not only did Tim confirm, he admitted later, "You could even see a little gobbler." I just remember being furious that nobody told me until after the fact—in fact, we instituted a rule after this that,

Even Peter Gammons and Dan Shaughnessy came out in favor of the new plan, mainly because the team promised to keep the name Fenway Park alive with the new stadium. The only person who still seems unhappy?

Me.

I hate this idea.

If you're going to build a new baseball stadium, then suck it up and do it. Don't kill off Fenway and say, "But hey, the new stadium's gonna look just like it!" Frankly, I think it's a little sick. For instance, if my father passed away—God forbid—would I immediately find another 51-year-old man with bad eyesight, ask him to grow a handlebar mustache, then take him to Celtics games just so I could keep calling someone "Dad"? Of course not. Fenway Park is one of a kind. You can't re-create it. More importantly, why would you want to re-create it?

See, that's the key to the whole thing. The worst part about being a Red Sox fan is the neverending baggage—Ruth, Buckner, Dent, Burton, Slaughter, Bearden, Clemens/Fisk/Lynn/Mo, Jackie Robinson's tryout, etc. —that makes rooting for this franchise such a suffocating, unbearable chore. Fenway isn't the biggest problem, but it's definitely a symptom. Since they built the Wall in 1930, the Red Sox have appeared in four World Series and squandered them all. Seven full decades have passed, each filled with some level of heartbreak. The media seems to relish our team's legacy of failure, and even some Sox fans seem to enjoy perpetuating our misfortune to some degree. It's a vicious cycle. This seems like an ideal opportunity for the franchise to distance itself from its tragic history, much like the way the Broncos distanced themselves from their Super Bowl failures by changing their uniforms two years ago (winning two titles in the process). Sometimes you just need to move forward—not backward or sideways—before you can change your own destiny.**62**

That's why a new baseball stadium in Boston should look *completely different* from the old one. Change the dimensions, change the outfield walls, change everything. They couldn't go far enough in my book. I would love to see them flip Fenway around—put Pesky's Pole and the bullpens in left field, stick the Triangle and the bleachers in left-center, then build another 37-foot Green Monster in right field. Seriously, what's wrong with creating Bizarro Fenway? It would be like that *Seinfeld* episode when George Costanza's life takes off as soon as he

if it ever happened again, someone at the table had to say "code red!" Anyway, after McLemore was being carried off the field, Jack-O said, "I can't believe that, that's the most unbelievable thing I've seen all weekend!" And Tim House quickly responded, "No way, I'm still going with **the girl with no underwear**." When they do a *SportsCentury* about Camden Yards, I just hope I have a chance to tell that story.

61 That was the understatement of the century—as it turned out, this project was blocked by the owners of the *Boston Phoenix*, who controlled the land next to Fenway.

62 Two years later, this would work for the Patriots.

starts going against his first instinct, only with some World Series titles at the end of the rainbow.[63]

Whatever happens, I just hope the new place ends up looking different from the Fenway we know and fear—er, love. Give us comfortable seats facing home plate, the chance to order a hot dog without heading into some underground dungeon, better food and drink options, a place that isn't dirtier than some college junior's off-campus apartment. Make it fun to see a game for the simple reason that *it's fun to see a baseball game.*

Here's the big question: Will the fans allow this franchise to move forward or are we content with being lovable losers? Think about it. Most people search for ways to move away from a tortured past; we would rather embrace it. We'll allow them to build a new stadium, but only if it looks like the old one. We want them to call the new stadium Fenway Park, but only if the original Fenway Park is still standing right next to it. What are we holding onto here? At the rate we're going, the team will keep breaking our hearts in this new ballpark, and everything will be just like it always was. Deep down, maybe that's what some people want in New England.

Let the record show that I'm not one of them.[64]

63 I'm very proud of this idea. Even though we ended up winning a title, I'm convinced that we would have won for 10 straight years with Bizarro Fenway.

64 Okay, so that's how I felt about Fenway at the time. But while we're here, three underrated things about seeing a game at Fenway in 1999:

1) You could point to Johnny Pesky in the dugout and make the "Do you think Johnny Pesky calls his dick 'The Pesky Pole?'" joke.

2) It remained the only place on the planet where you could urinate in a trough next to other men, really **the closest experience to prison** you could have in a baseball stadium.

3) Before they added Monster seats, when the Wave went around Fenway and reached the section next to the left field wall, two seconds always passed before the fans in Section 35 of the bleachers picked it up and started going again—an implicit pause, as if The Wave was being performed by imaginary people sitting on the leftfield wall. That always killed me.

THE LOST WEEKEND

September 14, 1999

One of the memorable weekends in recent Boston sports history and I missed it. On the bright side, I kept a running diary of, um, missing it. Here's what transpired:

THURSDAY NIGHT

2:00 a.m.: Tomorrow I'm headed to Pittsburgh for my buddy Stoner's wedding—leaving Boston during the same weekend as Sox-Yanks and Pats-Jets. To make matters worse, my Uncle Ricky offered me choice tickets for all three Sox games at Yankee Stadium—and I had to turn him down. If the Stoner ever gets divorced, I will retroactively kill him. And no jury would convict me.[65]

Now I'm packing my suitcase. My head is pounding. My contacts are putting headlocks on my retinas. My back feels like hell. The Sports Gal[66] went out with friends to a local bar and downed multiple mixed drinks—now she's lying on her side on the sofa, with all the blood settling on one side of her body, like in one of those HBO *Autopsy* shows. With one last ounce of strength, I set the VCR for Sunday's Pats game before heading to bed, dragging the Sports Gal by her hair like an extra in *Quest for Fire*.

FRIDAY MORNING

11:30 a.m.: Our plane to Pittsburgh is delayed by a little-known rule: the departures of all US Air planes must be delayed by at least one hour. Fortunately, this gives me time to read three newspapers. At least that's the plan. You've never sat next to the Sports Gal in the airport—she's commenting on every passenger at Gate B16 ("Oh my God, Bill, look at THAT lady's hair!") and asking me questions like, "Hey, where do you stand on gun control?" Finally, I give in and put the papers down. She wins. She always wins.

11:50: In a last-minute desperation move, I offer her some head scratches. If this doesn't work, I'll have to resort to Plan B: Strangulation.

11:55: She just fell asleep. And if you think I'm not capable

65 Still married, the Stoner's real name is Rob Stone, which explains why we call him Stoner. There are no marijuana connotations at all. As far as you know.

66 The Sports Gal's first appearance in the book! That's the pseudonym I gave to my girlfriend in lieu of using her real name. There were actually *two* Sports Gals during the four years I wrote for my old website (1997–2001), almost like there were two principals in ***The White Shadow*** (one in the pilot, one in the series). The first one held the crown from November 1997 to March 1998, when barely anyone was reading me except for family members, friends and a few 15 year olds. And since it was a fun gimmick, I had no problem transferring it to my new girlfriend when we started dating in June 1998 (as I started to gain more and more readers). The original plan was to keep calling whomever I was dating The Sports Gal in columns, almost like how there's a new Miss America every year—but I ended up marrying Sports Gal II. In retrospect, it would have been more entertaining if there were a slew of Sports Gals with escalating Roman numerals (like Super Bowls or WrestleManias), so I could have written things like, "As Sports Gal XIV said the other day...." Although I can't imagine anyone doing a better job (as a significant other and running character for the column) than the current Sports Gal. And yes, my attorney advised me to include that last sentence.

67 My Top 750 Underrated American Cities list: **1)** Milwaukee; **2)** Pittsburgh; **3)** Portland; **4)** Seattle... **750) Jacksonville.**

of reading two sports sections while scratching somebody's head at the same time...well, you just don't know me well enough.

1:55 p.m.: We're halfway to Pittsburgh and the Sports Gal is still unconscious, ruining my chances to join the Mile High Club. Here's what US Air has left in their magazine cabinet: *People En Espanol*, *BusinessWeek*, *Ebony*, and a 1984 *Sports Illustrated* with Alan Trammell on the cover. Is it a rule that airplanes can't carry good magazines? Is this a federal regulation? And remember the days when airplanes gave you snacks on lunch-time flights? Now they throw five peanuts at you, fill a Dixie cup with warm ginger ale and call it a flight. Plus, the stewardesses all kind of look like Brian Dennehy.

(That reminds me, what happened to the days of cute stewardesses? Years ago, if you told your buddies you hooked up with a stewardess who you met on an airplane, they would have been pumped for you. Now they would ask questions like "Was she pushing two bills?" and "How drunk were you?")

2:10: Hey, this month's issue of *People En Espanol* has an article on Ricky Martin! I can't believe it! I mean, I never, *ever* thought I'd see a Ricky Martin article in an issue of *People En Espanol*.

2:40: Just landed. My third time in Pittsburgh—very underrated city. Take the best things about Portland, Oregon, put them in Hartford and you'd have Pittsburgh.[67] Just to liven things up on the way to our hotel, I start a fight with the Sports Gal in our cab —it's always good to put on the gloves and spar a few rounds every so often. Keeps you fresh. Unfortunately, cab driver Grwdsxcdfsgstyg Jkksgsfagegegjj looks pretty terrified.

3:45: Few things are secretly more fun than checking into a hotel room. I always feel like a little kid. Should I nap or pay $8.95 for *The Things That My Wife Won't Do* on Spanktravision? Hmmmm...I need a nap.

5:30: Just woke up. Not only is the Sports Gal still asleep, she may have lapsed into an Adrian Balboa-like coma. As Mike Tyson would say, I think she's narcoscopic.

6:30: At church for the wedding rehearsal, the queasy groom (Stoner) has a "Trent Dilfer in the fourth quarter of a close game" look about him. Meanwhile, one of the ushers (Wiker) just accidentally dropped an F-bomb. It's always fun when somebody swears in church, realizes what they just said, then their eyes bulge out of their heads like an extra in *Total Recall*. Of course, this doesn't matter to me because I'm not religious—if there was a God, the Red Sox would have won a World Series by now.[68]

6:45: One of the bronze urns in the church would make a perfect trophy for our roto football league—it looks like a mini-version of the Stanley Cup. That prompted the inevitable, "Should we take this thing today or tomorrow?" conversation between Camp and me, leading to this exchange:

Camp: If you steal from a church, do you go to hell?

Me: We're already going to hell. Remember when we watched *Life Goes On* that time and made fun of Corky?[69]

Camp: You're right…we're taking the urn.

7:00: Well, the first wrestling jokes of the weekend have been made. When the best man (Jim) shows up late for rehearsal, Stoner imitates WWF announcer Jim Ross and screams out, "Good God! That…that's Jim Grady's music!" Meanwhile, Camp and I just spent the last 10 minutes thinking of every reason why a hardcore match would work in a church. You have urns, fire extinguishers, collection cups, wooden rows, candles, wine bottles, the altar podium, wooden chairs. Why hasn't Vince McMahon thought of this yet?[70]

7:30: Onto the Riverwatch for a gala rehearsal dinner, where I spend the next 45 minutes drinking bourbon-and-Cokes, socializing and trying to forget that Pedro is pitching the biggest game of the season. Every time you miss a Pedro start, you could be missing out on one of Those Games. It's a fact. I love him as much as I can platonically love another man. I'm not ashamed to admit it.[71]

8:45: Jim and I exchange good-natured barbs about the NY/Boston thing, with Jim finally announcing, "I don't care if the Yanks lose this year…I'll just go home and look at my replica World Series rings from '96 and '98." Am I bleeding? I think I just got tagged.

9:35: Just had the following conversation with the bartender:

68 Hah!

69 Camp used to do an imitation called "**Every Episode of *Life Goes On***" that started with Corky proudly announcing, "Dad, I washed the car!" followed by Corky's Dad looking out on the street and saying, "Uh, Corky, that's not our car."

70 At the time of Stoner's wedding, the WWF was more popular than ever—with the Rock, Stone Cold, Billy Gunn and the Road Dogg, Triple H, and everyone else, plus all the hardcore stuff they were incorporating because of ECW's influence, this was the golden era of modern wrestling. All of us were watching every Monday night. You couldn't help it. I don't care if you think less of me.

71 Because I never fully appreciated the Bird Era until it was over, that gave me a good perspective of the Pedro Era. Even when it was happening, I was savoring every moment. And I know, Randy Johnson's stats were just as good, and Clemens did it for longer, and Koufax has the rings, but I can't imagine that there was anyone quite like Pedro in 1999.

Me: Any chance of switching to the Sox-Yankees game?
Bartender: No. We don't have a satellite.
Me: You didn't catch a score, did you?
Bartender [perturbed]: No.

(Yep...he'll be giving me a Jack and Coke with some saliva a little bit later in the evening. And just for the record, there's nothing worse than having no idea how your team is faring during an important game.You just feel left out and helpless, like a male crew member in an all-female porn movie, but worse.)

10:00: Camp gives a rambling toast about Rob's hair in front of 100-plus people, breaking the old rule, "Don't speak in front of people if you've been drinking and have no point." Highest of high comedy. You know your toast is going poorly when you get *heckled* at a wedding rehearsal dinner.

10:20: Jim and I spend 20 minutes watching the Pirates–Cards game under the faint hope they'll show a Sox score. No dice. And for those of you wondering where the Sports Gal has been during all of this, not only is she looking good, she's talking to everyone and anyone. She's the Tim Wakefield of dates—throw her in any social situation and she can give you quality work. Need a spot start? Call the Sports Gal. Need help in the bullpen? She's your girl. Need someone to talk to the bride's cousin's father's sister's niece? Just give her the signal. She's got five pitches, she can throw them all for strikes, and she doesn't even need a scouting report for the other team's lineup.

11:35: Back to the Holiday Inn for late-night drinks. We never did get that Sox–Yanks score.[72] By the way, I'm drunker than Charles Nelson Reilly during your average *Match Game* right now. Could someone give me a navy-blue suit and a sailor's hat please?

11:45: There it is! Red Sox 4, Yankees 1! Woo-hoo! According to our friend Wyman, Pedro struck out 17 en route to a one-hitter—a ONE-HITTER?!?!?!?!?!?—even striking out eight of the last nine. Good God! Th-that's Cy Young's music!

12:05 a.m.: Just said, "You're lucky you're getting married because you made me miss the greatest game of all time" to Stoner for the 100th time in the past 20 minutes.[73]

72 If you're wondering, "Why didn't he call someone on a cell phone?" I didn't own one. Remember, this was 1999. Cell phones were for rich people and posse members.

73 Six years later and I haven't quite gotten over this. There were three transcendent Pedro games—the near no-hitter against Tampa, Game Five against Cleveland, and this one—and I missed one of the three. And, yes, that was a Yankees team that ended up winning their third title in four years.

1:00: While discussing the Transcendant Comedy Moments of All Time—with Camp's speech being immediately inducted in the Top Five, of course—we decide the no. 1 moment was Carl Lewis botching the national anthem, when players on both teams were cracking up and ESPN's Charley Steiner lost it on air while doing highlights from the game. Nothing will ever be funnier than that. That's the comedy ceiling right there.**74**

1:30–4:00: Room party in Camp's room. Things getting blurry...beers on ice in bathtub...speed quarters...things moving too fast...*Breakfast Club* showing in background...I feel like Kevin Kennedy during the 1995 playoffs...*Do I stutter?*...smoking cigs in a non-smoking room...*Answer the question, Claire*...things getting spilled...is this how Chris Farley died?...Wiker calls front desk for 6:00 a.m. wakeup call while Camp's in the bathroom (pure genius)...*I taped Larry Lester's buns together*...Red Sox within 5.5 games...Pedro for president.

SATURDAY MORNING

10:00 a.m.: Ugh.

11:00: Man.

12:00 p.m.: Yikes.

12:30: I force myself out of bed to call my father, who reports that Pedro was beyond belief last night. On the final pitch, Dad claims that Chuck Knoblauch was just starting his swing when Pedro's fastball zoomed by him for strike three, like a scene from a bad baseball movie where they use special effects to make the ball look faster. I haven't heard Dad this excited since I told him I was graduating college with a 3.0.

2:00: Las Vegas lists the Sports Gal as "Questionable (hangover)" for today's Stone-Carson wedding. I'm listed as "Probable (headache)."

2:20: I stop by Jim and Camp's room to pick them up. Jim looks paler than the half-eaten guy from *Jaws* who floats out of the boat and scares Richard Dreyfuss in the scuba diving scene. Meanwhile, I'm green. We make quite a combo. Well, at least we won't be posing for a bunch of pictures that Stoner and Lynn will be looking at for the rest of their lives.

2:30: During the limo ride to the church, the bridesmaids

74 This section eventually morphed into the Unintentional Comedy Scale, my column that ran on ESPN.com in 2002. Some other top-five candidates: Every Dikembe Mutombo interview; Ozzy Osbourne performing household tasks; Rickey Henderson's Hall Of Fame induction speech (when it happens); David from *Real World New Orleans* singing "Come On Be My Baby Tonight"; Corey Feldman's performance in *Blown Away*; Corey Haim's *E! True Hollywood Story*; the wedding video of Liza Minnelli and David Gest; **Dontae Jones high-fiving Henry Louis Gates** during pregame warmups of a Celtics home game in 1997; Journey's "Separate Ways" video; and Tom Cruise's 2005 appearance on *Oprah*. Of course, Joe Namath telling Suzy Kolber, "I want to kiss you" on national TV during a 2003 Jets-Pats game tops everything.

keep asking us questions like "Are you guys okay?" and "If you throw up, could you throw up in this champagne bucket?" All the puking talk isn't helping Stoner, who looks like Trent Dilfer on third and 19 from his own three right now. He's the color of skimmed milk.

2:35: Mmmmmm...Advil and Diet Coke.

3:00: Camp and I have the job of lighting the candles before the ceremony. After performing our duties, the wedding coordinator tells us, "I'll tell you, you guys make a couple of handsome acolytes." Good God! Th-that's the Acolytes' music!

3:30: With the wedding approaching, Wiker and I visit Stoner in the basement of the church and make about 15 Dilfer jokes. That's why I'm here, to keep things loose. I'm like the Jack Haley of this wedding.

(Seriously, as someone who's served as an usher or best man in six weddings, this is always my favorite moment—either backstage or in the basement of the church right before the ceremony, the moment of truth, when everyone collectively realizes, "Hey, this thing's actually gonna happen." There's nothing quite like it. What a rush. If the groom-to-be can get through that moment and keep going, it's definitely meant to be. As for the bride, she's not even thinking about stuff like that because it's much too late to return the dress. And yet, I digress.)[75]

3:59: With the wedding starting in seconds, everyone is dead-serious...well, except Camp and me. We're whispering about how funny it would be if the loudspeaker suddenly started blaring the Road Dogg's wrestling intro music ("Bowwwwwwwnah-nah NAHHH!"), followed by Stoner strutting down the aisle holding a microphone and screaming, "Oh, you didn't know? Your ass better caaaaaaaaall somebody!"

4:45: The Stoner is officially betrothed. If there's anything hotter than a tuxedo in a hot church after a night of drinking, please, let me know.[76]

6:15: Our wedding party just rode around in a stretch limo for the last hour, drinking champagne and taking pictures. Good times all around. Now it's off to the reception. Plus, our limo driver, Z, just reported that the Red Sox outlasted the Yankees, 11–10. Thank you, Z.[77] Four and a half games back.

75 When this happened to me four years later, Geoff Gallo (my best man) and I were stuck in a back room that had a piano, which prompted Geoff to play the "Laurie's walking across the street to see why Annie won't answer the phone" music from the end of *Halloween*—a funny idea except for the look on our priest's face, who just happened to be walking by at the time.

76 My old college roomie, Chipper, **fainted during his own wedding** in 1994—because of the hangover/hot tux/hot church trifecta—which was mortifying at the time and becomes 3 percent funnier every year. It's like Alan Alda's comment in *Crimes and Misdemeanors*, how comedy equals tragedy plus time. By 2025, even Chip will think it was funny. I think.

77 Only limo drivers, bookies and NBA centers could ever have the name "Z."

One downner: Camp and I just realized that we forgot to steal the urn.

8:00: After our party gets introduced at the reception, I can't stop teasing Jim about the Yanks (only because Clemens is going tomorrow). Stuff like, "Maybe they could hypnotize Clemens into thinking they've been mathematically eliminated, he'd probably toss a two-hitter." Jim doesn't say anything. He knows the truth about Roger.

8:30–11:00: The wedding reception carries on and on. Let's just say that I drank a lot and stepped on a lot of female feet.

11:30: Back to the Holiday Inn for more beers. Unfortunately, the wrestling jokes finally stretch too far as Camp performs Degeneration X's "I got two words for ya…SUCK IT" routine for Steve and Wyman, but the drummer for the Holiday Inn lounge's band mistakenly thinks Camp is talking to him. Enraged, the drummer takes a wild swing at Camp and misses, sending them plunging into a large plant before Steve pins the drummer against a wall. My God, it's a hardcore hotel lounge match! Things finally settle down, although we're all a little perturbed at the drummer. Nobody gets ejected from the game and Camp gets to shoot two free throws.[78]

78 I swear on Tom Brady's life, this happened.

11:40: The band packs up and leaves, maybe because we hissed and booed them during their last song, with your buddy Sports Guy leading the way. You don't mess with the Wedding Acolytes. No sirree. Everyone spends the next 45 minutes encouraging me to write about the wedding weekend. "Come on!" I tell them. "That's ridiculous. Nobody would want to read about a wedding weekend with people they don't even know!"

1:00 a.m.: Time for bed. Not by choice.

SUNDAY MORNING

5:00 a.m.: Does it get any worse than peeing in the dark in the middle of the night when you're so messed up that you can't even stand, and the pee won't stop coming but you can't stand anymore, and finally you pull an Austin Powers and hold your hand against the wall to remain upright? The answer of course, is "yes." When you can't stand anymore, so you have to pull the 180-degree spin and sit on the toilet like a chick…that's worse. Fortunately, I'm not at that point. But I'm damned close.

11:30: Overslept and missed brunch. Hey, it's not like I'm in the wedding or anything.[79]

12:30 p.m.–2:45: We say our goodbyes to everyone at the hotel, then spend the early afternoon sight-seeing around Pittsburgh with Steve and his girlfriend. Highlights include: A Harley Davidson convention, an outside look at Three Rivers Stadium (a big concrete blab), Mount Washington, Big Ben and Parliament. During the drive, we listen to ESPN Radio for game updates (Pats-Jets, Sox-Yanks) as they happen, encouraging the girls to discuss hairdos and makeup. One downer: Somewhere along the line, I stepped in dog poop. Hope that's not an omen for the '99 Pats.[80]

3:14: All right, the Red Sox are winning, the Patriots are winning...and I have to hop on a plane in 30 minutes.[81] Time for a tough decision: Should I watch as much TV as possible in the airport bar, leave the Pats game at the last possible minute, then let the up-in-the-air results eat away at me for the entire flight? Or should I ignore the TVs, head home, get a Sox score from the cabbie and watch the second half on tape? Hmmmm.

3:16: Screw it, I can watch the game on tape and pretend it's happening live, kinda like how I pull out old Celtics tapes from the '86 season and pretend Bird and the gang are still playing together. In fact, maybe I'll follow the Pats-Jets game with Celtics-Rockets, Game Four. Yeah. That's what I'll do.

3:17: Just informed the Sports Gal of my plan. "I'm breaking up with you," she says.

4:45: Dying. Considering paying $1.95 a minute on the airplane phone to see who won. Then again, going to those extremes might anger the Sports Gods.

6:15: After a smooth landing, the taxi drops us off in front of our house. I sprint up the stairs, forgetting the Sports Gal and our 200-pound suitcase and creating ill will for the rest of the evening. While rewinding the Pats game, I check ESPN2 for scores...RED SOX 4, YANKEES 1. You knew they were beating Clemens! Get your brooms out, baby!

6:25: I rewind the Pats tape exactly one hour, which should put me right near the end of the third quarter. At the 1:00 mark, I press STOP, then PLAY...

79 My least favorite part of any wedding: The obligatory Sunday morning brunch, where a bunch of hung-over people in their 20s heroically attempt to mingle with wide-awake parents, aunts, uncles, grandparents and little kids—an experience that's 10 times more awkward if you hooked up with somebody's daughter the previous night. Who invented this idea? My stepmom insisted on a Sunday brunch when I got married and wouldn't be denied; I'm still bitter about it. To anyone who's planning a wedding, just elope. I'm telling you. For $24.95, that's the best thing you're getting out of this book.

80 As it turned out, it was—they finished 8–8.

81 Remember the days when you could drive to the airport and board a plane 45 minutes before the flight? In a related story, Stoner and his wife were married on September 11, 1999.

Golf?

In one of those "Happens so slowly that it's almost in slow motion" moments, I glance over to the cable box, which is displaying Channel 5 (ABC). It's impossible. It can't be. I left the TV on Channel 4 (CBS) when I set the VCR timer. I'm absolutely positive. That leads to the following exchange:

Me [*voice shaking*]: Hey honey, did you turn on the TV Friday morning when you were getting ready?

Her: Yeah, I was watching *Regis and Kathie Lee* while I was getting ready. Why? [*Pause*] That didn't screw up your tape, did it?

[Wait a second! Good God, th-that's the Sports Gal's music!]

PEDRO SAVES THE DAY

October 12, 1999

I don't even know where to begin.

(Seriously, how would *you* start this column?)

In a three-day stretch loaded with great moments,[82] my favorite part was watching the Red Sox celebrate in Cleveland last night. Over any other sport, baseball games have the most satisfying conclusion from a fan's standpoint. Your team gets the third out…the camera shows your pitcher with his arms raised…your catcher bearhugs him and they start dry-humping like two black Labs in heat…the dugout guys sprint happily towards the mound, all looking like the girls from my college whenever the soft-serve yogurt line opened on Wednesday at noon…they switch to the closeup of the most bummed-out guy on the other team, who usually has a couple of whiteheads…they show the wide shot of the huge pigpile on the mound, as you hope that your winning pitcher doesn't get stampeded…they show the losing manager with that "Maybe I should put my house on the market" face…they show the coaches and managers in the winning dugout shaking hands and trying to act like calm adults…and so on.

[82] Down 2–0 in the playoffs against the Cleveland Indians, the Sox won Games Three and Four at Fenway by a combined score of 32–10, followed by a 12–8 win in Game Five. Now *that* is a comeback.

It's a wonderful thing, all of it. Boston fans watched it happen with the Mets in '86, the A's in '88 and '90, the Indians in '95 and '98, and it's a sickening feeling when you're on the other side. We were due. We were *due*. We needed a reason to celebrate. And the great Pedro Martinez provided it.

Here's what struck me: The ending of Game Five actually made me a little emotional. Jeez, I thought that side of me had been killed off long ago. Maybe it was Magic Johnson's skyhook that did it. Maybe it was Petr Klima scoring on his third shift in triple OT or Rulon Jones sacking Tony Eason in the end zone in '87. Maybe it was Stanley's wild pitch, or Clemens never doing *quite* enough, or (fill in the Red Sox reliever) giving up the big hit at the wrong time. Maybe it was the Bruins always falling one goal, one sniper and about $10 million short when it mattered most. Maybe it was Mark Price and Bill Laimbeer making those dagger jumpers at the Garden during Bird's final two seasons. Maybe it was that kickoff right down the middle to Desmond

Howard.[83] Who knows? When I saw my team jumping all over one another and spraying champagne in the dugout, it put a Hallmark-sized lump in my throat. Honest to God.

You see these people celebrating who you feel like you know, so you *feel* like you're a part of it. I watched Brian Daubach pouring champagne on teammates and thought to myself, "There's a guy who's been to hell and back, he deserves it." I watched Sabes celebrating and never considered his double-stinkbomb in Games Two and Five, but those 10 gutty wins during the season, when his body was always one slider away from giving out. And so on down the line. Unlike any other sport, the baseball season resembles a running soap opera—peaks and valleys, trials and tribulations, raging subplots, likable stars and memorable cliff-hangers. When you stick with a team for six months and everything culminates in a champagne party, it feels pretty damned good. Even if you aren't covered in bubbly.

The Cleveland series showcased every likable quality about the 1999 Red Sox. Sometimes they were a two-man team, other times they were a 25-man team; regardless, someone was always carrying the load. All season, my New York friends dismissed them with comments like, "Brian Daubach's your no. 3 hitter?" and, "Who's your closer again, Charlie Sheen?", but those same no-names proved everyone wrong over these last three games. Lewis, Stanley, Varitek and Nixon and Daubach all came through at various times. Valentin had 12 RBI in the last three games and made up for his putrid, lifeless, decrepit regular season.[84] O'Leary turned into Dave Henderson Jr. in Game Five. Offerman kept working the count and stroking those line drives, a true leadoff hitter in every sense. The unappreciated Rheal Cormier held the fort in Game Four for an overworked bullpen. Ramon Martinez came up mammoth in Game Three, like we knew he would, and Derek Lowe saved the series with clutch relief work in that same game.

(Some of the people who *weren't* on the above list: Butch Huskey did squat. Scott Hatteberg barely played. Sabes was hit harder and more frequently than a stolen ATM card. Wakefield was inept. So was Kent Mercker. Rod Beck and Flash didn't do much. The Blair Wasdin Project[85] was simply terrifying. Yet the team rolled on. They always roll on.)

Best of all, Nomar and Pedro came through when it mattered. No way Boston captures Game Five unless two things happen:

83 Did you notice how, in the first few columns of this book, I spent an inordinate amount of time rehashing unhappy Boston sports memories? We all carried scars from 1986 to 1998, and at the time of this column, nobody cared about the Bruins, **Pete Carroll had ruined the Pats**, and Pitino was ruining the Celtics (who weren't even playing because of the '99 lockout). Throwing in the Sox and their tortured history, well, that's why I spent a paragraph after the happiest Red Sox game in 13 years rehashing unhappy things.

84 In a running diary during Game Four, I wrote that Valentin's improbable October resurgence was "the Boston sports equivalent of O.J. Simpson finding the real killers."

85 That was my nickname for John Wasdin, who was so scary to watch, you ended up standing in the corner facing the wall like the about-to-die characters at the end of ***The Blair Witch Project***. Hey, it made sense at the time.

1) Nomar belts a homer in the first inning, forcing Cleveland to intentionally walk him those two fateful times (one for Troy O'Leary's grand slam, the other for his three-run homer).

2) Pedro slams the door from the fourth inning on.

So all 25 guys pitched in, some shined more than others, and the two money guys came through when it counted most. That was the Cleveland series in a nutshell; that was the '99 season in a nutshell. Go figure. It certainly wasn't conventional. The Red Sox only had one starter pass the fifth inning and scored 44 runs in the last three games, which jibed with the rest of the goofy season. And in the pantheon of Happy Boston Sports Moments, Game Five probably cracks the top 10 in my lifetime, and not just because no Boston team had advanced in a series since 1986, or the team had lost 18 of 19 playoff games before winning these last three. This was a game that could have been simulcast on Classic Sports. What about both intentional walks coming back to haunt Mike Hargrove, the first leading to O'Leary's grannie, the other leading to one of the few "Jump out of your seat screaming" Red Sox moments of the past 25 years? What about the "both teams might run out of decent pitchers" threat hanging over everything, or every terrifying Jim Thome at-bat? Or Pedro coming in for "maybe one or two innings" and throwing 97 pitches and a fucking no-hitter over the final six innings?

It's difficult to believe that someone could have overshadowed O'Leary, but Pedro cracked the pantheon of Ballsiest/Guttiest/Greatest Boston Performances from the past 25 years, right up there with John Havlicek finishing the '73 playoffs with a separated shoulder and Kevin McHale playing on a broken foot in the '87 playoffs.**86** Thanks to that aching shoulder, Pedro couldn't even have a long-toss catch on Saturday. Forty-eight hours later, he was throwing 97 pitches in 50-degree weather, with a terrifying, "This could be the one that makes Pedro wince and sends Joe Kerrigan sprinting from the dugout" aura hanging over every pitch. (A feeling vaguely reminscent of Terry Glenn catching a deep pass and getting gang-tackled, but multiplied by 100). At one point in the seventh inning, my father and I had the following exchange:

Dad: I can't take this anymore. I think I'm gonna have a heart attack.

86 Pedro's stats for the '99 playoffs: 3 games, 17 innings, 0 runs, 5 hits, 5 walks, 23 Ks.

Me: Can you wait until after the game?

Now factor this in: Boston pitching had given up 32 runs in 34 innings since Pedro left Game One with pain in his back.[87] When he returned, the Indians didn't even get another hit, much less another run. Unbelievable. For his first two innings, he was throwing semi-sidearm, avoiding the high heaters and struggling with control that wasn't up to the normal Pedro standards. Gradually, you could see him finding a rhythm and settling into an effective mix of changeups, curveballs, cut fastballs, and (intermittent) fastballs. You could see it on the faces of the Indians batters. They were done. Even better, their fans knew it. By the eighth inning, you couldn't hear a peep in Jacobs Field. I don't even remember seeing one person transform a baseball game, or a series, like that before. For six innings, Pedro turned into Keyser Söze.

So the Red Sox may have ended their prolonged playoff drought, but Pedro accomplished something far greater than that. To crack the Boston Pantheon, it doesn't just take 23 wins and a Cy Young, or 17 strikeouts and a one-hitter at Yankee Stadium. You need one or two of Those Moments to earn your keep. You need to come through when it matters most, when you're the only hope left, when the fate of the season rests squarely on your shoulders. You need to vanquish your opponent, destroy them, break their will. You need to resonate with people. Pedro Martinez did all of those things last night. His teammates lifted him on their shoulders when it was over. And it was a beautiful thing.

Bring on the Yankees.

(The world will now destruct in 30 seconds.)

87 Here's how scary that pitching staff was: In Game Four, with the Sox leading 15–2 in the fifth inning, you didn't feel even remotely safe. This was the season when Pat Rapp, Mark Portugal, Jin Ho Cho and Brian Rose started a combined 78 games and Tim Wakefield was used as the closer for half the season. Other than Pedro, nobody finished with more than 10 wins or 150 innings pitched. Did you ever think a team could win 94 games using 25 pitchers in all? It happened.

ESCAPE FROM NEW YORK

October 13, 1999

Instead of previewing the biggest baseball series in the history of mankind, let's play a little Q & A. I don't feel like Boston fans despise the Yankees enough right now. Remember, these are the Yankees! I know it's been a long time, but we're supposed to loathe these guys like the Nazis in *Raiders of the Lost Ark*. If you're having trouble working up some good old-fashioned antipathy for the Bronx Bombers, here's a little help (answers at end of the column):**88**

88 I borrowed this format from **David Letterman**, who also gave me the idea for a goofy mailbag (from "Viewer Mail"). In retrospect, I should have just colored my hair red and stuck a gap in my front teeth.

1) How did Paul O'Neill suffer a cracked rib this month?

a) Diving for a flyball in right field.

b) Throwing a tantrum after a called third strike.

c) Colliding with Joe Torre's nose in the dugout.

2) What was Roger Clemens' nickname from 1993 to 1996, when he was playing under his final Boston contract ($20 million for four years)?

a) Rocket Roger

b) The Rocket Man

c) Thief

3) Why do people normally become Yankees fans as kids?

a) They started liking the Yanks because their father rooted for them.

b) They grew up in the tri-state area.

c) They jumped on the bandwagon in second grade and never looked back, then made up an excuse later like "No, it wasn't because they were winning, I really liked their hats!"

d) The Yanks were the most popular team in juvie.

e) All of the above.

4) Why did Derek Jeter dump Mariah Carey?

a) She gained too much weight.

b) She's a slut.

c) He needed to start concentrating on baseball so he could realize his dream: "Someday I will be the second-best shortstop in the American League."

5) Why were Red Sox fans upset when former Boston manager Don Zimmer was struck in the head by a line drive during the playoffs last week?

a) Because it was such a scary moment.

b) Because the game was delayed for five minutes.

c) Because he was still breathing.

6) What's the funniest book written in the past 10 years?

a) *Sein Language.*

b) *The Collected Works of Dave Barry.*

c) *Roger Clemens' Greatest Playoff Moments.*[89]

7) When NBC's Bob Costas tells you that "Darryl Strawberry's average is .321," what is he referring to?

a) Darryl's postseason batting average.

b) Darryl's regular season batting average.

c) Darryl's blood-alcohol level.

8) What injury bothered Yankees lefty Andy Pettitte during the '99 regular season?

a) Tendinitis in his left elbow.

b) Back spasms.

c) Menstrual cramps.

9) Which Yankee gave the greatest movie performance by an athlete this decade?

a) Ricky Ledee in *For Love of the Game.*

b) Roger Clemens in *Cobb.*

c) David Cone as Miggs in *Silence of the Lambs.*[90]

10) Which TV show featured George Steinbrenner this decade?

a) *Seinfeld.*

b) *NYPD Blue.*

c) A&E's *Biography* during "Millionaire Assholes of the 20th Century" Week.

11) What does "260 million" stand for?

a) The Yankees' actual payroll over the last three years

b) The amount of money MSG pays the Yankees for TV rights.

c) The number of times Joe Torre picks his nose during the average Yankee game.[91]

12) What does the number 38 stand for?

a) El Duque's real age.

89 My antipathy towards Clemens was at an all-time high at the time—I was bordering dangerously close to DeNiro in *The Fan.*

90 This was a reference to the allegation that Cone pleasured himself in the Mets bullpen in front of two female fans, which turned out *not* to be true. Still, it was too good not to joke about. And yes, Miggs was the character who jerked off and threw his man-juice at **Jodie Foster**, which raised the question, "Was that real semen or fake semen, and if it was fake semen, where can I buy some to torture my friends with it?"

91 Torre and former Jets coach Joe Walton were like **the Russell and Chamberlain of Nose-Picking Coaches.** Torre was like Russell because he won more titles, but Walton was like Wilt in that his stats were absolutely mind-blowing.

b) The number of years Don Zimmer has spent as a coach or manager.

c) The number of Yankees fans who would still make the Wells-for-Clemens trade.

13) What's the most common first name for a Yankees fan?

a) Sal

b) Bobby

c) Vinny

d) Inmate

14) Why did Bernie Williams turn down a $91 million offer from Boston to play with the Yankees for $87 million?

a) He felt loyal to the Yankees organization and to his teammates.

b) He didn't want to move his family away from New York.

c) He's a dick.[92]

15) Why did the Yankees have to get rid of Tim Raines after the end of last season?

a) They wanted to give more playing time to Ricky Ledee and Chad Curtis.

b) They didn't want to pay $2 million per year to a backup outfielder.

c) Commissioner Bud Selig passed a new rule: "Only one former cokehead per team."

16) What's the "Big Apple"?

a) A nickname for Manhattan.

b) The name of Spike Lee's new movie.

c) The thing lodged in Roger Clemens' throat when he's pitching Game Three at Fenway this weekend.

17) Why did the Yankees use non-alcoholic champagne during their celebration after they swept the Rangers last week?

a) Chad Curtis convinced the players to have non-alcoholic champagne so Strawberry could take part in the postgame celebration.

b) The team manager bought the wrong champagne at the liquor store.

c) They were afraid wine coolers and Zimas would end up staining their uniforms.

18) What's the telltale sign that you're a Yankees fan?

92 My editors wanted me to soften this; I fought them off. Bernie strung the Sox along as leverage for a better offer from his team—in my book, that makes him a dick. Sorry.

a) You have curly black hair and a wispy mustache that hasn't quite grown in yet.
b) You're a backup infielder on six different softball teams and you definitely own baseball cleats.
c) Your girlfriend looks like Paula Jones, chews Jolly Ranchers with her mouth open, weighs 98 pounds and slept with at least four of your friends before you started dating her—although nobody has broken the news to you yet.
d) Your first name can easily be transformed into a two-syllable name ending in "y" or "ie."
e) You wear sweatpants to bars.
f) You really enjoyed *Summer of Sam*.
g) You failed the local fireman's test six times, but you're taking it again next week.
h) You think Deborah Van Valkenburgh was smoking-hot in *The Warriors*.[93]
i) You think Thurman Munson, Ron Guidry and Don Mattingly are Hall of Famers.
j) Not only would you allow Jeter to have sex with your girlfriend, you would high-five him as it happened.
k) All of the above.

19) What will be the most common theme of the emails I'll be getting from Yankees fans over the next 24 hours?

a) The Red Sox suck.
b) Sports Guy sucks.
c) 1918
d) Munson kicked Fisk's ass.
e) Jeter kicks Nomar's ass.
f) All of the above.

20) What's the most incredible thing about the first Yankees-Red Sox playoff series?

a) That it's taking place in the last year before the millennium.
b) That Clemens could potentially pitch Game Seven against his old team.
c) That the Sox could potentially win the World Series by beating their all-time nemesis (the Yankees), followed by either the team that broke their hearts in '86 (the Mets), or their old rival in Boston (the Braves).

93 She played the girl who hung out with the Orphans and their creepy leader (**the guy with the fish-eye**), then quickly jumped to the Warriors after the Molotov cocktail scene, leading to Swan's famous line, "Maybe we oughta run a train on you, you look like you might even like it." She looked like she'd been around. And then some.

d) That we might get through this next week without the apocalypse happening.
e) That the 1981 classic *Escape From New York* was set in the "futuristic" year of 1999.[94]

Because that's what this is all about, right? An *Escape From New York*? Starring Pedro as Snake Plissken; Steinbrenner as the Duke, Jimy Williams as Brain; Clemens as the Duke's psycho assistant; Dan Duquette as the President;[95] Adrienne Barbeau's boobs as themselves; and introducing Nomar Garciaparra as Nomar. Remember how that movie ended, with the President riddling the Duke's body with bullets while screaming, "I am the Duke! I am A-number one!" as Plissken happily looked on?

Expect something similar next week: Pedro vs. Roger, Game Seven, Yankee Stadium, winner goes to the World Series. The year? 1999. The movie? *Escape From New York*. The hero? Snake Martinez.

The pick? Sox in seven.[96]

94 After posting the column, I found out that the movie was actually set in 1997, not 1999—ruining my entire ending. I'm leaving it in as a pre-imdb.com cautionary tale.

95 Not sure why I didn't have Dan Duquette just playing The Duke. Maybe it was too easy.

96 As it turned out, we lost in five games—thanks to Bernie's bomb off Rod Beck in Game One, plus a number of shady umpiring calls—leading the fans at Fenway to litter the field with garbage during Game Five and nearly cause a forfeit. Needless to say, this didn't end well. Although **Pedro did destroy Clemens** in Game Three. As always with the Sox, you had to take solace in the moral victories. By the way, here are the answers to the questions: 1-a; 2-c; 3-e; 4-c; 5-c; 6-c; 7-b; 8-b; 9-a, 10-a; 11-a; 12-b; 13-c; 14-c; 15-b; 16-a; 17-a; 18-k; 19-c; 20-c.

THE BUZZ

April 18, 2000

We didn't make it through one homestand before Carl Everett started generating The Buzz.[97] And if you don't know what The Buzz is, you obviously haven't been to Fenway before.

First, a disclaimer: I think Fenway should be demolished as soon as possible. You can't find a good seat without connections. You can't sit comfortably in any seat unless you're built like a jockey. The concession stands underneath the park have a "prison facility" feel, with cardboard food and stale beer to complete the effect. Every sound coming out of the centerfield speakers sounds like this: "Mrrrmrmrmrmrmrmrmrm." The hot dog vendors never have napkins. Every usher has a glazed, "I wish I could help you find your seat, but they just bussed me in from a nursing home" look about them. The fat guy behind you is invariably bombed and sitting so close that you could get drunk off the fumes from his breath, especially as he shouts out "No-mahhhhhhhh!" and spits all over your back. And the Sox are so friggin' cheap these days, bat boys chase down foul balls and never consider tossing them into the stands.

That's Fenway in a nutshell. We know it, we love it, we forgive its innumerable faults. Now please, tear it down before I start bludgeoning myself in the head with a rock-hard pretzel.

There *is* one good thing about Fenway. Because they don't blare rock music between at-bats, thanks to the 40-watt speakers in center field, fans rely on themselves to make noise. It's a novel concept. I just spent a winter being manipulated by the Fleet Center Jumbotron—the loathsome, hateful electronic Satan, the bane of my existence, the root of all sports evil[98]—so it's refreshing to kick back and watch a ballgame, hampered by no distractions other than 14-inch seats that face in every direction but home plate. Because of the laconic Fenway atmosphere, you can always tell when something's happening (on or off the field). Some fans even park behind the left field wall on Landsdowne Street, then follow a few innings through the sounds of the crowd. Try it some time.[99] Could you do that at the Fleet Center?

97 The Red Sox acquired Everett the previous winter from Houston for shortstop prospect Adam Everett (no relation).

98 I was having trouble adjusting to **the Jumbotron Era**. Now I'm resigned to this stuff. It's like getting a new puppy and cleaning up shit and piss every day—after awhile, you don't even think about it.

99 I'm ashamed to admit that I actually tried this on a date once. Repeat: once.

Some of my favorite sounds at Fenway:

• When two drunken bozos suddenly start recreating Hearns-Hagler in the bleachers, you can hear that "HrrrrrrrAHHHHHHHH!" swell of excitement sweeping across the park even as the first punches find their mark.

• When Nomar boots an easy grounder, you hear the disappointed "Ohhhhhhhhhhhhh!" groan drift underneath the grandstand as you're ordering a $12 beer.

• When a Boston homer heads over The Wall, there's that initial burst of excitement—"Hrrrrrrrrrrrrrrrrrrrrrrrr"—followed by that classic moment when the ball hits the screen—"hhhrrrrrrrr....HAHHHHHHHHHH!!!!!"

• When the crowd pines for a rally, someone inevitably starts the "halting clap" thing and it sweeps through the whole ballpark within seconds CLAP...CLAP....CLAP...CLAP... CLAP... CLAP...CLAP...CLAP...CLAP...CLAP... CLAP... CLAP...CLAP...CLAP. CLAP. CLAP. CLAP. CLAP. CLAP. CLAPCLAPCLAPCLAPCLAPCLAP!!!

And then there's The Buzz. The Buzz is reserved for special players, the ones who makes us wait until *after* they bat before making a beer run. Sometimes it comes out of nowhere; if you're zoning out or making small talk, The Buzz snaps you back and makes you say, "Whoa, Player X is up!" Usually the seeds of recognition (rustle, soft cheer, applause) are planted as Player X leaves the on-deck circle and strides to home plate. That's followed by definitive recognition (more rustle, louder cheer, louder applause), spiced up by the PA announcer's introduction ("Now batting...no. 2...the centerfielder...Carl Everett") as the groundswell crests into full-scale appreciation.

If this happens four or five times a game, that usually means one thing: This guy has *arrived* in Boston. Usually fans reserve The Buzz for three scenarios: Player X has been enjoying an exceptionally good season, he always seems to come through in the clutch, or he possesses a healthy dose of *duende*, defined by former Boston columnist George Frazier as "an indefinable charisma."[100] Over the past few decades, only an esteemed group of Boston players reached Buzz-worthy status: Ted, Yaz, Pudge, Mo, No-mah, Jim Ed, Tony C., El Tiante, Rog-ah, Pedro and Can. Some random players were Buzz-worthy during spe-

100 Gammons has been trying to keep that phrase alive for the past 25 years. Not sure if it's working.

cific stretches and couldn't maintain the momentum: Don Baylor in '86, Mike Greenwell in '88, Lonborg in '67, Lynn in '75, Dick Radatz in the mid '60s and the Eck in '78, to name six. When it happens, you remember.[101]

Here's hoping that Everett remains Buzz-worthy. He plays baseball like a new-wave version of Dave Henderson, wearing his charisma like bad cologne, unleashing a never-ending stream of idiosyncracies. Everything about him stands out—the way he disdainfully snatches flyballs from the sky, his effortless ability to cover ground in center, even the goofy way he points to the sky after home runs. When he stands in the batter's box—bat waving, head moving, eyes blinking, sometimes chewing on a toothpick—he leans defiantly over the plate, almost daring the pitcher to plunk him. There's always something going on with him, only it never seems contrived (like with Antoine Walker).[102] This even translates off the field, as Everett offers opinions on everyone and everything, without fear of retribution. In the last two months, he slammed the Yankees, Mets, Astros, and even an opposing pitcher who had just tossed a four-hitter (Gil Heredia). He belted a walk-off home run against Oakland, then admitted afterwards that he was trying to go deep. In this respect, he shares the same refreshing qualities as Mo Vaughn, another star who ignited this town, although Everett is infinitely more reliable in clutch spots. You want Everett standing at the plate with the game on the line. You feel like you're in good hands.[103]

Mix everything together and you get The Buzz. If he stays healthy, the Everett trade could eventually be considered one of the great deals in franchise history. A multi-tool player, a switch-hitter, a centerfielder, someone just hitting his prime, someone who naturally clicks with the Fenway fans…and all they sacrificed was a single top prospect? It almost makes the Pedro-Carl Pavano deal pale in comparison. Almost.[104]

The fact remains, it's fun to attend games at Fenway again, despite the decrepit conditions. It's fun to watch Offerman and O'Leary at the plate. It's fun to watch Lowe, Varitek, and Nixon make The Leap. It's fun to watch El Guapo waddling in from the bullpen. It's fun to watch Everett, it's *really* fun to watch Nomar and it's pure joy to watch Pedro weave his magic every five days. Most of all, it's fun to feel The Buzz, even as you're sitting in seats facing the right field foul pole, even as you're

101 I had no way of knowing this at the time, but David Ortiz would shatter the Buzz Record during the 2004 Playoffs. For every Papi at-bat after Game Four of the ALCS, there wasn't just a buzz; it was a full-fledged rumble. Also, Manny ranks in the top five on **the Fenway Buzz Scale** in my lifetime, along with Rice, Yaz and Mo. Ranking last: Cesar Crespo.

102 Apparently this was one of the weeks where I was anti-Antoine. It vacillated, depending on the week, almost like Disney stock.

103 I'm trying to swallow my own tongue right now.

104 Still trying.

struggling to regain the feeling in your feet between innings, even as you're brushing beer and spit off the back of your shirt.

Then again, it could be worse. Flash-forward 10 years to a New Fenway nightmare. As the 500-foot Jumbotron implores us to make "Old Fenway Level" noise on the new Citizens Bank Noise Meter. As Wally the Green Monster races around high-fiving fans in the first row between innings. As dancing idiots desperately try to catch the attention of the centerfield cameraman while 600,000-watt speakers blast "Stayin' Alive." As we watch people hit infield popups in the Dunkin' Donuts "Dunk a homer over the Wall" contest between the second and third innings. As the PA announcer screams, "NOW BATTING, NUMBER TWOOOOO, CARLLLLLLLL EVERETTTTTTTTTT!!!!!!!" while Prodigy's "Firestarter" drowns out any and all applause.[105]

Would you miss The Buzz then? Would you miss the slow grumble of applause as The New Guy ambles up to the plate? Would comfortable seats, accessible concession stands and available tickets outweigh everything else, including the loss of our baseball soul?

As the old saying goes, "Be careful what you wish for, it just may come true."[106]

105 By the way, those last five sentences don't seem so outrageous, do they? **Tom Werner** is reading this right now and thinking, "The Dunkin' Donuts 'Dunk a homer over the wall' contest—I like it!"

106 Was that even the old saying? Was it "Be careful what you wish for, it just might come true?" Or "Be careful what you wish for, it may come true?" Was it something else? I need a ruling here.

FOUL BALL

May 12, 2000

We were about to lose the greatest baseball seats on the face of the earth. Our clothes were drenched, our sneakers soaked, our faces covered by invisible water masks. We didn't care. For five innings at Fenway, my buddy J-Bug[107] and I had been battling a swirling mist, more annoying than anything. You put up with these things when you get a taste of the good life. Unfortunately, the Weather Gods had other ideas. When the rain gained strength and thunder rumbled in the distance, we knew our time could be coming to an abrupt end. We needed a miracle.

At the start of the seventh,[108] many of the remaining fans in our section scurried toward the grandstand, leaving us behind like wounded soldiers. We could barely see El Guapo halfheartedly warming up on the mound, a swollen, blurry ball of white goo. Or Daubach at first, who was hucking grounders around the infield and glancing to the first base umpire, waiting for The Signal. The outfielders traded lobs and prepared for the inevitable sprint for the comforts of the clubhouse. All four umpires alternated between studying the sky and kicking the infield dirt (now a blanket of mud). Nobody made a move. What were they waiting for? Finally, the home plate ump raised his hands and started waving everyone off the field, like Bruce Willis waving the *Die Hard* hostages off the top of the Nakatomi Building. It was over.

They said it was only a rain delay, but we knew better. Umpires rarely mess around with thunder and lightning, not even when Leslie Nielsen is behind the plate. Bug and I glanced at each other and nodded sadly. That was that. Within a few minutes, we were limping towards his car, wet and depressed. We had just given up two seats in Row C, Section 74 at Fenway Park.

Lemme explain...

One of the unique things about Fenway is its complete absence of foul ball territory, especially on the third base side of the field. Next time you attend a game there, check out the structure. I mean, really, *really* examine it. It's messed up. The guy who designed the park in A.D. 1737 was smoking some serious opium. For instance, if you're looking at the visiting

107 Out of all my friends, the J-Bug (real name: Jason Buggy) makes the most appearances in the book. We became friends when we were bartending together in Charlestown, where we named every stool at our bar after an athlete so we could talk about the customers even if they were five feet away. For instance, if there was a half-decent girl sitting in no. 42 (Mo Vaughn's seat), Bug would be cleaning a wine glass and casually say, "Billy, what do you think of Mo Vaughn this season?" followed by my saying something like "I'm a little **worried about the extra weight**, but I think we could get something out of him." They would have no idea what was happening. And yes, these are the things that eventually come back to haunt you when God is deciding, "Should I give him a son or a daughter?"

108 Final score: Red Sox 5, White Sox 3

dugout on the third base side, you'll see a camera crew positioned to its left, toward the wall, followed by the next 11 sections of the field (sections 71–82, to be exact), which JUT OUT towards the field at a 40-degree angle to the dugout. No rhyme or reason. Even Tori Spelling's implants don't stick out that much.

But this is a good thing. Trust me. If someone ever offers you seats in that general area and you're thinking about turning them down, just know that you're passing up the chance to sit in the best foul ball seats on the planet.

See if you can follow this line of thinking...

• If you chart every foul ball during any given game, you'll notice that the first few sections after the dugouts (the sections starting at the first and third base bags and going towards the foul poles) attract a disproportionate number of line drives, grounders and pop flies.

• Throw in the righthanded hitters who keep pulling the ball foul because they're gunning for The Wall. [109]

• Throw in the lefthanded hitters who push the ball foul when they're trying to go opposite field. [110]

• Finally, throw in in the 40-degree angle factor for those third base/left field seats. See where I'm headed here? I'll spell it out for you.

F- O- U- L- B- A- L- L

It's the Holy Grail for baseball fans. I have seen grown men humilate themselves at games by bringing a glove, just to improve their odds. I have seen foul balls make fans inadvertently collide like punk rockers in a mosh pit. I have seen fans booed for dropping foul balls. I have seen people nearly come to blows over foul balls. When my buddy Bish caught one at Yankee Stadium, I actually remember hating him when he told me the story. *You caught a foul ball?Really?* Until Wednesday night's game with the Bug, I had never been with somebody who caught a foul ball. I had never sat within 20 feet of someone who caught a foul ball. I had never even held a foul ball.[111]

So when Bug and I were hunting for tickets outside a rainy Fenway, and a desperate scalper offered us "two lower boxes" for "face" ($90), I noticed they were in Section 74 and nearly

109 We were three years away from Kevin Millar shattering Carlton Fisk's unofficial record for "Most foul balls hit into Sections 71–82." If they ever moved the dimensions of a baseball field 30 feet to the left, Millar would have been the white Hank Aaron.

110 Two words: Wade Boggs.

111 Back in the mid-'70s, I have a vague memory of attending a Royals game with some elementary school buddies, sitting in the rooftop seats, heading to the bathroom between innings, then being told when I returned that a foul ball bounced off my seat. I'm pretty sure this happened and it ruined my week. Then again, I also thought I remembered getting my first boner when they showed Cheryl Ladd's ass at the nude beach during the **two-part Hawaii episode of *Charlie's Angels***, but when I watched a syndicated re-airing of that show about five years ago, the camera only went down to the nape of her back. So who knows?

did a backflip. But not before haggling him down to $60. Best deal ever. Can you put a price on snagging a foul ball?

In those six glorious rain-soaked innings, we came pretty damned close. Someone two rows in front of us (Row A) botched the old lean-over on a scorching grounder. (Note: If that ever happens to me some day, serve me the same helping of bullets parmagiana that Michael Corleone gave Solazzo and McCluskey in *The Godfather*.) Another foul ball ricocheted off the roof seats behind us and dropped like a grenade, bouncing off 10 pairs of hands, three heads and two pot bellies and sending everyone scattering under their seats to find it. Someone right behind us even snagged one, a little kid who was returning from the concession stands and HOLDING A FRIGGIN' ICE CREAM CONE. When the ball rolled right under his feet, he casually scooped it like a first baseman picking a one-hopper from the dirt, only he never dropped the cone. I wouldn't even have believed it if I had not seen it with my own eyes.[112]

112 Funniest part of this story: Bug and I asking the kid if we could hold the ball. Usually it works the other way around.

Best of all, Carl "The Truth" Everett cracked a tailing liner headed right at the Green Monster…then it started curving…and curving...and suddenly it was coming right at us…and it was getting big, like a softball...and I almost lost control of my bowels, because HOT DAMN! THIS THING WAS COMING RIGHT AT US!!!...(Holy FUCKING SHIT!!!)… and then at the last second, it stopped curving and smacked against somebody's chest about six seats down from us—THUD!—and rolled under his seat, where someone else picked it up. Imagine that one? You end up with a chest bruise *and* you've been emasculated in front of 25,000 people? Regardless, can you put a pricetag on that "Holy Shit" feeling? I'll always remember Everett's searing line drive coming right at us, as big as a grapefruit and getting bigger by the millisecond. Or shivering my way through the next five innings, on the edge of my seat, always ready, always hoping that *this* would be the pitch. Or heading home with the Bug, sopping and depressed, an opportunity lost. Maybe we never caught a foul ball that night, and maybe we nearly caught pneumonia. But that was the best time I ever had at a random baseball game.

Listen, there are a million reasons to rip down Fenway, and I probably agree with every one of them. But certain things can't be replaced, or recreated, or even explained, and I guess my biggest fear is that I'll take my children to New Fenway some day and wish for nine innings that the old joint was still kicking. Section 74, I hope we meet again. Next time, maybe you'll even have a foul ball for me.

PEDRO AND THE PANTHEON

May 16, 2000

Following Sunday's near-brawl against the Indians, after Pedro laid the smack down on Roberto Alomar like an angry stepfather,[113] I think everyone stumbled upon the same startling realization.

Williams, Russell, Orr, Flutie, Bird...Pedro.

The Pantheon.

That's the term my buddy House and I started using in college, defined then and forever after as "the highest level of transcendence."[114] Our six necessities for any Pantheon Guy:

1) The Kelly Leak Factor

Remember the way Kelly carried himself on the Bad News Bears? He didn't just come through with the game on the line, he was the only 13-year-old who could shag flies with a cigarette dangling from his mouth, or have the balls to drive a stolen van filled with underaged teammates from California to Houston. There was never a second when you forgot that he was better than anyone else. Here's the point: As soon as a professional athlete reminds you of Kelly Leak, they're in the Pantheon. For instance, MJ resided there for most of his career; Hakeem Olajuwon only had two Pantheon years (1994 and 1995). It doesn't matter who was better, only that both guys reached that rarefied state when they were just *dominant*. Just like Kelly Leak.[115]

2) You have to come through in the clutch

Remember when Jerry West buried a half-court shot to send Game Three of the 1970 finals into overtime? The best part happens right after the shot, when West bows his head and walks back to the bench while his teammates try—emphasis on the word "try"—to mob him. West would have none of it; he knew the shot was going in. He knew it. Resident Pantheon member Jimmy Chitwood sums it up best: "I'll make it."[116]

3) Rings

For basketball, hockey, and baseball (position players only), you need a championship to attain Pantheon Status. That's not

113 After getting plunked, Alomar did the classic "Glare out at the mound, then try to charge as soon as two people held him back" routine. What a wuss.

114 We were giddy about coming up with that phrase back in the day. Now I hear it from time to time and always wonder if we started it or if other people were using it irrespective of us, and that's how it spread. It's one of the only phrases I feel territorial about. This also happened when my high school buddy Jim and I used to use the phrase "That Guy" in college for people like **Joe Pantoliano and J.T. Walsh**—character actors who appeared in everything, only you never knew their names. Independently of us, www.fametracker.com started a page devoted to these actors called "Hey, it's That Guy!" Now I'm wondering if anyone ever comes up with anything on their own.

115 An absolute dead ringer for Phoenix's Steve Nash, by the way. That should have been enough for Nash not to win the 2005 MVP.

116 Other movie character-athletes in the Pantheon besides Chitwood and Leak: Paul Crewe in the original *Longest Yard*; Roy Hobbs in *The Natural*; Pele's character in *Victory*; Rifleman from *All the Right Moves*; Frank Dux from *Blood Sport*; **Ogie Oglethorpe** in *Slap Shot*, and the great Ty Webb from *Caddyshack*. I would throw Hustler from *Fast Break* in there, but I can't get over the fact that they called the last play of the Nevada State game for Swish.

117 One obvious exception after the fact: Barry Bonds. Although he's a cheater, so maybe it evens out.

negotiable.[117] Football is tougher because it's impossible for one player to affect a game; candidates should be evaluated on a case-by-case basis. With baseball, starting pitchers are exempt because they only pitch once every five days—but if they find themselves in a playoff situation, they better come through every time they get the baseball.

4) Reverence from one's peers

You can't crack the Pantheon unless your opponents are saying things like, "We just didn't have an answer for him" and, "I don't think I've ever seen a performance like that." Classic example: Bird's 60-point game, when the Hawks were rooting for him on the Atlanta bench by the end. Now that's respect.

5) The "What the hell?" factor

Ties in with #4. Any time Player X attempts something outrageous that sucks the life out of the other team—and he's doing it for kicks—it's a pretty good bet that Player X resides in the Pantheon. Not to keep bringing up Larry Legend (okay, twist my arm), but remember Game Six of the '86 finals, when Bird chased down an errant Bill Walton pass, dribbled back out to the left corner, then drained a fallaway three right in front of the Houston bench? That was the quintessential Pantheon Moment. That three didn't just finish off the '86 Rockets, it destroyed them in a "Nazis at the end of *Raiders of the Lost Ark*" kinda way.

6) The Orr Factor

My father once described Bobby Orr as being so good, you stayed home to watch Bruins games so you didn't miss anything. You don't necessarily need this trait to reach Pantheon status (just look at Kareem's career), but it definitely helps your case.[118] For example, Dwight Gooden will never make the Hall of Fame, but he sneaks into the Pantheon for everyone who watched him pitch in '85. Think Pedro with Jheri-curls. And he threw it all away.

The Pedro Experience featured all six requirements, only we didn't fully realize it until last weekend, almost like C. Thomas Howell not realizing that Lori Loughlin was hot until the tail end of *Secret Admirer*. There's a reason these things take so long: We're beseiged with information and opinions these days, with sports radio, cable TV, and the Internet fulfilling every possible need. Instead of seeing The Big Picture, we're inundated with thousands of little pictures, fleeting images that never add up to anything substantial, as we spend our days sifting through them and hoping for an occasional nugget. When we *find* that nugget, it usually gets shoved down our throats; after awhile, we don't even want to read/hear/watch anything about them anymore. Our senses become dulled, the complete opposite of the way things used to be.

When the Red Sox were fighting for the pennant in 1986, I was stranded in Connecticut, starving for information on a daily basis. All I could find were little scraps. Maybe Warner Wolf would show a 15-second clip during his CBS broadcast.[119] Maybe *USA Today* would print a cover feature on the Sox. Maybe *This Week in Baseball* would churn out a generic Sox feature. Maybe my dad would remember to mail up the Sunday *Globe* sports section (which I devoured like a homeless person throwing down a free sandwich). It was never enough; I always felt left out. I would climb onto my kitchen roof, catching Sox broadcasts on a temperamental 1080 AM frequency that always faded when the bases were loaded. My mother called me crazy, our dog Bee stood in the kitchen barking until I came down. I didn't care. Something big was happening that summer—you could feel it in the air, the logical third act to Squish the Fish and Sweet Sixteen. And I couldn't get enough of it, probably because I couldn't get any of it.

Things are different now. In Connecticut, you can follow Sox games on cbssportsline.com while listening to WEEI (on the Internet) AND watching the game (on your satellite dish). You can read the *Globe* and *Herald* online. You can catch highlights on ESPN and Fox. On message boards, you can argue with other fans about things like, "Why the fuck does Jimy pinch-hit Frye for Nixon?" You could buy Sox tickets on eBay and drive up for random games. And yeah, I guess it's better now. I just wonder if we're caught up in so many Little Pictures that we keep missing The Big Picture.

In Pedro's case, Boston fans were sifting through the wreckage of the Celtics/Bruins seasons and the Pete Carroll Era, bemoaning the dearth of championships since 1986, getting caught up in things like "Is Nomar carrying too much muscle?" and (again, because this was important) "Why the fuck does Jimy pinch-hit Frye for Nixon???" It's not like we ignored Pedro during this stretch (no local athlete received more positive

118 Eighteen NBA players in the Pantheon: Wilt; Russell; Walton; Bird; Magic; MJ; Hakeem; Duncan; Shaq; Mikan; Barry; Isiah; Pettit; Kareem; Moses; Oscar; West; and Doc. Although we're getting spots ready for Wade and LeBron, just to be safe.

119 During that same year, **Warner Wolf** appeared in *Rocky IV* and unleashed the Hall of Fame line, "I can't get over the size of this Russian!" Big year for Warner and me.

press over the last two years), but we were missing the real story. For everyone under the age of 20 who missed out on seeing Bird and Orr in their primes, THIS IS WHAT IT WAS LIKE. Over the past two seasons, including the '99 playoffs, Pedro has gone 31–5. 31–5!!! In 283.1 innings and 41 appearances over that stretch, he allowed 195 hits and 55 earned runs (1.72 ERA) and whiffed a whopping 401 batters (while walking just 69). Even the generic man-child who's five inches bigger and 50 pounds heavier than everyone else in Little League doesn't post numbers like that.[120]

Some of these beauties from the past 12 months are like works of art:

Date	Opp	W	L	IP	H	R	ER	BB	SO
5/07/99	Ana	1	0	8.0	6	0	0	0	15
6/04/99	Atl	1	0	9.0	3	1	1	2	16
8/24/99	@Min	1	0	8.0	4	1	0	1	15
9/04/99	@Sea	1	0	8.0	2	0	0	3	15
9/10/99	@NYY	1	0	9.0	1	1	1	0	17
9/21/99	Tor	1	0	9.0	3	0	0	2	12
5/06/00	TB	0	1	9.0	6	1	1	1	17
5/12/00	@Bal	1	0	9.0	2	0	0	0	15

Pedro snuck into the Pantheon before we even digested what was happening. This isn't about sports as much as someone so brilliant at their profession that even non-sports fans are getting sucked in. I hope every Boston fan under 20 takes a deep breath and enjoys this thing while it lasts. It doesn't happen too often. Believe me. If you don't believe me, consider these points:

1) Ever sat in the stands before one of Pedro's starts, listening to the buzz? It sounds like the crowd right before a Springsteen concert. And have you ever enjoyed the full "Pedro Kicking Ass at Fenway" experience? Words can't do it justice, but here are three that come close—festive, unique, and raucous. Like a Jimmy Buffet concert, only without the pot smoke.

2) Tell me you don't recognize this right away…

Boston	IP	H	R	ER	BB	K	HR	Pit
Saberhagen	1	4	5	5	1	0	2	27
D. Lowe	2	3	3	3	0	2	1	32
P. Martinez (W 1–0)	6	0	0	0	3	8	0	97

3) Check out the smile on someone's face as they tell you,

120 My friend Bish was like that—he was a missing birth certificate away from becoming the **Danny Almonte** of Greenwich, Connecticut.

"I'm seeing Pedro pitch tonight!" They look like they just won the lottery.

4) Try to concentrate on anything else when it's the top of the fourth, Pedro is pitching, and nobody on the other team has reached base yet. Katie Holmes could be filming live porn on Cinemax and I wouldn't turn the channel. All right, I'd toggle. But you get the idea.

5) Pedro could start Game One (first round), Games One and Four (ALCS) and Games One, Four and Seven (World Series) if everything fell the right way this October.

(Do you have an inexplicably giddy smile on your face? Me, too.)

6) Visit any dive bar in town when Pedro is pitching—everyone seems happier, even the old drunken Irish guys with red noses who hate everything.[121]

7) Check out this e-mail from one of my more rational readers, Steve Brown: "I think you should do a Pedro article every day. Even Lefty Grove in the '29–'32 era didn't do what this guy is doing. Even Sandy Koufax couldn't match what Pedro is doing considering how teams score these days. I'd have to say that I've never seen a Boston athlete dominate like this guy—not even Bird. I don't think we'll appreciate what we're seeing until 25 years later."

(Speaking of Bird, what would Larry have done if Einar Diaz stared him down in the seventh inning and Charles Nagy plunked Offerman in the top of the eighth...and Robbie Alomar was digging in to lead off the bottom of the eighth in Cleveland? Yeah. I thought so.)

8) Go online and read out-of-town sports sections when Pedro comes into opposing towns. Reverence. Respect. Gushing quotes. Just like the Bird days.

9) Remember this simple fact: Yankees fans fear Pedro.[122]

10) Finally, try and scalp good tickets for Pedro's starts at Fenway—they're nearly as tough to find as playoff seats. I always thought that was the best way to measure an athlete's impact. When Michael Jordan came to town, it didn't matter that ML was coaching and Todd Day was launching 30 shots a game at the Fleet Center...people wanted to see MJ. When

121 One of the dumber things I miss about Boston—right up there with the smell of Dunkin' Donuts staying on your clothes, **Joe the Alcoholic Counter Guy**, the people behind the counter at Newbury Comics, and the 1-800-54-GIANT commercial.

122 The underrated aspect of Pedro's prime: He put the fear of God into Yankee fans. That's easy to forget after the losing streak and the "Who's your Daddy?" stuff, but back in 1999 and 2000, they were petrified of him. They even admitted it.

Doug Flutie was scurrying around for daylight at BC, Boston became a college football town. When Larry and Kevin and Robert were walking through that door, nobody wanted to tear down the Garden; we were too busy trying find an extra ticket. Just like now. That's why Pedro Martinez is in the Pantheon.

I leave you with the following story, and let the record show that nothing like this ever happened when Clemens was pitching here.[123]

Last Friday, the Sports Gal and I were driving to Connecticut and listening to the Sox-Orioles game. I was enjoying the game because Pedro was toying with Baltimore's lineup like a cat pawing at a dead mouse; she was enjoying the game because she had been sound asleep since Cambridge. Through seven innings, Pedro had fanned 11 guys and allowed only two bloop hits, which Jerry Trupiano kept derisively referring to as "two cheap hits," like he was blaming the Orioles for ruining the moment. Then it happened.

Some Baltimore fans started cheering Pedro in the eighth, the most surreal subplot since the Russian fans started rooting for Rocky at the end of *Rocky IV*. When's the last time a pitcher *not* pitching a no-hitter ever got cheered by the opposing fans at a baseball game? I kept waiting for Barry Tompkins to burst into the booth and scream, "And now the Russians are *cheering* Pedro!"[124] Blown away, the WEEI guys discussed the Baltimore fans through an extended Sox rally, during which my girlfriend snapped out of her slumber and slowly awoke to the sounds of the game. When the damage was done, the Sox were leading 9-0, but according to the WEEI guys, most of the Baltimore fans were remaining in their seats. Unreal. Of course, Pedro came out for the bottom of the ninth and whiffed the first batter (#14) as the fans erupted and WEEI's Jerry Trupiano shouted, "This crowd is really behind Pedro now!" Still groggy, my girlfriend mumbled, "I thought you said this game was in Baltimore." "Yeah, it is," I answered. "The Baltimore fans are cheering for Pedro though. It's like a *Rocky IV* thing." She was still confused. "Wait, I don't get it. Is he pitching a no-hitter?" I shook my head no. "Then why would they cheer him? He's just so great that even the other team's fans cheer him?"

Yup. Pretty much.

123 Ah, yes… the inevitable Clemens dig.

124 I hate to ruin the moment here—really, I do—but there's an excellent chance that some of these fans were Boston transplants who settled in the DC/Baltimore area and attended the game to support the Sox. Living in Boston at the time, I wasn't fully aware of this phenomenon—and neither were the announcers, apparently. By the end of the Pedro Era, Sox fan transplants were making up 15 to 30 percent of the crowd in nearly every city. And the number keeps growing—by 2005, MLB could have counted any road games in Tampa, Toronto, and Oakland as home games for the Red Sox.

COME FEEL THE GUAPO

May 24, 2000

When you're catching a game at Fenway and hear an unmistakable rumble from the bleachers—"Haaaaahh RRRRAHHHHHH!!!!"—you know it means one of four things:

1) Two guys are beating the crap out of each other.

2) Somebody just threw a beer on someone wearing a Yankees hat.

3) Somebody's trying to start The Wave.

4) El Guapo.

Unless you're sitting in the bleachers, you never know what's causing the commotion in cases 1 through 3…but you *always* know when El Guapo is getting loose in the bullpen. It doesn't even matter where you're sitting; you could be crammed in a high grandstand seat in Section 26 (on the third base side) and *still* make out the big white blob with the giant red 3 4 stretched across his back. That's the power of El Guapo.[125]

His real name is Rich Garces, although that particular identity has fallen by the wayside, much like nobody ever says "Sean Combs" or "Hunter Hearst-Helmsley." When Guapo waddles-er, jogs in from the bullpen, he draws an ovation comparable to anything Pedro, Nomar or Carl Everett have been getting this year. People *love* this guy. It's the best level of appreciation, sincere admiration mixed with the inspired, rock-solid comedy that only a 275-pound middle reliever can provide. As one reader pointed out this week, "How can anyone not think that Rich Garces is the most amusing character we have had here in a long time? Anyone who has a 22-inch neck, a 48-inch chest, a 52-inch stomach, a 28-inch sleeve, and NO ASS, has got to get all the votes in a 'Most Amusing Fenway Subplot' poll. Do you think Pedro rides him mercilessly? Just thinking about Pedro and Guapo together makes me laugh."

Me, too. I love Guapo—and from the sounds of things at Fenway this season, so does everyone else. During a game against the White Sox two weeks ago, Guapo came huffing in

125 In the big scheme of things, the brief apex of **a comical set-up man**—during a season when the Sox didn't even make the playoffs, no less—means nothing in the context of this book. And yet, this piece brings back as many memories for me as any of them. So there.

from the bullpen to a raucous ovation. Sitting in my section, a bunch of Little Leaguers from Connecticut were mystified by the mammoth reliever. They couldn't tell if the Fenway fans were making fun of him or not.

"What are they calling him?" one kid asked me.

"El Guapo. That's his nickname. His real name is Rich Garces. People love him here."

"El Guaper?"

"El Guapo. It means 'The Handsome Guy' in Spanish."

"Are you serious? How did he get that name?"

"Apparently he gave it to himself. Swear to God."[126]

"Get out of here!"

Then the kid turned to the field, delighted, and screamed at the top of his lungs…"EL GUAPO!!!!!!"

Of course, Guapo shut the door on the White Sox, just like he's been doing all season. The overall Guapo experience makes it difficult to take him seriously, but looking at his numbers, you could make a solid case that he saved Boston's pitching staff this season. Remember, with Flash Gordon out for the season and Night Train Lowe[127] assuming the closer role, the bullpen looked shakier than Guapo's belly. Now it's almost June and the bullpen has emerged as the steadiest part of the team, with El Guapo as big of a reason as anyone. Check out his stats from the 14 months:

YR	W–L	ERA	G	IP	H	K	BB
1999	5–1	1.55	30	40.2	25	33	18
2000	1–0	2.05	17	22.0	14	24	5

Not bad, huh? The Guapster gave up three runs in a one-inning stint in Anaheim back on April 7th. Since then, check out some of these numbers:

- He's allowed just two earned runs and 11 hits in 21 innings.
- He's retired 13-of-14 of the "first batters" he's faced when coming into a game.
- He's eaten 56 hot dogs, 78 cheeseburgers, 840 chicken fingers, and polished off 123 burritos.
- With two outs and runners in scoring position, he's retired all seven batters he's faced.

126 Supposedly he gave himself the nickname, taking it from the El Guapo character in ***Three Amigos***.

127 That season I decided that Lowe needed a menacing nickname befitting his new status as closer, something that would obscure the fact that he couldn't grow facial hair and looked like an ESPN News anchor. Ultimately I settled on Night Train, and only because it worked in college with our friend Jim Kelly, a ROTC student who lived on my hall freshman year and was the whitest guy alive. The Night Train nickname gave Jim a whole new persona. It was unbelievable. Sadly, I didn't have enough readers at the time to pull this off with Lowe, who ended up becoming D-Lowe after other names like A-Rod and T-Mac had taken off. I blame Stu Scott and Linda Cohn.

• Lefties are hitting .133 against him; righties are hitting just .204.

• He's cleared out the bullpen bathroom three times from stall #2.

• He's only given up one run in May.

• When his first pitch is a strike, batters are hitting 3-for-40 against him.

• He set the record for "Most Ludicrous Sports Stat of the Year" when his weight was listed in this year's Red Sox program as "215."

Pretty convincing stuff. Garces always threw in the low-90s but lacked control until the latter part of last season, when he apparently purchased command of the strike zone on eBay. These days, he's throwing strikes, getting ahead of batters and giving the Sox everything that Lowe gave them last year. They haven't missed a beat since Gordon's elbow injury.

But can he keep it up? Having just turned 30, Guapo finally seems to be reaching his mammoth potential, literally and figuratively. Still, he hasn't topped the 46-inning mark for a season during his entire career, mainly because he can't remain healthy; Guapo spends more time in the shop than your average Jaguar, and it's pretty safe to say that his size has something to do with it. Top set-up guys usually throw between 75 and 90 innings per year, which means Garces will nearly double his career high for innings if he avoids the disabled list this season. Will he keep throwing heat in July and August if he's still pitching three times a week in 95-degree weather? That remains to be seen.**128**

Whatever happens, El Guapo has finally earned his keep in Boston. As far as set-up men go, he's pitching as well as anyone in either league. As far as characters go, he's moving towards Oil Can status at Fenway. As far as bizarre bodies go, he's right up there with Kevin McHale and the three-boobed lady from *Total Recall* in my book. And as far as great Boston nicknames go, nobody can remember a nickname with more comic potential than El Guapo.

It's a feel-good story all the way around. And around. And around...**129**

128 The famous Guapo story happened two months later, during a 95-degree game in Texas, when Guapo covered first base on consecutive grounders, then found himself so winded and overheated, pitching coach Joe Kerrigan had to come out and stall while Guapo caught his breath. And you're telling me this man doesn't deserve his own *SportsCentury* episode?

129 Guapo submitted one more solid season before falling apart in 2002 (21.3 innings, 7.59 ERA), leading to his ignominious release. In Janury 2005, a Venezuelan newspaper reported that he had been kidnapped; as it turned out, he was only "missing" for 10 days and blamed family problems for his unexplained absence. Regardless, couldn't the Sox hire him as a bullpen coach? Or **bring back the old bullpen car** and have him drive it? What's wrong with keeping El Guapo around?

THE OTHER SHOE

July 17, 2000

There's a scene in *Jerry Maguire* after Renee Zellweger's character falls for Jerry, the handsome, thoughtful, down-on-his-luck sports agent, when she tells her sister, "I feel like I'm getting a great break on a used car."[130]

Hey, we've all spent time with someone who seemed great on the surface, only we felt that nagging "used car" sense about them, even as we were still getting sucked in. *Why is this person still single? Why hasn't anyone else snapped them up yet? When will the other shoe finally drop?* Usually things remain fine for a few more weeks, until our beloved starts showing their true colors and we discover they're carrying more baggage than a Lear jet. Everything finally adds up…and we never feel the same again.

This doesn't just happen with relationships. Last Saturday at Fenway, Red Sox fans were collectively clobbered over the head with the other shoe. The New Guy flipped out. The New Guy bumped an umpire and head-butted him. The New Guy tossed aside teammates and coaches like blocking dummies. The New Guy stormed back to the dugout, broke some things, screamed at some more teammates. And then he stormed into the clubhouse and probably calmed down within 15 minutes. For him, it was over. But not for us. And not for me.

There was always something about the Carl Everett Era in Boston that didn't add up. Players with MVP potential don't get traded three times in five years. Players with MVP potential don't settle for cheap money (three years, $21 million). Players with MVP potential don't inexplicably surface on the discount trade rack, no matter how badly their franchises need to chop payroll. And as we watched him belting homers and pointing to the sky for the first two months, we all felt like Zellweger's character during those first few months with Jerry Maguire. Now we know. It all adds up. There *is* no such thing as a great break on a used car.[131]

Maybe we knew all along. It wasn't any one big thing, just a number of small things that kept building toward one conclusion, a conclusion nobody wanted to face: *The New Guy isn't all there*. He bashed the Yankees in spring training. Bashed Jeter

130 Don't kill me for quoting *Jerry Maguire*, which remains the most divisive case study in the history of the "Sports Movie vs. Chick Flick" debate. I actually call these movies "Spork Flicks"—they have enough sports stuff that guys can stand them, but enough chick flick stuff that women are happy. With *Maguire*, since **Rod Tidwell** was the most realistic sports movie character of the past 15 years, that fulfilled its sports movie requirements on its own. And yet, this is the kind of movie that will pop up on the Lifetime Network from time to time. Very difficult to pull all of these things off. Some other examples: *For Love and Basketball*, *Bull Durham*, *Vision Quest*, and *Rocky*. That was the problem with the loathsome *Fever Pitch*, by the way—it marketed itself as a Sports Flick, but it was really just a straightforward chick flick. The Farrelly Brothers still owe me $10.

131 Four years later, Corey Dillon proved me wrong. I guess you never know.

132 The vocal similarities between Everett and Mr. T were eerie. You could almost imagine Everett storming into the manager's office and screaming, "**Don't give me no jibber-jabber, Jimy Williams!** I pity the fool who stands up to me! I pity the fool!"

and Paul O'Neill and Joe Torre. Bashed the Mets. Insulted a pitcher who blanked the Red Sox in April for having mediocre stuff. Talked about dinosaurs and how he thought they never existed. Quoted psalms from the Bible despite the fact that we could see him swearing on the field at times. Griped about being rested for one measly game. Alluded to mysterious forces that were handicapping his manager. Laid an expletive-filled tirade on a sports columnist and a Red Sox employee.

We looked the other way every time. And why? Because the New Guy was exceedingly fun to watch—a riveting mixture of Oil Can Boyd, Mr. T and former Sox star Reggie Smith.[132] "That's just Carl," we said to ourselves. "The New Guy. He's a little loopy." Well, he's a little more than that. And if you think I'm wrong, then you weren't there at Fenway Park on Saturday afternoon. Sitting nine rows behind the Mets on-deck circle, I had a birds-eye view as Everett stormed away from the batter's box, turned toward the Mets dugout, walked a few steps and dropped an F-bomb loud enough for every child in our section to hear. I watched Everett whip off his helmet, charge forward, bump home plate umpire Ron Kulpa with his chest, then ram his head towards the bridge of Kulpa's nose. I watched the ensuing fallout, my heart pounding the entire time.

This wasn't fun or cute, and it certainly failed to fire anyone up. I read every account of Saturday's game over the past two days, but nothing accurately captured the emotions in Fenway. Remember, this was the final game of a heated Mets-Red Sox series; the stands were filled with fans from both sides, everyone screaming at different times like a European soccer crowd. And it was a gorgeous afternoon to attend a baseball game—on a weekend, no less—so everyone's spirits were high. When Everett and Kulpa started clashing, it meshed with the atmosphere in the stands and a jolt of electricity surged through the crowd. We were poised for a classic, old-fashioned baseball argument. Then Everett lost it. It was like someone pulled Warren's ears in *There's Something About Mary*, only with 35,000 people watching.

Quick tangent: Baseball crowds produce an eclectic variety of memorable sounds. There's the "We need strike three and…WE GOT IT!" roar. There's the "That ball looks like it might have a chance and IT'S GONE!!!" cheer. There's the "WOWWHATAPLAY!" sudden yelp. There's even the disturbing "Fred Lynn just ran into the centerfield wall at full-speed and now he's dead" groan, which you probably remember from Game Six of the '75 World Series. Basically, everyone's cheering and screaming and then BOOM—things turn silent and a horrified hush reverberates through the park. It sounds like this: "HRRRRRAHHHHHHHHHHH—ohhh (low murmur)."

Why is this relevant? When Everett and Kulpa butted heads, we made the "Fred Lynn is dead" sound: "HRRRRRAHHHH-HHHHHHH—ohhh." Nobody wanted that. Once his teammates pushed Everett toward the clubhouse to cool off, the fans weren't the same for a few innings (until the Sox rallied to tie the game). As far as I'm concerned, Everett ruined the afternoon. The Other Shoe smacked 33,288 people right in the forehead.

Everett's anger was justified—not his actions, his *anger*—and he deserved the right to make a commotion and plead his case (Kulpa had told him to move off the plate). But you could sift through history and find dozens of athletes who showed their true colors once they faced a little adversity, from Kareem Abdul-Jabbar sucker-punching Kent Benson to Clemens flipping out in Game Four of the 1990 Playoffs. Seriously, would Nomar *ever* butt heads with an umpire, even semi-accidentally? Good people don't react to situations that way. It's that simple.[133] Throw in Everett's reported struggles to control his temper in the past (as Gordon Edes tackled in yesterday's *Globe*) and the picture becomes a little clearer. *Just $21 million and one prospect for the right to play a potential MVP in center for the next three years?* Two months ago, it didn't add up. Now it does.[134]

I keep remembering the way I felt in April, when Everett's play inspired me to devote an entire column to him. Now I keep remembering the portly guy in my section who kept blaming the umpire and stealing the "She was asking for it" defense from Jodie Foster's attackers in *The Accused*. I actually ended up arguing with him—he was such a miserable moron, I couldn't take it—as we debated points until I finally hissed, "That's a good lesson for you to teach your son." I was half-joking, but that managed to shut him up. After all, his son had been sitting next to him for the entire time. The boy looked no older than eleven. His mouth was covered with metal. He looked awkward as hell. And he wasn't even listening to us, just staring intently onto the field, probably wondering when the centerfielder was going to run back out to head-butt the umpire again.

133 See: Ron Artest and Stephen Jackson.

134 In this paragraph, I removed two sentences about **Robert Horry** throwing a towel at Danny Ainge (then coaching Horry for the Suns)—which included the phrase, "I hated him ever since"— the only time in this entire book that I changed an opinion I had at the time. And here's why: I love Big Shot Rob now. He's the Nate Dogg of the NBA—doesn't get enough attention, always seems to be involved in a winning effort. And it's been going on for like 13 years. In fact, this spring I received the e-mail, "Whose career would you have rather had, Karl Malone's, Charles Barkley's or Robert Horry's?" and decided on Horry. Anyway, I wouldn't have lived with myself had that Horry slam remained in the column. The more I'm thinking about it, Ainge probably deserved it.

That was Saturday. Everett returned the following day and slammed a pitch into the centerfield bleachers against Montreal. The fans stood and cheered as Everett rounded the bases and reached home plate, where he touched his chest, kissed his hand, and pointed up towards the sky. Then he jogged back to his dugout, where his teammates slapped him on the rear and doled out high-fives. Life goes on. Two months ago, I would have felt giddy. Now? I'm just hoping he makes it through the season. I've rooted for guys I didn't like before, with Antoine Walker being the prime example, and I'll support Everett for as long as he wears a Red Sox uniform.[135] To put it coldly, he gives this team a better chance to win, warts and all.

With that said, I won't care about him the same way I care about Nomar and Pedro and Sabes and everyone else. If Everett called Kulpa and offered him an apology, everything would have been forgiven. Anyone with a good heart would have done that—*hey, sorry about yesterday, we were both wrong and I overreacted, my bad*—then served their suspension, upbraided and a little mortified, and the whole thing would eventually be forgotten. But Everett didn't apologize, nor did he seem contrite. Actually, he didn't seem to care at all—not that he certainly jeopardized his team's pennant chances with a long (and imminent) suspension, not even that his young son witnessed the sordid episode from the family section. All he cared about yesterday was circling the bases and remembering to point at the sky when he touched home plate.

And so nothing changed for him over the past 48 hours, even if everything changed for me. He didn't change...I changed. Maybe you did, too.

The Other Shoe strikes again.[136]

135 That proclamation lasted about 10 more days. Everett's career in Boston ended predictably the following season—just five days after 9/11, he cursed out manager Joe Kerrigan and was sent home for the season (they traded him to Texas that winter). Here's what I wrote in my end-of-the-year report card: "Not since Jim Rice developed rigor mortis between the 1986 and 1987 seasons has a Red Sox player declined so quickly and abruptly from one season to the next. Once a .300/30 HR switch-hitter with a decent glove and enough power to carry the team for a few games on end, Everett simply fell apart in 2001—put on weight, couldn't hit righties, couldn't run and made Manny look like a **young Fred Lynn** in the field. Just a shocking collapse. It's like he aged in dog years."

136 The creator of The Other Shoe theory: My buddy Joe House. Every time I met someone I liked, House would ask if The Other Shoe had dropped yet. Invariably, it always did. And then I met my future wife, and he kept asking when The Other Shoe was dropping, and I kept telling him, "I don't know if it's happening with this one." And it didn't. Although I guess there's still time.

DATE WITH DESTINY

August 29, 2000

Twenty thoughts after tonight's Red Sox game, which was simply the most mesmerizing regular season baseball game of my lifetime.[137]

1) Only 249 batters have hit for the cycle and 224 people have pitched no-hitters in the *history* of baseball. Tonight in Tampa, both things nearly happened in the same game. What are the odds? Infinity-to-one? Throw in the fact that an Italian guy[138] suffered a concussion in the same game and the odds are off the charts—and that's before we get to the bench-clearing brawls. Easily one of the weirdest games of all time.

2) If you were trapped under a rock, here's what happened: Pedro nailed the first batter of the game (Gerald "Ice" Williams) with a fastball, fought off Williams's charge and the ensuing brawl, endured the ensuing 25-minute delay, stewed in the dugout through two prolonged Sox rallies that were extended by more beanballs and more ejections…and ended up retiring 24 batters in a row before John Flaherty broke up his no-hitter in the ninth. Pedro is the Dominican Larry. There's nothing else to say.[139]

3) Okay, maybe there is. Did you notice how, after Williams charged him, Pedro was hitting 97 and 98 on the radar gun for the first time in months? Is it safe to say that he's been saving that extra-special fastball for the playoffs so he didn't endanger his arm, only the Devil Rays triggered his mean streak? Was he dusting that baby off like my Mom breaking out a bottle of '91 Sassacaia? Sure seemed like it.

4) A bench-clearing brawl with the first batter? Will we *ever* see anything like that again? It's just about the last thing you expect at 7:30 at night. The Sports Gal and I were so inspired that we decided to re-enact a few scenes from *What's Love Got to Do With It*, which is always fun because I get to break out my Ike Turner wig. *Eat the cake Anna Mae! Eat the cake goddammit!*

5) Why would Pedro throw at Williams in the first place?

137 I posted this column at 3:30 a.m. that night.

138 That was **Lou Merloni**, the quintessential "Sox player who nobody could judge accurately because he was a local guy." You could be a .240 hitter with no power, no range and a throwing arm made out of fettucini, but if you grew up in Framingham, that gave you permanent immunity in New England. If Buckner had grown up in Dorchester, everyone would have blamed Bob Stanley for losing Game Six at Shea.

139 If Pedro had ended up throwing a no-hitter, there would have been a precedent in Red Sox history: On June 23, 1917, Babe Ruth (did you know he once played for the Red Sox?) walked Washington's leadoff batter before being ejected for arguing balls and strikes. Ernie Shore relieved him and retired the next 27 guys in order for the pseudo-perfect game.

Made no sense. Old Gerald needs to scrape the ice off his brain. And can you imagine if Pedro actually got hurt in that fight in a "Lee-Nettles '76" kinda way?[140] We'd be holding an emergency induction ceremony for Williams for the Samuelsson/Quinn/Laimbeer/Hamilton/Ruhle wing of the Boston Villain Hall of Fame.[141] I don't even like *mentioning* this. Let's move on.

6) I had to go to the bathroom from the 3rd inning on, only I was afraid to move because I didn't want to miss anything—plus, I was sitting in a special position on the sofa that was helping Pedro out. (Yes, I believe in this stuff.) After the game ended, I had one of those Austin Powers pees. Had to rest the hand against the wall and everything. Just wanted to share that with you.

7) As far as I'm concerned, Pedro officially entered the bar for his date with Destiny[142] in the fourth inning (after that quick 1–2–3 inning with all the groundouts). He sat down with her in the fifth when he struck out the side. In the sixth and seventh, they did a few shots together and loosened up the mood. By the eighth inning, he was paying the check while she was in the bathroom sticking in her diaphragm. Then... boom! The cross breaks around his neck. And it's all over. Suddenly she's hailing a cab and Pedro's headed home for a date with Cinemax. Destiny's a bitch that way.

(Let's face it: As far as bad omens go, that cross snapping around Pedro's neck during the Flaherty at-bat made Bobby Brady's Hawaiian tiki[143] look like a rabbit's foot.)

8) We will never watch a potential no-hitter under those circumstances again, where you're worried that the pitcher involved will get thrown out for protecting his teammates. Every time Pedro threw a pitch, I cringed. By the seventh inning I was so antsy and nervous that the Captain almost turned off the no-smoking sign in Sports Guy Mansion for the first time in five months. Just seeing Miguel Cairo made me start hyperventilating—I felt like the "Looks like I picked the wrong week to stop sniffing glue" guy from *Airplane*. An agonizing three hours.

9) Why is it always schmucks like John Flaherty who break up no-hitters? It kills me that he almost chased that high fastball on 1–2, right before the cross broke. How does someone

140 On May 20, 1976 (my mother's birthday party), Lou Piniella and Carlton Fisk ended up fighting at home plate in Yankee Stadium, leading to a brawl in which **Graig Nettles ended up body-slamming Bill Lee** (separating his shoulder), followed by Mickey Rivers sucker-punching Lee and me calling someone a "fucking asshole" for the first time (which felt fantastic). The Red Sox couldn't even beat the Yankees in bench-clearing brawls.

141 Ulf Samuelsson injured Cam Neely's hip; Pat Quinn nearly broke Bobby Orr in half with an infamous body check; you know Bill Laimbeer's resume; Jack Hamilton was the guy who threw the beanball at Tony C in '67; and Vern Ruhle broke Jim Rice's wrist in '75.

142 This was a running joke between me and my buddy Gus, to the point that he would call me after some stiff like Joe Cowley pitched a no-hitter and start screaming, "Did you hear what Destiny did? What a tramp! How could she do that?" Gus' team (the Mets) couldn't throw a no-hitter, either—in fact, they still haven't had a no-hitter in franchise history, although their three most famous pitchers (Tom Seaver,

like Flaherty lay off that pitch? Damn him. Six years from now, he'll be an assistant coach at East Bumfuck High, telling the kids how he broke up Pedro's no-no while resting a can of Keystone Light on his pot belly. No, I'm not bitter.[144]

10) Pedro could retire tomorrow and I could live off last night's game, the Memorial Day game against the Yankees, the one-hitter in Baltimore, last year's one-hitter at Yankee Stadium, and Game Five of the Cleveland series for the rest of my sports fan life. I never thought anything would surpass Game Five for me, but last night came close. *You dare to charge the mound against me? Have some of THIS, bendejo!*

11) The best part of the game: when Tampa hit Daubach for the umpteenth time in the seventh and Sox players poured onto the field ready to throw down like the Warriors on Coney Island. Unfortunately we didn't have the one crazy guy on the team to escalate things by trying to pull a Kermit Washington on someone (a basebrawl standard). Darren Lewis showed the most potential but never really snapped. Too bad Carl Everett remembered to take his Prozac before the game.

12) I called my dad after every inning from the fifth on, just to make sure he didn't fall asleep. You have to love those games. You can always judge a great Red Sox game by the number of calls between my father and me. That was like a seven-call game.

13) Maybe I'm the only one who thinks about stuff like this, but can you imagine if Jose Guillen started up with Trot Nixon? Trot was giving him the Eastwood-eqsue "Make my day" stare. Other than the completely-insane Carl Everett, Trot's probably the one guy you wouldn't want to mess with on the Sox.[145] If I were ever matched up against the Sox in a bench-clearer, I'd seek out El Guapo and disarm him with a burrito.

14) The only time I really became angry tonight was when they threw at Nomar and I had the "Rice in '75" flashback. Ugh.[146]

15) I have now seen two Red Sox pitchers take a no-hitter into the ninth inning—Pedro last night and Rick Wise during the '75 season, which I barely remember because I was five at the time. And both of them lost it. Life sucks.

16) One word: Sabes. [147]

Nolan Ryan and Dwight Gooden) all ended up throwing ones for other teams. I'm telling you, Destiny is a big-time bitch.

143 Probably my most over-used pop culture reference over the years, harkening back to my college days at Holy Cross. Since the three-part Hawaii episode was a defining moment in my childhood, I always forget that nobody under 25 remembers how scary it was when Greg's surfboard overturned, or how confusing it was that **Vincent Price tormented the Brady Boys** in a cave for an entire episode, then Mr. Brady inexplicably invited him to the final luau. I don't think I will ever get over this.

144 Flaherty ended up having a decent career for a mediocre catcher—at age 37, he's backing up Jorge Posada for the 2005 Yankees instead of coaching East Bumfuck High. There's still time.

145 As it turned out, Jose Guillen makes Carl Everett look like Fred Rogers.

146 Four weeks later, Baltimore's Al Reyes nailed Nomar in the right wrist—Nomar's career was never the same. I blame myself.

147 I have absolutely no idea what this means—maybe he was fun to watch during the brawl. I dunno.

148 Reason no. 2455 why I could never be a professional athlete—I would absolutely put myself over the success of the team. Seriously, 10 years from now, nobody would remember that the Sox beat Tampa in late-August of a season where they both missed the playoffs, but I bet they'd remember that cycle.

149 If this happened four years later, there's about a 100 percent chance I would have added a joke about Landon from ***The Real World: Philly*** right here. Do you think Daubie owns a yellow "Huggable" T-shirt?

150 He was the 120-pound star of that MTV show about the boy band, *2gether*. I know we're only on page 88, but I guarantee he's the most obscure reference in this book.

17) When Everett needed a single for the cycle and jacked that second homer in the stands, do you think he ever considered "forgetting" to touch second base? Hell, it was a 5–0 game and Pedro was pitching. No jury would have convicted him.[148]

18) What about the bizarre subplot with Daubach, who was getting picked on more often than Daniel LaRusso in the *Karate Kid* trilogy? *Sweep the leg, Mr. Eiland. Do you have a problem with that?* Daubie got thrown at four times! Just what the hell happened at the bottom of that first pile? Did he put the Walls of Jericho on somebody? Did he pull out a salt packet like Mr. Fuji and try to blind someone? Have you ever seen a baseball team go after somebody that way? And how come Daubie always seems to take these things to the next level? He's like that unassuming buddy everyone had in college who always ended up picking fights with football players after a few beers.[149]

19) As much as I've been enjoying NESN's new Bob Rodgers-Jerry Remy tandem, why do announcers jinx no-hitters by saying things like, "There have been 10 hits in this game and the Red Sox have all them"? Drives me crazy. Anyone who says this should be beaten with reeds after the game. And then they have ESPN cut into the game during the Flaherty at-bat in the ninth? Why not throw a black cat on the field and have Pedro walk under a ladder?

20) Finally, will Pedro ever pitch a no-hitter for us? Everything seemed ripe last night—extra motivation from the fight, an especially-popping fastball and an opposing lineup so lame and punchless that I think Jason "QT" McKnight[150] led off the seventh for Tampa—and you only have so many nights where everything falls into place. Ironically enough, I watched ESPN Classic's re-broadcast of Roger Clemens' 20K game against Seattle recently and was bowled over by Seattle's lineup of stiffs. Ken Phelps? Steve Yeager? Spike Owen? Gorman Thomas? Talk about the stars aligning at the right time. Anyway, Tampa's lineup gave me that same "Mmmmmmm" feeling.

And so another opportunity goes by the wayside. Destiny just doesn't seem to like anyone from Boston, does she?[151]

151 Funny postscript to this one: Exactly seven months later, during the first week of the season, free agent acquisition Hideo Nomo pitched the first Red Sox no-hitter of my lifetime, which was strangely bittersweet because Pedro wasn't involved. At the time I wrote, "**I feel like a 17-year-old girl** who was saving her virginity for the star QB on Prom Night...and ended up losing it to some transfer student who couldn't speak English on the second day of senior year."

152 Or unless you're writing sports columns on a little-known website and borrowing money from your parents every few months.

153 I scalped tickets for more games in 2000 than any other season, to the point that certain scalpers started recognizing me. **Three tips for scalping:** **1)** Always go to the same guy, because good scalpers are more prone to sell premium seats for return customers; **2)** if you're looking for one ticket, keep an eye out for three-person groups where the lead guy is glancing around and looking nervous, almost like he's trying to complete a drug deal, because their fourth didn't show up and he just wants to get rid of their ticket for face value (only he's not sure if it's legal); and **3)** the best times to scalp are either 90 minutes before the game (when the most tickets are out there) or right before the game (when people are panicking to get rid of their tickets). I always enjoyed the whole scalping thing—it's like trying to buy pot in a foreign country. You never know how it might turn out. Um, not that I'd know about buying pot in a foreign country.

154 That July, I wrote an entire column argu-ing that the Red Sox should *not* trade Nixon

WRESTLING WITH SHADOWS

September 21, 2000

The shadow inched forward every inning, creeping closer and closer to the mound, a menacing portent of doom. The Sox were trailing Cleveland, 1–0. Sitting in Fenway, we were more anxious than 34,000 chainsmokers trapped on a cross-country flight, the biggest game of the season slipping away. Everyone hated to see another Pedro masterpiece getting wasted. But it was happening. Again. We were a few more outs away from another lost season.

So we did our best to affect the game. On Wednesday afternoons in September, you don't play hooky and head over to Fenway unless you care.[152] Pedro was on his game, but so were we. We yelled. We hollered our support. We battled our doubts about this team, the nagging feeling that your favorite team just plain *sucks* (only you can't admit it to yourself). We knew they were a group composed largely of castoffs, washed-up veterans, overrated young players and guys who couldn't speak English. We knew the coaching staff was inept. We understood the effects of Everett's meltdown against the Mets, how a team predicated on chemistry and camaraderie had somehow sold its soul. We just weren't ready to give up on the season yet.[153]

But that damned shadow…

Halfway through the game, the sun shone directly behind the 600 Club, so the shadow reached the back of the batter's box. It was becoming more difficult for the batters to see; we knew this because it was becoming more difficult for us to see. In the bleachers, they hadn't moved fans out of those two sections in dead-center—Sections 34 and 35, right over the pitcher's shoulder—so batters were peering into a background littered with white T-shirts and baseball caps. These weren't exactly optimal conditions for a rally. And we knew it.

Normally during Pedro's starts, fans head for concession stands and bathrooms only during Boston's at-bats. That wasn't happening yesterday; 34,000 people were stapled to their seats. Sometimes you know when a game is turning into one of Those Games, those three or four games in a season that decide a team's fate. The Sox needed to beat Cleveland four times in

as the centerpiece in a deal for Sammy Sosa. Sadly, all records of this column have been lost. As far as you know.

155 Five seasons later, neither Jimy Williams, Jim Rice, Joe Kerrigan nor Wendell Kim (**the core of that putrid coaching staff**) are working in the majors. And neither is GM Dan Duquette. I find this interesting. Speaking of Kim, it's a little-known rule that the Sox always have an incompetent third base coach, but Wendall was the worst of the bunch. Here's one of my Wendell rants from the 2000 season:

"Out of anyone I know, Wendell's the absolute worst at what he does, and that includes everyone working in the Charlestown area—including the lady at the Store 24 who asks if you're all set after you've already paid for your items and the three post office employees who go on their lunch break from 12–1:00 p.m. while 47 people are waiting in line on their lunch break. Forget that he looks like he should be standing next to Mr. Roarke, that he has worse depth perception than Keith Olbermann, that he's gotten 43 guys thrown out at home by a combined 1500 feet this season. Unless somebody fires him ASAP, Wendell could blow out somebody's knee with those ultra-late stop signs. I attended the Kansas City game three weeks ago when Varitek rounded third on a single and went 10–12 feet past the bag before Wendell threw up the emergency stop sign. Poor Varitek screeched to a halt like a stationwagon trying to avoid an accident, limped back to the bag, called time, and proceeded to lay into Wendell. And dumb old Wendell was standing there clapping his hands trying to pretend that the starting catcher wasn't bitching him out, but it was happening and every fan on the third base side could see it. When someone like Nomar blows out a knee putting on the skids because Wendall suddenly changed his mind for the umpteenth time, would *that* be enough to remove this man from third base? I keep waiting for Wendell to show up on ***South Park*** and wave Kenny onto a three-lane highway."

five games to keep their wildcard hopes alive, and that wasn't happening if the Indians defeated Pedro. Fortunately, Pedro was throwing seeds, allowing hits to the first three batters of the game, then mowing through the next few innings hitless and untouched. Only Pedro could do that. I've found myself saying that a lot over the last two years—*only Pedro could do that*. Who else would allow three hits to start a game and then retire the next 16 batters in order? Only Pedro.

By the sixth inning, it was impossible to conceal our contempt for certain Boston batters. O'Leary had looked dreadful all season—save for a three-week hot streak in July—and even worse this month when it mattered most. He was practically a Section Eight. Offerman had appeared slow and uninterested since April, which gave him something in common with my reactions to every one of his at-bats. Daubach was trapped in one of his "Ed Norton from *Primal Fear*" slumps, when he inexplicably turns into Mario Mendoza for weeks on end. Nixon had been pressing for months, ever since the Sosa trade rumors, when every Sox fan overrated his value (including me).[154] Manny Alexander was manning the third-base spot, which would have been fine if we were playing in Japan. Varitek had been slumping all season, replacing Carl Everett in the 3-spot for this game because, well, our manager is nuts.

How could this team even finish over .500? Between the limp offense and struggling pitching staff, there wasn't much left other than Nomar and Pedro. In denial for much of the season, we directed most of our anger toward our inept coaching staff[155], an overmatched group that cost the team 8–10 games (and I'm being kind). But we still had Pedro. He was the X-factor, the Dominican Larry, the Jimmy Chitwood of this whole thing. When Pedro's involved, you always have a puncher's chance. Surround him with a few competents (Everett, Lowe, Bichette and Arrojo) and a superstar (Nomar) and maybe, just maybe, the other mediocre pieces will fall into place. At least that was the plan. *Just get there.* That's all we wanted. Get into October and Pedro will take care of the rest. That's what we had become, a group of fans pinning our hopes for a 25-man team on a 160-pound pitcher.[156]

Against the Indians, Pedro kept throwing darts and fanning our hopes. There was a great moment in the eighth, after he was squeezed on third strikes to consecutive batters: One of them

(Travis Fryman) ended up reaching base on an infield hit, the other (Russell Branyan) remained alive thanks to a mysterious "foul tip" call. Jimy and Mr. Weebles[157] ended up getting thrown out of the game, punctuating their exit by kicking dirt on home plate as the crowd roared in delight. Now we were *into* it. In any other situation, the pitcher invariably gives up the back-breaking 3-and-2 single for the insurance run; we've seen that scenario a million times over the years.

Not this time.[158]

First, Pedro needed to express his disapproval. That's what the great ones would do. So he stood defiantly behind the mound, his hands on his hips, looking like a little kid who wouldn't play until he got a do-over, the drama building. Finally, he stepped back onto the mound, having worked himself into enough of a lather. Not only was he angry, the Indians would have to pay. As we stood and pounded our hands together, Pedro reared back and fired another pea past Branyan...swingandamiss...strike three!!!!!

And we went crazy. Really, we went *crazy*. You had to be there. Standing and hollering near the visiting on-deck circle in Section 24, carrying on like everyone else, I could actually feel a lump welling in my throat. Sometimes Pedro lifts me to a higher place, the same way Bird and MJ did, the way Tiger does now. Every time you count Pedro out, he responds. Every time he gets challenged, he roars back. Every time you think he's extraordinary, he does something to make you think he's just a little bit greater. And honestly, I don't know what else to say. I love the guy. I've never even met him, but I love the guy.

Pedro ended up getting a double play to end the eighth. Of course he did. In the bottom of the inning, the Sox stranded a one-out pinch hit by Everett. A 1–0 defeat seemed inevitable. And cruel. And fitting. And since the shadow had almost reached the mound, the time seemed ripe for another edition of "What the hell is Jimy doing???" This one had two parts:

1) Even though Pedro had been hitting 95 in the eighth, even though he was working on five days rest, even though he had thrown 122 pitches and probably had another 15–20 left in him, Mr. Weebles told Jimy to yank Pedro so they could save his arm for the stretch run in September. Apparently it didn't matter that this *was* September (September 20th, to be exact) and

156 During this particular season, the local media made a big deal about how the Sox had trouble scoring for Pedro. But wasn't that inevitable? Athletes always raise their level of play against superior opponents, whether they're playing Wimbledon against Sampras, Golden Tee against Simmons or baseball against Pedro. At one point in 2000, the Sox played 14 games featuring a total of three runs or less, and Pedro was involved in 10 of those 14. That's no accident.

157 Jimy made so many crazy, inexplicable moves during the course of this season, I started pretending in columns that there was a crazy man named Mr. Weebles who lived in his mouth and ordered him to make these moves. **I got the idea while watching *The Shining*** one night. When you're watching a movie about a caretaker who slowly goes insane and tries to murder his family, and that movie reminds you of the guy managing your baseball team, it's probably not a good sign for your World Series hopes.

158 I stand by everything in the next two paragraphs, no matter how gay you may think I am.

Pedro was only pitching in the most important fucking game of the season. Go figure. I challenge you, go figure.

2) In the previous night's game, with a 7–4 lead in the pouring rain, Mr. Weebles ordered Jimy to warm up closer Derek Lowe and pitch him in the ninth. Keep in mind, this was the first game of a five-game series over the next three days. Normally you would think to yourself, boy, I'm not pitching Lowe unless I absolutely, *positively* need him over the next three days. And yet here was Jimy, wasting Lowe in a lost cause, then bringing him back 16 hours later.

DOES THIS MAKE SENSE TO ANYONE?????????[159]

So Kenny Lofton's ninth-inning homer was inevitable. Now the Sox were trailing by two. Normally fans would start fleeing Fenway like the Lutz family fleeing the Amityville Horror house,[160] but not this time. If the boys ever needed us, this was it. We stayed. And like a scene from a Poe story, the menacing shadow finally reached the pitcher's mound. My mind started racing about ways I could work the shadow into a column; it was just too strange. I didn't even notice when Offerman walked and Varitek grounded out, then Nomar belted the second pitch to left and...

(Wait a second...)

(That ball's carrying...)

(Hey, WAIT a second...)

(Noooooooooooooooo!!!!!)

The ball struck the middle of the Green Monster, right near the top of the wall. And I mean, the VERY top. Two more feet and it would have been gone. Nomar kicked the dirt behind second base in disbelief, a rare display of emotion from him. In any other ballpark, the fans would have been going bonkers, but not in Boston; we were so stunned, we forgot there were runners on second and first and just one out. These are the moments when you hate rooting for the Red Sox. You feel those familiar doubts surfacing every time something like "Nomar's game-tying homer hits 35 feet up a 37-foot wall" transpires. We've all been burned too many times. [161]

(Quick tangent: I can't stand the Curse, the media's doom-and-gloom routine, certain Red Sox fans expecting the worse at all times...but even I have to admit, there are *clearly* larger forces at work here. Goofy things happen to this team. Personally, I

159 That paragraph was co-written with Stephen A. Smith.

160 Another pop culture reference I used WAAAAAY too much, right up there with Bobby Brady's Hawaiian tiki. Although *Amityville Horror* was the lost scary movie of my childhood—every bit as creepy as *Halloween*, *Friday the 13th* and *The Shining*, only nobody ever mentions it now. I'm pretty sure this is James Brolin's fault—he's been impossible to take seriously for 15–20 years, which renders all of his previous work pretty much impotent. But my favorite part is when the family finally escapes the house at the end, **black goo is coming out of the walls**, the whole house is shaking, and it's already been established that the portal to hell is in the basement, only they forgot to bring their dog with them. So they're about to drive away, only Brolin's wife and kids are giving him the "Come on, Daddy, we can't leave the dog" guilt trip. What happens? He takes a deep breath, then runs back to save his black Lab. The lesson, as always: Don't get married.

161 Jets fans are nodding silently right now.

think Fenway Park is haunted; the list of feel-good Red Sox moments in Fenway Park pretty much starts and end with Fisk's homer in '75. If our baseball park was an automobile, it would be Arnie's Plymouth Fury in *Christine*.)

The ending seemed inevitable. They teased us with a run before Bichette feebly grounded out to the pitcher, then Daubach whiffed to end the game. That last at-bat typified the past six months: Daubach battled back from two strikes, worked a full count, then swung at a pitch that bounced in front of home plate. I mention this only because those are the types of at-bats the Yankees never seem to have. Like it or not, we measure up to them. Everyone in their organization seems to be on the same page. When they face Pedro, every Yankee hitter works him for 6-to-7 pitch at-bats; usually he's cooked by the sixth or seventh inning. You wonder if the Yankees love playing the Red Sox, if they believe they will always have an edge in close games. And maybe they will.[162]

So that was it. We watched the Indians celebrate for a few moments—by the pitcher's mound, in the shadows—and nobody really wanted to leave. For all intents and purposes, the season was over. We turned and headed for the exits, depressed, beaten, exhausted, cooked. Our team may have been alive mathematically, but we knew better. We had the best pitcher in baseball, maybe the best pitcher of our generation, and even *he* couldn't make a difference in the end. Hey, we've lived through those seasons when everything goes right, when we win quirky games, when everyone stays healthy, when every break goes our way. This wasn't one of those years. More things went wrong than right. Something bad always seemed to be happening—clubhouse outbursts, lame acquisitions, unfortunate injuries, mindless coaching moves, short-sighted trades, tough breaks, somebody always bitching about something—and in the end, the season wasn't all that much fun.[163]

Baseball isn't a very forgiving game; usually you get what you deserve in the end. Maybe that's why this season's finish seemed so poetic, because a shadow loomed over this Red Sox team all season. On Wednesday, it finally finished them off.

Eighty-two years and counting.

162 In light of what happened in the 2004 playoffs, that was a pretty interesting paragraph, wasn't it?

163 One bonus: The season did prompt one reader to send me the mailbag question, "If the 2000 Red Sox season was an episode of *Saved By the Bell*, **who would play Zack, Pedro or Nomar?** What about Slater, Screech and Kelly? Here were my responses:

• Nomar (Zack): Figures in every plot, gets all the cute women and routinely comes through in the clutch. Let's just hope that Nomar's career doesn't turn out like the career of the guy who played Zack.[163.5]

• Pedro (Slater): The coolest guy on the team, singlehandedly carries episodes, even travels with his own posse. Plus he has a secret rivalry with Nomar than never gets discussed but you *know* it's there—just wait until they battle over a groupie and start pouring fruit punch on each other at the next team party.

• El Guapo (Screech): Just because of the inherent comedy involved every time either guy enters a room or ballpark. The mere sight of them makes you giddy. Plus, both of them will be MIA in five years.

• Carl Everett (Jessie): Both of them look good on paper, both of them are completely insane. If you want proof, check out the head-butting incident or the episode where Jessie became addicted to diet pills. "I'm so excited, I'm so excited, I'm so...scared."

• Trot Nixon (Kelly): Kelly needed a boob job, Trot needs to start hitting for more power, but both of them give you hope for the future. Just look how Kelly turned out on *90210*.

• Derek Lowe (Lisa): You don't really notice him, but he moves the plots along and gives **Screech** someone to hang out with.

• Jimy Williams (Mr. Belding): You feel strangely safe with him...even while you're wondering if he knows what the hell he's doing.

163.5 Zack's career actually turned out better than Nomar's—he ended up on *NYPD Blue* as Dennis Franz's sidekick. Seriously, would you have rather been Nomar (Rookie of the Year, two Hall of Fame seasons, rapid decline by your early 30s) or Mark-Paul Gosselaar (the lead of the most memorably ridiculous show of the '90s, followed by a nice stint on one of most famous cop shows ever)? I'm going with the latter. Call me crazy.

THE RED SOX ARE FOR SALE

October 6, 2000

In case you missed it, the Yawkey Trust announced that they're selling the Red Sox after 67 snakebitten years. Here's a quick recap of everything that happened over that span.

Number of championships: Zero!

Number of state-of-the-art baseball stadiums built: Zero!

Number of star players pushed out of Boston: (Hmmmm... Tiant, Fisk, Lynn, Clemens, Vaughn... and we don't have to count Nomar until 2004.) Five![164]

Number of black players signed before 1959: Zero!

Number of happy Red Sox fans right now: Zero!

Through the past seven decades, through all the heartache, we've only seen two constants with the Red Sox—the ownership and the ballpark—and both have needed to go for years. We need a fresh start. We deserve it. This team has been run like a bad chain restaurant: escalating costs, tons of employee turnover, managers battling management, unhappy customers, an insolent waitstaff, arrogant executives, filthy tables, disgusting bathrooms, the whole shebang. We might as well be a Friendly's in Revere. As one of my readers once joked, CEO John Harrington is so friggin' cheap, he probably wonders why Michael Corleone paid for Carlo's plane ticket to Vegas when he was going to kill Carlo, anyway. One thing's for sure: The new owner couldn't do much worse.

I'm hoping that Owner X will have one of those strong, vibrant, "take charge" personalities, along the lines of Patriots owner Robert Kraft. Even if Kraft ended up being a little too hands-on during the Carroll Era—and that's an understatement—he still makes Patriots fans feel like he's committed to building a winning team. Sure, much like Ike Turner, he *cares* a little too much. But that's besides the point. You feel like you're in good hands with him, especially now that he's not scouting players and pushing out Hall of Fame coaches.

Contrast the Kraft Era with everything we witnessed with the Red Sox this season. By the end of September, it was obvious that none of the higher-ups even remotely cared about the fans, as evidenced by the way Dan Duquette ran amok over the

164 Notice how I nailed the EXACT year that **Nomar was pushed out of town.** And this was coming off a season when he batted .372. Talk about a predictable franchise.

past few weeks, or how they kept Fenway Park filthier than your average third world country during that final September homestand, when the Boston front office decided, "Hey, since we have so many games in such a short time span and Fenway is such a dump to begin with, let's not even bother cleaning up between games!" During the Thursday night game against Cleveland, I paid a scalper $28 for what turned out to be a partially-obstructed grandstand seat, my legs banged against someone's chair all night, my back went out by the third inning and my shoes were stuck in some sort of retroactive ginger ale/saliva/beer/puke liquid mix that had been festering in the sun for two days and looked like *Ghostbusters* goo. At one point, I dropped a quarter on the ground and spent the next 20 seconds debating the pros and cons about picking it up. It was like sitting in an X-rated movie theater.[165]

Still not convinced? Look at everything that happened with the Redskins last year. All jokes and potshots aside, new owner Daniel Snyder threw cash around like Mo Vaughn at the Foxy Lady, transforming the Skins into an elite NFL team in less than a year. So why couldn't that happen in Boston? Why couldn't Owner X ride in on his white horse, clean house and exterminate the second-class attitude that developed and festered during the 2000 season (a terrible, unhappy season by all accounts)? I already hate myself for writing this, but let's be honest: Wouldn't it be interesting if the new Red Sox owner was chiseled out of that Snyder/Steinbrenner mold?

(Admit it—that would be loads of fun for us. Come on...admit it...)[166]

Let's say the Red Sox were purchased last winter by a meglomanical, eccentric billionaire whom we'll call "Mitch Cumstein."[167] Imagine Mitch makes Snyder seem like a cross between Jeremy Jacobs and Marlee Matlin. Now imagine Mitch dealing with everything that the Red Sox ownership shied away from this year.

Is Dan Duquette shuffling players in and out of the clubhouse like a casino pit boss shuffling blackjack dealers again? BOOM! Mitch slams the Duke in newspapers and promises that his job will "be evaluated" unless he calms down. *Is the publisher of the Boston Phoenix vowing to block New Fenway again?* BOOM! Mitch laughs off the threats and makes some derisive "alternative newspaper" jokes. *Is Carl Everett bullying his teammates*

165 That joke was an homage to my freshman year at Holy Cross, when eight friends and I went downtown to the Paris Theater and caught 40 minutes of an X-rated movie. One of our friends (The Worm, Sean Krause) accidentally dropped his keys on the floor; we spent the next 10 minutes debating whether he should reach down to pick them up before we were shushed by someone two rows behind us. The night ended with a guy sitting in our row, then dropping his pants down to his knees while we sprinted out of there at warp-speed. That's right, college... $21,000 a year at the time.

166 Daniel Snyder?!?!?!?!? What was I thinking???? I'm so ashamed.

167 Mitch Cumstein: Painfully forced *Caddyshack* reference. Although it looks pretty funny in print. I'm torn on this one—at gunpoint, I would say it didn't work. On the other hand, it's not too often you get to work "**Mitch Cumstein**" into a column. So I don't know.

again? BOOM! Carl gets summoned to the owner's office for a reminder of eight million reasons why his behavior will improve, or else. *Is Boston Mayor Tom Menino threatening to squash New Fenway again?* BOOM! Mitch vows that he'll move the team to Somerville, Quincy or even—gasp—Hartford if he has to get a new stadium built.

Imagine seeing a Red Sox owner acting instead of reacting? As far as I'm concerned, this team can't get sold fast enough. And since it's finally happening, here are ten pieces of advice for Owner X:

1) You need New England roots. You need to understand what it's like to be a Red Sox fan—the pain, the horror, the torture, the history, the perverse sense of hope. Or else nobody will take you seriously.[168]

2) You need to have that rare Steinbrenner/Snyder, "Maybe I'm a jerk, but it's all in the name of a good cause and you'll potentially get a title out of it" quality. Billionaires are usually rich for a reason: They know how to get things done. This Red Sox team has needed someone like that for the past 25 years; the fact that Fenway Park hasn't been put out of its misery yet speaks for itself. [169]

(Which reminds me...)

3) Get the new ballpark done. Buy the team, hold your press conference, pat yourself on the back...then go to work threatening Boston politicians (and greasing their palms) until they agree to help. A new ballpark on the waterfront in Southie would rejuvenate that entire area, much like Pac Bell invigorated the Embarcadero in San Francisco. There's a reason you never see a happy movie filmed in Southie or Charlestown.

(And by the way, if you have trouble swaying those politicians, watch *The Godfather* and *The Godfather Part II* over and over again for tips and ideas...even if this leads to Mayor Menino waking up in a local whorehouse covered in blood and screaming "Oh my God! What did I do? What did I do?")

4) Spend some cash this winter. Make a splash. The team's payroll already hovers around the cost for a James Cameron movie, and you'll have already shelled out $350-400 million to purchase the team. What's an extra $75 million for Mike Mussina?

5) You need to spend a weekend hanging out with Carl Everett.

168 Who ended up buying the team and bringing Boston its first baseball championship in 86 years? Lucchino, Werner and Henry—three guys who weren't from New England. I'm an idiot. By the way, one of those "local guys" who ended up trying to purchase the team was penny-pinching Bruins owner Jeremy Jacobs—at the time, I wrote that Jacobs buying the Red Sox would spur the largest local revolt since the Stamp Act was enforced.

169 I was half-right: Lucchino ended up doing the "pompous prick who gets things done" role perfectly, only he wasn't a billionaire.

Take him skiing or hunting. If you can't stand him after 48 hours, imagine how his teammates feel. He needs to go. Or else we need to keep him heavily sedated.

6) Fire Dan Duquette. The man has been an outright menace, metamorphosing from Boy Genius into one of the wardens from Oz in the space of two years. *Nobody* likes this guy. Boot him out of his office, shave his head, and take his pants.[170]

7) Keep Jimy Williams, but only if he agrees to undergo a series of mental competency tests. Once he fails those miserably, jettison him and Mr. Weebles and bring in a new manager with an IQ above the Guerrero Line.

8) Find Nomar. Meet with him. Rip up his contract. Ask what he wants for the next seven years. $80 million? $90 million? $100 million? Done.

(And if you don't think that sounds like a good idea, ask yourself one question: Why would Nomar want to stay here? He's from California, his family still lives there, he's not married and he doesn't have any real roots in the Boston area. What's keeping him from fleeing this place when his contract expires in four years? If you were him, wouldn't you pull a Will Hunting, throw all your luggage into your car, and head West in October of 2004? I sure would.)

9) Hold meglomaniacal press conferences where you say outlandish and inane things, just so I have some column fodder. We haven't had a crazy owner in Boston since John Y. Brown in the late '70s. Sure, John Y. nearly ruined the franchise and drove Red Auerbach to the Knicks, but that's beside the point. Give me a crazy-competent owner over a cheap-quiet-incompetent owner any time.

10) And this is imperative...

Let people know that there's a new sheriff in town. That you're not going to stand for an 82-year legacy of losing. That you're not letting all the crap that happened during the 2000 season happen on your watch. That you're going to kick ass and take names. That you will even frame Everett for involuntary manslaughter if it comes to that. Do these things and you'll have my unyielding support for your entire stay. Well, until we start losing again.

One final thought: If you read those 10 points carefully enough,

170 Don't you love the dated pop culture references in this one? Already we've had **James Cameron**, Oz, and an Ike Turner joke alluding to a Tim Meadows *Saturday Night Live* skit. Where was the joke comparing Pedro to Charlie from *Party of Five*?

171 The main reason I wanted to include this column in the book: In a weird way, Henry-Werner-Lucchino ended up fulfilling pretty much every wish. They cleaned house, spent the extra money, fixed up Fenway, made their presence known locally and nationally—especially with the Yankees feud—and went out of their way to connect with fans. Just what the doctor ordered. And since we won a World Series with them, I can honestly say that I would rather have had these guys than **Vince McMahon** over the past three years. Although it's pretty close.

it should be *painfully* clear who needs to purchase the Boston Red Sox. I mean, painfully clear.

(Wait a second, what's that? Good God! Th-that's Vince McMahon's music!) **171**

HERE COMES MANNY

December 12, 2000

It can't be true. Manny Ramirez is coming to Boston? We're positive? He's coming here?

The numbers are staggering...and I'm not talking about the $160 million contract. I'm talking about a .313 lifetime batting average, 236 home runs and 1,086 career hits before the age of 29. I'm talking about a career OPS (slugging + on-base percentage)[172] sitting just .002 away from 1.000, a slugger who belted 127 homers and 432 RBI over the past three years and reached base 20 out of 42 times against the Yankees last season. I'm talking about the most dangerous power hitter in the American League, a potential Triple Crown threat, a 28-year-old superstar entering his prime. I'm talking about Manny Ramirez actually playing in Boston.

172 Notice how I had to define OPS. Back in 2000, writers like **Bill James** and Rob Neyer were still considered lunatics. By the way, I started writing this column at midnight—I just remember walking to my local Store 24 for coffee that night and Joe the Alcoholic Counter Guy was there, and I said to him happily, "What about that Manny signing?" and he looked at me like I had three heads.

Every diehard Sox fan was hoping for the best and expecting the worst with the Manny chase, including me. And if that previous sentence didn't make sense, well...neither do Red Sox fans. There are two mistaken perceptions about us:

1) We fear the worst at all times

2) We're cynical as hell.

In reality, we're oddly optimistic, always hoping that this trade will be The Trade, this move will be The Move, this player will be The Savior, this year will be The Year. We torture ourselves, overlooking the fact that our team hasn't deviated from the game plan of the past eight decades—placing a premium on hitting because we play in a haunted bandbox called Fenway Park—and now they're escalating ticket prices *before* signing free agents. Clearly, something's not working. Pitching wins in the World Series every October, yet our team always seems to gravitate toward sluggers and middle-tier pitchers (Pedro excepted). And it's okay. It's okay. Look up the definition of "unconditional love" and you'll see a picture of a drunken Sox fan wearing a Jack Clark jersey and looking like he just got socked in the stomach.

So during those rare times when management makes the

correct move, we become so giddy that it's almost embarrassing. When I heard about the Ramirez signing last night, I actually stood up, yelled my fake crowd noise ("Hrrrrrahhhhhhh!") and unleased a fist pump right out of Tiger Woods' playbook. Swear to God. You know you're feeling giddy when you find yourself saying, "Man, I wish I owned that Baha Men CD" so you could scream out a couple of "Woof woofs!" [173]

That's what happens to Sox fans when something good happens: We turn into grinning, giggling idiots. I checked my unread reader e-mails from last night and one stretch of consecutive subject headings looked like this (in order):

MANNY!!!
WE GOT 'EM!
MANNY!
Manny!!!
MANNNNNNNYYYYYYYYYYY!
THE EAGLE HAS LANDED!
MANNY
MANNY!
MAN-NY! MAN-NY!
WE GOT HIM!

I felt the same way. Yesterday I was fighting a nagging sense of déjà-vu—that we had traveled this ground with Bernie Williams and Kirby Puckett, that we were getting used again, that something rotten was about to happen. And it ruined the rest of my afternoon. I couldn't bear the thought of another winter spent complaining about our local teams. The Sox haven't signed a marquee free agent since I was seven (Bill Campbell). Other teams were consistently landing the Reggie Jacksons and Greg Madduxes while we were stuck with the Danny Darwins and Steve Averys.[174] With the exception of the Pedro trade—and let's be honest, nobody knew Pedro would be *this* good—I can't remember the last time the Red Sox made me shriek, "WOW! THEY GOT HIM!" So I was a little skeptical.

When my buddy Gus called to say hello that afternoon, I immediately started bitching about the Manny Sweepstakes, mentioning how the Sox were always used to drive up prices for free agents. We decided that the Sox resembled Charley, the dork on *The Brady Bunch* who landed a date with Marcia, only to get blown off because school hunk Doug Simpson asked her out. Something always seems to "suddenly come up" when the

173 Do **the Baha Men** deserve their own footnote? (Thinking... thinking...) Actually, no. They don't.

174 Boston's "major" winter signings since the dawn of free agency in 1976, in order: Campbell; Skip Lockwood; Mike Torrez; Tony Perez; Tony Pena and Jeff Reardon (ending a 10-year drought from 1980-89); Jack Clark, Danny Darwin and Matt Young (yikes); Frank Viola; Andre Dawson and Jeff Russell; Otis Nixon; Erik Hanson; Flash Gordon; Steve Avery; Bret Saberhagen; Jose Offerman. See what I mean? This team had a knack for landing someone a good four years past their prime.

Sox are involved. And the other teams never seem to get hit in the face by a football.[175]

This time? We landed the date with Marcia, and desperation was the reason: Management needed to make a splash after raising ticket prices last month. For the first time since the Buddy LeRoux Era, Boston fans were simmering about the direction of the franchise. Some season ticketholders were even recruiting friends and co-workers to purchase shares of the 81-game home schedule (to defray costs). From the e-mails I received and WEEI calls I heard, it was clear that fans would forgive the ticket hike as long as the team landed Ramirez or Mike Mussina at any price. When Mussina joined the Yankees and the pressure mounted, there was a genuine sense of urgency for the first time since Clemens's prime. Without Ramirez, the team would have been forced to make a panic trade for someone like Sammy Sosa or Jeff Bagwell that would have done more harm than good.[176]

As Internet reports earmarked Manny for a possible Cleveland return, I found myself dreading the upcoming 2001 season. The three-time champs had gotten better again, this time with Mussina. What had the Sox done? It looked like a classic Dan Duquette winter. He already signed his token "question mark starter with arm problems" (Lt. Frank Castillo); all that was missing was the token Asian pitcher, the token washed-up reliever and the token veteran bat who would be waived by June. We were supposed to pay as much as $55 a ticket for this crap?

Then...BOOM!

On Monday night, word broke that the Sox were still in the mix with Manny. By 10 o'clock, the *Globe* was reporting that the Sox had trumped everyone else with a $160 million offer for eight years (featuring a $16 million signing bonus and $31 million worth of deferred money). And suddenly I was doing fist pumps and wishing I owned the Baha Men CD. That's the beautiful thing about sports...just when you think you're out, they pull you back in.

Is the money absurd? Absolutely. But you can't get killed by overpaying a superstar...it's overpaying the Jose Offermans and Vitaly Potapenkos that kills you in the end. Maybe Manny's contract seems tough to digest, but with the way baseball is going these days, it might be a bargain in five years. Remember what happened when Clemens signed with Toronto for $31 mil-

175 Re-reading these older columns, I was surprised by the number of *Brady Bunch* references/analogies versus the lack of *Gilligan's Island* material. I actually liked Gilligan's Island more as a kid—the Skipper killed me. He was right up there with Norm Peterson, George Costanza, J.J. Evans and Hank Kingsley in the "Sitcom characters who could make me laugh by doing pretty much anything" Pantheon. **Why didn't Alan Hale Jr. ever get his proper due?** This has been nagging at me for like 30 years.

176 Pretty simple lesson here: Don't raise ticket prices until *after* you sign a marquee free agent.

lion and four years? Seemed like a buttload of money at the time—now those numbers couldn't land you Kevin Appier. Maybe when Vlad Guerrero signs with someone for $400 million in 2003, Manny's contract won't seem so outrageous.[177]

Then again, what do we care? These shortsighted morons were the ones who raised prices before adding anyone of consequence. It's like a butcher raising meat prices by 25 percent and telling you, "Don't worry, I'm gonna get better filet mignons one of these days," then trying to sell you London broil. Frankly, the Red Sox owed this to us; they needed to land a superstar. We needed Manny's star power, we needed his charisma and we desperately needed his bat. If they overpayed for him, so be it. We're over-paying for tickets. Quid pro quo, Dr. Lecter.

As for the 2001 Red Sox, Manny probably bats fourth between Nomar and Crazy Carl. Suddenly a team that battled to score runs won't be struggling anymore. Last season's team squandered too many close games because they missed that game-changing presence in the middle of the lineup, the slugger who carries you for seven to 10 days and always seems to make a difference in those 3–2 games. Can you place a price on somebody like that? Would you rather have seen them spend $60 million on Denny Neagle and $50 million on a trade-and-sign for Jeromy Burnitz? Me neither. When in doubt, throw the big bucks at the big gun. And that's what the Red Sox did. For once.[178]

Flash-forward to this summer...

Manny emerges from the Boston dugout as a happy murmur swells from the first base side of the stands. Fans start hollering his name, hundreds of versions of the same sound uttered at once. He swings two bats over his shoulder, stretching his muscles, watching the pitcher, preparing himself, getting ready. And now it's his turn, so he flings the second bat to the ground and strides to the batter's box as the Fenway buzz builds, and finally everyone in the park realizes, "Hey, Manny's up!" and excitement sweeps through the stands like a brisk breeze, and anything seems possible, and the only thing you know is that wild horses couldn't drag you from your seat right now. Then you hear the chant emanating from the bleachers—"Man-ny! Man-ny! Man-ny! Man-ny!"—and you join in, and now everyone's standing and chanting his name, and Manny's digging in, and it's summer, and we're at Fenway, and the sun is beating down

177 Um...no. Not even close. Salaries leveled off after the A-Rod/Jeter signings the following winter; within three years, the Sox were desperately trying to extricate themselves from Manny's contract, even placing him on waivers, which culminated in the disastrous A-Rod chase that inadvertently led to us winning the World Series. Vlad ended up getting $70 million from the Angels for five years.

178 This strategy also works in fantasy baseball: Every year, two or three studs (A-Rod, Johann Santana, Ichiro) go for 5–6 bucks more than anyone thought, but you never hear anyone say that summer, **"Man, I wish I didn't spend $43 on A-Rod."** Either the studs help you contend, or you can trade them to a contender for a whopping package. And this happens every season. I'm telling you. By the way, didn't the mere sight of that Neagle-Burnitz combination give you chills? Can you imagine?

and nobody is mentioning salaries or ticket prices or anything else. We just want to see what happens.

Every home game won't have a moment like that, but some of them will. And that's enough for me.

OUTSIDE THE LINES: THE MANNY SIGNING

December 18, 2000

I thought my winter peaked when Manny Ramirez signed with the Red Sox...and then I watched ESPN's *Outside the Lines* documentary where they followed Manny's agent around for two months. In case you missed it, here's a running account of the most captivating Boston-related TV show in recent memory.

SEGMENT ONE

October 23: Jeff Moorad (Manny's agent) and Scott Parker (Moorad's associate) are riding around a limo in Cleveland. Moorad looks like a cross between Dan Fouts and Rob Reiner and has a bubbly, "Hey, I'm on TV!" glow about him. You have to question the motives of any agent who allows cameras to follow him for a pivotal six-week period of his career (he's obviously seen *Jerry Maguire* one too many times). Anyway, Moorad tells the camera that he hopes to make Manny the highest-paid player in the game. Somewhere A-Rod giggles.[179]

179 The following winter, A-Rod's Texas deal dwarfed Manny's deal by two extra years and $92 million. Two winters after that, the two players were nearly traded for one another in the **first Double Contract Dump trade**. You have to love baseball.

That same day: After finishing an off-camera meeting with Tribe GM John Hart, Moorad calls Manny to recount the details of the negotiation. You just *know* Manny's playing Nintendo or watching the *Flintstones*. Where's the Manny-cam?

November 2: Moorad tells Hart by phone that he wants $200 million over 10 years, adding, "You have to swallow hard on something if you want the guy." That choice of words narrowly edged the runner-up choice, "You're gonna have to bend over and hold onto your ankles if you want the guy."

November 9: Yankees GM Brian Cashman calls Moorad to express a "strong interest" in Manny, adding that they're considering a few other big-name guys (like Mike Mussina) and that "whoever decides they want to be a Yankee the most, first, obviously is gonna take us in the direction we want to go." Moorad responds with a hint of indignation: "Well that doesn't sound like a real compelling reaching-out to Manny Ramirez." Apparently grammar isn't a major priority when you're a big-time agent. At least his power play scares Cashman, who hems and haws before rushing off the phone. "Now we've got our 300-pound gorilla," Moorad says, dollar signs dancing in his head.

That same day: Moorad eavesdrops on a conference call between Cleveland beat writers and Hart, who says that Moorad "made it very clear that this is going to be an economically-driven contract," prompting Moorad to nod with a "You're fucking-A right" look. That was fun. Later Moorad calls another associate and admits that he doesn't know where the Indians are headed, wondering why they're "almost daring us to go on the market." Why is it so much fun to watch sports agents squirm?

November 11: The Indians fax an offer for $119 million over seven years. Moorad calls Hart and "respectfully" declines. All we're missing at this point is a follow-up scene with Moorad driving in the car and belting out the words to "Freefallin'" by Tom Petty.

SEGMENT TWO

November 13: A Seattle meeting features Moorad (who used the *Miami Vice* beard trimmer for the El DeBarge[180] look), ancient Mariners GM Pat Gillick (wearing a bright red sweater and looking ready for a bingo game); and Mariners president Chuck Armstrong (I'm pretty sure that's a stage name). Moorad relays a special message from Manny ("Tell them to put up the money and I'm there!"), then giggles like a hyena. Mesmerizingly awkward.[181] When Gillick asks if Manny would consider coming to Seattle, Moorad mentions Manny's concerns about Safeco Field and wonders if they would move in the fences for him, prompting Armstrong to give one of those stammering, "Um, can I borrow your towel, my car just hit a water buffalo?" answers like John Koktostin in *Fletch*.[182] Buh-bye, Seattle.

November 14: By phone, Moorad updates Manny on his offers, tells him that the process won't get going until the winter meetings, then adds this tidbit: "I told Dan Duquette that, listen, Pedro is a good friend of yours, that your preference was to stay in the American League. I also like the fact that there's a significant Latino population in Boston...you know, when Pedro pitches up there, they have the entire ballpark filled with Dominican flags." Apparently, Jeff hasn't heard about the

180 I thought about changing this to the "Jerry Bruckheimer look," just to make it a little more current...but there's something funny about seeing **El Debarge** in a Red Sox book. Even when I wrote that one, that reference was dated. Now it's almost prehistoric.

181 When he watches a tape of this show now, Moorad must feel like one of those *Real World* castmates watching footage from that drunken threesome they couldn't quite remember in Mexico. By the way, Moorad ended up leaving the sports agent business and signing a deal to run the Arizona Diamondbacks in 2004.

182 Huge internal debate on how to spell that one—was it Koktostin, Cocktoasten, Kocktostine...I mean, that could go 20 different ways, right?

recent ticket hikes at Fenway; the only Dominican who can afford to go to Red Sox games anymore is Pedro.

(By the way, maybe it's just me, but Moorad sounds more and more like Fouts every minute. I keep waiting for him to say things like, "One of the keys to this negotiation will be which team offers the most money" and, "Any time somebody offers you $160 million, that's more money than $119 million.")

December 1: One day after Mussina signs with the Yankees, Red Sox assistant GM Lee Thomas calls Moorad in a quivering voice and asks, "Dan wanted me to ask you and, to kinda put it bluntly, would there be any need for us to get involved with Ramirez? Are we out of the box already or is there any chance for us to talk about him?"

(Translation: "We screwed up with Mussina, we need Manny to save face, money is no object whatsoever, and we're so embarrassed about this whole thing that my boss didn't even have the balls to call you, he had me do it. Any interest on your end? Any at all?")[183]

December 5: Duquette and Thomas arrive at Moorad's hotel room in Miami to meet with Team Manny. After everyone sits down, Duke hands a sheet of statistics to Manny that shows "how we think you can really help the Red Sox," which Manny examines like somebody checking out an unexpected subpoena.[184] Not a good idea. They should have gone with Plan B: A $50 bill and the latest Marc Anthony CD.

(Please note that, for the duration of this show, Duquette wields the on-camera charisma of a seven-state serial killer being interviewed on an HBO *America Undercover* special. At every point in every conversation, you keep waiting for him to spring forward and jam a pencil into Moorad's neck. You know it's killing him that Moorad made him pitch that "Come to the Red Sox" spiel to Manny in front of ESPN's cameras. Comedy galore.)[185]

Duke and Manny then combine for one of the most awkward exchanges ever captured in television history:

Duke [*monotone*]: The fans in Boston appreciate your unique skill and your ability to hit.

Manny [*sounding like Chico Escuela*]: I'm one of those guys that don't talk a lot you know and just go and try to play the game and that's it you know.

183 The "Mussina or Manny?" debate was the no. 1 sports radio topic in Boston that winter, with the Sox targeting Mussina and losing out because Duquette was outworked by Cashman and the Yanks. For some insane reason, the Sox decided to raise ticket prices at the same time, forcing Duquette to either land Manny or risk being drawn-and-quartered in Kenmore Square. This explains Boston's sudden urgency.

184 Funniest moment in the whole show, by the way.

185 **Duquette was a dead ringer for Sam Neill** in *Omen III: The Final Conflict* to the point that I called him Damien Duke on my old website.

186 That was an inside Boston joke: John Harrington was the longtime Red Sox CEO; Will McDonough was the legendary *Globe* columnist who consistently defended certain players in the Boston scene (Harrington, Red Auerbach, Bill Parcells) and ripped others (Roger Clemens, Mo Vaughn, the late Reggie Lewis, Bob Kraft) before his death in 2003. You could always count on him to defend Harrington, no matter what the circumstances were, even if there was videotape of Harrington **tossing babies off the Green Monster**. McDonough's son, Sean, the longtime broadcaster for the Red Sox, later confessed to me that this was his favorite joke in the whole column. Although he winced when he read it.

187 This is one of those shows where you know the ending, but every time the Yanks and Indians get involved, it's still frightening for some reason—like every time the Nazis take a 4–0 lead in *Victory*.

Duke: Yeah. [*Stifling silence*] You've always been, uh, quiet and business-like and ready…[*forced smile.*]

Manny: That's the only thing you could do…you know, just work and see what happens. [*Dead silence.*]

Duke: Sometimes I pick up prostitutes, bring them back to my apartment and strangle them to death.

(I made that last part up, sorry about that. Couldn't resist.)

And then the phone rings…it's No-mahhhhh! Manny looks and sounds like a 13-year-old girl getting called for her first date. Unfortunately we can't hear what Nomar is saying on the line, but still...

Manny [*talking into phone, heavy Chico Escuela effect here*]: Eh-lo?…Hey, wass goin' on, man?…Everything's fine so far… Yeah, everything's cool…Yeah, well, joo know…I hope this will work out…Yeah, I like joo guys, joo know...

(Another scene that simply can't be done justice in print. Oh, well.)

December 6: Boston's offer: Eight years, $136 million. Cleveland counters with five years and $100 million. Narrating the show, Bob Ley ominously says, "The numbers can only go up. The question is, how far?" Hmmmm.

SEGMENT THREE

December 9: One day after Duquette arrives in Moorad's California office—and let the record show that there was a *Jerry Maguire* poster in the lobby—Moorad pushes Boston to increase its offer, forcing Duke to call Red Sox CEO John Harrington to seek approval for the extra funds.

(Now *there's* a phone call that should have been broadcast on live TV: "Hey, Mr. McDonough? It's Duke. Is Mr. Harrington there? Can you roll over and wake him up?")[186]

Moorad tells an associate, "We're close," but that doesn't stop him from calling Hart for leverage. Hart explains that he's trying to get Cleveland's owners to accept eight years and adds, "I made it clear that if all things were equal or close to being equal, you're going to send Manny here." Moorad replies that Manny's no.1 request was a competitive deal in Cleveland. He doesn't elaborate on Manny's no. 2 request, which was probably something like, "I want a neverending supply of mint-flavored toothpicks!"[187]

December 10: Moorad arrives in Dallas for the winter meetings and updates Manny by phone, explaining that things should be settled soon. Cleveland finally raised its offer and went to eight years, but some money was deferred. Being a money-grubbing whore-er, talented agent, Moorad will use that offer to squeeze the Red Sox. Riveting stuff.

Later that night: Cut to Moorad and Duke negotiating in a hotel room. Duke looks like Nicholson at the end of *The Shining*; he's only missing the five o'clock shadow, the typewriter and the axe. They have the following exchange:

Duke [*monotone voice, glazed expression, looking like an airplane crash survivor*]: Our-our preference would be...to defer...two (million)...out of each of the years.

Moorad: I know that at one point you proposed those without the deferrals.

Duke: Um...[*long pause, psychotic look, weight of Red Sox Nation on his shoulders*]...I would say that, um...I would say that we would just prefer it, um...on a, uh, cash flow basis.

Moorad: So you're talking years nine and 10.

Duke [*staring straight ahead*]: Correct.

Moorad: So you'll do the 20 (million per year) if you can defer two (million) each year. Correct?

Duke [*practically flat-lining*]: Yes.

Moorad: Both club options?

Duke: Yes, yes.

Moorad: I don't think I have anything to ask for...other than more money!

[*Moorad unleashes a loud, grating laugh as Duke fantasizes about slitting his throat.*]

With Boston's offer in hand, Moorad scurries back to the Indians even after telling Duquette, "My gut is that (Manny) chooses Boston." The Indians crunch some numbers and Moorad makes plans to fly Ramirez to Dallas for a final decision.

December 11: Moorad awakens to a morning phone call from Manny, who has a surprise announcement: He's ready to accept Boston's offer, but only if they agree to hire (Cleveland clubhouse attendant) Frankie Mancini as well. There's comedy, there's high comedy, there's transcendent comedy, and then there's the moment when Moorad relays this request to his associates by phone and explains, "Frankie Mancini...he sets up the pitching machine for him...[*realizes how ridiculous this is,* *starts giggling hysterically*]...are you kidding me??? [*more giggles*] That's why he's Manny."

(There are a million different reasons why we'll adore Manny over the next decade, but I can't imagine anything topping, "I'll move to Boston, but I have one last request—the guy who sets up the pitching machine for me gets to come, too."**188** Manny seems like one of those media-hyped "quirky characters" who really *is* quirky. The possibilities for the next eight years are limitless. In a good way. I keep telling myself this.)

Later that day: Mancini doesn't want to leave Cleveland, but Ramirez still accepts Boston's offer. GO SOX! Cut to Moorad and Duquette hammering out the final numbers, with a nodding Duquette looks like he just fought off another electroshock treatment. My only regret here is that I'm not talented enough to describe how freaking strange and disoriented the Duke seemed for this entire show. He should have been strapped to a stretcher and forced to wear a triple-pronged metal mask like Hannibal Lecter. Anyway, Moorad calls Manny to give him the good news, then puts Duke on the phone for one final dose of comedy:

Duke [*monotone, strange smile*]: "Hi Manny, how are you?... congratulations...we're so happy to have you with us, I think it's gonna be great. You're gonna love Boston, the fans are gonna love you, and you're gonna able to get recognized among the great hitters in the history of the franchise. We're so excited to have you. And you know what the good news is? You don't have to hit against Pedro!" [*Loud, excited, startling, out-of-character laugh.*]

The end.

The question remains: Will we ever be able to take Duquette seriously again?**189** Is he always like that? Did the cameras make him uncomfortable? Is part of his negotiating process to make other people feel uneasy? Does he remind anyone else of Johnny Depp after the explosion in *The Astronaut's Wife*? Did anyone else even see *The Astronaut's Wife*? Why does all the acrimony from the first six years of the Duquette Era suddenly make sense when you witness this man in action? I mean, seriously...should a man lacking any discernable social skills be allowed to run a major league baseball team?

Let's save those questions for after the holidays. If you didn't realize how close the Sox came to losing out on the premier

188 This is actually now my second-favorite Manny story of all time. The first? When his mother revealed that **Manny was breast-fed until he was four** years old. Never has one sentence revealed so much.

189 Not only was the Duke fired 14 months later, he hasn't worked in baseball since. And here's the weird thing: He still lives in Massachusetts, attends Red Sox games, even calls in to local radio shows. If Theo Epstein ever disappears without a trace, here's your no. 1 suspect. By the way, after the 2001 season (Duquette's last with the team), I wrote that he "failed *spectacularly*" and "even Sofia Coppola's casting in *The Godfather III* wasn't this big of a misfire." I also handed out 50 quotes from *The Godfather* as awards for the 2001 season, with Duquette receiving five in all, including "What guarantees can I give you, Mike? I am the hunted one. I missed my chance"... "Dammit, if I had **a wartime consigliere**, a Sicilian, I wouldn't be in this shape! Pop had Genco, look what I got!"...and "Barzini's dead. So is Philip Tattaglia. Moe Greene. Stracci. Cunio. Today I

righthanded slugger in baseball, check out the replay of this show on Christmas Day. My preference is, um…that…you watch…the show…just for the, um…Duquette stuff…because it's, um…it's that phenomenal…and I really, um, think it's um, a special show…and, um, Merry, um, Christmas…

settled all family business. So don't tell me you're innocent. Admit what you did. Don't be afraid. Come on, you think I'd make my sister a widow?"

March 2001–December 2003

THE ABYSS

CURSE WORDS

Heading into spring training for the 2001 season, expectations for the Red Sox had never been higher. For the first time in franchise history, they had the best pitcher (Pedro), best hitter (Nomar), and best slugger (Manny) in the American League. To justify skyrocketing ticket prices, the team was casually throwing around big contracts like Ben Affleck tossing around $100 chips at a casino, knowing that someone else would be footing the bill before long. The sale of the team seemed imminent, which was turning into an interesting story in itself (we were like beaten-down foster kids hoping to get adopted by real parents at that point). Around the country, more and more fans were trickling into opposing stadiums and cheering for the Sox, most of them children of the Impossible Dream. And with the Bruins, Celtics, and Patriots floundering beyond recognition, the success of our baseball team had never seemed so important.

Little did we know that we were headed for the roughest stretch in franchise history, culminating in an epic collapse at Yankee Stadium. Remember the scene in *The Shawshank Redemption* when they show Andy Dufresne walking around outside with fresh bruises on his face, and Red narrates how the Sistas had been attacking him for almost two years, and then Red casually mentions, "I do believe those were the worst two years for Andy." Really? Getting repeatedly gang-raped for 24 straight months was the low point? I wouldn't have guessed. With that said, this 2001–03 stretch was the "I do believe those were the worst two years for Andy" stretch for Red Sox fans. We kept walking around with those fresh bruises on our faces, hoping things were about to get better, and then somebody would jump us from behind again.

There was one crucial difference between this 2001–03 stretch and every other agonizing stretch: The Curse of the Bambino was in full bloom. In my first column for ESPN.com (see page 131), I tried to explain that the experience of supporting the Red Sox couldn't be stereotyped with something as trite as a curse, a piece that seemed to resonate with readers around the country (and eventually led to my getting hired full-time that summer).[190] In September of the same year, I wrote one final column about the Curse before adding it to the ever-expanding list of Things I Refuse to Discuss in My Columns, along with the time my Mom made me wear a brown corduroy blazer to my first day of prep school in eighth grade, the time I cheated on my A.P. Bio exam and still ended up with a 2, and the time I uttered the words, "I think the Spin Doctors will be around for years to come." But after what happened in October 2004, it's okay to bring up The Curse again. You know, since it's dead and all.

190 In the reprehensible *Fever Pitch*, **the Farrelly Brothers**—allegedly Sox fans from Rhode Island—kept an entire scene where season ticketholders at Fenway happily recapped the history of the curse for Drew Barrymore's character. As if that would ever happen. These are the things Red Sox fans dealt with for 86 years—even visible Sox fans were perpetuating this crap.

In lieu of re-running the entire thing (you're not missing much), here's an excerpt from that 2001 column:

We need to set the record straight about The Curse for three reasons:

1) It's the *Blair Witch Project* of sports legends. In other words, the vast majority of people don't understand it, so it has assumed a life of its own.

2) The only people who keep mentioning The Curse are members of the media and uneducated non-Boston fans.

3) Sox fans don't discuss the Curse—not because we're afraid of it, but because it's so absurd, we wouldn't bother discussing it in the first place. The Curse rose to prominence with Dan Shaughnessy's 1990 book about the history of the Red Sox, coincidentally titled, *The Curse of the Bambino.* Looking for a hook to invigorate 70 years of rehashed stories, Shaughnessy borrowed a Scituate preacher's theory that the Red Sox were haunted ever since they sold Babe Ruth to the Yankees in 1920. It was a cute way to weave together every Sox-related heartbreak over the past eight decades. It also placed Shaughnessy on the map, made him a best-selling author, and put his kids through college (as WEEI's Gerry Callahan likes to joke). Of

course, since nobody has more to gain from The Curse than Shaughnessy—given that his 11-year-old book keeps pumping out printings and royalties—he keeps bringing up The Curse in his highly visible *Globe* columns.[191] And since casual fans and outsiders believe everything they see in print, they mistakenly believe that Shaughnessy's Curse-laden rhetoric represents the thoughts of every Red Sox fan. Trust me, it doesn't.

Another passage near the end of the column summed everything up:

Admittedly, Sox fans are depressed and touchy right now. Just remember, it was only six months ago when Pedro, Nomar and Manny were healthy and we were printing World Series tickets. We're not "fulfilling our annual prophecy of doom" or any of that crap; we're just disappointed, that's all. Even the concept of a "Curse" is moronic. Do you really think Babe Ruth devoted his afterlife to haunting the Red Sox franchise because they sold him to New York, undoubtedly the best thing that could have happened to his career? For instance, my father and I discuss the Red Sox every time we talk on the phone, which is quite often. And under no circumstances have either of us ever uttered a sentence like "I can't believe the Sox are doomed" or "I wish we didn't have this Curse on us." That has never happened. I can't emphasize that strongly enough. I mean, *ever*.[192]

We complain about the same things that everyone else complains about when they're discussing their favorite baseball team—what's wrong with the manager, why can't so-and-so get his act together and so on—and when the season ends, we move on to the other local teams, like everyone else in Boston. Deep down, we worry that our lives will pass us by without ever seeing the Red Sox win a World Series...which is what this whole thing is *really* about in the first place. That's why Red Sox fans are so insanely passionate about our team. We're haunted by the possibility of living an entire lifetime—80–90 years, followed by death—without celebrating a World Series title. That's not a curse; it's an imaginary guillotine that hangs over us every season. We're just waiting for it to go away, that's all. And only Cubs fans can truly understand.

And with that, I vowed never to mention The Curse again. Unfortunately, most national discussions of the Red Sox were

191 When the Red Sox won the World Series, Shaughnessy moved briskly, releasing a quickie book about the 2004 season called *Reversing the Curse* AND re-releasing his previous book, now called *The Legend of the Curse of the Bambino*. At the home opener of the 2005 season, when the Sox were **raising the 2004 banner** and handing out rings, he appeared at Barnes and Noble in Kenmore Square to sign copies of his books. The only reason I know this? My dad happened to stop by there on his way to the game, reporting that Shaughnessy was sitting at a table by himself, surrounded by books, with maybe two or three people coming up to him in 10 minutes. See, there is a God.

192 That's one of the five or six most important points in this book.

invariably (and unfairly) tied to The Curse, as certain writers and networks took peculiar delight in torturing Sox fans. Believe me, we were already tortured enough. For one thing, the Duquette Era looked shakier than ever. His much-ballyhooed farm system kept coming up empty, with prized prospects like Brian Rose, Tomo Ohka, Wilton Veras, Paxton Crawford, and Sunny Kim falling short of expectations (killing their own trade value as well). That meant Duquette had to keep rolling the dice with washed-up veterans (Dante Bichette, David Cone, Mike Lansing, Rod Beck) and health risks (Bret Saberhagen, Frank Castillo, David Cone) to fill those spots.[193] He also couldn't grasp the importance of team chemistry, as evidenced by his bizarre grudge against popular Mo Vaughn, followed by the acquisition of the moody Everett (before the 2001 season, I was joking that "the thought of trading Everett will be almost as fun as the thought of the XFL's imminent demise,[194] only without the cheerleaders"). And his relationship with the media was more clumsy and surreal than ever, personified by a peculiar WEEI pre-game show where he routinely second-guessed decisions made by his own manager (Jimy Williams).

193 My favorite move that Duquette made: Signing utility man Craig Grebeck, who looked just like the **Unfrozen Caveman Lawyer** from *Saturday Night Live*. Every time he messed up during a game, I found myself saying things like "I don't understand your 'turning the double play,' I'm just a caveman—I saw your relay throw and thought to myself, 'Is that a ball coming at me or did the sun hurtle off its axis?'" That 2001 team actually had the most lookalikes in Red Sox history, including: Hideo Nomo (the bad guy from *Karate Kid 2*); Lansing (Chuck Norris); Morgan Burkhart (Babe Ruth); Daubach (the *Return of the Jedi* version of Mark Hamill); Castillo (Solazzo the Turk from *The Godfather*); and Bichette (Private Pyle from *Full Metal Jacket*).

When John Henry, Tom Werner, and Larry Lucchino purchased the team during the winter of 2001, they quickly changed managers (hiring Grady Little), signed a marquee free agent (Johnny Damon, the team's first quality centerfielder since Freddie Lynn) and allowed Duquette to twist in the wind for much of spring training before ultimately firing him (with assistant GM Mike Port taking over in the interim). The following winter, they made a celebrated attempt to hire Oakland's Billy Beane—two years before the groundbreaking GM was immortalized in ***Moneyball***, Michael Lewis's superb book about the use of statistical analysis to find players—with Beane actually accepting the job before changing his mind and staying with the A's. Unhappy with the other available names, the team promoted a highly regarded 29 year-old assistant named Theo Epstein—a Brookline native, Yale grad and Gammons favorite—and hoped he would grow into the job. While absorbing the inevitable digs about his age from the local media, young Theo moved quickly with a number of Beane-like signings and trades, eschewing bigger names for bargain hitters who could reach base and hit for power (Todd Walker, Kevin Millar, David Ortiz and Jeremy Giambi) and proven bullpen arms (Mike Timlin,

Ramiro Mendoza). Four of those six moves ended up working out (you can guess which ones), although Theo's big in-season deals (for Jeff Suppan and Byung-Hyun Kim) bombed spectacularly. Still, the Red Sox ended up winning 93 games and the wildcard, setting up a potential showdown with the Yankees in the 2003 playoffs.

But that was still 30 months away. In the spring of 2001, all hell was breaking loose. The media was getting angrier, the fans crazier, the expectations more and more dizzying. Even a good-natured soldier like Nomar was starting to wear down, as you'll see in the first column of this section. In retrospect, we weren't battling a simple curse, we were battling something deeper... and you can't face your demons until you hit rock-bottom. Which is where our story continues.

June 2005

194 Note to everyone reading from 2020 on: The XFL was a rough-and-tumble professional football league started by WWF owner Vince McMahon that only ended up lasting one year. In retrospect, his biggest mistake was not trying the same idea with hockey, which would have worked brilliantly.

THE OTHER SIDE OF NOMAR

March 1, 2001

You wonder if the next few weeks will blow his cover. Reporters dogging him with the same questions, day after day after day. *How's the wrist? Does it feel any better? When will you be back? Has there been any progress? Will you consider surgery?* It won't end, not any time soon, not until the injury heals. Will he snap? Will he reveal his true colors?

Will we finally glimpse The Other Side of Nomar?

For the past two years, the worst-kept secret in Boston was that Nomar Garciaparra—our beloved shortstop, the biggest threat to hit .400 since George Brett, maybe the most popular local athlete since Larry Bird—can be an absolute prick to the media. I learned this revelation from a media friend when our conversation turned to difficult athletes; my friend claimed that Nomar made Jim Rice seem bubblier than Richard Simmons. I couldn't believe it. Nomar? Our Nomar? The guy who climbed out of his dugout and applauded the Boston fans during the '98 playoffs? The guy with the engaging smile and "Oh, shucks, I'm not that good" demeanor? The guy who won the "Which local athlete would be most fun to have a beer with?" poll on my website two winters ago? *That* Nomar?

"Yup," my friend said. "Turn the cameras off and he can be a world-class prick. Inconsiderate and unfriendly. Sarcastic if he doesn't like your question. It's like pulling teeth to get him to say that the sun came up today."

Wait a second. *Nomar?*

"Yup. After games, he takes his time showering and getting ready, even though he knows some of us are on deadlines. It's like he thrives on it. The cameras flash on, he livens up. The cameras shut off, so does he. The only reporter he'll talk to is Gammons, and that's usually in private. He does the bare minimum with the rest of us."

If I didn't know better, I could have sworn my friend was describing Rice, whose frigid demeanor cost him a spot in the Hall of Fame. Jim Ed's reputation surpassed "prick" status; he was alternately surly, distrustful, and just plain rude. When reporters approached, he acted like they were pissing on his shoes. Miserable guy. I had the misfortune of interviewing him once, one of the few times in my life that someone regarded me with complete indifference and disdain. And it wasn't me—it was the fact that I was holding a notebook and wanted a few minutes of his time.[195] For Jim Ed, that was enough.

Maybe Nomar doesn't treat reporters *that* badly—the fear factor isn't there—but he has his share of Jim Ed moments. Last week at Fort Myers, Nomar reported to camp and kept the media waiting for 90 minutes before holding court, remaining concise and humorless throughout, to the infinite frustration of anyone hoping to drag a 75-line story or column out of him. Following the announcement that Nomar will take two weeks to rest his ailing right wrist, his uneasy relationship with the media will inevitably become an issue. For the first time, the media needs specific information from him: They need to know about his wrist. If he isn't forthcoming, it could be the first public blemish of his career, as well as our first taste of The Other Nomar.

Should we re-evaluate our relationship with him? We like him, we feel like we know him...we don't know him at all. How is that possible? Ask me to describe Pedro's personality and I would need 2,000 words. I *know* Pedro. Feel like I do, anyway. But Nomar pulls the Ray Bourque routine, never offering anything beyond cliches and jock-speak. He's a blank slate. This last happened with Larry Bird in the early '80s, but as his career evolved, Larry grew increasingly more comfortable around reporters. We learned about his biting sense of humor and round-the-clock competitiveness, the anecdotes adding up: He loved drinking beer and getting rowdy with Rick Robey, saved every dime he ever made, remembered every small wager he ever won, felt most comfortable with his friends from Indiana, thrived on tweaking teammates and reporters ... all the little pieces added up to a bigger picture. By the time he was winning MVP awards, we felt like we knew him.

Nomar? He loves soccer, his name is Ramon spelled backwards, he eats, drinks and sleeps baseball and he may or may not have dated Lauren Holly. That's all I know.[196] His distrust of the media supposedly started in the minors, when he made a sparkling defensive play for Trenton and expressed disappointment that the crowd hadn't responded adequately, saying after the game, "You could hear crickets chirping after I made that

195 I was writing a Mo Vaughn profile for the *Boston Phoenix* that never ended up running. Two outcomes made up for it: I stepped onto the field at Fenway for the first time, and my disturbing encounter with Rice convinced me that I would stop thinking like a fan if I spent too much time in clubhouses. That's why I avoid them. Every time I think of Jim Rice, I think about how he was an asshole to me. And yes, this is why so many sportswriters secretly hate sports.

196 Over those first four seasons, only one Nomar incident stood out: A post-game attack on Sox announcer Sean McDonough, who angered Nomar for counting out the Sox in the later innings of a blowout loss.

play." Of course, that went over as well as a bomb joke on an airplane. After the Trenton newspaper splashed one of those "Nomar slams the fans!" headlines on their sports section, the fans responded with jeers at the following home game. As the story goes, Nomar hasn't trusted a reporter since. His unspoken message to the press remains the same every year: *I hate doing this. I wish you would go away. I don't really like you. This is the part of the job that I hate most. I'm not going to make your lives easy. I will not give you anything good. I don't trust any of you. I just want this to be over. You will get nothing and like it.*[197]

Here's the real question: Is that a bad thing? Does Nomar have every right to act like a prick? Consider these four questions.

1) Why shouldn't players be wary of reporters?

Remember three things about reporters: They travel in packs, they like to eat, and they're always pursuing the next story.[198] The same guy who just shook your hand and thanked for your time could be slamming you in the paper 24 hours from now. For instance, imagine being Carl Everett, knowing that you're a little "out there," knowing that reporters will print every one of your ill-advised quotes, knowing that they'll slam you for every one of your errors in judgement. Why give them 15 minutes of your time? Why help somebody when they come up to you, smiling and deferential, and say, "Do you have 30 minutes to talk to me for a magazine piece?"...and you know that they're getting paid to write that piece? Basically, they're making money off *your* time. Why do them a favor when you could get screwed in the end? I sure wouldn't.

2) Since reporters serve as the fans' lifeline to the locker rooms, shouldn't the players respect this?

Absolutely. And most of them do—including Nomar, who spent 20 minutes answering questions about his injured wrist yesterday. We needed to know two things: "What's wrong?" and "How bad?" Nothing else mattered. Whether he displays similar patience over the next few days remains to be seen. In a strange way, yesterday's incident demonstrated why we endure the media in the first place. Imagine if they didn't allow reporters at spring training, if TV cameras showed Nomar sitting in the dugout with an air cast covering his right wrist? HUH??? The fans would suffer a collective coronary.

197 I want a hamburger...no, I want a cheeseburger...I want a hot dog...

198 Three more things I should have mentioned: They feel totally comfortable in a Hawaiian shirt even when it's 35 degrees outside; there's a good chance they keep mustard and ketchup packets in their cars; and they practically go into heat any time they see a girl who's remotely passable in the press box. That's one of my favorite sayings—when a girl is "Press Box Hot." In other words, she's mediocre, but stick her in a press box and she's like **the next Natalie Portman**. This phenomenon extends to NESCAC schools, Fenway Park, prisons, and Irish-Catholic weddings.

199 Poor Antoine. He's taking more abuse in this book than Grady Little, John McNamara, and Wendell Kim combined.

3) What do players really have to say, anyway?

Probably 90 percent of game stories, mini-features, sidebars and recaps contain useless quotes from players and coaches. And that's not always the reporter's fault; they have to fill space and rely on quotes to prove they attended the game. Can you ever remember a sportswriter posting a game story with a message in italics that read, "I went to the game tonight but nobody said anything interesting, so I'm running my recap without quotes." Would never happen. Maybe one out of every 300 quotes is truly memorable; for the most part, it's just sludge. Either the athlete doesn't feel comfortable talking in public, or they don't want to appear boastful, disrespectful or overly candid. So they end up saying nothing.

Most reporters compound the problem by failing to push athletes in the right directions with provocative, pertinent questions. During a Celtics loss in Dallas last week, Antoine "I'm allegedly getting it" Walker[199] attempted 17 shots with Eduardo Najera defending him for most of the game. Of those 17 shots, 10 were three-pointers, meaning that Walker only attempted seven shots from less than 24 feet. *Seven.* That raises a simple post-game question: "Antoine, why in God's holy name were you shooting threes all game with an undersized rookie covering you?" Right to the point. No way Twan can answer that without actually giving an answer. Of course, nobody asked him or mentioned those curious numbers in either local newspaper. We deal with this stuff every day—people covering teams who don't know enough about the sport they're covering. Let's move on before I start jamming toothpicks in my ears.

4) Would you want somebody in *your* face asking *you* questions after a hard day's work?

People always say "It's part of the job," but does that always have to be the case? Let's say that you're Bret Saberhagen. Battling back from shoulder surgery, you just allowed eight runs and 10 hits in two innings to the B.C. varsity baseball team, including two homers by a redheaded kid named Smitty. Now your right arm feels like somebody tried to hack it off. You're looking forward to jumping in the whirlpool and forgetting about a dreadful afternoon.

(But first…)

What happened out there today, Bret? How's the arm feel? Was this a setback for you? How come you weren't effective out there today? What went wrong out there? Can you take anything good from this? Why didn't you pitch well? When do you think you'll be ready to pitch for the Red Sox? Are you considering retirement?

And you have to figure out 10 different ways to say "My arm hurts, I sucked, I couldn't locate my pitches, and I have no f-ing idea whether this comeback will work."

Doesn't that sound terrible? In a weird way, I can relate.**200** The life of a sports columnist resembles a professional athlete in some ways—we're in the public eye, people have strong opinions about us, we keep plugging away week after week, we feel underappreciated because people take us for granted, we only have a shelf life of 8-10 years before we start to lose it, we're only as good as our last column or game, and we're always thinking, "Can I keep it up?" I can't imagine dealing with a barrage of questions about a subpar column. Would I go on auto-pilot and avoid saying anything substantial, just to get out of there alive? Absolutely.**201**

Maybe that's what happens with Nomar. In the now-infamous *Sports Illustrated* cover story, Tom Verducci infiltrated Nomar's inner circle and chronicled the shortstop's rigorous off-season training regimen. We learned that Nomar trains for five hours a day and has added 35 pounds of muscle since college.**202** We learned that Nomar doesn't watch videos of pitchers; sometimes he doesn't even know if he's facing a lefty or a righty until he steps into the batter's box in the first inning. "It doesn't matter who's out there," he told Verducci. "If I'm swinging the bat real good, I feel like I should hit anybody."

We learned that he fields grounders with a Little League-size glove that forces him to stay low for every ball. We learned that he hits pitches on the middle of his bat so often that his bat barrels become harder than those of his teammates. We learned that he possesses enough locker room presence that David Cone muttered last week, "When he walks through the room, you know it." We learned that Nomar grew so tired of Jimy Williams' lineup shuffling during the season that he pleaded with his manager in midseason, "Just leave me fourth." And we learned that "he advises new teammates to ignore the Boston media." Over the next few weeks, it will be interesting to see if he can heed his own advice.

From what I gathered from Verducci's article, Nomar is just *that* driven. When he acts prickly to members of the Boston media, it happens for two reasons: He doesn't trust them, and

200 Brace yourself: The pilot just turned off the "No Self-Pitying" sign.

201 Here's what my answers would sound like: "Well, I really wanted to post something but things just never fell into place for me…I need to keep plugging away and hopefully get that thing posted tomorrow…hopefully the fans will understand that I'm working hard out there and keep supporting me…I just have to take things one column at a time…all right, guys, GET THE FUCK AWAY FROM ME!"

202 There were always rumors about Nomar and steroids in Boston, mainly because he was a scrawny soccer player type as recently as the 1994 College World Series. Also, he suffered two tendon injuries (one to the wrist, one to the Achilles) and had aberrational statistical seasons in 1999 and 2000. At the time, you thought, "Nomar? No way!" Now, since that there's a black cloud over everything that happened from 1994 to 2004, I would believe just about anything. That's right, it's America's pastime! Good times!

they interfere with his responsibilities to his team. There's a reason why Verducci landed that access during the winter. As Nomar explained in the article, "My very first thought when I wake up is the game that night. There is a feeling in my body that begins right away, knowing I have to prepare myself."

Reporters? They're probably just in the way. So be it.[203]

203 Within a few days of this column, the team revealed that Nomar had suffered a major wrist injury. Here's what I wrote in my season preview at the end of March: "Well, spring training went over like a fart in church. Everett did everything short of peeing on Ted Williams. Valentin blew out his knee again, making him eligible for Shea Ralph's ACL support group. The David Cone Bandwagon careened off the tracks and left 15 dead and more than 100 wounded. We found out that Arrojo suffered from ADD, Manny was breast-fed until he was almost four and Pedro thought of Everett 'like a brother.' Worst of all, not only did Nomar's wrist tendon mysteriously split like an atom, the *Globe* printed **a disturbing photo of no. 5 hugging Merloni from behind** (just in case Yankee fans didn't have enough ammunition against us)."

THE NOMAR REDEMPTION

April 4, 2001

There's a small place inside us that they can never lock away, and that place is called hope.
—Andy Dufresne[204]

Act I: The Jinx

It all started with that damned *Sports Illustrated* cover four weeks ago. There was Nomar, inexplicably shirtless, flexing a bat in front of his waist, grinning broadly, looking like they cut-and-pasted his noggin onto Stone Cold Steve Austin's body. Surprised Red Sox fans had three immediate reactions:

1) No-mahhhh!

2) Damn, he's ripped.

3) Hey wait a second...NOOOOOOOOOOO!!!!!!!!!

Yup, it was the dreaded *SI* Jinx. In retrospect, they should have dressed up a black cat in a no. 5 jersey and photographed it standing under a ladder. As word spread about the issue, panic slowly rippled through Red Sox Nation. We were titillated that Nomar received some much-deserved ink, rattled by his impressive, "It doesn't make me gay to say that Nomar's ripped, right?" physique, and infuriated at *SI* for jeopardizing our beloved shortstop's health. In that order.

And then it happened. Midway through the afternoon—the same freaking day!—word filtered down that Nomar had injured his right wrist.[205] Details were scarce, early reports weren't encouraging...and everything just *stopped*. New Englanders sleepwalked through the rest of the workday, searching for updates, sending out e-mails, calling friends, and engaging in Group Commiseration. Rumors appeared in various message boards that included the dreaded phrase "Out for the year." We quickly tied the injury to September 1999, when Nomar was struck by an errant fastball from former Orioles pitcher Al "Burn in Hell!" Reyes. *Was Nomar suffering lingering problems from that pitch? And should we organize a witchhunt to find Reyes?* Nobody knew. Subsequent reports confirmed that Nomar was suffering from extreme discomfort and a sudden loss of strength.

204 This was my first ESPN.com column. On a Monday night, Page 2 editor Kevin Jackson e-mailed me and asked, "Will you write a column for us about Nomar?" Less than three days later, it was running on the front page of the website. Historically, the moment ranks somewhere between Will Ferrell's first *SNL* sketch and Margaret Cho's first *Tonight Show* appearance. I'll let you decide where.

205 There wasn't nearly enough made out of this, by the way. **Has the *SI* Jinx ever worked faster?** They should have just swung the photographer's chair over his head right after the photo shoot.

Yikes! The 2001 season was going down in flames faster than the Spin Doctors after "Cleopatra's Cat" was released.[206] We waited for positive news—something, anything—but deep down, we knew it wasn't coming.

The next three weeks of spring training were agonizing; every morning felt like another kick to the collective groin. For a season brimming with so much promise—every year we believe that "This is the year," but after the Manny signing, we were *really* believing, "Hey, this is the year!"—the sudden collapse seemed almost cruel.[207] This team can tread water for two to three months without Nomar, but no reasonable fan would expect them to contend unless Nomar, Pedro, and Manny were 100 percent. It will take months to recover from major wrist surgery, especially for a hitter like Nomar who relies on his bat speed. Even if he returns near the end of the season, he won't be the same.

We know this. We *know* this.

Act II: The Void

Somewhere in the middle of this mess, the season commenced in Baltimore, a disheartening 11-inning loss that summoned many of last year's problems. Once again, the Sox offense wasted a fine effort from Pedro, who could have married Derrick Thomas and gotten better support over the past few years. Once again, shoddy defense cost the Sox a crucial run in a close game. Once again, Jimy ("The dealer's showing 6 and I'm sitting on 18...hit me!") Williams made some strange decisions, highlighted by his refusal to pinch-hit for soft-hitting Darren Lewis with runners in scoring position in the 9th and 11th innings. The more things change, the more they stay the same.[208]

Well, except for one thing: A Red Sox season without Nomar felt like a cheeseburger without ketchup, or even a Cinemax skin flick without Shannon Tweed. At least four different times during Monday's game, I fell off the wagon and suffered legitimate "Goddammit, why does Nomar have to be injured!?!?!" moments that caused me to shake my head, drop a few F-bombs, and question the morals of the Baseball Gods. Quite simply, the Nomar-Pedro tandem was the best thing to happen to the Boston sports scene since the Larry Bird Era. We *love* these guys. Outsiders can't fully appreciate that.[209]

On the one hand, there's Pedro, the most dominant pitcher since Koufax, a no-hitter waiting to happen every five days, one

206 I will bet you anything that this is the only Red Sox book released in 2005 with two Spin Doctors jokes in it.

207 One positive from spring training: Brian Daubach won a place in every Boston fan's heart by unveiling a cheesy mustache that he bought on eBay from either Jeff Hostetler, Tom Byron or Jeff Gillooly. It was right up there with the time **Ray Bourque grew that bushy beard that covered his whole body** during the 1990 playoffs in the Boston Sports Pantheon of Classic Facial Growths.

208 Everyone was turning on Jimy that season—even Duquette, who refused to give Jimy an extension and suspiciously added two "managers in waiting" to his coaching staff (Rick Down and Gene Lamont). At the time, I wrote it was like my refusing to propose to the Sports Gal, then moving two attractive female readers into the guest room of the BSG Mansion just to "shake things up" around the place. "Honey, they're just here to cut down the rent and help out with the cooking and cleaning... Both of them are single, but neither of them are home that much because one's a stripper and the other is a personal masseuse..."

of the more charismatic Boston athletes in recent memory. Every one of Pedro's starts is an event. That's the best way I can put it. And Nomar was on pace to become the best all-around right-handed hitter since DiMaggio, approaching every at-bat the same way, right down to his manic-obsessive, "Nicholson in *As Good As It Gets*" routine with the batting gloves. He never studies pitchers, freely admitting that he doesn't know if the team is facing a righty or a lefty on some days. He swings at everything, and I mean *everything*, belting more frozen ropes than anyone you've ever seen. He's a line drive machine. It's uncanny. You really have to watch the Sox day in and day out to appreciate it.

209 Out of any column in this book, this is the strangest one to read after the fact, if only because I wasn't exaggerating any of these feelings at the time. Within four years, *both* guys were gone from Boston. Would anyone have guessed that at the time? In a million years?

After Boston fans suffered through a catastrophic 10-year span ('87 to '96) that featured the rapid decline of the C's and B's, the Tuna's bitter departure to the Jets, the stunning deaths of Reggie Lewis and Len Bias, Bird and Neely having their careers cut short by injury, and Clemens fleeing to Canada, watching Pedro and Nomar arrive in the same calendar year was like hitting the lottery. Suddenly we had two heroes again—the artist and the everyday grinder—Pedro playing the role of Hendrix, Nomar playing Springsteen. We came to marvel at the unique contrasts between the two superstars. Pedro doesn't just get batters out, he buries them. He breaks them. On those special days when Pedro has all four pitches working, it feels like somebody stuck Fenway Park into a light socket. You stand on every two-strike count, you scream at the top of your lungs, you pound your hands together until they throb, you high-five strangers...*you give yourself to this man*. Everything you have. Everything. I'm telling you, he's a comet.

Nomar? He's more like a family member; we immediately adopted the California native as one of us. Even the way we scream his name speaks volumes. That always cracks up outsiders at Fenway, those four or five moments a game when Nomar glides toward home plate, bat in hand, and you hear a rustling buzz, followed by general recognition and giddiness, followed by a genuine roar and a cacophony of "No-mahhhhhhhhhh's!" His consistency makes him more endearing than anything—the bottomless reservoir of line drives, the way he runs out every grounder, his uncanny ability to avoid slumps, how he carries himself and plays the game. Even without Pedro's outgoing personality, Nomar's "average guy" charisma

210 Again, for a national audience, nobody had ever properly explained **the psyche of Red Sox fans** (at least to my knowledge). For decades, everyone was getting spoon-fed the "Boston fans feel sorry for themselves" and "They think they're cursed by Babe Ruth" routine, which simply wasn't true. I couldn't have been happier to set the record straight on ESPN.com—I felt like Allison finally confronting her child molesting father on *Melrose Place*.

makes up for it. Yank him off the Red Sox for a few months and everything changes. It's like watching an episode of *The Sopranos* without Tony involved—maybe every plot doesn't have to revolve around Tony, but you still need him around. Together, Nomar and Pedro equal Tony; remove one of them and the Red Sox aren't the same show anymore. As we're finding out.

Act III: The Comeback

To understand why we haven't given up hope for the season—even though Nomar probably won't return until August; even though this could be the worst defensive team to play in a major league stadium since the California Bears ignited the Astrodome; even though the starting rotation goes Pedro, Nomo, Castillo, Tomo and Uh-Oh; even though $14.3 million worth of washed-up second basemen rot on the bench; even though our manager openly works on his resume between innings—you have to understand us. Red Sox fans are complicated and perennially misunderstood.[210]

You probably think that 82 years of sweeping failure, as well as some beyond-scarring losses, a haunted ballpark and the fact that we came within one pitch of winning the World Series *13 different times* would jade us beyond repair. Nope. For whatever reason, we always believe that this will be The Year. When it doesn't happen and things fall apart, we react as if our hearts were broken for the first time. Those first three months after Manny's signing exemplified everything: We went from sizing World Series rings to popping Prozacs in 10 weeks. Nobody overreacts quite like us, good and bad. We're a rollercoaster ride. We're insane. And it's all because we're terrified that we might live a complete life—I'm talking seven to eight decades, followed by death—without seeing the Boston Red Sox win a World Series.

The local media preys on this fear. Manipulative, mean-spirited, agenda-ridden (pick an adjective, because all of them fit), this current crop of writers overrates our weaknesses (the "woe is me" complex), dwells on negative issues and delights in tweaking our stars. Outsiders read them and think, "All Boston fans are like that." Not true. The media members are just trying to rile us. Usually, it works. Again, we're insane over this whole thing; we're not rational. But at least we care. And at least we never stop hoping.

If Sox fans were defined by a movie, you know what the obvious choice is? *The Shawshank Redemption*. That's why I led with Andy's quote up top. *There's a small place inside us that they can never lock away, and that place is called hope*. That's us! Andy didn't deserve to spend 20 years in jail; we didn't deserve to root for a baseball team responsible for so much heartache over the years. Andy planned his escape every day; we think about winning the World Series every day. Andy battled the Warden and lost; we battled the Yankees and lost. People thought Andy was crazy because he had hope; people think we're crazy because we always think, "This is the year!" Andy was gang-raped for more than two years by The Sistas; we suffered through the '86 World Series. And so on.[211]

But here's the key: Andy escaped. He dug out of Shawshank with a rock hammer, for God's sake. He crawled through 500 yards of shit-smellin' foulness the likes of which we couldn't imagine. He stole millions from prison and caused the Warden to decorate his office with his brains. He fled to Mexico and settled in Zihuatanejo, but not before hiding a letter and money in a Maine cornfield, just in case his buddy Red was released some day. And Red was released, and he found the money and the letter, and he skipped town and headed to Mexico, and he found Andy, and hell, for all we know, they're probably playing chess on that boat right now.

Yeah, it's only a movie, but it makes you wonder about the Red Sox and what would happen if they win the Series. Everyone has their own fantasy about this, but we all agree on one thing: Downtown Boston would turn into a three-day Mardi Gras. Back in my raging 20s, I worried that I would go overboard, that they would find me like the late Chris Farley—butt-naked, bleeding, incoherent, beyond drunk and crawling toward a hooker with a smile on my face. I feel differently now that I'm 30. I see the whole thing unfolding like a giant group hug, like when Andy and Red greet each other at the end of *Shawshank*, but multiplied by 10 million people. Does that make sense? And that's the lure: The giant group hug. That's why we keep the faith every year. That's why we overreact to everything. That's why Sox fans were doing backflips over Manny's signing and chugging Drano after Nomar's injury.

And that's why we're waiting...and hoping...and praying... and that's why we're quietly pining for July, when the Sox somehow keep treading water and remain alive in the A.L. East, and then Nomar starts taking BP, and then he heads down to

211 Every time I wonder why I kept (almost pathologically) comparing the Red Sox and *Shawshank*, this paragraph sums it up. We were like Andy. That was the thing. **As it turned out, beating the Yankees was the equivalent of Andy finally escaping**, winning the World Series was the combination of Andy driving in his convertible to the Pacific as the Warden blew his brains out, and 2005 Opening Day (unveiling the 2004 banner while the Yankees stood there and watched) was the Andy-Red reunion at Zihuatanejo.

Pawtucket for the rehab stint, and then he returns, our secret weapon down the stretch, reunited with Pedro, spraying line drives once again, the missing piece that puts us over the top and pushes us closer to the giant group hug.

Will it happen?[212] Maybe, maybe not. But I *hope* it happens. When all else fails, just remember that hope is a good thing, maybe the best of things, and no good thing ever dies. I think I heard that somewhere once.

212 Actually, no. They finished 82–79. Nomar's final stats: 83 ABs, .289 BA, 4 HR, 8 RBI. His career was never the same.

CLEANING UP

May 15, 2001

Well, we have a cleanup hitter again.

Ever since Jim Ed Rice's glorious apex in the late '70s, Boston fans have been waiting for another slugger who made everything *stop*. Rice's stretch from '77 to '79 has always been the Power Hitter Standard here, with the hallowed exception of Yaz's Impossible Dream season. But after six weeks, it seems possible that Manny Ramirez could become a more memorable cleanup hitter than both of them. Quite simply, it was $160 million well-spent.

Through six weeks, Manny is batting .408. He reached base at least once in 35 of the 37 games this season. He's hitting .391 with nobody on, .423 with runners on, .449 with runners in scoring position and .565 with runners in scoring position and two outs (13 for 23, 16 RBI). He has 46 RBI this season; the Sox have 187 RBI *total*. In 22 games at home, he's hitting .424 with 35 RBI and a 1.302 OPS (on-base + slugging percentage). His OPS is 1.251 overall, 1.332 against lefties. According to baseball-reference.com, only Ted Williams and Babe Ruth have topped the 1.250 OPS barrier for an entire season in the *history* of baseball. And he's been doing it with the struggling four-headed monster of Daubach, Bichette, Varitek and O'Leary behind him.[213]

213 Manny ended up leveling off a little, finishing with a .306 average, 1.014 OPS, 41 HRs and 125 RBI as the nonstop clubhouse dysfunction sent him into a relative funk. After the season, when I was handing out those aforementioned *Godfather* quotes as awards, I gave Manny the scene when **Johnny Fontaine started crying,** "I don't know what to do, I don't know what to do" to Don Corleone and the Don slapped him and screamed, "You can act like a man! What's the matter with you?"

Of course, numbers can't capture that wonderful buzz at Fenway when Manny strides to home plate. Or how it feels to chant "Man-ny! Man-ny! Man-ny!" along with 35,000 strangers. Or the fact that nobody leaves their seat (for the bathroom, for a food break, for a beer, etc.) during an inning when Manny's coming up. Or that awed, "Holy shit, that's slicing fair and it's still going up!" sound that everyone made Saturday during Manny's 468-foot "sliced back onto the fairway" homer that nearly reached the Mass Pike. Or the fervor of a crowd chanting someone's name during an entire at-bat, then being rewarded by a game-tying home run, leading to a Garden-level roar (like what happened on Sunday).

Numbers don't describe those moments during a Yankees-

Sox game when one of your friends (a Yankee fan) calls just to tell you, "I am scared shitless of Manny Ramirez."

Numbers don't describe those moments in an 8–4 game when there are two outs in the eighth and Manny's still four batters away, but you're saying to yourself, "If the next three guys get on, we can tie this thing!"

Numbers don't describe what it's like to watch a Sox game on TV this year—even if you're watching five different channels, you always remember when Manny's coming up. It's like watching an erotic thriller on cable; even if you're not watching the entire movie, you develop a sixth sense for the next nude scene. That's Manny, only every night.

If there has been a revelation, it's the way he battles pitchers from at-bat to at-bat. You can't judge a baseball player unless you watch him every day. Remember how the Yankees (especially Knoblauch and Jeter) battled Boston pitchers over the past two seasons? Remember how frustrating it was to watch them foul off pitches before finally settling on one they liked? Remember how you always said to yourself, "Man, I wish we had a guy like that?" Well, we finally do. Manny *works* pitchers; he wears them out.[214] You can see their wheels turning around pitch #6, like they're saying to themselves, "Crap, what should I throw now?" It's comical. For whatever reason, Manny possesses the innate ability to foul off certain pitches *and* lay off pitches that just miss the strike zone, never unleashing his full-fledged "Here's Manny!" swing until he gets the exact pitch he wants.

How does he consistently make correct decisions in one-tenth of a second? I have no idea—it's mystifying, almost like watching a well-done card trick. But since Manny pulled the same routine in Cleveland, it can't be considered a fluke or a "hot streak." Call him a savant, call him an artist, whatever. Some guys just have a gift. Bird and Gretzky knew where each of their teammates was headed at any given time. Pedro makes his delivery of two different pitches look exactly the same, even though one travels 17 miles an hour faster than the other. Barry Sanders consistently made defenders tackle air in the open field. John McEnroe played the net like nobody you've ever seen. Keith Hernandez didn't just play first base, he mastered it.[215] And Manny can do this. Day in and day out, he's the best hitter I have ever seen.

(What about Nomar, you ask? Remember, Nomar hits just

214 After watching him for four years, this is the one way to tell whether he's struggling or he's in a groove: The long at-bats. If it looks like he's just trying to get his ABs over with, either he's slumping or he's bothered by something goofy like "I wish they hadn't painted the pitching machine" or "I can't believe my favorite parking attendant was off today."

215 **He gets my Hall of Fame vote,** by the way. I've never seen anyone play first base like Hernandez—it was like seeing Dominique Wilkins dunk in traffic for the first time.

about any pitch, no matter where it is, and he smacks more line drives than anyone I've ever seen...but he swings at everything. He's a freak of nature. Manny is more of an artist; his at-bats are a cerebral experience, a chess match of sorts. It's like comparing McEnroe and Ivan Lendl in their primes, two special players who went about their craft in completely different ways. Not to lump Nomar with someone as hideously uncharismatic as Lendl, but as a hitter, he's Lendl. You won't ever have a 10-minute conversation about a specific Nomar at-bat. Manny? That's a different story.)

Boston fans quickly embraced him, the first "You like me! You really like me!" experience of his career. Could that explain why he batted .323 at home and .324 on the road from 1998-2000, yet he's batting 38 points higher at Fenway than on the road?[216] From everything I remember about his Cleveland stint, the fans supported him, liked him, didn't love him. He even took heat for "nursing" an injury and missing 39 games last summer, the 160,000,001st reason why he wanted to leave town. In Boston, he homered on his first Fenway swing and the fans adored him ever since. It just feels like various elements are colliding at the same time—fresh start, unconditional love from the fans, right city, superstar entering his prime, even the spiteful side effect of "sticking it" to a former team (like Clemens in '97). Everything feels right about this.

There have already been some sweet moments along the way. My favorite happened after his RBI single toppled Mariano Rivera and the Yankees, when his teammates mobbed him and he looked almost sheepish, like he wanted to sneak off the field before anyone embarrassed him. My father attended last Sunday's game (when Manny belted the game-tying homer after five minutes of "Man-ny! Man-ny!" chants) and deemed it the best baseball game he ever attended, comparing Fenway to a mid-'80s Celtics crowd—the highest praise he can give. Again, something's happening here. I find myself becoming more and more fascinated by no. 24, trying to figure him out. When I was reading David Halberstam's book *Playing for Keeps* recently, the following passage jumped out:

"There was a certain unspoken undertow of tension between [Larry Bird and Kevin McHale] because of their very different personalities. McHale was by most standards hard-working and committed, but he might not have been as dedicated as Bird. That was a source of great irritation for Bird...

216 Starting with the 2000 season, the sophistication of the **Sons of Sam Horn** posters had a dramatic effect on my Sox columns—you couldn't throw arguments out there without backing them up or those guys had you for lunch. Once I started doing my homework, studying stats and taking notes during games, my baseball columns really improved. So thank you, random guys on the Internet who post under anonymous names. I appreciate the kick in the ass.

McHale, on the other hand, the most gregarious man, a man who with his love of talk could have been a great pol or the most charming saloonkeeper around, a man who came to work each day not only to play basketball at a high level but to luxuriate in the social pleasures of being with his teammates, seemed to think that Bird was too monodimensional, that he had no life other than basketball. There was some truth in that."

Sounds like Manny. Supposedly he arrives at the ballpark earlier than any of his teammates, sometimes eight or nine hours before game time. He hits the weight room for a couple of hours, takes extra (early) batting practice, studies videos to pick up tendencies about the day's opposing pitcher, even studies videos of his own swing (just to make sure he isn't developing any bad habits). Eventually he heads back outside for more batting practice. Then he returns inside again and watches more video. Apparently he's consumed by his swing—sometimes he walks around the clubhouse holding a bat, practicing his stance or taking check swings—and his relationships with his teammates revolve solely around baseball. Hobbies? Please. From all accounts, his life revolves around eating, drinking, going to the bathroom, and swinging a baseball bat, and not in that order. Some people were placed on the earth for one thing, whether it's Pamela Anderson, Stephen King, Kurt Cobain, Manny Ramirez or whomever. It's our gain.[217]

When an athlete peaks like this—the way Manny crested over the past few weeks, or the way Bird crested during those infamous Larry Streaks he unleashed from time to time—the sense of drama heightens as it keeps going. *Can he come through again? Can we just hold on until he gets going? Will he do it again? Will he top yesterday?* You feel more attached because, when they're cresting, anything seems possible. Pedro possesses many of those Bird-esque qualities as well, like the rare ability to raise his game in big moments, the eye-popping talent, the competitive charisma, the Maximus-esque ability to "win the crowd." But you have a better grasp of an athlete when you're watching him every day. Pedro weaves in and out of our lives; during a 162-game season, he feels like a luxury, like an expensive bottle of wine once or twice a week.[218]

Manny? He's *always* there, just like Bird was. More often than not, he comes through, just like Bird did. Occasionally, he exceeds our expectations and takes us to The Higher Place, that

217 Originally this column was called "Ten Reasons I'm Enjoying the Manny Ramirez Era"—I dumped the top-10 list, stripped the fat, shifted some paragraphs around and VOILA! Coherent column.

218 I've always believed that fans feel more attached to position players than pitchers. **Position players are like dogs**—you see them all the time, they're loyal, you have to walk them three times a day and so on. Pitchers are like cats—they disappear for days at a time, they're fussy and they can't be trusted. And when they end up fighting, the hitters always end up chasing the pitchers.

small window we always leave open where we're hoping something happens and cheering for something to happen *and then it actually happens*...the best feeling you can possibly have as a sports fan. With Pedro, we're constantly expecting it (because every one of his starts feels like such an event). With Manny, we're constantly surprised. And any time an athlete making $20 million per season can surprise a grizzled bunch of baseball fans—in a good way, no less—that moment alone warrants its own column. We have a cleanup hitter again. It's about time.

IS ROGER THE ANTI-CHRIST?

May 29, 2001

My bosses gave me a simple assignment this week: "Please explain why Boston fans believe that Roger Clemens might be the Anti-Christ."[219]

With pleasure. Even the most ardent Rocket-hater would concede his Hall of Fame resumé. Clemens certainly won enough games: 265 and counting, including five 20-win seasons. He rang up enough Ks: 3,575 and counting, not to mention children with names starting with the letter "K" (Koby, Kory, Kacy, Kody, Kodachrome, Kornonthekob and so on). He owns more than enough Cy Young trophies (an astounding five), World Series rings (two and counting) and records (including the hallowed Only Guy to Strike Out 20 Batters Twice mark).[220] He made enough money during his career to fund a Michael Bay movie— $60 to $70 million at least, not including endorsements and other goodies. All the elements are there, except one.

Fans.

He doesn't have any.

And that's what makes Clemens so unique: He sails along in his late-30s, pitching as well as ever, only nobody cares about him. Can you recall another superstar squandering his emotional connection to every possible city? Boston fans loathe him. Toronto fans despise him. Yankees fans will never fully embrace him because of his Boston roots. So who's left? Name any superstar over the past 30 years; within a nano-second, you instinctively link that athlete to one city. Rose? Cincinnati. Reggie? New York. Rice? San Fran. Isiah? Detroit. The list goes on. In every case, the superstar enjoyed his prime in a particular city and reaps the benefits of that relationship to this day. Not Clemens. He drifts along like the Wolf in *Pulp Fiction*—no attachments to anyone or anything, a hired hitman, the superstar who sold out his fans for a few extra bucks. Instead of a team's logo, the cap on his Hall of Fame statue should have a dollar sign on it.

Casual fans associate Clemens with the Red Sox, regardless of his current team (the Yankees), or with enough residual bad blood back in Boston to rival the Overlook Hotel's main eleva-

219 This was my third assignment for ESPN.com. I probably got the nod because I was the guy who once wrote the sentence, "**The only time I would ever root for Roger Clemens again** is if he was standing on top of a 10-story building and the crowd started a 'Jump! Jump!' chant."

220 At the time, I never imagined Clemens would still be thriving four years later, or that he would finally find a home in Houston. Now he's on pace for 350 wins and 4,500 Ks. You could even make the case that he's the best pitcher of the last 50 years. I will now wander into oncoming traffic.

tor at the end of *The Shining*. The prevailing feeling is that Boston fans will soften during the twilight of Clemens' career, when he enters that cuddly "aging and vulnerable" stage that turns everyone nostalgic, and we'll bury the hatchet and accept Clemens back into our good graces.**221** Then the Rocket will retire, and he'll make the Hall of Fame, and heck, he might even wear a Boston cap as a gesture of good will. That's what people seem to think. Well, I'm here to tell you, this will *never* happen. Sometimes relationships pass a point where they can be salvaged, as Ike and Tina, Nicole and O.J., and Sam and Diane all proved over the years. In the Rocket's case, too much has happened. We *can't* let it go. We *won't* let it go. When you give your heart to someone and they basically drop it on the ground, stomp on it a few times, then ask, "What did I do?"...well, you don't forget something like that. Ever.

Clemens splashed onto the scene in 1986, putting himself on the map with a record-breaking 20-strikeout game and 14 consecutive wins. We quickly anointed him as our next local legend, the logical successor to Orr and Bird. Over the next seven years, the Rocket played his part reasonably well (136 wins, three Cy Youngs, three playoff appearances one World Series trip), only he lacked Orr's panache and Bird's sense of The Moment. After awhile, we stopped measuring him against them. We adored him, we supported him, we worried about him. You never worried about Bird and Orr.

The first doubts surfaced during the '86 World Series, when Clemens could have closed out Game Six and emerged as an authentic hero. He pitched valiantly through the seventh, leaving with a 3–2 lead and a blister on his throwing hand. And that's where the story gets interesting. Fifteen years later, the principals involved (Clemens, manager John McNamara and pitching coach Bill Fischer) still argue whether or not Clemens asked out of the game. McNamara vehemently claims that Clemens told him, "That's all I can pitch";**222** Clemens steadfastly maintains that he was yanked after the seventh; and prosecutor Jim Garrison claims there was a second pitching coach ordering Clemens to leave. Nobody knows the truth, but we know one thing: Under similar circumstances, Bird would have remained in the game unless he was forcibly removed and hogtied to the Celtics bench.

Clemens started eight playoff games before 1991, with Boston winning two of them: Game Seven of the '86 ALCS

221 Much to my horror, this almost happened during the 2004 trading deadline, when rumors started flying that the fading Astros would deal him to Boston. And much to my horror, many Sox fans seemed okay with this. Me? I was mortified. I'm not sure what I would have done—it's like imagining how you would react in an airplane that suddenly started free-falling. I couldn't even consider it.

222 My take: Clemens asked out. McNamara was many things, but he wasn't a liar. Everyone who covered the team at the time agrees that Mac was a salty, cut-to-the-chase guy who didn't sugarcoat anything. In Clemens' case, we have documented proof that he lied (claiming that he signed with Toronto to win a championship) and cheated (the handshake clause that landed him on the Yankees). So I'm voting for him.

(against a shell-shocked Angels team), and Game Two of the '86 World Series (where he didn't stick around long enough for a decision). To be fair, the bullpen blew two other potential wins, but one statistic keeps jumping out: 2–6. We watched Orel Hershiser ('88), José Rijo ('90) and Jack Morris ('91) shine over that same stretch, quietly waiting for a similar "Get on my back, boys" run from Rog-ah. Never happened. We wondered if Clemens only peaked in meaningless games—like the time he tossed a shutout during the final game in '87, clinching a second Cy Young when the Sox had been eliminated for months. It didn't help that Oakland's Dave Stewart thrived on beating Clemens in their matchups. (My math might be a little off here, but if I remember correctly, Stewart's lifetime record against Clemens was 982–0. Even the Globetrotters-Generals feud wasn't this one-sided). Things boiled over in Game Four of the 1990 ALCS, when the Rocket was tossed by Terry Cooney for arguing balls and strikes, punctuating his exit with a memorable, Whitney Houston-esque tantrum.

Our concerns deepened after the '92 season, when Clemens signed a four-year, $20 million contract and took much of the next three-plus years off, almost like a professor who gets tenure and doesn't feel like grading papers anymore. Unveiling a historic double chin in '93, Clemens battled arm problems en route to his first losing season. After re-dedicating himself for the strike-shortened '94 season (9–7, 2.85 ERA), he arrived the following spring looking like he was auditioning for The John Goodman Story.[223] Fueled by an increasingly vicious Boston media, Sox fans starting turning against Clemens after his inevitable breakdown (an extended DL stint), which coincided with an improbable playoff run. When Clemens squandered his only playoff start against Cleveland, that only fueled those "can't win the big one" doubts.

That brings us to '96, the final season of Clemens' aforementioned contract. Chunky, disinterested, and increasingly agitated about Boston's failure to offer him a contract extension, the Rocket turned on his jets once the team fell out of playoff contention, going 6–2 over his last 10 starts and striking out 20 Tigers in mid-September. Classic Roger, through and through. You could always count on him when it mattered least. Understandably, the Sox were dubious about handing the 34-year-old another long-term deal, given that he had battled health prob-

223 My father's favorite joke that April was, "Would you like another slice, Roger?"

224 At the time, this was **the musical equivalent of U2 asking for a lucrative extension** from their record company on the heels of "Zooropa" and "Pop."

lems and hibernated through much of his last mega-contract.[224] Tensions escalated between Clemens' agents (the hideous Hendricks brothers) and Dan Duquette, exacerbated by the Duke's steadfast refusal to negotiate during the season or recognize the Rocket's market value. We were headed for a divorce, an ugly one, and the sad thing was this: We knew things were headed that way all along. When Clemens ultimately jumped at Toronto's $28 million offer, deep down, we understood. Sometimes you just have to move on.

So what happened? Why the sudden change of heart? Why did the Rocket practically become the modern-day Sirhan Sirhan of New England? Five things happened over the next three years that turned Boston fans against Clemens for life. If any of those five things had unfolded differently, the bad blood would have been averted.

1) The Slap in the Face

When Clemens held his first press conference with the Blue Jays, he only needed to take one minute—just one—to say something like this: "I want to say something to the Boston fans who stuck with me over the past 12 years: Thanks for all your support. I'll always remember the time I spent in Boston. I hope you guys finally win a Series some day and I'm just sorry I'm not going to be a part of it when it happens. I wish things didn't deteriorate with the front office, but they did, and I didn't feel like they wanted me around anymore. Toronto makes me feel like they want me, and they did everything they could to make me a Blue Jay. For that, I'm grateful, and I'm happy to be here. But I hope the Boston fans realize that I'll always remember them and I'll miss pitching in front of them at Fenway. Thanks for 12 great years. You guys are truly special."

Would have taken 35 seconds. That's all.

Instead, Clemens spent the hour stroking his new Toronto hat and showing as much emotion as Mr. Spock. His only concern seemed to be making everyone aware—repeatedly, painfully, flagrantly—of how "excited I am to be a Blue Jay" and "how grateful I am that the Blue Jays have treated me so well." It was like they offered him an extra 50 bucks every time he praised the Jays. Reporters kept giving him chances to rectify the mistake, repeatedly asking him about Boston, but no. 21 stubbornly stuck to his guns. He was moving forward. He was a Blue Jay. And so he brushed off every Boston question while we watched in disbelief, our anger mounting. That wasn't just an oversight, it was a hanging curveball right over the plate. Later, when we learned that Toronto had offered the most cash—about $3 million more than the defending champion Yankees, after Clemens maintained that he signed with Toronto because he wanted to win a championship, no less—that made him a liar, too.[225]

2) The Kick in the Gonads

Suddenly and mysteriously motivated by the slight from Boston's front office, Clemens embarked on a rigorous conditioning program, determined to prove Team Duquette wrong. He arrived for spring training in Jamie Lee Curtis in *Perfect*-level shape, repeatedly telling reporters that he had never been better prepared to start a season. That revelation should have prompted questions like, "If you're so motivated this season, why weren't you as motivated after signing the most lucrative deal in Red Sox history?" and, "Will you be training with a feedbag and a vat of chicken wings like you did in 1995?" Nobody went there. Apparently, star athletes aren't obligated to get themselves in shape until they feel slighted. Anyway, we watched in horror as Clemens rolled off *consecutive Cy Young seasons* for the Jays. Here were his average stats from '93 to '96 in Boston, followed by the '97 and '98 seasons in Toronto:

YR	W–L	ERA	G	IP	H	SO	BB
93–96	10–10	3.78	27.5	186.1	179	204	76
1997	21–7	2.05	34	264.0	204	292	68
1998	20–6	2.65	33	234.2	169	271	88[226]

Put it this way: Watching Clemens lighting it up in Canada was like breaking up with your girlfriend, then watching her hire a personal trainer, shed 15 pounds, spend 10 Gs on a boob job and join the cast of *Baywatch*. Clemens saved his best for his former team, going 2–0 with a 1.73 ERA in four starts (including a memorable "Fuck you!" start in Fenway in '97, when he glared at the owner's box after leaving the game) and dropping hints that free agent-to-be Mo Vaughn should join him in Canada. Now it was becoming personal, and when the Boston media started hammering him (with Will McDonough leading the pack),[227] the tide shifted against Clemens for good. We felt jilted and used, and we started rooting against him. Vehemently.

225 In 1997 and 1998 with Clemens, Toronto finished two games over .500; the Yankees finished 96 games over .500.

226 Admittedly, this column is skewed against Clemens and I went a little overboard to argue my case. But you can't deny that those stats are fishy.

227 The late McDonough was relentless with Clemens, calling him **The Texas Con Man** and skewering him every six to eight weeks. Needless to say, he's sorely missed.

3) The Revelation

As Clemens sparkled for a .500 team in a foreign country, the double-barreled emergence of Nomar and Pedro (coupled with Clemens hooking himself up to the Rejuvenation Machine) made us realize that the loss of Clemens wasn't as important as we thought. If anything, the new guys were more fun to watch, while Clemens was a self-serving, greedy jerk who didn't care about us when he played here. If baseball were wrestling, this would be the point where Clemens came into the ring carrying the Canadian flag, shouting epithets about Nomar and Pedro, making unflattering jokes about Boston and forcing everyone to stand for the playing of the Canadian anthem.[228] In other words, all ties had been severed—he was an official Bad Guy.

4) The Ultimate Violation

After missing the playoffs for two straight seasons, a disenchanted Clemens forced a trade to the Yankees—the Yankees!!!—with help from an illegal "You can ask for a trade two years into this deal if you're not happy" handshake clause that drew the ire of the commissioner's office. It wasn't bad enough that the winningest pitcher in Red Sox history wanted to play in New York; he actually cheated to get there. Even the staunchest Clemens sympathizers in New England couldn't defend him anymore. He had crossed over to the dark side. He was Darth Vader with a Texas accent. He was the enemy.

(By the way, if you're keeping track, Clemens was officially a quitter, a cheater, a liar, *and* a traitor at this point).

5) The Final Straw

During opening ceremonies for the '99 All-Star Game at Fenway, Clemens took part in the Greatest Players of the 20th Century introductions, as every living legend wore the cap of the team with whom they were most prominently associated. Clemens wore a Yankees hat, which made perfect sense because he had been playing in New York for a whopping three months. Here was his last chance—I mean, ever—to salvage his ties with Boston fans. And he blew it. At this point, we were like Michael Corleone in *Godfather II* after finding out that Fredo knew Johnny Ola. *Roger, you're nothing to me now. I don't want to see you. I don't want to know you. Which if you visit our mother, I want to know a day in advance. You're dead to me.*[229]

We savagely booed him during an unforgettable Game

228 Sometimes I wish pro sports were more like pro wrestling. For instance, coaches of defending champs should always wear championship belts onto the field or court; starting fives in hoops should be introduced as a "Combined weight of 1230 pounds"; and **a sneering Dirk Nowitzki** should absolutely force everyone to stand for the German national anthem before games.

229 A better movie analogy for this night: Remember in *Midnight Run*, when the Duke finds out that Jack was forced out of Chicago by the same mobster (Serrano) who was trying to kill him? Duke knows that Serrano will have him killed in prison and pleades with Jack to let him go, but Jack needs the bounty ($100,000) so he can retire and open a coffee shop. So the incredulous Duke says: "Serrano was the heroin dealer you told me about, the guy who owned your buddies and destroyed your life, that's Serrano? That's the guy that you're taking me in to? That's the guy who's gonna kill me? [Disgusted pause] I hope it's a wonderful coffee shop, Jack." That's how I felt when I saw Clemens in that

Three in the '99 ALCS, as Pedro outdueled him and officially became The Man. When Clemens' wife whined about the hostile response of the Fenway fans (including the infamous quote, "I don't know what Roger ever did to them"), that inflamed us even more. We winced when Clemens finally captured his first-ever ring a few weeks later, taking solace that the Yankees would have won without him. We enjoyed his goofy feud with Mike Piazza the following season, including the bizarre bat-tossing incident that inadvertently tainted that fourth title for the Yankees and their fans. Now he's practically old news. The "Everyone hates Clemens" angle has been done to death. So has the "Clemens vs. Pedro" angle. And the "Fallen hero returns home" angle. Done, done, done. Next time Clemens pitches in Fenway, only the Yankee fans in attendance will be cheering him.

That begs one final question: Will Roger Clemens ever be loved?

Say what you want about Yankee fans, but at least you know where you stand with them. When they love somebody, they *love* somebody. Especially pitchers. But Clemens hasn't clicked with New York fans; any diehard Yankee supporter would admit that. They're cheering him now, but you always get the sense that they're wary of him, that they would turn on him in the drop of a hat.**230** He gives them a better-than-good chance to win every five days, and as soon as those odds drop, they'll discard him and find someone else. Those are the stakes. He's a hired gun, a means to an end, a necessary evil. He's a temp. And maybe he'll end up topping 300 wins and getting another ring, and maybe he'll make $25–30 million more before it's all over...but everything about those final few years will feel hollow. He'll have his family and friends in the end, and that's it. The real fans will be long gone.

For Boston fans, the most disappointing outcome was the retroactive emotional void from 1986–1996, almost like dating someone for an extended time, then enduring a dreadful breakup that tainted every aspect of the time you spent together. It's not that you forgot the good times; you simply choose not to think about them anymore. What's the point? For instance, when I was in college, my then-girlfriend bought me an autographed, limited edition photo of Clemens' 20K game, which I hung in every one of my apartments from 1990 to 1996. After the Toronto press conference, in a fit of rage I yanked

Yankees cap. "Hey Roger? I hope it's a wonderful coffee shop."

230 Watching the movie *61*, you can't help but notice the similarities between Roger Maris and Clemens, both All-Star imports who never won over the Yankee fans (through no real fault of their own). When Clemens screwed them over by "retiring"—after a year of farewells, no less—then coming back to pitch for the Astros in 2004, he burned that bridge as well. Seriously, can you think of another athlete who burned bridges in three different cities? That has to be a record, right?

down that picture, never to be seen again. More than four years have passed and it's still buried in my bedroom closet. That's what I think of Clemens. He's stuck in a closet with useless college notebooks, eclectic magazines, yellowed photos, letters from old flames and sweaters that I stopped wearing long ago.

Does that make him the Anti-Christ? Probably not. But I have been following sports for nearly three decades, and no athlete ever let me down quite like Roger Clemens. Fortunately, I can take solace at the thought of Clemens standing on the field at New Fenway, maybe 40 years from now, being introduced on Old Timer's Day 2041...and getting showered with boos from Boston fans. "I can't believe they still haven't let this go," he'll mumble to himself, a thin smile spread across his face, oblivious to the bitter end, still waiting for the fans to come around.

Not a chance.

ENJOY THE GAME!

July 25, 2001

We're not even into August and Red Sox fans have already learned more lessons than Ben Savage learned during the entire 1996 season of *Boy Meets World*. The $100 Million Little Engine That Could keeps chugging along, and we keep counting them out, and dammit, they keep chugging along. Fifteen games over .500? Tied for first place in late July? It's amazing, it's dumbfounding, it's downright baffling. And honestly, it hasn't even been that much fun.

Without further ado, here are 10 lessons that Sox fans learned from this season.

1) Ongoing, sweeping team dysfunction isn't necessarily a bad thing.

Even the Manson family didn't have this many problems.**231** There's a For Sale sign outside Fenway. The GM (Dan Duquette) and manager (Jimy Williams) have one of those frosty, phony "Bill and Hillary" working relationships, with just as much public affection. The team has used four different closers and tried so many Nomar Replacements at shortstop, I think Moonlight Graham gets his chance next week. Players kept going down like a platoon in a Vietnam War movie, and not just soldiers, either; we're talking *big* guns, including four of the best players on the team (Nomar, Pedro, Everett, and Varitek). An astounding 18 (and counting) players have bristled at the manager at various points this season (mostly overpriced veterans platooning in their contract years), and the ones who didn't gripe also didn't speak English (giving them something in common with their manager). Somehow, the ongoing dysfunction hasn't affected the team on the field.

Have you ever rooted for a baseball team that staged enough comebacks to provide that constant feeling of "Hey, we're still in this!" even when they're down by five in the ninth on a 100-degree afternoon at Comiskey Park? That's the 2001 Red Sox. These guys are a 25-man homage to Jason Voorhees. Even after backbreaking losses (like Derek Lowe squandering a two-out, two-run lead in Toronto in the span of about three nanoseconds),

231 In June, reader J. Contoyannis sent me the mailbag question, "If the 2001 Red Sox were the cast of *90210*, who would be who?" Here were my answers:

- Nomar (Brandon Walsh): Goody two-shoes, the rock of the show, incredibly consistent, you can't imagine life without him.
- Pedro (Dylan McKay): Mysterious, floats in and out of episodes, his best work is better than anyone else's best work. I mean, can't you imagine Pedro saying something like "May the bridges I burn lead the way"?
- Manny (Valerie Malone): A late addition that pushed the show over the top...took things to the next level from her/his previous show/team (*Saved by the Bell*/ Cleveland)...every scene/AB keeps fans in their seats...both have made out with **Mark-Paul Gosselaar**.
- Dan Duquette (Mr. Walsh): Butts in a lot, very high self-esteem, fallen light years from the promise of a few years ago. Although Duquette has

never come up with anything remotely approaching Mr. Walsh's intro in the opening credits, when James Eckhouse whirls around with the "That's right, I'm Mr. F-ing Walsh" smile.

• Jimy Williams (Andrea Zuckerman): You never stop hoping that they'll go away.

• Derek Lowe (David Silver): Cheesy, entertaining, battled some personal problems, and the team relies on him more than you think. Bonus points: **I bet Derek Lowe knows the words to "Baby It's You Girl."**

• Troy O'Leary (Josh Richland): They're both dead.

• Jason Varitek (Donna Martin): Improves every year and came a long way over the years. Although Varitek doesn't have anything on his body approaching Tori's creepy cleavage that looks like when you press your finger in hamburger meat and the print sticks.

• David Cone (Kelly Taylor): Kelly was been burned in fire, joined a cult, was raped by a mugger, and shot in a drive-by, suffered amnesia, suffered a miscarriage, nearly burned to death in a fire, became addicted to diet

these Sox have an uncanny knack for bouncing back and winning the following game. As David Cone described them this week, they're "unflappable."

My theory is that constant chaos actually *helped* the Red Sox as a team. When goofy things happen day after day after day, you become immune to the distractions after awhile. Nobody represents the 2001 Red Sox better than the utterly unflappable Manny Ramirez, who looks exactly the same whether he's chewing tobacco in the dugout, playing catch with a teammate, sharing a burrito with Rich Garces, or batting in the ninth inning at Yankee Stadium in front of 60,000 screaming fans. You could land a small plane in right field during a Manny at-bat and he wouldn't notice.

2) It's never a good idea to anger the Babe, not even if you're the best pitcher in 35 years.

Curse schmurse. Do you *really* think Babe Ruth is devoting his afterlife to haunting the Red Sox franchise? Wouldn't he devote his energies to haunting Roger Maris and Hank Aaron, or taking revenge on the extended families of William Bendix and John Goodman? With that said, follow this timeline:

May 30: Pedro follows a shutout over the Yanks (four hits, 13 Ks) by telling reporters, "Wake up the Bambino and let me face him—I'll drill him in the ass." At this point, he's 7–1 with a 1.44 ERA and 121 strikeouts in 81 innings (as well as 67–18 with a 2.16 ERA in his three-plus years in Boston).

June 4: Pedro gets yanked after 90 pitches in an eventual loss at Yankee Stadium.

June 9: Pedro gets racked by the Phillies. Days later, we find out that he's suffering "shoulder stiffness" and might miss a start.

June 21: Pedro pitches five innings in Tampa Bay, barely topping 93 on the gun.

June 26: Pedro leaves an eventual home loss against Tampa in the fifth inning and goes on the disabled list. Eventually we find out that he's suffering problems with his rotator cuff and these problems may require surgery.

(Translation: Even if there's no such thing as a curse on the Red Sox, just to be safe, let's all avoid trash-talking the Babe ever again.) **232**

3) The more foreign-born players on the roster, the merrier. Would someone like Hideo Nomo or Hipolito Pichardo pay attention to a media-driven "curse" or worry about a fan base that overreacts to every loss and bad break? Are those things even on their radar screen? Could that be one of the reasons why this year's team (featuring a sizable collection of Asians, Dominicans, and other Latinos) has seemed so unflappable? Might that make the crucial, push-us-over-the-top difference between the Pedro Era teams and the Yaz/Rice/Williams Era teams? Should we just build a team with 25 guys who can't speak English? Or am I grasping at straws here?

(Wait, don't answer that.)**233**

4) Few things in life are more enjoyable than a reliever with a cheesy mullet who comes out of the bullpen with Foreigner blasting.

For further evidence, please refer to the Rod Beck Era in Boston (1999–2001).

5) The only thing more fun than one 300-pound Latin reliever is *two* 300-pound Latin relievers.

Rich Garces and Carlos Castillo—wait, that's more than 600 pounds of fastballs! There hasn't been a tag-team with this much ooomph since Tugboat and Earthquake teamed up in the WWF back in the early '90s. I'm giddy just writing about it. When will the Red Sox bring back the bullpen car, for everyone's safety? And while we're at it, why did they ever get rid of the bullpen car in the first place? Was there a greater invention than the bullpen car? Didn't the mere sight of the bullpen car send you into a veritable frenzy as a kid? Why are younger generations of baseball fans getting gypped out of the bullpen car experience? ANSWER ME!!!!!!!!

6) Apparently, anyone can manage a successful baseball team as long as you have a head, two arms, and two legs.

We've actually known this for years, but Jimy's performance this season drilled it into our heads for life. Before we delve briefly into Planet Jimy, please remember that baseball managers have the easiest coaching job of any professional sport. How difficult is it to pick a five-man rotation, fill out a starting lineup every day, make sure all 25 players stay awake, juggle the bullpen so it doesn't get burnt out, handle the wide array of egos and handle the media as well? It's hard…but it's not that

pills, battled an eating disorder, and thought she had AIDS. And she still didn't struggle over the past year as much as David Cone did.

• Mo Vaughn (Brenda Walsh): She shouldn't have left the show; he shouldn't have left Boston.

• Carl Everett (Claire Arnold): Always complaining about something, produces decent numbers, has the rare ability to take things off the table and put things on the table at the exact same time.

• Tim Wakefield (Steve Sanders): He's great to have around, you had some good times with him…but you never actually want him involved in key plots.

• El Guapo (Nat Busichio): Incredibly entertaining, for reasons you can't possibly explain. My favorite Nat moment of all time was the time he screamed at Dylan during the watershed "Dylan's Drinking Again" season, **"Come on Dylan, SHOW ME SOME TRUST!"** Even Guapo couldn't top that one.

232 You have to admit, this was a crazy coincidence—Pedro was *never* the same after that May 30th game. Well, until he signed with the Mets.

233 Obviously I didn't know it at the time, but I was writing a blueprint for what unfolded with the "Idiots" on the 2004 team.

234 When Jimy was finally fired in mid-August, I wrote a column called "Inside the Manager's Studio," where Jimy went on James Lipton's show and gave crazy answers like "If you keep searching for answers you drive yourself crazy and end up feeling like **a kangaroo with a hangover**" and "You don't get bonus points for a good parachute landing." I planned on including it in the book, but it didn't hold up that well. By the way, Jimy went on to manage the Astros, who fired him during the 2004 All-Star Break, and then rolled off something like a 65–3 streak and came within one game of the World Series.

hard. Coaching an NFL team, now that's hard. When you're managing a baseball team, you're basically steering a boat—as long as you don't ram into anything, you're fine. As the old saying goes, "Managers can't win baseball games, but they sure can lose them."

(Actually, I just made that up. Sounded good, though, didn't it?)

Jimy apparently believes that managers *can* win baseball games. Although history has proven that baseball teams thrive on continuity and defined roles, Jimy thrives on insecurity and general chaos. He tosses out goofy lineups, relies on game-to-game whims, inexplicably shifts people around in different roles from week to week, drives his players batty and explains everything with his two-word, Rain Man-esque catch phrase: "Manager's decision."[234] Somehow it's working, even though the best compliment you could give him is, "He keeps everyone on their toes" (which makes it sound like you're describing a Doberman). I've given up trying to figure it out. For instance, there have been a variety of links between Hatteberg and the phrase "no. 2" this season, but the batting order shouldn't be one of them. And yet there's Jimy sticking Scott Hatteberg in the no. 2 spot against Toronto last night…and Hatteberg goes 2-for-4. Of course he does. Sometimes you wonder if Jimy could walk back and forth across the Mass Pike at rush hour without getting hit.

7) Note to every Sox opponent: Don't give Manny anything to hit with the game on the line.

I mean, *ever*.

(Actually, there might be some AL managers who don't know about this one yet. Lemme re-write this one…)

8) When Manny comes up with the game on the line, definitely challenge him and definitely throw him a fastball.

That's right. This guy's a bigger choke artist than Inari Vachs—he has been killing us all season. The $160 million fraud, I call him. What a waste of cash.

9) Nothing's more frustrating than a closer who can't be trusted.

Statistically, Lowe has been decent: 4.06 ERA, 20 saves in 23 opportunities, seven losses, one brief demotion in April. Dig deeper and you'll find Lowe has allowed 88 baserunners in 57.2 innings and squandered leads or ties *8* times in 45 appearances. Yikes! Those numbers don't tell the whole story. You can have faulty field-goal kickers, up-and-down goalies, point guards who never seem to make that clutch 15-footer. For my money, a shaky baseball closer tops them all on the Agonizing Scale. You become paralyzed by this constant feeling of dread. Even when you're winning in the late innings, you can't enjoy the lead because you're too busy thinking to yourself, "Oh God, *he's* coming in."

In Lowe's case, you spend the ninth rooting for things to go smoothly, but something happens (a single or a walk), so you start searching for signs that he's okay, and he is okay, but maybe something else happens (a stolen base, a walk) and then... BOOM! He makes the face. My buddy J-Bug calls it The Derek Lowe Face,[235] a distant cousin to The Troy Aikman Face. Remember when Aikman would suffer a concussion, and TV cameras would catch him on the sidelines (glassy-eyed, totally shellshocked) as the Dallas trainers would shove 10 pounds of smelling salts in front of his nose? And Aikman would continue to stare onto the field, undaunted, looking like he just saw Milton Berle naked? That was the Aikman Face. Lowe's face freezes like Aikman's did, only with considerably more anguish. Imagine someone taking a dump and suddenly realizing that there's no toilet paper in the bathroom. Exactly. As soon as Lowe starts making that face, the umpires should halt the game and award it to whomever the Red Sox are playing. I have to admit, I'm *haunted* by The Derek Lowe Face. I spend every one of his appearances saying to the TV, "Don't make it, don't make the face, stay cool, come on, stay with us, hang tough kiddo." It never ends.

(Note to the Red Sox: I'd like to order the Ugueth Urbina please? And hold the mayo.)

10) "Enjoy the game!"

This was the Phillies' promotional slogan in the late '80s. Remember how teams used "catchy" phrases to promote ticket sales back then? Philly was so woeful one year that they simply told their fans, "Enjoy the game!" In other words, here's a ballpark, two baseball teams, and a seat. Enjoy the game!

There's a lesson there. Sometimes you have to overlook your nutty manager or your closer who doubles as a human roller-coaster ride. You have to forget that your bullpen can't ride in the same elevator without risking a calamity or that three days can't pass without somebody bitching about something. You

235 This is one of my favorite running gimmicks over the years, dating back to The Troy Aikman Face on my old website, carrying over to ESPN.com with The Derek Lowe Face and continuing with The Peyton Manning Face to this day. More on page 158.

can't dwell on the fact that your team only sent one representative to the All-Star Game, and worse yet, it didn't even piss you off because nobody else deserved to go. You can't get caught up in the jarring possibility that bad karma knocked your two best players out for the season. Sometimes, you simply have to enjoy the game. On Tuesday, I watched a rejuvenated Cone scatter six hits, three runs and about 15 "at-him" balls over six-plus innings for his sixth win. I watched a team full of .270 hitters grinding out two-out RBI hits like they were going out of style. I braced myself in the late innings for a Toronto comeback that never happened, even listening with both hands covering my face as Lowe slammed the door in the ninth. And when I was leaving wretched Fenway and regaining the feeling in my legs, I realized to myself, "Hey, I *enjoyed* that game."

And yes, there's another lesson here, the one about pathetic Red Sox fans who always think "maybe this is the year" and "something strange is going on here" and "I just have a good feeling about this team" and everything else that makes us feel more comfortable about the Sox Team Du Jour. But you know what? Maybe this *is* the year. Something strange is going on here. Maybe we *should* have a good feeling about this team. Maybe we should kick back and enjoy the game.

(Just remember to load up on ulcer medication first.)**236**

236 Within a few weeks, the team quickly self-destructed. Lowlights over the last two months of the season included: A 6–22 streak down the stretch; Everett cursing out interim manager Joe Kerrigan five days after 9/11, then getting sent home for the season; Ugie Urbina almost fighting Nixon and Varitek on the team charter after they told him to lower the volume on his boom box; pitching coach John Cumberland getting fired because of an alleged drinking problem; and Pedro throwing a bullpen tantrum in mid-September and going MIA. As I wrote in September, "Did any team in the history of baseball have worse chemistry? **I keep waiting for them to sign Shannen Doherty** and Janeane Pettibone for the final week."

DO I HAVE ANYTHING LEFT?

July 31, 2001

You probably don't remember Tom Seaver's aborted comeback...but I remember. Probably because he hummed a fastball at my head.

I'll explain.

Seaver was eight months removed from playing in Boston, where his right knee buckled during the pennant stretch in 1986. You can drive yourself crazy thinking about these things, but a healthy Seaver would have started Game Four against the Mets, and there's a good chance that no. 41 would have submitted one of those turn-back-the-clock starts that make baseball so special—something of the "seven innings, four hits, two earned runs and six Ks" variety against his former team—as a deafening Fenway crowd swayed with every pitch. Maybe that game would have turned the series around. Maybe there wouldn't have been a Game Six. Maybe it would have been the perfect swan song for Seaver's career.

Instead, Al Nipper pitched Game Four and was summarily shellacked.[237] Seaver became a relative afterthought, tossed aside after the season and quickly forgotten by the Boston fans. Probably gnawed at him, too. Even at 42, with nothing else to prove—311 career wins, 3,640 strikeouts, three Cy Youngs, one ring, unofficial title of "Best Pitcher of His Generation"—Seaver couldn't walk away. Not yet. Hoping to finish his career in New York, he spent the winter awaiting a phone call from the Yankees that never came. Naturally, everyone assumed the old man was finished. But when Dwight Gooden submitted a dirty urine sample to the Mets, the lightbulb over Seaver's head started flickering. After David Cone and Bobby Ojeda suffered injuries in May, the bulb was officially beaming. Did Tom Terrific have another season left in him? Was the risk (potential humiliation) worth the reward (the perfect ending to a Hall of Fame career)?

In a nutshell...did he have anything left?

As Seaver was mulling over his secret comeback, he was involved in a business deal with the father of my buddy, Gus Ramsey, who lived in Seaver's hometown of Greenwich, Connecticut.[238] Since the deal brought him over to Gus's

237 Nipper could have been the worst pitcher to start a World Series game in the last 25 years; his combined ERA in 1986 and 1987 was 5.41. But here's why you had to love Nipper: When hitters charged the mound in the '80s, pitchers usually reacted in one of three ways: **1)** attempted tackle; **2)** wild punches; **3)** fled for their life. Nipper changed everything in '86, after Seattle's Phil Bradley objected to a fastball planted between his fifth and sixth vertebrae. When Bradley dashed for the mound, Nipper ripped off his glove, stepped quickly to his right (avoiding Bradley's rush like a matador) and pummeled him with his *left* hand (so he wouldn't injure his pitching hand). This genius move paved the way for **the watershed Robin Ventura-Nolan Ryan beating** in 1993. Nip also threw at Darryl Strawberry in spring training, 1987—retaliation for Straw's HR trot in Game Seven of the World Series. And he was one-third of the infamous 1996 Boston coaching staff (along with Tim Johnson and Kevin Kennedy) that stood motionless on the top step of the dugout, wearing matching bushy mustaches, Raybans and warmup jackets, looking like they were participating in a photo shoot for gay baseball porn. I guess what I'm trying to say is this: The Al Nipper Era, at the very least, was entertaining.

238 This was the great **Wally Ramsey, my eighth grade english teacher and basketball coach** at the Greenwich Country Day School, as well as the guy who inspired my ESPN.com column about remodeling the Baseball Hall of Fame into an Egyptian pyramid (five levels in all, with the top level reserved for mega-legends like Ruth and Mays). Every writer has one person who came along in their formative years and made them think, "Hey, maybe I'm good at this." He was mine. I even thought about dedicating this book to him before realizing that my own father would hang himself. But hey, a tiny footnote in a 353-page book is almost as good as a dedication, right?

239 Looking back, that was a Hall of Fame Face, right up there with some of these: The Derek Lowe, Peyton Manning, Stan Humphries, and Troy Aikman Faces (the Mount Rushmore of this list); The

house a few times, Seaver quickly befriended Gus, a lifelong Mets fan who was only 19 at the time. Eventually, Seaver popped the question: "I brought my glove with me, you feel like throwing?"

After prying his own tongue out of his throat, Gus found himself heading outside, on his own front yard, with one of the 10 greatest pitchers of all time. Within 10 minutes, Seaver worked up a sweat and started putting some mustard on the ball. Five more minutes passed, and given that Seaver was standing about 60 feet away, Gus squatted down like a catcher. Just felt right. Seaver didn't mind. He started ripping off pitches and punctuating them with different questions. You can catch a curveball, right? *(Pop!)* Okay if I throw a slider? *(Splack!)* Your hand starting to hurt yet? *(Ka-pow!)* Once he realized Gus could handle everything—and, more importantly, that Gus was willing to squat for the next three to four years straight—Seaver stopped talking and concentrated on his mechanics. They threw for 10 more minutes in relative silence, the ball popping back and forth between two gloves, Seaver grunting with every pitch. When it was over, Seaver dropped the bombshell, confessing that he was secretly considering a comeback with Gus's beloved Mets. He asked if Gus wouldn't mind catching him over the next week or so—a clandestine testing of the waters, if you will—and Gus quickly agreed before blacking out.

(Here's how random this whole thing was: Pick your favorite athlete of all time, then imagine that entire sequence of events somehow unfolding with you and that athlete. Seems unbelievable, right? Couldn't happen, right? Well, this happened.)

Over the next few days, Seaver kept dropping by Gus' house for not-so-impromptu games of catch. I started stalking the premises, dropping by more frequently than the mailman in hopes of a Seaver sighting. No dice. One afternoon, right after I had gotten home from school, Gus gave me the word: "He's coming over…*right now.*" After shattering the land speed record and beating him to the house, Seaver seemed friendly enough when we were introduced, despite the fact I was staring at him with the "Holy crap, it's Tom Seaver!" Face.[239] We made some small talk. And then it happened.

"Hey, why don't you grab a bat and come outside with us?" Seaver asked me. "You can pretend you're a batter. I want to see what it's like with somebody standing there."

(Well, that's what he probably said. All I can really remember is the "Hey" part, then seeing little white dots.)

Outside, I watched from the sidelines as Gus and Tom warmed up. They started out playing long toss, looking like two outfielders killing time between innings, before Gus settled into his crouch. Seaver kept throwing soft fastballs and loosening up, finally barking out, "All right, I'm ready." And it wasn't like he went from throwing 60 to 80 in two pitches. The early throws were all motion—a rock back, a rock forward, a twist of the hips, a flick of the wrist—as he slowly started getting his body involved. Within minutes, he was bringing his glove over his head, rearing back, whipping forward and firing the ball, his left leg swinging around for the finish, his right knee inching closer and closer to the ground with every pitch (the Seaver trademark).

(Quick interjection: Witnessing this evolution in person was simply incredible, like seeing the birth of a child or something. For whatever reason, we take professional athletes for granted and ignore the little things, like the effortless way Robbie Alomar starts a double play, or the way Randy Moss finds that extra gear and breezes by an unsuspecting cornerback. Watch enough games and you forget to notice these things. But to see this 42-year-old man round himself into pitching form over a 15-minute span in my buddy's front yard was breathtaking to watch. One of those moments in your formative years that you don't forget.)

Once Seaver was ready, I stood in front of Gus, who had the same look on his face that Wyatt and Gary had in *Weird Science* when Kelly LeBrock first walked into the room. The previous summer, Gus and I had finished a 162-game, simulated Micro League Baseball season between the All-Time Mets and the All-Time Red Sox on my Apple computer,**240** and the 1973 Tom Seaver won our Imaginary Cy Young Award. Nine months later, he was pitching to us on Gus's front lawn. Undaunted, I dug into the imaginary batter's box, unveiled my finest impersonation of Carl Yastrzemski's stance—rigid posture, bat circling about my head—and stood there as Seaver chucked pitches by me.**241**

Ssssssssssss. That's what every pitch sounded like. Like a snake's hiss. Every pitch was accompanied by a barely audible grunt from Seaver, followed by the ball smacking into Gus' mitt, so it really sounded like this:

Huhhhhhhhh...*ssssssssssss*...SPLAT!!

Admiral Stockdale "Who am I? How did I get here?" Face; the Andrew Shue "I can't believe I'm being out-acted by David Charvet right now" Face; the Ashton Kutcher "Holy shit, **I'm banging Demi Moore!**" Face; the Byung-Hyun Kim and Calvin Schiraldi "Please, come out and get me" Faces (distant cousins); the Michael Corleone "You had a fucking abortion?!?!?!" and "Holy shit, I'm about to shoot Solazzo and McCluskey" Faces; the Eli Manning "How long do I have to hold up this Chargers jersey?" Face; the Tom Cruise "I'm trying to cry after Goose's death but I can't make the tears come, so I'll look like I'm taking a dump instead" Face; the Smiling Jack Ross "I can't believe he asked Col. Jessup about the Code Red" Face; the Jeff George "I might get waived at halftime" Face; the Jon Gruden and Mike Shanahan "I'm very, VERY angry" Faces (distant cousins); the Mike McD "I just lost my shirt to Teddy KGB" Face; the Brian Billick "I can't believe these officials are so fucking dumb" Face; the Karl Malone "I wish I hadn't pushed so hard for the '97 MVP" Face; the Steve Spurrier "I should have fucking stayed at Florida" Face; the Thomas

Seaver: "Fastball."

Huhhhhhhhh...*sssssssssssss*...SPLAT!!

Seaver: "Slider."

Huhhhhhhhh...*sssssssssssss*...SPLAT!!

His fastball seemed somewhat hittable, as long as you knew it was coming. The slider looked like a fastball, only it suddenly and inexplicably darted down and to the right. (How does *anyone* hit a slider? You got me.) And he threw two types of curveballs: a standard curve (a slow fastball heading straight for my head that would miraculously swerve across the imaginary plate), and a lollipop curve (like the one Bill Lee blooped to Tony Perez in the '75 World Series). I had no illusions about hitting the standard curve, but the lollipop looked positively inviting. During one stretch, he ripped off five or six in a row...and by the last one, I had the curve timed and everything.

"I think I could hit that one," I yelled out.

"Oh, really?" Seaver smiled. "Why don't you dig in there and wait for it again?"

So I did.

Huhhhhhhhh...

(Wait a second, that's coming at my head...)

Sssssssssssss...

(Good God, run for your lives!)

Splack!!

He actually aimed that fastball about a foot over my head, but I got the message. I wouldn't be digging in for the lollipop curve again. As I pulled my heart out of my small intestine, Seaver smiled—a thin smile, but a smile nonetheless—and waited for a giggling Gus to toss the ball back to him. After 20 more minutes, Seaver called it quits and everyone went on their merry way.

As it turned out, the Seaver-Ramsey battery lasted one more week before the Mets finally contacted Seaver, setting off a round of comeback talks that came to fruition in June. Tom Terrific was coming home to the Mets. Considering that the comeback made the back page of every New York paper, and considering Gus and I shared his secret all along, we held an enormous stake in the whole thing. Maybe that's why it hurt so much when Seaver's comeback sputtered in Triple-A. In his final simulated start for Tidewater, the Mets hitters gave no. 41 a beating straight out of a sports movie; a no-name catcher named Barry Lyons even went 6-for-6. Six-for-six! Seaver called

Hill "We beat Kentucky oh my God!" Face; **the Kobe Bryant "Everyone hates me" Face**; the Bill Cowher "Get that linesman over here so I can scream at him and unintentionally spit all over him" Face; the Dan Reeves "I have to stay totally, completely calm or I might go into cardiac arrest" Face; the Nick Anderson "I Just Blew Game One of the '95 Finals" Face; the Joel Goodson "Are you ready for me, Ralph?" Face; Shaq's "I really need to make this free throw" Face; and, of course, the "Stop staring at my daughter" Face (works for any father of anyone under 18).

240 In a related story, both of us were single at the time.

241 Upon further review, I probably looked more like Bob Bailey in the '78 playoff game against the Yanks—you know, since my bat never moved.

it quits two days later. Gus donated his catcher's mitt to the Clandestine Comeback Hall of Fame. I had a lively "Seaver threw a fastball at my head" story to tell my friends. And Seaver had his answer.

So why am I telling you this? I was thinking about Seaver last Sunday, as David Cone gritted his way through another six-inning effort at Fenway Park. Sox fans didn't expect much from the 38-year-old after he struggled famously last season, but Coney quickly emerged as a clubhouse leader, bona fide good luck charm, and potential no. 2 starter in the playoffs.[242] Other than their impressive resumes and the Boston connection, there are eerie parallels between Cone's revival and Seaver's aborted comeback. Both peaked as pitchers in New York, on the biggest stage possible. Both waited for one last phone call from the Yankees that never came. And both felt a nagging need to return one final time—not for financial reasons, but because they needed to find the answer to one question: *Do I have anything left?*

Invariably, you find out the hard way—by Barry Lyons rocking you for six hits and a high school punk telling you, "I think I can hit that"—or you keep chugging along and staving off Father Time. Maybe you even get into a groove, like a musician or writer, and you tune out everything and reach that elusive zone where everything falls into place, and you're painting corners, and you're keeping hitters off-balance and playing them like the cello, and you're reaching back for that extra oomph for your fastball and somehow finding it, and even though you're on a 95-pitch count, it feels like you could throw 300.

That's what it feels like to be David Cone right now. Unlike Seaver 14 years ago, Cone's tank isn't empty yet. He has something left. He has his answer. And in a memorable Red Sox season with more twists and turns than a Grisham novel, that's been the most pleasant surprise of all.

Coney's back.[243]

242 It's hard to believe that this 2001 Red Sox team self-destructed because of bad clubhouse chemistry when they had two Hall of Fame "Great guys to have in the clubhouse" guys—Cone and Bret Saberhagen. I always pictured them hanging out in a Baltimore hotel bar until 4 a.m. and buying Tony Massarotti tequila shots until he throws up, or taking Hillenbrand into **the Champagne Room at the Gold Club** for an extra-special "You hit your first major league homer" lap dance, or even sitting in the clubhouse during a rain delay, playing poker in their underwear and ragging on El Guapo. Not sure why this didn't work out.

243 Pretty much right after this column was posted, the Red Sox went into the tank and Jimy Williams was fired two weeks later. Cone finished with a 9–7 record and a 4.31 ERA in 135 innings. In the irony of ironies, he tried a comeback with the Mets in 2003 and only lasted four starts (18 IP, 13 ER) before calling it quits. Just like Seaver.

THAT GAME

October 25, 2001

You can drive yourself crazy just thinking about it.

Fifteen pitches. Fifteen. Any of them could have brought the Red Sox their first championship in 68 years. Four Mets came to the plate with two outs. Boston came within one strike three times. The Mets scraped together a flimsy three-run rally on consecutive line-drive singles, a bloop single, a wild pitch and an error. Ray Knight crossed the plate with the winning run, so overwhelmed that he was running full-speed with his hands behind his head. Everything unfolded in just twelve minutes. And nothing would ever be the same.

For many Sox fans, Game Six changed the way we approached sports—the pain was *too* intense, *too* overwhelming—and that feeling of devastation seemed much more consuming than the flip side (being on the winning side). The sacrifices were too great. Before '86, we feared the worst. After '86, we expected the worst. There's a difference. That night linked every Red Sox fan for life, a collective sports catastrophe that nobody else can fully comprehend. We remember our whereabouts on October 25, 1986, the same way people remember JFK's assassination and the O.J. Bronco Chase.[244] We blame ourselves for what happened in our own little ways. We rehash those 12 minutes in our minds, again and again, and it never really goes away. We're connected by Game Six, all of us, inexorably. Sports shouldn't mean this much, but sometimes, it does.

244 If I was writing this column today, I would have thrown in **Kathy Bates' nude scene** in *About Schmidt*.

I watched That Game at a friend's house in Connecticut, one of those classic, impromptu "Somebody's parents are away for the weekend!" high school parties straight out of a John Hughes movie. That afternoon, I had agonized over being Mr. Social (attending the party) or Mr. Sox Fan (staying home for the game), eventually deciding that I wanted to party after the Sox captured their first World Series of my lifetime.

(I probably should have stayed home.)

(I wish I had stayed home.)

(I was only 17.)

I went to the party.

It never dawned on me that they would lose. We had a 3–2

lead in the series and Clemens was pitching, and Dave Henderson's series-saving home run in California (Game Five, ALCS)[245] had reversed the franchise's deadly karma (or so we thought). Raising the stakes, that '86 team was my team. Everybody has one baseball team that meant a little too much, a season where you lived and died with every pitch, every mood swing, every losing streak, every foible, every mistake, every triumph, *everything*. Usually that team arrives in your teens, when sports carry too much weight in general. As you grow older and your priorities fall in line, you realize that sports doesn't warrant that level of devotion, especially when many athletes couldn't care less about their fans (like when Clemens skipped town in '96 and never looked back). When enough of these slights pile up over the years, you find yourself not caring as much.

Back in '86, I cared. Fifteen years later, I can still rattle off everything from April to September off the top of my head. Clemens whiffed 20 Mariners on April 29. Boggs was hitting over .400 in late May before wrenching his back while putting on cowboy boots (or so the story goes—wink, wink). Don Baylor delivered a three-run double at Yankee Stadium in June, and the cameras showed him pumping his fist toward the bench...and there were all the Boston players, standing on the top of the dugout and pumping their fists back (so much for "25 guys in 25 cabs")[246]. They started winning wacky games, like the time an Angels third baseman dropped a game-ending pop-up, or an Indians game that was called after five innings because fog had rolled in from Lake Erie.[247] When those wacky victories start piling up, you start saying to yourself, "Hmmmmmm, maybe it's our year." And since the Patriots and Celtics had just played for championships (with the Celts winning their 16th title), we naturally assumed that our good fortune would continue with the World Series. Our collective confidence had never been higher.[248]

And I was only 17.

Come playoff time, every pitch mattered. During the Angels-Sox series, I remember bristling because Angels catcher Bob Boone kept pulling errant pitches into the strike zone and stealing calls. Now, I wouldn't care. Back then, it infuriated me to the point of near-hyperventilation. I spent three weeks feeling that way, 14 playoff games in all, always on the edge. When Hendu struck his series-saving home run in Game Five, I blacked

245 Al Michaels' second-greatest moment: "Deep to left and Downing goes back. And it's GONE! Unbelievable! (Incredulous pause and Hendu skips happily towards first base.) You're looking at one for the ages here. Astonishing! Anaheim Stadium was one strike away from turning into Fantasyland! And now the Red Sox lead 6–5! The Red Sox get four runs in the ninth on a pair of two-run homers by Don Baylor and Dave Henderson!"

246 Gammons's famous phrase that described the not-so-close Red Sox teams from the Yaz-Rice Era.

247 Prompting Oil Can Boyd's quote, "That's what you get for building a ballpark on the ocean."

248 That was a once-in-a-generation team: Gifted stars (Clemens, Boggs, Rice, Bruce Hurst); likable vets (Evans, Buckner, Baylor, Seaver, Henderson); one world-class goofball (the Can, who nearly became a Section 8 in August and earned himself an *SI* cover); the token Reliever Who Drives Everyone Crazy (embattled closer Bob Stanley, who ended

out for the only time in my life. Watching the game at my Aunt Jen's house, apparently, I leapt from the sofa and sprinted around the first floor before bursting through the kitchen door and ending up outside. All I remember is standing outside in the middle of the street, jumping up and down and wondering to myself, "How did I get out here?"

Hey, I know I've changed over the years—matured, softened, all that jazz—but still, that was the last innocent baseball season for me. I wasn't jaded, wasn't cynical, wasn't fearing the worst. Every Sox fan remembers the moment when they lost their baseball cherry; for me, it happened when they collapsed at Shea. I never saw it coming. Blame Buckner, blame Schiraldi, blame Stanley, blame Gedman...you could make a case for all of them, but you'd be wrong. Blame me. I'm the one who called his mother with a 5–3 lead in the 10th, asking her to record the rest of the game because, and I quote, "I want to have it on tape when we win the World Series." It never entered my mind that they would blow it. Call me naive, call me a fool, blame the success of those Bird Era Celtics teams for spoiling me. All I remember was that the Red Sox were about to win the World Series and I wanted it on tape. Well, I got it on tape all right. Right between the eyes. You only lose your cherry once.

I remember everything. Vividly. Thirteen snapshots from a photo album of baseball hell.

1) Hendu belts one into the left field stands in the 10th. Pandemonium.

(There are few sure things in life, but this is one of them: Had the Red Sox prevailed in Game Six, Dave Henderson would have become a New England legend. L-E-G-E-N-D. This would have extended far beyond a mere statue in Faneuil Hall; I'm talking "Paul Revere" proportions here. Maybe the most underrated subplot of that entire night.)

2) Same inning: Boggs doubles home Dewey Evans and then scores an insurance run. You could smell it. It was going to happen.

(Here's where I made the infamous phone call to Mom. In a surreal subplot, Mom accidentally used my tape of Game Five of the ALCS, somehow taping over the entire ninth inning, including Hendu's homer, with the tape ending as they were showing the replay of Hendu hopping around the bases. The lesson here, as always: Never let your mother, wife, sister, daughter, girlfriend or mistress near the VCR under any circumstances.)

up losing his job to Schiraldi); and The Manager Who Drives Everyone Crazy (John McNamara, who graduated with honors from **Professor Don Zimmer's school** of Resting Your Players as Little as Possible). They had something for everyone. Even the writers covering them were memorable: Gammons, Shaughnessy, Montville. Right team, right place, right time.

249 During Game Four of the 2004 World Series, when Keith Foulke came in for the ninth inning, let's just say that there were no "What happens now?" thoughts.

3) Bottom of the tenth: Schiraldi quickly mows down Wally Backman and Keith Hernandez.

(We later found out that Hernandez departed for the clubhouse, where he removed his uniform, poured a drink, and smoked a butt. Nice leadership there. No, I'm not bitter.)

4) Now I'm standing. The Red Sox are about to win the World Series.

(I remember feeling a weird twinge in my stomach, like, "What happens now?" What happens when something that you've wished for your entire life actually happens? What's the proper display of emotion? I remember an empty feeling, almost like The Chase was more fun than The Payoff. Later on, I would hate myself for thinking this.)[249]

5) Carter rips a line-drive single. No biggie. I'm still standing.

6) Mitchell follows with another single. Second and first. Still two outs. I'm sitting.

(In baseball, two or three innings serve as a microcosm for an entire season. You probably don't remember this, but Boston's bullpen crapped the bed all season—they were about as reliable as a used condom. In the moment of truth, they failed. That's why New York ended up winning and Boston ended up losing. I firmly believe this.)

7) Everything starts to slow down. The camera shows Clemens sitting in the dugout—*why does he look as nervous as me?*—followed by one of those prolonged, so-close-you-can-count-his-whiskers closeups of Schiraldi, who suddenly has the proverbial deer-in-the-headlights look going (and yes, in the storied history of deer-in-the-headlight looks during sporting events, Schiraldi's face remains the one to beat), followed by Bob Stanley frantically getting loose in the Sox bullpen. In succession, these images felt like a punch in the stomach, followed by a kick to the groin, followed by a chair shot over the head. Oh, God. Oh, my God. OH...MY...GOD...

(That's when we knew: Something bad was going to happen. You could feel it in the air. One of those Hall of Fame "Pit in your stomach moments" that you don't forget. I will never forget. I will never, ever forget. This was bigger than all of us.)

8) Schiraldi somehow gets two strikes on Knight, who fists a bloop single that drifts over second base and falls in. You can't

have a cheaper hit than that. You just can't. Carter scores, Mitchell to third, Mets trailing by one. I am frozen. I cannot move. I am frozen. I cannot move. I am frozen. I cannot move.

(In a movie, this would be the moment when the CD skips to a stop and the room goes silent.)

9) McNamara strolls out. It takes forever. Schiraldi limps off and, unfortunately, doesn't get pancaked by the bullpen car. Stanley jogs in wearing a Grim Reaper outfit. We need one more out, the Mets are trying to pull off the greatest World Series comeback ever, and only one man can stop them...the Human Rollercoaster Ride, Bob Stanley.

(Imagine the reliever who frightened you more than anyone else over the years. Now imagine this exact situation, only with that reliever jogging in to save the day. See what I mean? This was a sports event crossed with a horror movie. And I fucking called my mother to tape the ninth inning. It was my fault. This was all my fault.)

10) Now Mookie Wilson strides to the plate. The fans at Shea are absolutely beside themselves, like Mardi Gras revelers watching Jennifer Aniston flash them from a balcony. They can smell it. NBC's cameras keep showing the Mets standing on the top dugout step, looking alive, looking confident, looking hungry. Then they show the Sox dugout—guys chewing their nails, guys staring onto the field in shock, guys looking like they might start dry-heaving. Pure torture. Somehow, Stanley gets two strikes on Mookie, including a foul ball chopper down the third base line (THIRD OUT! THIRD OUT!) that cruelly curves foul. Pure agony. This can't be happening.

And then...

11) Trying to come inside for strike three, Stanley throws his next pitch at Mookie's feet, which—given the situation and the stakes—was probably the worst pitch in the history of the sport that didn't involve Tim Robbins. Mookie jumps out of the way and Geddie (who played in something like 175.9999999 of a possible 176 games that season) can't slide over to block the pitch in time. Wild pitch. Tie game. Utter despair.

(One of the five worst moments of my life. Sad but true. The 1986 World Series ended right here. No way the Sox could have bounced back. Ever. Simply impossible. Somehow Stanley,

Schiraldi, and Gedman escaped relatively unscathed in the historical sense; the common fan blames Buckner. True Red Sox fans know better.)

12) NBC's cameras show a smiling Carter hastily putting on his catcher's equipment in the dugout, as if this game was actually headed into the 11th inning. Not a chance. Between the delirious fans at Shea and the suffocating bad karma vibes emanating from New England—and let's face it, we deserve some blame here, too, because every diehard Sox fan stopped believing the moment Ray Knight's single landed behind the second base bag, if not before then, and if you don't think karma matters at all then you've obviously never played at a hot craps table in Vegas—they don't make salad forks big enough to resemble the collective one sticking out of the Red Sox.

(Heading into the next paragraph, I don't have enough space to defend Billy Buck, but let the record show that, along with Baylor, he was the heart and soul of this team; he had 110 RBI that season; he deserved to be out there; he couldn't have beaten Mookie to the first base bag if there was a CO_2 cannister attached to his butt cheeks; and the Mets would have won the damn game, anyway. Give him a break. Please.)[250]

13) Three pitches later: Mookie slaps a grounder to first base... it rolls between Buckner's legs and into rightfield...Knight scores from second. Mets 6, Red Sox 5.

(There are no words.)

After the Mets won the seventh game (the most ironclad lock in gambling history), they dismantled that Boston team faster than DeNiro knocking off his Lufthansa Heist cohorts in *Goodfellas*. Nine key members were sent packing within the next 15 months.[251] Buckner went from Borderline Hall-of-Famer and Gritty Competitor to Hall of Fame Goat and Punchline, eventually fleeing to Idaho and relative anonymity (the most unfair outcome of all). Henderson became "Just another random-yet-memorable postseason star," no more or less memorable than Francisco Cabrera or Buddy Biancalana. Clemens' mysterious departure from Game Six ignited questions about his intestinal fortitude for the rest of his career. Stanley, Gedman, Buckner, Schiraldi, and McNamara became part of Red Sox folklore, along with Galehouse, Pesky, Burton, Torrez and everyone else.

After Game Six, everything changed. With any hint of trouble

250 During the 2004 World Series, Buckner angrily denounced the whole **"Let's get Buckner off the hook"** angle, correctly pointing out that it was too little too late. And it was. Nobody received a more unfair deal from a single sporting event. Everyone forgets this now, but during the ninth inning of Game Five at Anaheim, Buckner screamed obscenities at Angels starter Mike Witt during his at-bat, looking for any possible edge... and ended up singling to start the big rally. I loved that guy.

251 McNamara, Buckner, Baylor, Hendu, Schiraldi, Can, Seaver, Al Nipper, Stanley and Shag Crawford.

during a big game, you can feel everyone tense up in Fenway. *Here we go again. Oh God.* Maybe that always happened, but I never noticed it until 1986. The media-created (rhymes with "schmurse") hasn't helped, although that affects the way others evaluate us more than anything. Red Sox fans are good fans—passionate, loyal, and perceptive almost to a fault—and we have an uncanny knack for blindly throwing ourselves behind our team and supporting them through thick and thin. Few franchises could say the same about their fans. It's just that we expect the worst now, which won't change until this team finally wins a championship.

Hey, I'm as guilty as anyone; Game Six haunts me to this day. If I'm flipping channels and stumble across the last few innings on Classic, I feel like Fred Goldman coming across the opening scene of *The Naked Gun*. And yet I never change the channel. Why? I don't know. It's the sports fan's version of penance. I watch. I can't help it. I can't believe what I'm watching. And it drives me crazy all over again. Fifteen pitches, any one of which could have won the World Series, and none of them did.**252**

252 I thought this predilection would disappear after they won it all… but during the winter of 2004, somebody was showing Game Six one night, I ended up watching the last 45 minutes, and it made me just as sick. When something scars you, no matter what happens after that you still have scars, right? For instance, in *Shawshank*, Andy may have escaped and had some good times in Mexico, but do you really think he looked back at **those two years with the Sistas** and thought, "You know what? That was a long time ago, I'm in a different place now."

At least I know I'm not alone. Three years ago, I attended a wedding in Nebraska of all places, eventually talking outside the reception with an old college friend named Dan Hausman, a diehard Sox fan whom I hadn't seen in seven years. Somehow we started talking about Game Six…and 45 minutes later, we were still out there. We were like two Vietnam War veterans remembering the time our entire platoon was wiped out. When I wrote a column about that conversation on my old website, the e-mails immediately started pouring in, one after the other. The experience seemed cathartic for many. I heard from fathers who blamed themselves for waking up their children to watch the 10th inning; sons who lost a parent within months of Game Six; brothers who wobbled out of Shea that night in an absolute fog.

In the big scheme of things, our experiences as sports fans don't matter nearly as much as we previously believed; September 11 rammed that lesson home the hard way. But for everyone who believes that 9/11 "put everything into perspective" and "proved that sports don't matter in the big scheme of things," well, I'm telling you, sports *still* matter. What happened with the New York Yankees over the past two weeks proved that, irrevocably and indisputably. September 11 demonstrated the fragility of life, the strength of human will, the depths of human compassion and understanding; the 2001 Yankees demonstrated the power of baseball and all its capabilities—how it can galvanize an ailing city, lift fans to a higher place, help us appreciate true greatness, remind us of how it feels when a group of people are screaming and cheering and feeling happy just to be alive.

Game Six of the '86 World Series? That was the flip side, for Red Sox fans, anyway. And let's just leave it at that.

SILENCE OF THE RAMS

February 4, 2002

NEW ORLEANS (Monday, 5 a.m. CT)—Now it all makes sense.

You bleed for your team, follow them through thick and thin, monitor every free-agent signing, immerse yourself in Draft Day, purchase the jerseys and caps, plan your Sundays around the games...and there's a little rainbow waiting at the end. You can't see it, but you know it's there. It's there. It has to be there. So you believe.[253]

Of course, there's one catch: You may never get there. Every fan's worst fear. All that energy over the years just getting displaced, no release, no satisfaction, nothing. Season after season, no championship...and then you die. I mean, isn't that what this is all about? Isn't that the nagging fear? That those little moral victories over the years won't pay off in the end—that one moment when everything comes together, when your team keeps winning, when you keep getting the breaks and you just can't lose?

And if none of this makes sense, well...it does to me. My team just won the Super Bowl. Patriots 20, Rams 17.

I was there. The Superdome. February 3, 2002. Section 347, row 15, seat 10. And I'm not writing this for you right now, I'm writing this for me. I don't want to forget anything that happened Sunday night. I was...

...Walking down Poydras Street before the game, seeing all the Patriots jerseys and sweatshirts, slapping strangers on the back, high-fiving people just because they were wearing a replica Grogan jersey, joining in random "Let's go Pats!" chants, feeling alive.[254]

...Finding my seat in the end zone, being pleasantly surprised that I was so close to the field, feeling like I could reach out and touch one of the uprights, telling everyone in my row that the Patriots were about to win the Super Bowl, noticing the doubt in their eyes, then reiterating it to them: "You don't understand, we are *winning* this game."

253 The most underrated part about seeing your team in the Super Bowl: seeing everyone in the stadium wearing jerseys from various years. It's like re-living your childhood all over again. Can you really put a price on the sight of a drunk Masshole wearing a no. 39 **Sam Bam Cunningham** jersey?

254 Why am I including a Patriots column here? By the fall of 2001, everyone in New England was in such a sports funk, we wouldn't have invested ourselves in a Red Sox comeback during the 2004 ALCS—we would have been sitting there waiting for something bad to happen, like in the "Wrestling With Shadows" column. But the Patriots changed that mentality. If the Fredo of the Boston sports scene could win a championship, then anything was possible. Even a Red Sox title.

255 Why hasn't "America" taken its rightful place alongside "The Star Spangled Banner" and "America, the Beautiful" in the rotation of patriotic songs before sporting events? Would anyone be against this? Is there a rule that these songs have to be at least 75 years old?

...Sitting through the interminable pregame show, trying to figure out why Paul McCartney was involved in a September 11-USA-Freedom angle when he's from freaking England, feeling *verklempt* when they showed Leon Gray and Dick Rehbein during the "Every NFL-related person who died this year" montage, staring at those giant Rams/Patriots inflatable dolls that looked like the Stay-Puft Marshmallow Guy from *Ghostbusters*, trying to decipher the difference between the "Let's go, Pats!" and "Let's go, Rams!" chants. Just waiting.

...Giggling as the PA system blared Neil Diamond's "America," only because the wacky Pats fan sitting behind me kept screaming out "TO-DAAAAY!" during the chorus.[255] High comedy. And since he was joking, I made the quick decision that we needed to be friends, so I introduced myself to him and his buddies (Eric and Craig) and told them, "I'm gonna be coming to you guys for high fives all game."

("We're ready for you," they told me. "We're ready.")

...Wondering why the Rams offensive starters were introduced to the crowd one by one, yet the Patriots all came out as a team. Then wondering to myself, "Maybe they wanted to come out as a team" and thinking that would be pretty cool if it were true. Like a Norman Dale/Hickory High "This is your team!"-type move. And it was true. It was true. Can I emphasize how much I love this team? Is it possible?

...Glancing around the stadium during the Completely Insane Mariah Carey performance of the national anthem, all of us holding up glow-in-the-dark thingies. Everyone in the top section had a red one; everyone in the middle section had a white one; everyone in the bottom section had a blue one. Dark stadium, 80,000 people, red, white, and blue. Pretty damned cool.

...Following the kickoff as it hurtled through the air, flashbulbs clicking everywhere. Didn't even seem real. Were the Patriots *really* in the Super Bowl?

...Feeling terrified of Kurt Warner and Marshall Faulk. Is there a more frightening sports experience than playing the Rams? Warner goes back, you're scared. Faulk gets the ball, you're even more scared. (Does anyone in sports consistently make you say "He's so damn good" more than Faulk?) It's like a three-hour horror movie. All this backfield was missing was Jason Voorhees and Michael Myers.

...Telling the Pats fans behind me that I was jotting down notes for my ESPN column, then having one of them say, "Wait a second, shut up, you're Simmons?" Two readers, both Pats fans, both sitting right behind me! Had to be a good omen, right?

...Holding on for dear life at 3–0 midway through the first quarter, Rams with the ball, Tom Brady looking like crap, some serious blowout potential...and then Warner gets hit...and the ball's floating in the air forever...and Ty Law's turning around...AND HE CATCHES IT!!!! And he's sprinting down the sideline toward us, coming right at me, and the Patriots are about to take a 7–3 lead, and we're jumping up and down and hugging one another, one of those joyous, unexpected sports moments that defy description.

(Probably ranks second for me behind Bird stealing the ball against Isiah in the 1987 Eastern Conference finals. I'm not kidding.[256] If this game were the Drago-Balboa fight, this was the moment when the announcer screams, "He's cut! The Russian is cut!" I can still see Ty Law running down the sidelines. Some things you just don't forget.)

...Watching in disbelief as the Pats defense kept shutting down the Greatest Show on Turf. Sitting behind me, my new friend Craig summed it up best: "Silence of the Rams!!!"[257] The perfect title for this column. I could even see the headline: SILENCE OF THE RAMS. Something just felt right about it.

...Seeing the Rams fumble in the final two minutes, then seeing the underdog Pats roll down the field and score again (Brady to David Patten, corner of the end zone, we couldn't even see it). 14–3, Patriots. Are you KIDDING me? That's followed by the scoreboard showing graphics like, "The Patriots are 11–1 this season when leading at the half" and "10 points is the largest deficit that anyone has overcome in Super Bowl history." And then the obligatory *Karate Kid* jokes with the guys behind me as the Rams ran off the field at halftime: "Get 'em a bodybag, yeahhhhhh!" and "Sweep the leg, Johnny!" Those never get old.

...Sitting there in awe as U2 (my first favorite band) ripped

256 See page 307 for the complete list.

257 Starring Bill Belichick as Hannibal Lecter, Tom Brady as Clarice, and Mike Martz as Miggs.

off an electric version of "Beautiful Day." Another good omen. Sweet Jesus, it's a beautiful day. **258**

258 Looking back, this was one of the most astounding moments of my life. Here were the Patriots, 14-point underdogs, pretty much throwing a no-hitter in the first half—gunning for the first Boston sports title in 16 years—and then U2 comes out at halftime and sings "Beautiful Day." I can't remember sports and music ever coming together more perfectly, at least for me. I had goosebumps on my goosebumps' goosebumps.

...Thinking we were ready to put the Rams away, wincing as the Pats kept letting them off the hook (especially when Brady just missed Patten on a bomb to start the second half, a potential backbreaker), glancing at the clock again and again. Faster. Faster. Keep moving.

...Shaking my head in disbelief as the third quarter ended. *The Patriots are one quarter away from winning the Super Bowl.* I can't even come remotely close to being in the relative ballpark of even broaching the point of considering that there's the slightest chance that under any circumstances beyond the realm of possibility that I should be believing this could be happening (if that makes sense).

...Seeing the Pats throttle them on fourth-and-goal, seeing them force Kurt Warner's fumble, seeing Tebucky Jones sprinting down the sidelines right at us, jumping up and down in disbelief, hugging the Pats fans behind me, practically crying because the Pats have just clinched the Super Bowl. And then, there it is: The yellow flag. Absolutely surreal. One of the all-time stomach punches.

(How 'bout the disturbing parallels between the Tebucky non-TD and the Allies' fourth goal from *Victory*? *The goal has been disallowed! The goal has been disallowed!* Why does this game have me thinking of so many sports movie parallels? Is it just me?)

...Dying in the fourth quarter. Just dying. Pining for that clinching first down, agonizing when it doesn't come, knowing the Patriots have to punt. Up 17–10, less than two minutes left. And the Rams have one last chance. And the Pats defense has been on the field for the entire second half. And everyone in the building knows the Rams are about to score.

...Dying some more. Dying a slow death. Almost feeling like I can't breathe. 17–17. *How many times can this happen to Boston fans in a 16-year span? How many times can we endure this? When will we turn the tables? Will it ever happen?*

...Watching in disbelief as Brady strings together a little last-minute drive, trying not to get my hopes up, heart pounding out of my chest, unable to speak, officially passing the point of no return. *I believe.* Looking up at the scoreboard, seeing that there's 0:33 remaining on the clock, thinking that was a good omen (being Larry Legend's number and all), then hearing Eric screaming behind me, "Thirty-three seconds left! Larry Bird! That's gotta be an omen, right? Larry Bird!!!!!" Too weird. The best guy on the last Boston team to win a title, as well as the Basketball Jesus. Thirty-three. 0:33.

(Of course, Troy Brown caught a pass on the next play, broke a tackle and brought the Pats close to field-goal range. You couldn't make this stuff up.)

...Watching Jermaine Wiggins bulldoze his way to the 30-yard line, watching Brady spike the ball, watching Adam Vinatieri run onto the field, thinking to myself, "My life as Patriots fan will never be the same after this kick. I mean, NEVER."

...Staring at the ball as it traveled through the air, right toward us, and it seemed straight, and it seemed long enough, and...

GOOOOOOOOOOOOOOOOOD!!!!!!!!!!!!!!!!!!!!!!!!!!!

I don't remember much after that. The crowd went bonkers. The Patriots sprinted onto the field, everyone hugging everyone else. I was climbing over my seat for a four-way hug with the Pats fans behind me, accompanied by confetti and fireworks galore, and I just kept thinking to myself, "This is my team! This is my team!" Finally, I ended up standing there, my hands behind my head, looking like Thomas Hill after Christian Laettner made his famous shot against Kentucky.[259]

(I don't think I've ever felt that way before. I mean, have you ever been totally dumbfounded by something? Have you ever been completely overwhelmed? I'm telling you, keep the faith, keep believing, keep supporting your team—there's a slight chance that it might be worth it some day. Just trust me.)

Sitting behind me, an older Patriots fan had turned bright red—I couldn't tell whether he was laughing, crying, or both. He just kept screaming "Fifty years! I've been waiting for this for 50 years!" and "They gave us no respect! None!" And he just kept screaming those things again and again. And again. And again. Meanwhile, the other Patriots fans in our section were hugging and carrying on; none of us knew what to do. We were

259 At the time, nobody could have imagined that the Pats would become a legitimate dynasty. As Gene McDonough (my freshman year roommate) wrote in an e-mail after their third title, "This is the same franchise that 13 years ago was owned by Victor Kiam and had a roster of four quarterbacks: a frightened Tony Eason, **a decrepit Steve Grogan**, a talentless Marc Wilson, and a five-foot-seven Doug Flutie. It's completely unfathomable how far they have come. It's the equivalent of waking up 15 years from now and discovering that Bangladesh has become a military and economic superpower."

collectively incredulous. Total disbelief. Nobody could ever make jokes about the Patriots again. We had arrived. And then they were bringing the championship trophy out, and Pats owner Bob Kraft was accepting it, and I kept standing there like Thomas Hill. Just a wave of happiness and disbelief. Can't even be explained unless you've been there. Sitting behind me, Craig summed it up best: "Every year I watch them present the Super Bowl trophy to somebody… now it's…it's us, baby! It's us!!!! YEAAAAAAAAAAAAHHH!!!!!!!!!!!!"

Well after the game, I met some of my buddies on Bourbon Street to celebrate.[260] The J-Bug was there. And Grady, Rusty, Vinny, Murph, Nate. And Doons. We threw down some Hurricanes, hugged one another, hugged one another again, kept hugging. We traded high-fives with every Pats fan in our immediate vicinity. We started "Here we go Patriots, here we go (clap clap!)" chants. And we kept having conversations like this:

Me: "Hey, have I mentioned that the Pats won the Super Bowl?"

JBug: "How 'bout the fact that we're the world champions right now?"[260]

Murph: "Dude, we just won the Super Bowl."

Doons: "Hey, you guys… we're the world fucking CHAMPIONS!"

And that went on for three straight hours. No lie. We were the champs. The champs. The champs. The champs. Have I mentioned that we were the champs? We couldn't stop talking about it. *Sports Illustrated* is coming out with their annual Super Bowl video…and the Patriots will be the main attraction. *Madden 2003* needs an intro and a team for their cover—it's going to be the Pats. Letterman needs a Super Bowl-related guest for his show this week—it's going to be Brady or Vinatieri. We're having a victory parade on Tuesday, a day-long Mardi Gras—it's taking place in Boston. Good God, does it get any better than this?

True story: At around 3:30 a.m., we were huddled in the back of Pat O'Brien's, an infamous bar right off Bourbon Street, when the theme song from *The Greatest American Hero* started blaring from the speakers. And we started singing along. *Believe it or not…I'm walking on air… I never thought it could feel so free-ee…flying away on a wing and a prayer…who could it be?….believe it or not, it's just meeeeeeeee.* Sounds corny? It wasn't.

260 This was the only column that I've ever handed in drunk. After the game ended, I raced back to my hotel room, typed as fast as possible for 90 minutes (finishing the first two-thirds of the column), then **raced down to Bourbon Street** to meet my friends, promising myself that I would only have "two drinks." Six hurricanes later—I mean, the Pats just won the Super Bowl, for God's sake—stumbled back to the Embassy Suites at 4:15 a.m. and pumped out the remaining third of the column. The following morning, I woke up thinking, "Wait a second… oh God!" and immediately called my editor, KJ, in a panic. But KJ said, "Yo, great job, everyone loved it!" As it turned out, it was probably the most popular column I ever wrote; I get more e-mails about it then any other column. Go figure.

261 I missed J-Bug's highlight at 4:30 a.m. in the morning, when my remaining friends met Leonard Davis (the 350-pound rookie Cardinals tackle) and the Bug started screaming at him, "Hey Leonard, you WISH you could play for the Patriots! You WISH you played for us!" Finally, the Bug got Davis to sheepishly admit,

I'm telling you, you had to be there. The Patriots had just won the Super Bowl and we were celebrating in downtown New Orleans, belting out the lyrics to *The Greatest American Hero.* Some moments you just don't forget. I'm not ashamed to admit that this was one of the five or six happiest days of my life.

"I wish I played for the Patriots," followed by the Bug climbing on top of a table and leading the bar in a series of raucous "P-A-T-S PATS PATS PATS!" chants. It's like the Bug had been preparing for that night his entire life.

So what happens now? I don't know. Vinatieri takes on Eruzione/Revere proportions in Massachusetts. Brady could throw 3,500 straight incompletions and never get booed. Belichick becomes the next Auerbach. Brown becomes a cross between… I don't even know (we *love* Troy Brown). The vibe is so good, the love is so strong, that honestly, I wouldn't be surprised if this Patriots team decided to take a collective walk across the Charles River this week. Nobody would stop them.

There's another dynamic here: We needed this. Badly. After the Celtics cruised to the NBA title in '86, there were a ton of hits, one after the other, from Lenny Bias' death to Clemens and Parcells skipping town within two months of one another. During the 2000 season, all four local teams missed the playoffs for the first time since A.D. 383. In other words, we were starting to develop a complex. And then the 2001 Pats came along, and they kept winning, and they kept winning…and they kept winning. Until it was all over. Until the confetti was flying, until the players were hugging, until the coach was being carried off the field, until tears were streaming down our cheeks. Now we have a 10-year grace period. No matter what happens over the next 10 years, we won the Super Bowl. Nobody can take that away from us. **262**

262 After further review, I made this a five-year grace period. Ten seemed a little long.

Nobody.

One last story…

After the game ended, I was walking back to my hotel so I could slip on my brand-new "Super Bowl Champions" T-shirt, but not before noticing a Patriots fan slumped on the ground along O'Keefe Avenue. He was wearing a leather Patriots jacket, collapsed against a park bench, almost like he had crumbled there after taking a right hook to the face. I didn't know whether he was drunk, unconscious or dead, only because I couldn't see his face. Concerned, I tapped him on the shoulder.

"Yo, man, you all right?" I asked him.

He looked up. Tears were streaming down his face. He looked at me, unable to speak, totally overwhelmed, well past the point of being able to express himself coherently.

"You all right?" I asked him again.

"The Patriots just won the Super Bowl," he mumbled. "The fucking Patriots just won the Super Bowl."

And he slumped back down in a heap.

END OF AN ERA

April 2, 2002

Maybe it's over. Maybe.

During yesterday's Opening Day shellacking by the Blue Jays, Pedro Martinez seemed human for the first time in years. Once untradeable, once beyond reproach, you would be hard-pressed to count Pedro among the best 10 pitchers in the league. The Red Sox simply can't keep him healthy. He isn't reliable. Another trip to the disabled list seems inevitable.

Is this a baseball eulogy? Who knows.[263] Even if Pedro never throws another fastball, there isn't a Red Sox fan alive who would feel cheated. Other than Koufax, no pitcher since Lefty Grove slapped together a more dominant stretch than Pedro's last three years in Boston. Statistics can only cover so much. They don't describe the buzz at Fenway before every Pedro start, the collective swagger, the electricity in the air, the giddy anticipation that something special could happen. You would sit there in your seats, hoping for a perfect game, hoping for a no-hitter, hoping for 20 strikeouts, hoping for something dramatic, just hoping. Anything was possible. This was a man without limits. Usually during home games, fans head for the concession stands when the opposing team comes to the plate. Not when Pedro was pitching. We were clapping on every two-strike count, standing and clapping for every two-strike count in the later innings. I remember leaving Fenway some nights, looking at my hands and noticing that they were actually swollen. Pedro always left his mark, on everybody.

When he was cruising along in one of those infamous Pedro grooves, you planned your nights around him. *Let's go down to the sports bar, Pedro's pitching tonight.* That kind of stuff. During that surreal stretch from 1999 to 2001—48–13, 2.02 ERA, 547 innings, 372 hits, 94 walks, 760 strikeouts (that's right, 760)—there were maybe a dozen Pedro starts in which he simply destroyed the other team, broke them down, broke their will, left them for dead. Seventeen Ks, one hit, one run at Yankee Stadium (September 1999). Fifteen Ks, two hits, no walks against Chicago (July 2000). Fifteen Ks, two hits, no walks against Baltimore (May 2000). The list goes on. And on.[264]

263 From Boston fans, I took more heat for this column than anything I'd ever written, mainly because the original headline ("Eulogy for Pedro" before I made my editors change it) made them think I was giving up on Pedro, so hundreds of e-mailers claimed I was "**turning into another Shaughnessy**." Normally, it's the writer's fault if someone misreads a column; in this case, the column was clearly about the end of someone's invincibility, not the end of someone's career, which is an enormous difference. And as it turned out, I was right. So there.

264 According to ESPN's Jeff Bennett, this was the best Pedro stretch: From August 8, 1999 to April 9, 2000 (including the postseason), Pedro pitched 16 games, started 13, finished 12–1 with an 0.96 ERA in 103.1 innings, gave up just 53 hits and three homers, and struck out 165 guys.

265 In *Wait 'Til Next Year*, one of the best ten sports books ever written, William Goldman called this the *Shane* sound—from the movie *Shane*—describing it as the sound everyone in the bar made when someone had the audacity to punch Shane for the first time.

Watching him every five days, we learned to appreciate the way he set up batters, how he changed speeds and pitches depending on the situation, how he found that extra gear when it mattered. Pedro usually stayed in the 93–95 mph range with his fastball, relying on his pinpoint control and three superb complementary pitches (slider, curve, and a devastating change-up), then doing his "picking the wings off a butterfly" routine. When he needed a strikeout, he would reach back for his Uber-Fastball (in the 97–98 mph range) and slam the door. It was almost like watching a video game with a glitch, where they accidentally made one of the pitchers a little *too* good.

The definitive moment happened in Game Five of the Cleveland series in 1999, and only because it involved every aspect of the Pedro Experience: his unforgettable talent and charisma, his unparalled sense of The Moment, the damning physical limitations that threatened to derail him with every pitch. When Pedro jogged out of the bullpen before the fourth inning to save the season, you could feel the air leave Jacobs Field. They *knew*. It was positively Eastwood-esque. Pedro's teammates ended up carrying him off the field, and they should have: He saved the season. I remember watching that game with my father and dying with every fastball, wondering which pitch would cause Pedro to double over in pain as the trainer sprinted in from the dugout. You never knew when the whole thing would suddenly end.

His whole career in Boston has been like that. Just one glimpse of that wispy frame—skinny legs, skinny arms, no ass—made us wonder how long he might last. For God's sake, he was built like a batboy. We were seriously supposed to expect 240 innings per season from this man? As it turned out, we rode him for three and a half years, two Cy Youngs and a boatful of memories before his body finally started breaking down. There were warning signs every season—two extended stints on the disabled list, the final breakdown last summer—which we learned to identify as they were happening. When Pedro is on his game, he barely ever steps off the rubber. Varitek throws him the ball, Pedro peers in, Pedro hums another BB. Lather, rinse, repeat. That's the beautiful thing about watching him in person: the breakneck pace, the utter command he holds over everyone and everything.

So when he isn't feeling it and he isn't healthy, the diehards can tell. He wears a resigned look on his face, like a fat guy laboring on the treadmill and realizing he still has 20 minutes to go. There's no pace to his pitching. He keeps stepping off the mound to loosen his back or stretch his right arm over his head. His control seems off, just a tad, but enough. Batters aren't swinging through his high fastball, so he relies on too many change-ups. Instead of hitting the mid-90s on the Fenway radar screen, he's hovering between 90 and 93. You just know something is wrong.

When Pedro struggled in the past, he exuded enough confidence that it seemed like an unexpected aberration, just a patch of bad luck. On those rare occasions when Pedro was getting kicked around at Fenway, the crowd made a strange sound with every hit—a muffled, incredulous hush, as if something absolutely unthinkable was happening. I haven't heard that specific sound at a sporting event before or since.**265** That's just the way he was. You could bring someone who didn't know anything about baseball to Fenway and within 15 minutes, they would be totally drawn to Pedro. Some people are just larger than life.**266**

Not on Monday. Pedro hadn't seemed confident all spring, seemingly afraid to let loose because he didn't want to injure his shoulder again. And you could see it. He looked tormented. Rattled. Even a little scared. His mojo had pulled an Austin Powers and vanished.**267** That's why there was an inevitability about Monday's beating—four innings, eight runs, nine hits, two hit batsmen, only four Ks—because true Sox fans could feel it coming for five weeks. Deep down, we knew. The fans always know.

Still, it was painful to watch. One of my readers compared it to the scene in *Superman II* after Clark Kent gives up his superpowers to marry Lois, when Clark gets beaten up by the truck drivers and you keep thinking to yourself, "Wait a second, this is Superman! This can't be happening! It's Superman!" And that's one of the worst things about sports: those *Superman II* moments when the invincible hero finally passes his prime and gets knocked down to size. Every superstar experiences it at some point; Pedro's turn came Monday. Whether he lives to fight another day remains to be seen.**268**

And so the great Pedro Martinez had his butt handed to him on Opening Day. At Fenway Park. In front of everybody. His ERA stands at 21.00. And for the first time in four years, I'm not looking forward to watching him pitch in five days.

Maybe this isn't the end of an era, but it sure feels like it.

266 I always called that the MJ Test. When Michael Jordan was in his prime, you could have brought **a Zulu tribesman** straight from Africa to an NBA game, had him watch pregame warmups, then asked him who he thought was the dominant person on the court... and he would have picked MJ. Some people are just destined to be the alpha dog.

267 I'm surprised by all these Austin Powers references—has any popular comedy held up worse over the years, with the possible exception of *Wayne's World*? Or am I just not smoking enough pot anymore?

268 For Larry Bird, the other superduperstar whose prime I had the privilege of following regularly, that moment happened during Game Five of the 1990 playoffs, when Bird botched a reverse dunk during an eventual loss at the Boston Garden to the Knicks. And yes, we all made the Shane sound.

BLOOD FEUD

April 10, 2002

I'm staging an intervention.

Remember when the gang from *Beverly Hills 90210* lured Dylan McKay over to the Walsh house, then pounded him over the head with those "You're killing yourself and you're killing us!" stories so he would quit boozing and doing drugs? Okay, it didn't work—a whacked-out Dylan drove his Porsche off a cliff in the very same episode—but that's irrelevant. Dylan's buddies tried to knock some sense into him, just like I'm trying to knock some sense into Red Sox fans.**269**

269 You could make a pretty good case that *90210* peaked when Dylan fell off the wagon. I always thought Fox blew a golden opportunity here—I would have spun Dylan off into his own show called *Last Call,* then had everything revolve around his partying so we could have seen one-sentence *TV Guide* synopses for each episode: "Dylan narrowly avoids another DUI" and "Dylan's first threesome ends in tragedy." No way this could have missed.

To put it simply, Sox fans need to stop obsessing about the alleged "rivalry" with the Yankees. Why? Because it doesn't exist. When one side consistently beats up on the other side—not just for years, but for decades—you eventually reach a point where the word "rivalry" no longer applies. Harvard-Yale, Bird-Magic, Ali-Frazier, Borg-McEnroe, Hulk-Andre...those were rivalries. The Red Sox-Yankees "rivalry" is about as competitive as a wet T-shirt contest between Britney Spears and Janet Reno.

You hate reading the numbers as much as I hate writing them, but here they are: Since 1920, the Yankees have captured 26 world championships, while the Sox have appeared in four World Series and squandered them all. The teams have collided in two playoff situations (1978 and 1999) and the Yankees prevailed both times. For that matter, the Yankees have won four championships just in the past six years. And we're still calling this a rivalry?

Here's an analogy: Let's say two guys named Murph and Sully have been drinking at Paddy Burke's for 35 years, and, for whatever reason, they don't really get along. Every six months, they get into heated arguments that degenerate into fisticuffs—and Murph has beaten up Sully 48 out of 50 times. Over the years, Murph has KO'd Sully 15 times; broken his ribs, his nose, his jaw, and his cheekbone; and cracked six teeth while knocking out another 10. Conversely, Murph has suffered just three busted knuckles and two fractured hands. As an added kicker, back in 1971, Murph bought Sully's beaten-down house in Wellesley for $12,000 and renovated it into a $5 million showplace. And just last month, he started banging Sully's daughter.

Now...

Even if Paddy Burke's patrons are evenly divided between Sully fans and Murph fans, does this constitute a rivalry? Of course not. Here's how Webster's defines the term "rival": *One of two or more striving to reach or obtain something that only one can possess*. In the case of the Sox and Yanks, both sides have been striving year after year, only the Yankees keep doing the possessing.

So why do Red Sox fans keep fanning the flames? It's okay to despise the Yankees and their abrasive fans. It's okay to root vehemently against them. It's okay to pine for that wonderful day when the tables finally are turned, the Yankees are banished to baseball hell and the Sox finally capture the World Series.[270] But until then, shouldn't we keep a low profile? Shouldn't we collectively agree to shelve our ubiquitous "Yankees suck!" chant unless the Yankees are actually playing at Fenway? Do we really want everyone believing that we have an inferiority complex about the Yankees, that we're pathetic and desperate, that we start "Yankees suck!" chants to make ourselves feel better about rooting for a star-crossed franchise?

Hey, I understand the whole "Yankees suck!" thing. It gives us an advantage over New York fans (since the chant rolls off the tongue a lot better than "Boston sucks!"), gives everyone in the Fenway bleachers a way to pass the time and provides a tremendous tension-breaker during any Yanks-Sox game. But when we're chanting it during a meaningless Red Sox-Devil Rays game in June, we're carrying this thing too far. The post-Super Bowl rally for the Patriots at City Hall pushed me over the edge. We were celebrating our first local championship since 1986, the final chapter of the most memorable/improbable/unbelievable season by an area sports team since the '67 Red Sox—with the added bonus that the Patriots freaking won! Giddy fans crammed the streets of downtown Boston in 20-degree weather. We were beyond happy. Borderline Mardi Gras happy.

Then it happened. Second-string linebacker Larry Izzo couldn't think of anything interesting to say and started a "Yankees suck!" chant.[271] An estimated 1.25 million fans happily chanted "Yan-kees suck! Yan-kees suck! Yan-kees suck!" And we looked like idiots. Would Jets fans start "Boston sucks!" chants at their

270 Wait, that pretty much happened!

271 The reaction to Izzo's comment was the impetus for this column—I was legitimately *mortified* when it happened—which ran two months later in the April 2002 issue of *Boston* magazine. In the two-plus years following the column, a number of other writers would tackle the rivalry/feud angle, most notably **Frank Deford**. So if it sounds a little familiar, that's why. I'm not claiming I invented the wheel here, because it was a pretty easy angle to take. Just pointing out that mine was first.

Super Bowl parade? Would Yankees fans even think about doing this at a World Series rally? Of course not. We're not even on their radar screen. That's why New Yorkers don't take us too seriously. If we give them crap about the Yankees, they start giggling. Which dagger should they use as a retort? The Bambino? Bucky Dent? 1918? Roger Clemens? Wade Boggs? When we start with that Sox-Yankees stuff, they think it's amusing, the same way it's funny when you're watching a dog hump somebody's leg. Harmless, juvenile fun.[272] So when we celebrated our first Super Bowl win with a "Yankees suck!" chant, New York fans shook their heads. *Look at those idiots in Boston. Could they BE more pathetic? Could they BE more obsessed about us?* And they probably smiled to themselves, satisfied, knowing they were still winning the war.

And they were. And they are.

Deep down, we know it's true, which might explain why our inferiority complex reached staggering heights during the Yankees' most recent run of success. You wouldn't believe some of the e-mails I got from frustrated readers. One guy sent me a detailed comparison between the Yankees logo and the Nazi swastika. Another wrote an essay comparing Roger Clemens to Benedict Arnold. Another sent me a 1,500-word treatise entitled "Why I Hate Paul O'Neill." And those were the more reasonable messages. Our deepening hatred for the Yankees has been fueled by resentment more than anything, a loser's mentality fermenting in Boston ever since the '86 World Series. There's a reason *Boston Herald* columnist Gerry Callahan deemed Boston "Loserville": Not only were our teams losing, we were becoming insufferable about it. Curses, conspiracies, bad karma — we listened to excuses for everything, excelling at the role of Jilted, Disillusioned, Spiteful and Hopeless Fan. Chanting "Yankees suck!" at every opportunity played right into that. It was the mark of a loser: people trying to make themselves feel better at the expense of someone else.

When the Patriots rolled to the Super Bowl, we remembered why we loved sports in the first place. We didn't need to measure ourselves against our past, or against the Yankees, the Lakers, the Avalanche,[273] or anybody else. We were champions again. We were happy again. Sports was fun again. It wasn't about rooting against someone, but rooting *for* someone. There's a difference.

So now that we're winners again, let's keep a low profile and

272 Back in the late '80s, when I was completely insane, I attended a Yankees game in the upper deck wearing a Red Sox hat, Bruins jersey, and Celtics shorts. People made fun of me, but they seemed more amused than anything—like, **"Look at the pathetic Red Sox fan, he's so cute."** I would rather have had someone take a swing at me.

273 Something truly terrible happened in 2000 that illustrated how far the Boston sports scene had fallen: That season, Bruins icon Ray Bourque was traded to Colorado so he could pursue a Stanley Cup one last time. This would have been a much bigger deal if anyone in Boston still cared about hockey. Anyway, the Avalanche ended up winning the Cup (with many New Englanders jumping on the bandwagon), leading to the inevitable "Should we have a parade for Bourque?" controversy, with the obligatory "Look how pathetic we've become" counter-angle. Just a miserable time to be living in Boston. I'm convinced that the Patriots Super Bowl season was God's way of avoiding one of those Jim Jones/Guyana tragedies.

stop trying to revive this one-sided Sox-Yankees feud. Take solace in the fact that budding Yankee fans follow the team simply because they're winning and lack the creativity to buck the bandwagon. Better yet, bear in mind that the typical Yankees fan is obnoxious, condescending, and exceptionally arrogant—and those are his better qualities. You really want these fans to feel superior to you? Just because they support a superior baseball team doesn't mean they're superior. Keep telling yourself this.

And if our Red Sox finally topple the Yankee dynasty and start rolling off world championships, maybe there will be a Royals-Yankees game in the Bronx someday, and a "Boston sucks!" chant will start up—for absolutely no reason whatsoever. Then, and only then, will we have a rivalry on our hands.[274]

274 The more I'm thinking about it, this will never happen. Yankee fans would never give us the satisfaction.

THEY DON'T HAVE IT THIS YEAR

September 24, 2002

Since it's late September, you know what that means. That's right, it's time for my annual Red Sox eulogy! The 2002 season was weirder than most, as they trotted out seven All-Stars, including two 20-game winners, a potential batting champ, and a shortstop on pace for 200 hits and 120 RBI—and yet they weren't one of the best four teams in the American League. How does that make sense? Normally when baseball teams fall short, you can latch onto something: incompetent managing, back-breaking injuries, shaky chemistry, or whatever. Not this year.

As usual, my father summed it up best. About six weeks ago, we were talking on the phone for the first time in days, catching up on anything and everything. As the phone call wound down, I wondered, "Hey, we aren't gonna talk about the Red Sox?"

Dead silence on the other end.

Finally…

"Nahhhh. They don't have it this year."

Best piece of analysis I heard all season. *They don't have it this year*. Perfect. I could find 500 different stats and anecdotes that, collectively, would piece together the complicated "What's wrong with this team?" puzzle. But only one observation truly matters, an intuitive point, not a statistic: If the 2002 Sox were trailing by one run or more in the final three innings, they were done. Stick a fork in 'em.[275] Following this team every day, absorbing the body language, seeing how the parts assembled into a whole, watching the inability of Player A to pick up Players B through H with a big hit (with Player A changing every game), feeling helpless as opponents kept slamming the door in close games…after awhile, you just knew. They don't have it this year.

Either they were either winning 10–2 or losing 4–3, and every contender would have them for lunch. Watching this day after day was unbearable; one time, I actually cued up the ending of *The Natural*, just to remember how it looked when someone slammed a game winner and his teammates joyously skipped out of the dugout.[276]

275 They were 13–23 in one-run games that season; they also went nearly three months without rallying from behind to win a game after the sixth inning.

276 That wasn't a lie. I do things like this. When the Celts and Sox were floundering in 1996, I was bartending at the time—we used to go back to my apartment at 3 a.m. and watch the old Bird tapes. **After enough beers** and bong hits, it was almost like they were playing live.

A little misfortune didn't help. Manny broke a finger and missed seven weeks, then took another month to regain his hitting stroke. Damon wrenched a knee before the All-Star break, free-falling faster than Tony Montana in the final hour of *Scarface*. They brought in Cliff Floyd and Alan Embree before the trade deadline and both went down within two weeks (Floyd never really recovered). Even during their last-gasp run in September, Pedro's body broke down just long enough for him to miss a crucial Yankees start. It was that kind of year.[277] Throw in two horrible offseason moves (millions given away to washed-up veterans John Burkett and Tony Clark);[278] the baffling demise of El Guapo; a crummy season from Ugie Urbina (six losses, five blown saves); broken-down veterans like Arrojo and Hermanson; way too many innings from Lt. Frank Castillo; and maddeningly inconsistent hitting from Varitek, Nixon, and Daubach...I mean, was it surprising that this team didn't have "it"?[279]

They just weren't that good. And after everything I just wrote, you probably think they're on pace for 80 wins this season.

Wrong. Try 95.

That's why a trite explanation like "They don't have it this year" simply doesn't fly in Boston. We're like Lt. Kaffee interrogating Col. Jessep—we want answers, we want the truth, and dammit, we aren't going to be denied. Not only has this team gone 84 years without winning a World Series, New Englanders are dying every day without having seen the Sox win a championship in their lifetimes. Throw in an especially muggy summer, dizzying expectations, a ravenous media, and a particularly perplexing team and by August we were practically homicidal. Last winter, I remember thinking that the residual Patriots karma (from their Super Bowl season) would transfer to the Red Sox, their fans, and even the local media this summer. Boy, was I wrong.

The emotional breakdown started in June, when we derided Manny for getting injured on a risky head-first slide into the catcher. That shifted to the typical "What's wrong with these guys?" whining during interleague play. By the All-Star break, we were panicking ("Seven All-Stars and we still can't beat the Yanks?") and debating life-or-death issues like "Why is No-mah swinging at the first pitch so much?" As July chugged along, reporters kept unearthing evil stats that sent us into a frenzy (29–30 since May 17, 6–14 in one-run games, etc.). And all hell

277 For the first 10 months of 2002, I was living in Boston and writing three columns a week for Page 2 on ESPN.com. Needless to say, I was always looking for stuff to write about—this was the same summer that I wrote a running diary of the Spelling Bee, as well as a fake *Sports Century* episode about **Michael Myers from *Halloween***. But from Opening Day to late September, this particular Sox team was so disappointing and predictable, I didn't write a single column about them. Nothing interesting to say.

278 Two years later, Clark had a semi-improbable resurgence with the Yankees, leading to two terrifying moments in the ALCS: **1)** when he nailed a ground rule double in the top of the ninth in Game Five, which some people feel could have scored Ruben Sierra from first for the go-ahead run (although I vehemently disagree); and **2)** when he struck out to end Game Six, one of those classic "Guy who sucks on the Sox, goes to another team and ends up killing us" moments that didn't happen (like Pena's homer in the 1995 Playoffs).

broke loose in August, after those deadline deals couldn't halt a collective swoon.

It's Grady's fault. No, it's Manny's fault. No, it's Nomar's fault. Actually, it's the bullpen's fault. Don't forget about the starting pitching. This team has no heart. This team needs a leader. These guys look too complacent. There's no urgency here. They're just unlucky. They're choke artists.

Sure, the Red Sox fall short every year, but something felt different this time around. The griping was more mean-spirited than ever, a nasty edge stemming from the intense competition in the local media. With Boston already a crowded landscape for sports talk, a second all-sports radio station and two daily TV shows pushed things to another level. You couldn't turn on a radio or television without hearing someone rip apart the Sox like Dirk Diggler's Mom. The swollen number of radio/TV gigs spawned a cottage industry for local writers and personalities. Radio co-hosts pocket $300 for four hours of work; five-minute TV appearances can yield another $250, sometimes more. Some guys shamelessly exploit these opportunities, juggling as many as six radio/TV gigs during a single week, making the same points every time and laughing all the way to the bank. Desperate for programming and unable to find new blood, the local stations keep throwing the same guys out there, similar to how the same six guys appear in every porn movie.[280]

With a potential second income at stake, there's an inherent pressure to "up the ante," to come up with "something good," to produce an "angle" that nobody used before (yes, I'm doing my Chris Farley impersonation). For instance, maybe Manny isn't the sharpest tool in the shed, maybe he's a little infuriating at times, maybe he shouldn't have chosen "I Get High" as his entrance music for an at-bat,[281] maybe he should have run out that ground ball a few weeks ago...but jeez, the local press made him out to be a cross between the Rain Man, Method Man, Harpo Marx, and Satan. Satisfied that they found the right "hot button" topic, everyone divided into Pro-Manny and Anti-Manny camps like they were choosing sides in kickball, and the ensuing chaos dominated the airwaves and newspapers for most of September. I found this very confusing. When they signed Manny two winters ago, we knew he was a head case and we knew they overpaid, yet 99.9 percent of the fans were delighted. So Manny arrives in Beantown, posts his typically gaudy num-

279 Look at the names in this paragraph. And you wonder why they didn't make the playoffs.

280 By 2005, the Boston stations softened their requirements: If you have a head, two arms, and two legs, you're now eligible to appear on any of these shows.

281 Without question, the highlight of the 2001 season. That nearly surpassed the highlight of the 2000 season—when Wendell Kim coached an August doubleheader dressed like the Gimp from ***Pulp Fiction***.

bers and turns out to be just as quirky as advertised. Now he's an untradeable cancer?

And then there was Nomar. Say what you want about no. 5, but he always plays hard and seems like he cares—I mean, *really cares*, like in a "He heads home after a loss and broods about it for 45 minutes" kinda way. Maybe he hasn't improved as an all-around player since his rookie season, maybe he carries a Sean Penn-like edginess with the media, and maybe he could emerge as a potential Ewing Theory candidate if they trade him some day.[282] But that doesn't mean you go after him—he's practically an institution at this point, isn't he? That didn't stop the *Boston Herald*'s Steve Buckley. Spurred on by some harmless, sarcastic comments made by Nomar about playing in Boston, Buckley waited four days, then skewered the shortstop in a back page column for Wednesday's paper ("coincidentally" running the same day that Buckley co-hosted WEEI's drive-time show, no less).

Well, guess who the media star was last week? That's right... Mr. Steve Buckley! Other writers and hosts nitpicked at some of Buckley's facts, keeping him in the limelight. Poor Nomar met with everyone in the local media save for the *Globe*'s second-floor janitor, just to quell rumors that he hates it here (keeping the story alive). On Sunday night, Buckley triumphantly appeared on Bob Lobel's *Sports Final*, the centerpiece of a segment geared around the fallout from his five-day-old column. In other words, Buckley ended up getting exactly what he wanted. But that's how it works here in Boston now. If you're lucky enough to break into the inner circle—as a TV reporter, radio host or writer—there's money to be made if you make enough of a commotion. Just remember to wash the blood off your hands at the end of the day.

So how does this stuff affect the 2002 Red Sox? Because it made a disappointing season practically unbearable, like HBO following an *Arli$$* marathon with 12 hours of *The Mind of the Married Man*. What could be more frustrating than an enigmatic, charisma-less, $110 million group of underachievers, coupled with a rabid, opportunistic media picking them apart at every turn? Does that sound like fun? All I know is that the park hasn't changed, the fans haven't changed, the media seems to be getting worse...and for the 84th straight season, the Boston Red Sox have fallen short. Just another fitting epitaph for the

282 The Ewing Theory was created by longtime BSG reader Dave Cirilli, who was trying to explain the strange phenomenon when certain teams play better after losing their alleged superstar (either by injury or trade) who usually ended up not being as good as you thought at the time (named after **the wildly overrated Patrick Ewing**). The all-time best Ewing Theory example happened when the Pats won the Super Bowl after Drew Bledsoe's injury/benching. Some other classic examples: the 2001 Mariners (won 116 games without Griffey or A-Rod); the 1998 Tennessee Vols (won the title without Peyton Manning); *The Daily Show* (became a monster hit without Craig Kilborn); the 1999 Knicks (made the Finals without Ewing); the 1999 Lions (made the playoffs without Barry Sanders); whatever Colts team ends up winning the Super Bowl after Peyton Manning gets hurt; and, of course, the 2004 Red Sox (let's just say that Nomar was involved, as predicted).

annual eulogy. Only one thing keeps me sane: Maybe next year, I won't have to write one.

(Repeat after me: There's always next year...there's always next year...there's always next year...there's always next year...)

HERE COMES YOUR 19TH NERVOUS BREAKDOWN

October 7, 2003

If you're looking for an unbiased perspective, you came to the wrong place. Hours after the Red Sox finished their improbable comeback in Oakland, there isn't a discernable emotion remaining in my body. I'm tapped.[283]

Was it fun?

(Yeah, I guess.)

Did I enjoy it?

(Ummmm...I think so.)

Would I ever want to go through it again?

(Definitely not.)

How can you celebrate when you've been rendered an emotional cyborg?

(You can't.)

At what point does unbridled joy give way to relief and stunned shock?

(Right after the final out, and within 2.3 seconds.)

Ever spend four hours doing the "Let's break up/let's get back together" dance, then ultimately reconcile in the end? That's what this Oakland-Boston series felt like. My team won three straight "do-or-die" games—each by the skin of its teeth, each in crazier fashion than the last, each with an overmatched manager who almost appears to be crying out for help—and now we need to regroup for a seven-game series with the Yankees, only the most evil franchise in the history of sports.

Well, I can't regroup. Not yet. I can't get over what happened over the past three days. For starters, Game Three featured two Oakland runners thrown out at home: One who failed to understand the logistics of something called Rule 7.06(b);[284] the other because Varitek blocked the plate so perfectly that the runner tripped over his foot, twisted an ankle, hopped around like a failed skateboarder on Hollywood Boulevard, shoved Varitek as he tried to retrieve the ball, then got tagged out (while the home plate umpire stood there and twiddled his thumbs like Frank Drebin).[285] Two of the strangest plays in recent history...and they happened within minutes of each other. Go figure.

283 If you're wondering why a year passed since the previous Sox column, in November 2002, I started writing for *Jimmy Kimmel Live*. None of the Sox columns I wrote over that time were book-worthy.

284 I wanted to run the entire definition of Rule 7.06(b), but it's 401 words long and reads like **an SAT reading comprehension question**. Let's just say that Miguel Tejada shouldn't have assumed the home plate ump would call interference at third base before jogging home.

285 Even though Eric Byrnes had a solid 2004 season, I could never take him seriously after this play. He could hit .390 and I would still remember him hopping around like a moron. And while we're here, Oakland never received nearly enough credit for blowing this game, or the series for that matter.

After those breaks, we were feeling fairly optimistic: It was like the Tuck Rule all over again. So we were waiting and waiting...and Mike Timlin held the fort...and then Nixon ended things with a magnificent 11th-inning blast into the centerfield bleachers, which was ironic because **a**) Trot should have started the game; and **b**) Grady Little pinch-hit for him in Game One. The guy finishes fourth in the league in OPS, suddenly he's a situational hitter in the playoffs? Somehow, everything worked out in the end, as they often do with Grady. And Trot had his Bernie Carbo moment, a home run which I'll probably watch 1,500 more times on TiVo before everything's said and done (while fast-forwarding through the part when he thanks the Lord). **286**

Just 14 hours later, when Tim Hudson exited after one inning with a strained oblique muscle—which might or might not have been suffered in a Boston bar fight against five guys who looked exactly like CT from *Real World: Paris*—it looked like we were headed back to Oakland. Not so fast. Former Tiger Steve Sparks somehow held the Sox in check just long enough for Grady to allow 38-year-old John Burkett to start the sixth—after 97 pitches and five gruesome, excruciating, "He's one pitch away from getting shellacked" innings, capped by Eric Byrnes' near-grand slam that narrowly missed Pesky's Pole—and Burkett promptly gave up FOUR STRAIGHT (FUCKING) LINE DRIVES (!!!!!!!!!) before Grady mercifully yanked him. **287**

Now...

There are two kinds of disastrous managerial moves: the ones you second-guess after the fact and the ones that make you scream "Wait a second... what the hell is he doing????" right as they're happening. Well, Grady sending Burkett out for the sixth was my all-time "What the hell is he doing?" baseball moment. I still can't believe it happened. Burkett was playing with house money at that point. Everyone in the ballpark knew it. Except one man. **288**

With the Sox trailing, we were headed for a classic battle: the resourceful, never-say-die Boston offense against a superb closer (Keith Foulke) who had been "lights-out" (as Steve Lyons would say, and may I never quote that man again in my life). So Nomar starts things off with a double off the wall. Manny raps a two-out single, then runs down the line with his arm raised for no reason. (Just Manny being Manny; even Jamie Quirk wasn't this quirky.) Then David "Papi" Ortiz shakes off an 0-for-16

286 Trot's homer wasn't even the memorable moment of that night. Why? Because that was the same night **I went to the Playboy Mansion** for the first time, as well as the night I almost ended up getting divorced. Here's what happened: Jimmy Kimmel was invited to appear at *Playboy's* 50th Anniversary Bash, and since the Sports Gal was out of town, I thought I could sneak over to the Mansion for a few hours without her finding out. Since they provided a limo for Jimmy, he was swinging over at 8:00 with his girlfriend and the rest of his Caucasian posse. When the game went into extra innings, I had to meet them at the Mansion—but Jimmy never thought I would find it, since it's in Bel Air, so he sent the limo back to pick me up. Of course, the driver calls when I'm on the other line, then leaves a message asking, "Hey, it's the limo driver who's taking you to the Mansion, call me back on my cell and give me your address." And since I never knew he left a message, and since the Sports Gal was checking messages later that night...well, you can guess how this one turned out. It was like a bad episode of *Dharma & Greg*. On the bright side,

slump with a Hendu-esque two-run double off the wall.[289] Unbelievable. Two of the 10 most memorable hits in Fenway history—Trot's homer and Papi's double—and they happen 16 hours apart.

Even better, the possibly-rejuvenated Scott Williamson closes the game in the ninth—looking lights-out, by the way—as Byung-Hyun Kim stews in the bullpen, one game removed from flipping off Fenway fans before Game Three. In one week, Kim has gone from "Let's trust him with a Game One save opportunity" to "Let's leave him off the playoff roster and stick a straitjacket on him." Just another day in the life of the Red Sox bullpen.

Before we get to Game Five, you should know three things:

1) I wore the same shirt for the past three days—a white T-shirt with a Jack Davis cartoon of a Sox player on the front. I settled on this outfit after my game-worn 1986 Sox jersey of Rob Woodward failed in Game One and my lucky Sox cap failed in Game Two. Also, my buddy Hench wore the same T-shirt and underwear for three straight days. I wish I were making this up.[290]

2) While we were watching Game Three at my house, Hench made me switch seats in the fifth—I moved to the sofa, he moved to the comfy leather chair. Shortly after that pivotal move, Tejada was tagged out on Rule 7.06(b). We ended up sitting in the same seats for the rest of the series, wearing the exact same clothes.

3) Neither of us believe in the Curse of the Bambino, but we believe in everything you just read in the previous two paragraphs. You figure it out.

Anyway, Game Five was a beauty: Pedro against Barry Zito, winner takes all. Vegas listed the Sox as an 8–5 favorite, only because Zito was **a**) pitching on three days rest; **b**) reportedly partying on Friday night in Boston; and **c**) enough of a ringer for Eric Roberts that it made everyone uncomfortable. Just before 5 o'clock, Hench arrived in a tortured frenzy, already agonizing about how Grady would screw up the pivotal game. That's when we decided that, if the Sox win Game Five, Grady should be left off the playoff roster for the following series. They can do it to players, why not managers?[291]

So Pedro and Zito match a few zeroes as we wonder about things like "Is Gabe Kapler available to pinch-run on Yom Kippur?" Down 1–0 in the sixth, Varitek smacks a homer into

all the waitresses at the Mansion wore body paint, and I got to meet David Hasselhoff and Joe Millionaire.

287 This was also the inning when J-Bug—sitting in the first row behind the Sox bullpen—was kicked out of Fenway for heckling Ricardo Rincon in Spanish. The Bug is 100 percent Irish. You figure it out.

288 Eleven days later: Pedro, eighth inning, Yankee Stadium, same thing. Say what you want about Grady, but at least he didn't even remotely learn from his own mistakes.

289 Historic moment here: The first time I ever included the words **"Papi" and "Hendu"** in the same sentence. Let's just say this will happen again in this book.

290 After the Red Sox lost Game Seven to the Yankees, that Jack Davis shirt took its rightful place alongside **my white linen Miami Vice blazer** and Tony Simmons no. 81 Pats Jersey in the Pantheon of "Things I still own but would never wear again under any circumstances."

left field. Beautiful. Suddenly, Zito is laboring and that swooping curveball is bouncing on home plate, and two guys are on, and Manny's up, and my God is he due, and...

BOOM!

A three-run homer!

Sox lead 4–1!

Manny spends four seconds admiring it, skips around the bases and jumps into the arms of Papi, Millar, Varitek, Ace, Gary and everyone else in Boston's "overly-friendly, bordering on Apollo and Rocky's awkward beach hug at all times" dugout. Regardless, a nice moment—one that even prompted a victory jog around my house.[292] Up by three in the bottom of the 6th, Grady brings in a defensive replacement for his no. 3 hitter—Damian Jackson for Todd Walker, a 15-percent upgrade at best. It's like watching *The Handler* instead of *Hack* on CBS; you're not really making or breaking your Friday night either way. More importantly, IT'S THE SIXTH FREAKING INNING! As Hench says, "I've watched probably 500 baseball games this year. I've been watching baseball all my life. And never, *not once*, have I seen a defensive replacement in the sixth inning! WHAT THE HELL IS GOING ON???"

Both of us know instantly: This is coming back to haunt us. Either Jackson screws up a double play, or his spot comes up in a big at-bat. Something's going to happen. It's too dumb, too illogical. This is the way sports works. It's the Mike Hargrove Corollary: When a manager makes an indefensibly moronic move in a big game, that move always rears its ugly head in the end...well, unless you're Davey Johnson. In the playoffs, you shouldn't deviate from what you've been doing all season, unless it's an emergency or someone is trapped under something. When you start panicking, that's when you get into trouble. You don't take out your no. 3 hitter in the sixth inning, not with *this* bullpen. End of story.

(Now we're waiting for the Other Shoe to Drop...)

Fast-forward to the seventh: 4–2, Jermaine Dye pops one into shallow center, the Unfrozen Caveman Center Fielder (Johnny Damon) scurries under it...and here comes Jackson, and he won't stop running...and SPLAT! A sickening collision of heads, shades of Vinnie Johnson and Adrian Dantley in that Pistons-Celtics playoff game. Somehow, Nomar (the good sense to back up the play) and Bill Mueller (the good sense to cover

291 My favorite part of this joke: Imagining Grady sitting in the dugout for the next series as Joe Buck said, "There's Grady Little, the embattled Red Sox manager, shockingly left off the playoff roster for this round after a rocky ALDS. To his credit, he's here and cheering the team on..."

292 One downer: Fox's Thom Brennaman vented that Manny violated the sanctity of the game. Isn't this the same sport where Barry Bonds preens—that's right, *preens*—after every blast? So Manny couldn't get excited because he broke out his slump and knocked one of the biggest homers of his career? That made him a bad guy? Please. That's a new 21st century trend: Play-by-play guys interjecting their own opinions during games like they're a panelist on *Around the Horn*. I blame Bob Costas for this. Actually, I blame Costas for a lot of things. But this one's justified. Joe Buck is now the champion of this trend.

the base) combine to nail Dye at second, yet another baserunning blunder by the A's (five in three games). But the carnage is immeasurable. We lose our leadoff hitter—poor Damon gets carried off on one of those depressing stretchers, the ones they should use in Vegas after a gambler gets demolished by a blackjack dealer. Damian Jackson remains in the game, woozy and a little disoriented, which gives him something in common with his manager. The team loses its momentum and then some. And Pedro has to endure a 10-minute delay, plus Boston's round of at-bats, before he returns for the eighth.

Now Hench and I are dying. We're *dying*. We spend 10 minutes trying to remember if anyone won the World Series with an incompetent manager, finally taking solace that it happened with Arizona and Bob Brenly just two years ago. Of course, Grady isn't done: He pinch-runs for Ortiz in the top of the ninth, meaning Grady has managed to eliminate our first, third, and fifth batters from the game—a game destined for extra innings, no less. Just an unbelievable run for Grady Little this week. He did everything but order the tiger to attack Roy.[293]

Anyway, thanks to the extended delay, Pedro comes out and gives up two seeds. Now it's 4–3. I can't even remember what happened next—I just remember Mike Timlin getting us out of the inning. Thank God for Timlin, our only consistently reliable reliever all season. And with the walk-happy Scott Hatteberg leading off the ninth, Timlin's clearly coming in since he only walked nine batters all season.

(Um, right?)

Of course not.

Williamson comes out for the ninth. Injured for much of the season, he threw two innings and 28 pitches at Fenway on Sunday. Perfect choice. Immediately, he walks Hatteberg, one of the five most predictable things that ever happened in the history of baseball. For good measure, he walks the next guy before pulling an Exit Stage Right. As Derek Lowe comes in, Hench and I are standing. We're not even sure why. The life has been sucked from our bodies; Manny's homer in the sixth seems like it happened in 1996. It's down to Saturday night's starter, as well as the guy who once owned the dreaded Derek Lowe Face, to save the season.

My right leg is shaking. Hench is rocking back and forth

293 Notice how "Montecore" wasn't enough of a household name yet? The attack happened three days before this column was written. In fact, the A's haven't won a playoff game since **Montecore attacked Roy**, which could make for a fun running subplot if the team ever moves to Vegas. Someone page Shaughnessy—this sounds like his next book, *The Curse of Montecore*.

like he just witnessed a murder. As Lowe warms up, we have the following exchange:

Hench: Did you ever think about what a nervous breakdown feels like? Like, you're so nervous, your brain literally collapses onto itself? Can you imagine that?

Me: Um...yeah. You're not going to have one, are you?

Hench [still rocking back and forth]**:** Well, not tonight. But I can kinda understand what it would feel like to have one. I mean, after tonight. Does that make sense?

Actually, it kinda did.

That's what the baseball playoffs feel like. Every pitch matters. Every decision has ramifications that could last 50 years. When cameras zoom in for closeups of the players, you can see their nose hairs and those little white pimples you get from shaving too many times in the same week. No game lasts less than three hours. You can't relax for a second. Your stomach churns. Your heart pounds. You're totally helpless. You can't breathe. You don't want the season to end.

And that's the happy part: My season didn't end. Derek Lowe came through. After Ramon Hernandez bunted the runners over and Grady moved the infield in—you know, just so any grounder could get through for the winning run—Lowe whiffed the backup catcher on an unhittable sinker. He pitched around Chris Singleton to load the bases, Grady moved the outfield back toward the fence so any single would win the game...and then Lowe whiffed the always-atrocious Terrence Long on that same nasty sinker. Piece of cake. Never a doubt.

(Note: The preceding paragraph was infinitely more dramatic when it happened, even causing me to see those little white dots at one point. I wish I were kidding.)

We won. Well, I think we won—I could barely see straight. Hench and I exchanged an awkward beach hug and about 35 high-fives. Our cell phones started ringing off the hook. The Sox mobbed one another, then headed to the locker room before visiting Johnny D in the hospital. A confused Grady tried to pinch-run the clubhouse attendant for an A's security guard. And Hench and I headed out to get some chicken, two punch-drunk Red Sox fans who had just been through hell and back. What a game.[294]

Part of me wants to win the title so we never have to hear about the stupid Curse again, so the Yankees fans can shut the

294 We ate dinner at a place called California Chicken on Melrose, which was near my apartment between LaBrea and Highland and had the nickname "Gay Chicken"—since it was **a notorious restaurant for gay men**—although we didn't know this until my wife told me after the fact. Funniest part of the story: Since we were so drained from the game, we probably said 10 words during the entire dinner. Everyone probably thought we were on an awkward date or something.

hell up, so I can watch a grounder roll down the first base line in the ninth inning of a pivotal playoff game—which happened Monday night, by the way—without a condescending announcer eagerly dropping Buckner's name five or six more times. The other part—the happier part—wants to be in Boston when we win, just to hear what the city sounds like. I want to hug my Dad, see the look on his face. I want to get drunk with Sox fans that night, just like New Orleans and the Pats all over again. I want to call my friends who suffered through the ups and downs. I want to accept congratulations from everybody I know. I just want to win. And I think every Sox fan feels that way.

That's why people shouldn't argue things like "Deep down, Sox fans would be disappointed if they won the World Series" and "The whole region would lose its identity." What a load of crap. No true Sox fan feels that way. We want to win the World Series, and we want to go through the Yankees to do it. There's no other way. And if we're going to war with a shaky manager and a shaky bullpen, so be it.

PARADISE LOST, AGAIN

October 17, 2003

Twenty minutes after the Yankees eliminated the Red Sox, I called my father to make sure he was still alive.

And that's not even a joke. I wanted to make sure Dad wasn't dead. That's what it feels like to be a Sox fan. You make phone calls thinking to yourself, "Hopefully, my Dad picks up, because there's at least a 5 percent chance that the Red Sox just killed him."

Well, he picked up. And we talked it through. We always do. Dad's voice was barely audible. He sounded like he just got out of surgery. Like every other Sox fan on the planet, he couldn't understand one simple question: Why didn't Grady take out Pedro? In the eighth inning, Pedro was running on fumes. Everyone knew it. Everyone but Grady. Little did we know, our overmatched manager was saving his worst for last.

"He screwed up the season," Dad grumbled. "He screwed up the whole season."

So it happened again. Nothing was worse than Game Six against the Mets, but this was damned close.[295] I don't need to tell you why. If the Red Sox were a girl, you would probably just break up with her. You would call her on the phone, calmly explain that you can't take it anymore, let her down as gently as possible and move on with your life. But sports aren't like that. You're stuck with your teams from childhood. It's like being trapped in a bad marriage. You can't get out.

Hey, this is my team. I came to grips with that a long time ago. They're part of my life. Sometimes they lift me to a higher place, sometimes they punch me in the stomach and leave me for dead. There are thousands and thousands of diehards just like me, all trapped in that same bad marriage, united by our experiences and memories. We wear Sox caps, we pack Fenway Park, we travel insane distances to support our team on the road. We always have each other. And some days are better than others. This was one of the bad days. Given that the fucking Yankees were involved, and the way things unfolded, it may have tied for the worst.

I can't emphazize this strongly enough: I will spend the rest of my life wondering why Grady allowed Pedro to wilt to death

295 Upon further review, it was just as bad as 1986—I was in denial when I wrote that sentence. The following day, when I was working my then-day job at Kimmel's show, I was so morose that I ended up leaving early at 4 p.m. It took me about three weeks to bounce back. I'm not even kidding. At the very least, if '86 was 1A on the Depressing Scale, then 2003 was 1B.

in the eighth inning. This isn't Pantheon Pedro anymore; honestly, it's been more than two years since his last Mozart routine on the mound. Even if his ceiling is higher than just about anyone else's ceiling, asking him to throw 125-plus pitches over three-plus hours in Yankee Stadium—in the most nerve-wracking setting imaginable—was indefensible at best and catastrophically moronic at worst.[296]

296 Since this column was written, we found out four things: **1)** before the game, the owners and **Theo Epstein had ordered Grady to remove Pedro** either after the seventh inning or at 100 pitches, whatever came first; **2)** Pedro thought he was done after the seventh; **3)** Grady asked Pedro between innings if he could give him one more inning (what was Pedro supposed to say, "No"?); and **4)** after the game, Grady hugged Pedro, thanked him for pitching the eighth and admitted that he would be run out of town. So, yes, it turned out to be catastrophically moronic.

Unlike the other devastating defeats over the years, you couldn't blame any of the Red Sox players for losing the series this time. Not even Nomar. This was a great group of guys, a resilient, likable team that almost always came through (like they proved in Game Six). Every time you counted them out, they came roaring back. I loved that about them. Unfortunately, they couldn't manage themselves. Switch Grady Little and Joe Torre and the Red Sox advance. The teams were that close.

I would rehash the eighth for you, but frankly, I'm not in the mood. Nobody in his right mind would have allowed Pedro—struggling heroically with a three-run lead, 115 pitches on the odometer, running on the fumes of his fumes—to pitch to Hideki Matsui. Not with flame-throwing lefty Alan Embree waiting in the bullpen. The ensuing disaster (Matsui's ground-rule double, followed by Posada's bloop double to tie the game) wasn't just predictable, it was downright sickening. This was '86 all over again. Aaron Boone's homer in the eleventh wasn't just inevitable, it was practically preordained.

Of course, the TV networks and newspapers got what they wanted after spending three weeks gleefully rehashing "Curse" stories for the Cubs and Sox, flashing graphics like "RED SOX WORLD SERIES WINS AFTER 1918: 0" and showing so many Babe Ruth pictures, you would have thought John Henry Williams had brought the Babe back to life. It was almost pathological. Fox even hired Boone's brother as a guest announcer for the Sox-Yanks series; apparently, Plan B was one of George Steinbrenner's kids. Well, here's your reward, guys: a Yankees-Marlins series that absolutely nobody will watch. Well done.[297]

297 I nailed this one—not only were ratings way down, I'm not even sure the Yankees cared who won that series. It was like they had already played their championship.

That two star-crossed franchises blew three-run leads with five outs to go...sure, that's a little kooky. But the 2003 Cubs didn't lose because of a goat, and they didn't lose because of poor Steve Bartman. They lost because Dusty Baker, like Little, stupidly left Mark Prior in the game for too long. They lost because their bullpen, shaky all season, imploded at the worst possible time. They lost because Alex Gonzalez botched an easy ground ball, and because Kerry Wood didn't rise to the occasion in Game Seven. That's why they lost.

The demise of the 2003 Red Sox was a little more simple: They fell short because of their overmatched manager, to the surprise of absolutely no one who followed the team regularly. I'm sure he's a nice man and everyone likes him, but when it comes right down to it, you don't want Grady Little managing your team in the Biggest Non-World Series Game of All-Time. I could give you about 150 Grady examples from the last two weeks—including him breaking the unofficial major league record for "Consecutive games with a failed hit-and-run that resulted in a double play"—but that would waste everyone's time. This man would hit on 19 at a blackjack table because he "had a feeling." That's all you need to know.

As for me, I feel like Andrew Golota just spent the last two weeks punching me in the protective cup. The excruciating A's series sucked up 90 percent of the residual emotion in my body, with The Debacle That Was Game Three—Pedro petulantly throwing at Karim Garcia, Manny overreacting after Clemens threw a fastball four feet over his head, Don Zimmer and Pedro re-enacting the Clubber-Mickey tangle in *Rocky III*—wiping out the rest. For the past few days, I was walking around with one of those weird, Daryl Hannah-like half-smiles on my face, like the lights were on and nobody was home. I was tapped.[298]

But that's the baseball playoffs for you. My friend Jack-O (a Yankee fan) called me on Thursday to say, "No matter what happens, I'm a carcass right now." That's the perfect word. Carcass. Of course, he doesn't feel that way anymore, the bastard. His team came through. Mine failed. Again. You know it's a bad loss when one of your friends is saying, "I just spent the last 15 minutes reflecting on everything that's good about my life, and I guess I just have to keep doing that for the next couple of days to get through this" (an actual quote from Hench). I'm sure this game will be a staple on ESPN Classic, and that it will definitely cost Grady his job—thank God—but honestly, the last two weeks took something out of me. You spend six months following a team, you devote something like 1,000 hours to watching-reading-discussing them, and then everything vanishes just like that, and you feel like a moron for devoting so much of your time to something so, so, so...(I can't even think of the right word).

298 Why the random **Daryl Hannah** reference? Earlier that month, when she was a guest on Jimmy's show, I walked into his dressing room when she was with Jimmy's girlfriend, Sarah—just the two of them—and Hannah was freaking out because she had a severe case of stage fright, so she was sucking down a mixed drink working up the courage to go out there. And poor Sarah was stuck talking her off the ledge. Unfortunately, Hannah was so far gone, she was rocking back and forth on her high heels, and I remember thinking she was going to tumble through the coffee table like Chris Farley in *Tommy Boy*. Anyway, that was one of the craziest faces I've ever seen—the Daryl Hannah "I'm wasted and terrified and I was crazy to begin with" Face.

Only one thing still bothers me: As one of the more optimistic Sox fans around, I take pride in my ability to ignore the past. I don't believe in the Curse. At least, I think I don't. Because I watched the first 10 innings at my office last night, surrounded by a support system of friends from work.[299] When the clock turned midnight at Yankee Stadium, I noticed the "NY 5, Boston 5" score…

And I started thinking about it…

(Haven't I been down this road before?)…

And I finally made the connection…

(Oh God!)

And it weakened my knees like Kerry Wood's curveball.

It was like seeing the Ghost of Eighty-Six. Suddenly, I *knew* they were going to lose. I grabbed my stuff and quickly bolted out of there, looking like a guy grabbing his clothes after a bad one-night stand. My friends were in disbelief—it was like Montecore the Tiger was dragging me off the stage.[300] I couldn't possibly explain it to them. Ten minutes later, I walked through my front door, sat down next to the Sports Gal (dutifully watching the entire game on the sofa), and watched Boone crush that Tim Wakefield knuckler into the stands.[301]

I had been home for about 45 seconds. No lie.

Looking back, I can't say I was surprised—just like Cubs fans can't say they were surprised when the wheels came off after Gonzalez's error. As a sports fan, sometimes you know when bad things are about to happen. You recognize the depressing signs because you've been there before. So maybe that's the real "curse," those moments when you turn into Haley Joel Osment in *The Sixth Sense*…only you aren't seeing dead people, you're seeing a dead ballgame. And when that realization happens to hundreds of thousands of fans at once, the collective bad karma ends up killing your team.

(Does any of this make sense? Of course not. I'm completely insane. The Red Sox have driven me insane. It's official.)[302]

Anyway, my wife understands now. She only jumped on the bandwagon a few years ago, thanks to me. Now her Sox virginity has been taken; she was near tears last night.[303] "I finally understand why you're so crazy about this team," she said. "I can't imagine going through this for my entire life. This is horrible." Add another one to the list.

As for my Dad, he's still alive. When we were hanging up

299 Something I didn't know at the time: The boys at Jimmy's show rigged the room with hidden cameras, just in case anything crazy happened, for a possible segment on the show. Well, something crazy happened. My friend Paul Raff, who was in charge of the segment, claims that **my head slowly turned a reddish-purple color** during the course of the tragic eighth inning. But since the loss was so traumatic on so many levels, they destroyed the footage and never aired it. Also, I threatened to kill everyone at the show like Sly Stallone at the end of *Cobra*. That was another reason.

300 "The tiger" officially makes the leap to "Montecore" as a pop culture reference. Only took a week.

301 Notice how this was the only mention of Wakefield in the whole column? Shows you how valuable he was during the series, as well as how egregious Grady's performance was—in a column following one of the most memorable homers ever, I barely mentioned the pitcher who gave it up.

last night, right after rehashing Grady Little's mistakes, I mentioned how I had to stay up late to write my column.

"You have to write something *tonight*?" my father said, incredulous. "Damn. I'm going to bed."

"You can go to sleep right now?" I asked.

"Of course not. I'm just too depressed to do anything else."

That's my Dad. He's 55 years old. I hope he gets to see the Red Sox win a World Series some day.

I hope.

302 These last two paragraphs are a good example of why you shouldn't be allowed near a keyboard when you're an emotional wreck. I have no idea what I was talking about here. But I think that's why it works—the game had obviously turned me into a rambling lunatic. I handed this column in at 3:30 a.m.

303 When I was writing the column, I remember writing the sentence "Now **her Sox virginity had been taken**, and by force." Part of me thinks that's still a funny joke; part of me thinks I would have gotten fired for handing it in. But that's how I felt at the time.

FUNERAL FOR A FRIEND

October 21, 2003

A sampling of the 2200-plus e-mails that drifted into my ESPN mailbox since Game Seven, running in chronological order from "Sent immediately after the game" to "Sent Monday afternoon."[304]

Why????
—John C., Dudley. Mass.

It hurts so bad. It's honestly worse than when my (ex-)girlfriend broke up with me out of the blue. It's that same loser feeling: you're gonna sleep on it, wake up, hope that it never really happened, but it did. Except this is far worse.
—Chris T., San Diego

I just laid in bed for an hour and a half staring up at the ceiling. I'm too weak to cry, get drunk, or break something. I don't know why I'm getting some solace from e-mailing you; maybe it's just that you know how all of us are feeling right now. I don't know what else to say.
—Mike, San Diego

www.firegradylittle.com is an available domain name.
—Robert F., Cambridge, Mass.

If the *Chicago Sun-Times* can go off and print [Steve Bartman's] name, place of business, and Little League team, don't we deserve to know Grady Little's home address after what just happened?
—Ryan A., Atlanta

Am I too young to have historical perspective, or is Grady Little the worst manager in the history of postseason baseball???
—Marin, Cambridge, Mass.

At least the Grady Little Era is over.
—Frank M., Pittsfield, Mass.

Please tell me why Pedro stayed in for the eighth.[305] You needed the executioner from *Scarface* to take care of Little before

304 I ended up getting 4,500 e-mails in seven days. And it would have been more if my AOL account didn't keep filling up. Yes, I'm the one guy on the planet who still has AOL.

305 The Red Sox owners and Theo Epstein were also asking themselves that question: Once again, a *very* reliable source told me during the 2004 season that, before Game Seven, Grady was ordered by management to remove Pedro either after 100 pitchers or after seven innings, whatever came first. That's why Pedro was shaking hands after the seventh, that's why he told *Sports Illustrated* that he was so surprised when Grady asked him to go back out for the eighth, and that's the real reason Grady got fired after the season. When I asked my source why Grady disobeyed management, they replied, "Honestly? **I just think he choked.** He panicked." And Grady's quotes after the game, as reported by *Sports Illustrated*— when he hugged Pedro and thanked him for pitching the eighth, then said, "Petey, I might not be here anymore" seemed to confirm that fact.

306 I'm *huge* in Singapore.

the eighth inning. Can't you just see him walking up behind his back? Maybe next year.

—Tim C., Middletown, Ohio

I guess Grady was saving his bullpen for Game Eight.

—Steve M., Baltimore

What was a worse managerial decision: Duke and Rocky letting Apollo face Drago in the second round, or Grady letting Pedro face the Yankees in the eighth?

—Jon C., Singapore[306]

I know you probably don't need any help writing your column on the Yanks-Sox series, but I thought I would add the following (fair warning: I'm a Yanks fan). As I sat watching this series, and Grady Little in particular, I was often reminded of one of my favorite sports quotes. Bobby Knight (who hated Dale Brown) said after Indiana came back after being down 12 points with 12 minutes left, "I was worried about losing until I looked down the floor and saw Dale Brown. Then I knew we had a chance." That's pretty much what I felt on every shot of Grady Little in the Sox dugout.

—Jim D., Richmond, Va.

I'm sorry. I'm a Cubs fan; we're tied together in misery. I was at Wrigley for Game Six. I can't make any coherent points. I'm numb, and I'm sure you are too. It's like we're bad alcoholics. Red Sox and Cub fans are...you know you'll never improve your life by it, and you still can't stop. You keep finding ways to justify it, and it bites you every time. Hang in there.

—Jack M., Illinois

All I can say is that it was like watching *The Godfather*. Every time I see that movie, I get all bull about Carmine beating on Connie, and you can't wait for Sonny to pull up in that car and kick him all over the street. And then the phone rings later, and you know what's going to happen. You hope to God that he doesn't storm off to his car. You hope to God that he doesn't stop at that toll booth. And right before the bullets start flying, something in the back of your mind says, "Hey, wait. Maybe Sonny doesn't die this time. Maybe the script has changed."

And then the toll collector drops the quarter. He ducks down. The glass breaks. And Sonny gets caught in a hail of bullets. It's one of the most gruesome deaths ever. Just like last night's game.

Bill, our time will come.

—Timothy O., Boston

My boss grew up in Houston but his parents are from Massachusetts so he became a Sox fan. His 13-year-old son has joined the Nation. My boss didn't know what to say to his son after the loss in Game Seven. I said, "Tell him, 'Welcome to the Brotherhood.'"

—Joe H., Arlington, Texas

I just finished reading your "Paradise Lost, Again" column. It actually brought tears to my eyes. I'm not kidding. I was laughing uncontrollably and nearly crying at the same time. I finally broke down. I am a blubbering shell of humanity. That is what this playoff run has reduced me to. I haven't slept for more than five solid hours in two weeks. I can't remember my own telephone number. My eyes are so red I'm certain people think I've been toking like Marley in his halcyon years. When I got home last night, my wife (who could bear no more and left the bar after the tenth) was wimpering like a scared puppy, completely unequipped to deal with her first Red Sox cannonball to the gut—she is bitter at me for subjecting her to this life and keeps muttering, "I don't know what to do, I don't know what to do, I can't handle this…you did this to me!!" And (in the too-much-information category) I haven't had a solid bowel movement in six days. This is my life.

—Lance D., Somerville, Mass.

My buddies and I TiVo'd Game Seven last night, including the shows right after which overlapped with the game. So, guess what show the segment for the end of the game is listed in our TiVo under? *Just Shoot Me*.

—John M., Lawrenceville, N.J.

Last night I shut off the TV, then threw my Sox cap to the floor and kicked it into the corner. I was almost to the point of tears. But this morning I did something that just last night I didn't think I would ever be able to do again. I picked it up, shook it off, put it on and walked out the door with my head up high. Unexplainably, after everything, I'm still damn proud to be a Red Sox fan.

—Charles K., Mass.

Think about *Braveheart*. Think about how amazing it would be to fight for your freedom and win. That's probably the best feeling imaginable. Well, barring a takeover by Al-Qaeda, that's not going to happen in our lifetime. So sports is the next best thing. To me, the opportunity to achieve that feeling of solidarity with my fellow fans, the chance to celebrate wildly, totally, and unabashedly, to feel an intimate connection, a shared sense of accomplishment with millions of strangers IS important. These Yankee fans don't, and can't, understand our pain. It [ticks] me off, but really, it's not their fault. As angry as I am right now, I'd still rather be a Sox fan than a Yankee fan. Because if we ever do win, our celebration will make any of theirs look like a day at the DMV. Even if we don't, at least I have something to believe in. Last night, and even this morning, I felt like I never wanted to watch sports again. I've changed my mind. 'Tis better to have rooted and lost than never to have rooted at all.

—David S., Brooklyn

My God. I can't believe I had to go to work after that game last night. Today is like the day after your girlfriend breaks up with you. Everyone keeps coming over and patting my on the shoulder or hugging me and saying things like, "Are you okay?" and "How are you feeling," and I keep saying, "I'm okay," and, "I'll be fine," and, "It's not my fault, it's not theirs, we just weren't meant to be." This sucks.

—Mark H., Sacramento

Seriously, why do I feel like Gary from last scene in *The Last American Virgin*...sitting in my car, crying after having my heart ripped out and listening to Quincy Jones and James Ingram sing "Just Once?"

—Jon-Luc D., Boston

With a buddy in from Boston last night. Walking up to grab a slice after dismantling the shrine of pics of Larry Bird, Ted Williams, Patriots, Yaz signed bat. Taking off my Red Sox shirt and the hidden Larry Bird shirt trying to figure out why we are so deeply affected by a baseball game we have no control over. Why two 30-something men are jumping up and down as millionaires play a game. Why the same guys are now silent and sooo depressed because of it. Awake at 3 a.m. trying to figure it all out. It's just a baseball game right?

—Mark H., San Francisco

Three moments are etched in my brain forever:

1) Pedro comes off the field after the seventh pointing to the sky thanking his God for a strong performance...he's done.

2) Nomar's hug in the dugout after the seventh, thanking Pedro for his work and letting him know they'd take it home from here.

3) Jaw hitting the floor as Pedro climbs the stairs to come out in the eighth.

Everything after the tie was just white noise. Like a tough night of drinking, I'm not sure when, how I got to my bed last night, or for that matter how I got to work today. I will never utter HIS name (GL) again. Like Fredo, he's dead to me now.

—Mark F., Hamilton, Mass.

Rooting for the Yankees is like rooting for the house in blackjack.[307]

—Adam M., Los Angeles

307 One of the five greatest e-mails I've ever received.

My son, like you, has learned from his father. But not completely. His loyalty to the Red Sox, not yet completely tarnished by years of "what ifs," compelled him to go to the game at Yankee Stadium so he could possibly enjoy the "taste of victory." Father stayed home to await the "agony of defeat."

—Murray, Potash, N.Y.

I am a lifelong Yankee fan due to a long familial history in New York. Now I am back in New England living with a man who, if he had to choose between his parents and the Red Sox, would have a hard time doing the right thing. A man who believes that you and Hench are his friends. A man whose veins pump with a rich red blood not because of science but because of the Red Sox. Because I love baseball and because I love him, I have watched the Red Sox all season long. And so here it is—the morning after the series that offered me an ulcer the size of Zimmer's bowling ball-sized head. My team won. Am I overjoyed? Am I ecstatic? Not by a long shot. I am going to tell you something that I haven't told anyone: I was rooting for the Sox. How could you not? When it was all over and Boone crossed the plate, I saw the tears in the eyes of the man who was sitting on the couch next to me and I wished they had been mine. More than anyone (except Cubs fans), Sox fans deserved that victory. The Yankees might have a $160 million team, but like the

MasterCard commercials, what the Sox have is priceless. They have heart.

Am I becoming a Sox fan? A turncoat? A bandwagon fan? Possibly. Can I think about it first? Only true love can break your heart, and I know that most people wearing Sox jerseys these days are busy taping their hearts back together. It's something to see, that's all I can say. It's incredible to know, and quite frankly, the passion makes me a tad bit jealous. You might not have as many World Series rings as those who wear pinstripes, but you might just have something there in Beantown that the Yankees will never have. It can't be bought with George's stacks of green, and it can't be won over with a Frank Sinatra song...it's just in you. And I am beginning to wish it were in me, too.

—Steph G., Manchester, N.H.

Does it make me a bad person if I was cheered up by the local postgame newscast when they showed despondent high school and junior high kids in the street saying, "No joke, this is the worst day of my life. I'm not even kidding, this sucks"? I was pretty bummed too until I saw that, then I started laughing at the TV, shouting, "Welcome to Red Sox Nation, boys!" I think I saw myself as I was 17 years ago in them. It's the circle of life, man; a beautiful thing.

—Bill K., Dracut, Mass.

There was only one analogy I could come up with to describe your latest column. For me, your article seems to be reminiscent of a eulogy at a friend's funeral. It is beautiful, but you never want to hear it.

—Ethan B., Durham, N.H.

While watching the NFL, my wife once asked me, "Which guy is the quarterback?" She literally knows nothing about sports. Yet last night after the Bernie Williams hit in the eighth, she kept asking, "How come that guy is still pitching?"[308]

—Al H., Los Angeles

I saw my eight-year-old nephew, just like me in '78, refuse to get out of bed this morning after watching his favorite team rip his heart out for the first time in his life. I feel guilty for giving him a lifetime of heartache. Please tell me I'm still a good person.

—Steve E., Rochester, N.Y.

308 Ugh...even though they won the World Series the following year, these e-mails still kill me.

Morbidly depressed all day Friday. Had to put up with co-workers who just didn't get it. Had to put up with Yankee fans who apologized and looked like they'd gotten away with something but knew better than to rub it in for fear that I would remove their head from their body and kick it around for a little while. Didn't go to church on Sunday because my pastor is a Yankee fan, and I knew I would end up going to hell if I ran to the front of the congregation and beat him senseless when he made some snide remark. Then, a long bomb fell into the hands of Troy Brown, and I clapped out loud. Deep down, somewhere inside, a feeling stirred, one that had been dormant since Ortiz took Boomer deep. Later on Sunday night, Sergei Samsonov received a nice feed and scored the game-winning goal in OT and I clapped out loud once again and exclaimed a joyful sort of noise that hadn't been heard since Nomar and Manny took it to Contreras on back-to-back pitches. The healing begins.

—Jon S., Burlington, Vt.

As a die-hard Sox fan transplanted in NYC, I expected to receive a constant barrage of ridicule and downright humiliation from my Yankee fan friends after Game Seven on Thursday night. But on Friday morning I unexpectedly received friendly phone calls from them and e-mails titled things like: "Thinking of You" and "Are You Alive?" Yes, this loss was so painful that they chose to care for my health and well-being over ragging me. I couldn't help but feel like Corey Haim at the end of *Lucas* when everyone was clapping in unison and cheering for him while he put on that ridiculously large jacket. Their good-natured concern for me, however, has not brightened the dark, vengeful contempt I have deep down in my soul for each and every one of them.[309]

—Doug C., New York

309 Very good point here—Yankee fans were surprisingly subdued in the **Trash-Talking Department** after Game Seven. It was like even *they* knew the anguish of that game had crossed some sort of invisible line.

Ever feel like Red Sox fans are the sports equivalent of Sissy Spacek's character in *Carrie*? Just as you are handed everything you want, success, popularity, accolades...all your dreams are coming true, and WHAM! You are splashed with blood and mocked by the choir. The humiliation, the pointing! The cackling! "They're alllll gonna laugh at you...!"

—Jenny, Boston

My girlfriend and I have been going out for a little less than a year. She was never a sports fan, much less a baseball fan.

When I took her to Fenway for the first time, on the drive to Boston she asked me who the Green Monster was. I almost crashed into the wooden guard rail on the Merritt Parkway. Now I understand that she hasn't followed baseball, but I almost lost it. After putting her in the middle of the Sox-Yanks rivalry for a weekend, she became a full-blown Yankee hater. Which is a very good thing for the prosperity of our relationship. Anyway, on Thursday night she is watching the game with me and before I can even get the words out, even though I am screaming them in my head, she says "Why are they not taking Pedro out?"

This from a girl who seven weeks ago thought the Green Monster was actually a person. Now she even sees that Pedro needs to be pulled. Is this unbelievable or what?

—Greg E., Philadelphia

So I'm pulling out of my parking garage in downtown Boston on Friday. The Ethiopian guy who collects the money looks awful. Like he hasn't slept in days. I ask him if he's doing okay. He says, "I have never felt so awful. Not even when my own father died...my own father. I have only been in this city for a few years, so I'm new to this. I don't know how you people do this. In my neighborhood are lots of college kids from New York, and they were cheering after the game ended. I am a peaceful man...a PEACEFUL man I tell you...but I swear to you I went outside looking to fight some Yankee fans. Just awful."

—Paul L., Swampscott, Mass.

www.firegradylittle.com is now taken.

—Robert F., Cambridge, Mass.

A LONG DECEMBER

December 5, 2003

A long December
And there's reason to believe
Maybe this year will be better than the last.
—Counting Crows[310]

One day after Thanksgiving, the Red Sox officially acquired Curt Schilling. The trade happened six weeks after the defining Sox collapse of this generation: Game Seven, Yankee Stadium, the night of Grady's Boner.

(Please note: I'm calling it "Grady's Boner" because it sounds more dramatic than "Game Seven," less pretentious than "The Night Grady Blew the Biggest Non-World Series Game In 52 Years," less wordy than "The Night Grady Hung Pedro Out to Dry," and less offensive than "The Night Grady Fucked Up." Besides, it's always enjoyable to hear the word "boner" used for baseball purposes, isn't it? I thought so. Back to the column.)

After Game Seven, I suffered through the same grieving process as everyone else. The first few days are miserable. Your friends can't maintain eye contact without helplessly shaking their head. You go days without shaving. Wear the same pair of jeans for a solid week. Can't stop thinking about the game, so you watch it again…and that only makes it worse. You end up with that glazed, weathered look of Andy Dufresne after the Warden lets him out of the hole. Finally, you glimpse yourself in the mirror and think, "My God, it's only a game, this can't possibly be worth it." And you feel better after that.

I took solace in minor diversions—the Yanks losing the Series at home, an improbable Patriots winning streak, frequent trips to the Neverland Ranch—but the Sox hovered over everything. Only in a positive way. Because here's the thing: *We were damn close.*

This wasn't like '86, when an aging, flawed team came within one strike of the title, then self-imploded and left everyone with the Glen Campbell Mug Shot Face. This time around, there was a clear scapegoat, a proven nucleus, and hope for the

310 I'm a Counting Crows fan from the mid-'90s, when their lyrics mirrored my goofy relationships at the time. Hard to explain and I want to hang myself when I think about it now. But it's true. Anyway, when they appeared on Kimmel's show two weeks after this column was posted, **someone in the Green Room introduced me to Adam Duritz**, who said, "Hey, you're the guy who quoted us in the ESPN column, that was cool." And I totally froze—deer in the headlights, stammering, the whole thing. That was the only time in two years that I was ever completely flustered by a celebrity. Finally, I just scurried away.

311 Now that we won the World Series, my father's last words will probably be, "How did we not get Tim Duncan?"

immediate future. And yes, I repeat this to myself in the mirror every morning. This time, we could have beaten them.

(No, seriously. We could have beaten them.)

And so a curious sense of hope emerged from the abyss: *It's a good team, we have the right people in charge...shit, we can TAKE these guys.* I can't remember another winter like it: depression and optimism battling for the upper hand. Even as certain media nitwits eagerly rehashed Grady's Boner—unable and unwilling to write about anything else, feeling vindicated by this latest setback, their status as the collective Scrooge of Baseball safe for another season—the organization and its fans were moving forward. Say what you want about Sox fans, but we never stop believing.

Better yet, the owners and front office feel the same way. Sox fans are accustomed to monosyllabic GMs with crewcuts and a God complex, or jolly storytellers who openly discuss potential trades with reporters, radio hosts, cameramen, waitresses, and anyone else with a pulse. These new guys (Epstein, Henry, and Lucchino) are different. They don't tip their hands, aren't afraid to take chances, act instead of react. Even last year's clunkier moves were defensible, like the hideous Freddy Sanchez-Jeff Suppan trade, which nearly caused me to drive into a telephone pole upon hearing the news. At least they weren't afraid to roll the dice.

This winter, they made three big decisions in two months. First, they canned Grady Little (Big Decision no. 1) in swift, succinct, "Tony taking care of Big Pussy in the boat" fashion. Let the record show that Grady was a nice enough guy...he just happened to be playing checkers when everyone else was playing chess. We'll remember him for his congenial personality and Forrest Gump accent, his unparalleled ability to substitute for his hottest hitters in late-game situations (only to have their spot in the lineup come up again two innings later); and his uncanny knack for keeping pitchers in three and four batters too long. Thanks to Grady, instead of "Take care of my wife," my Dad's final words on his death bed will now be "Why didn't he take out Pedro?"[311] Excellent. Anyway, Grady will be missed... by the other 29 teams. No, I'm not bitter.

Speaking of those 29 teams, nobody nibbled on Manny when Team Henry placed him on irrevocable waivers (Big Decision no. 2) in a last-ditch attempt to kick him in the ass.

Despite typically flashy numbers last season, Manny wasn't the same hitter. When he worked pitchers in his prime, he had an uncanny way of manipulating the pitcher to throw him the perfect pitch, like that buddy in a strip joint who doesn't stop circling the place until he finds the right stripper (the guy who won't settle for anyone less than the brunette with 36D's). Last year, Manny was going for blondes, redheads...he just didn't care. And it showed. So maybe the waiver move will wake him up. Then again, Manny could show up for spring training with ice-blue hair, a "Free Lee Boyd Malvo" tattoo,[312] and a batting helmet made out of chorizo and I wouldn't be surprised. Hey, it's just Manny being Manny. We knew this could happen, remember?[313]

Unable to come to agree on an extension with Nomar, Team Henry quietly floated no. 5 around the league (Big Decision no. 3), most notably in a potential three-way deal sending Manny to Texas, A-Rod to Boston and Nomar out West. The lack of outrage in Boston was telling. There's a nagging sense that, like Julia Roberts, Nomar's best days are behind him. It's not like he's washed up; you just don't see him mentioned in those "Who's the next guy to hit .400?" articles anymore. At his absolute apex, he strode to the plate, did his *Rain Man* routine with his gloves, swung at the first pitch—whether it was at his head, his feet, rolling to the plate, or whatever—and belted the living shit out of it. Then he broke his wrist, three years passed, and he settled into that ".301 BA, .340 OBP, 25 HR, 115 RBI" stage of his career. Yeah, it's good enough to make the All-Star team. But it's not the same Nomar.

The bottom line: You can pitch to this guy. Good teams can get him out (as we discovered during the playoffs), and there's a difference between **a**) somebody slumping because they're in a funk; and **b**) somebody slumping because they don't study pitchers, swing at bad pitches, and watched their reflexes slip just enough (maybe just 5 percent, but enough) that they can't get away with the "I'm going up there and swinging away!" approach in their 30s. Barring a dramatic reversal, Nomar seems destined to follow Jim Rice's lead, another physical marvel who peaked early in his career, then became a solid All-Star—but not a superstar, and certainly not your ideal choice when you needed a hit—for the remainder of his career.[314]

(Can you win a World Series with Nomar? Absolutely. Will

312 He was the apprentice of the Washington, D.C., sniper. Always a feel-good reference for a baseball column.

313 Three months earlier, I wrote the following paragraph about him: "Remember in *Life Goes On*, when Corky would put laundry detergent in the dishwasher or something—his parents would just laugh it off and you always admired the way they handled the situation? Well, that's how Sox fans are dealing with Manny at this point. You laugh it off. He's just Manny. There's nothing you can do. That's what you get when your team signs a hitting savant. I mean, it's not like any of this was a surprise, right?"

314 We'll see...

I tell my grandkids that I watched him play some day? Not this current version. He couldn't hold a candle to the guy from the 1999 and 2000 seasons. It's not even a fair comparison—it's like comparing Jessica Biel to Jessica Alba. Hey, you're fine with Jessica Biel. She may even appear in a few All-Star Games. But Jessica Alba…good Lord.)[315]

315 This paragraph started a major controversy with my readers: Many of them arguing that the Beil-Alba debate was closer than I acknowledged. But both Jessicas appeared on Kimmel's show when I was working there; at the time, everyone agreed that Alba blew Beil away. In fact, Alba and **Jennifer Garner** were the only two female celebs who caused a legitimate commotion from staff members when I was there, although Josie Maran apparently took the crown from them after I left. Sorry, I think this is important.

And then there's Pedro. You know what you're getting at this point: 30 starts, 180 to 200 innings, 17 to 20 wins, three or four gems, at least one trip to the disabled list and an entire group of Sox fans praying that he makes it through October with his right arm still attached to his body. Remember the guy who struck out 17 and allowed two baserunners in Yankee Stadium, against a team that won the World Series about seven weeks later? Well, that guy's gone. Truth be told, he's been gone for awhile. I wrote about this 20 months ago; nobody believed me. This isn't the same guy. Nobody can perform at that high a level for more than three or four years. It's impossible.

So why did they pick up his $17 million contract extension last April? Partly out of respect, partly to avoid any potential distractions, partly because they didn't want to be known as "The New Guys Who Drove Pedro Out of Town." Unfortunately, the way this current playoff system is set up, a champion's ace makes six quality starts in a month, plus two or three emergency bullpen appearances. Does Pedro have that in him anymore? Probably not. Could he do what Josh Beckett did in Game Six of the Series on three days' rest? Again, probably not. You wouldn't bet your life on it, that's for sure. For $17 million, I want a sure thing. Maybe I'm crazy.

Anyway, that's the foundation of the team: Manny, Nomar, and Pedro. By the 2005 season, all three of them could be gone without ever playing in a World Series together. Yet because the current braintrust seems to know what they're doing, and because there's a definitive plan in place, and because they're always acting instead of reacting, nobody seems too worried.

We're in good hands. Finally.

That brings us to Schilling. Team Henry (especially Theo) simply would not be denied. Schilling didn't want to pitch for a team without a manager…they convinced him. He didn't want to pitch in Fenway…they convinced him. He didn't want to give up his no-trade clause…they convinced him. Yesterday, they even stole his old buddy Paul Shaffer (real name: Terry Francona) away from Letterman and made him manager, just to make Schilling happy. And now he's coming to Boston, ready to play Don Drysdale to Pedro's Koufax (at least that's the plan).

There were two intriguing subplots to this signing, in order:

1) The Cold War

Once Schilling signed with the Sox, you knew Steinbrenner wouldn't, um, handle it very well. You just knew. Like many Sox fans, I derived a perverse sense of pleasure from the whole thing…

George hearing the news, angrily cancelling his yearly eye lift, then calling Cashman into his office and berating him for five straight hours, followed by a sobbing Joe Torre coming in as Steinbrenner spends the next 30 minutes consoling his emotional manager, telling him "It's okay, Joe, we'll overpay for Gary Sheffield and Tom Gordon and trade for Vazquez, and we'll do it within the next week," then sending Torre off so The Boss could call Howard Spira to dig up dirt on Andy Pettitte.

All right, maybe it didn't happen that way. But Sox-Yankees is the greatest feud in sports. Watching these two teams battle for supremacy in the ridiculous sport of baseball—which is quickly turning into English soccer before our very eyes—has been undeniably enjoyable. At least for me. If I lived in Kansas City or Pittsburgh, I'm sure I'd feel differently.

One other note: Peter Gammons wrote that Yankee players were just as nervous as Boston players during Game Seven, mainly because none of them wanted to play for the team that lost to the Sox. I also know two Yankee fans who swear that, after Game Seven ended, the on-field celebration was more emotional than any of the World Series celebrations (as crazy as that sounds). This feud seems to be reaching new heights these days—because of the events from last October, the neverending battle over quality players, the considerable history and everything else. When you think about it, it's the last great feud in professional sports. Nothing else comes close. It reminds me of Thomas Hauser's quote in Ali's *SportsCentury*, when he's talking about the third Ali-Frazier fight and says, "This wasn't for the heavyweight championship; it was for the championship of each other."[316] That's what every baseball season is starting to feel like. And it's a good thing.

2) The Message Board

On Thanksgiving night, Schilling submitted a lengthy post on the MLB's Red Sox message board, then chatted with Sox

316 My second favorite *SportsCentury* moment, behind **the Cooz** breaking down during Bill Russell's show.

317 I have been a SOSH member since July 11, 2000. My only regret is that you don't get an ID card like you do with Triple-A. While we're here, I always thought it was ironic that the most prominent Sox board would be named after Horn. During spring training in 1988 or 1989, I was visiting my buddy Gus at Rollins College in Winter Park, right near where the Twins used to have spring training at Tinker Field. Just my luck, the Red Sox were in town, so we ended up sitting through eight innings of a game until Gus wanted to leave to beat rush hour traffic. I didn't want to go because Horn (a towering rookie with much-ballyhooed power) was coming up in the ninth, but since Gus was driving, I didn't have a choice. As it turned out, **Horn hit the farthest homer in the history of Tinker Field**—it landed in the press box of the adjoining football stadium, something like 520 feet. It took me like eight years to get over the fact that we missed this. I'm not even kidding.

fans until the wee hours on another Sox message board called The Sons of Sam Horn (SOSH).[317] I'm actually a longtime member of SOSH, a den for diehards that weeds out weaker members and has 250-post threads on subjects like "Does Casey Fossum's delivery point seem different to you?" and "One Man's Thoughts on Nomar's Last 500 At-Bats, In Order." These guys know more than me; I'll freely admit it. During this past year in California, I clicked on SOSH twice a day for breaking Sox news (if something happens, SOSH usually has a thread going within about 1.23 seconds). Believe me, I'm not defending message boards—they can be evil places in the wrong hands—but some of them aren't that bad. And SOSH isn't that bad.

An admitted internet junkie hoping to get a handle on Sox fans, Schilling couldn't have picked a better place. He stumbled into a chat room and found about 20 fans in there, which is my favorite part of the story—only the guys from SOSH would be chatting about the Sox at 2:30 a.m. on Thanksgiving night. After introducing himself, they verified Schilling's identity with a barrage of questions, then spent the remaining 90 minutes pleading for him to come to Boston. The next day was even stranger: After Schilling landed a SOSH account and word spread, Friday afternoon (the deadline for Schilling to accept his Boston trade) turned into a pitch session from SOSH to Schilling. Hell, I was on vacation in Santa Barbara, and I ended up posting something (much to the chagrin of the Sports Gal, and I can't emphasize this strongly enough).[318] Since Schilling solicited SOSH's input in the first place, we figured these posts could help him with a difficult decision—he knew his place in history, that pitching for a championship team in Boston would push him into the Hall of Fame. You never know.

The deadline arrived...and Schilling accepted the trade, specifically mentioning the passion of the SOSH guys as one of the deciding reasons. Can you remember another instance of fans directly influencing a player's destiny, or another player seeking the input of fans in such a way? Sure, it's nearly impossible to determine an athlete's character from what we read and hear. (Note: Gammons does this all the time—according to his columns, he's apparently met more special people over the past two years than I've met in my whole life.) But Schilling seems like the exception, passionate and knowledgable, the kind of

318 Here's what I posted: "Thank God for SOSH. This is fantastic. I'm anxiously awaiting the official dawning of **the Curt Schilling Era** in Boston. Curt, if you're reading this, part of the beauty of this board is that there isn't a single person here who feels like their life would be complete until the Sox win the World Series. It's pathetic, it's endearing, and it's true. We would love to have you aboard."

guy who just *gets it*. Sports fans aren't asking for much these days; just give your best, take nothing for granted, show us some appreciation, and we're happy. Schilling did all of these things, even donating $500,000 to the Jimmy Fund on the day of the trade. In many ways, he was the complete opposite of Clemens, who played in Boston for 13 years, tossed on a Blue Jays cap and never looked back. I can't imagine Curt Schilling doing something like that.[319]

I'm not sure why these things make me happy, but they do. And to think that a future Hall of Famer could finish his career in Boston—one of the better big-game pitchers of his generation, playing on the biggest possible stage, and a good guy to boot—seems too good to be true. It's an unexpected development that makes you write a message board post when you're supposed to be on vacation. It makes you dream about Opening Day when you're shoveling snow, or when you're stuck 3,000 miles away from your favorite team. It makes you peruse every "A-Rod might be coming to Boston" story, because you never know what could happen. It makes you think ahead to next October—Pedro and Mussina in Game One, followed by Schilling and Vazquez in Game Two—best-of-seven, winner-take-all, for the championship of each other.

And so it begins. Again.

319 Phillies fans would probably argue with this assessment, although Schilling left Philly on much better terms than Clemens with Boston. I'll be honest: I just felt like taking another unprovoked shot at the Rocket.

3

February 2004–October 2004

HOPE IS A GOOD THING

CHASING A-ROD

We understand John Henry must be embarrassed, frustrated, and disappointed by his failure in this transaction. Unlike the Yankees, he chose not to go the extra distance for his fans in Boston.

—George Steinbrenner

Fucking Steinbrenner. In just 32 knife-twisting words, he managed to capture an entire winter for Red Sox fans.

The Boss made that statement on February 15, 2004, nearly six weeks after Boston's elaborate plan to land Alex Rodriguez unraveled and became a microcosm of every dark moment in franchise history. It all seemed so familiar, like one of those formulaic plots from an '80s movie, the one where the Aryan-looking prom king steals the prettiest girl from the tortured wiseass with a good heart. The Sox spent their winter pursuing one of the best players in baseball, raising everyone's hopes, ultimately falling short...and then the Yankees coldly stepped in and nabbed him. Unlike the typical '80s movie, there was no happy ending. The movie just ended. Abruptly.

Of course, losing A-Rod turned out to be the best thing that could have happened; we just didn't know it at the time. But you couldn't have concocted a more damaging turn of events for Red Sox fans. If Game Seven was the sports equivalent of walking in on your spouse banging your best friend, then the A-Rod chase was like getting shafted in the divorce hearing. Only worse.

The seeds for the A-Rod saga were planted in the spring of

2003, when Nomar Garciaparra's agent, Arn Tellem, rejected a $60 million extension that would have started after the following season. After Boston's front office was sufficiently frightened by Nomar's performance in the 2003 playoffs, they were intrigued when Texas owner Tom Hicks floated A-Rod's name later that month. Here was the marquee star they needed, the everyday stud who would become the face of their TV network, a personable go-to guy for every media request and franchise-related function.[320] With Hicks drowning under the shortstop's mammoth contract (seven years and $188 million remaining) and demanding Nomar in return, young Theo Epstein countered with an intriguing idea—what if they substituted Manny and some prospects for Nomar?[321]

Once Hicks agreed to keep negotiating, the Sox needed to figure out Nomar's situation...and that happened right before Thanksgiving, when Tellem told Theo that he wouldn't consider any offer starting at less than $16 million per year. If that couldn't happen, Tellem suggested that Boston trade Nomar, never thinking they would take him up on the threat.[322] Theo quickly swung a conditional trade with the White Sox—Nomar and Scott Williamson for slugger Magglio Ordonez and prospects—which would only happen if Boston consummated the A-Rod deal. Of course, the trade leaked to ESPN and poor Nomar heard the news on his Hawaii honeymoon with Mia Hamm. Now the fans were impossibly excited, Nomar looked like the aggrieved victim; and Hicks finally had leverage over Boston (because they had just napalmed their bridges with Nomar). With neither side willing to bend any further, it became clear that Rodriguez would have to restructure his preposterous contract. Or else the deal was off.

As the holidays approached, the A-Rod talks were practically holding Red Sox fans hostage. First the deal was on, then it was off, then it was kinda on, then it was kinda off, then it was in grave danger, then it looked promising...this was like Ben and J-Lo's engagement, but 100 times worse. As I wrote at the time, "I just wish somebody would give me the last two weeks of my life back. Like the 100 phone calls I made with my friends. Or the 56,000 times I reloaded ESPN.com at work to see if anything happened. Or the endless stream of message-board threads I sifted through. What a waste of time and energy. The entire saga started to feel like one of those five-overtime

320 In other words, they thought he was **the anti-Nomar**.

321 The new owners had quickly soured on Manny, who had been especially moody and enigmatic during the previous season, blaming the Green Monster for stealing home runs from him and publicly pining to play for the Yankees. On October 28, they even placed him on irrevocable waivers, just to prove to Manny that nobody wanted to assume his monstrosity of a contract. Nobody picked him up.

322 Looking back, this was like Jennifer Aniston telling Brad Pitt, "If you don't spend more time with me, I'm leaving you" and having no idea that **Angelina Jolie was waiting in the wings**. By the way, Nomar ended up signing a one-year $8 million deal with the Cubs before the 2005 season, then blowing out his groin three weeks into the season. It's safe to say that Arn Tellem cost him between $40 and $50 million. The lesson, as always: Whenever a player ends up getting screwed in baseball, there's usually a greedy agent running away from the wreckage covered in blood.

323 Note the sarcasm of the quotation marks "afford." Boston's owners made it seem like they were cracking piggy banks open

hockey games—after awhile, you don't even care how it ends anymore, you just want an ending."

Everything crested for three days in mid-December, as Selig granted a 72-hour window for everyone to come to terms. When A-Rod ultimately agreed to reduce his contract by $28 million so the Sox could "afford" to trade for him,[323] the player's union allowed only a partial reduction ($13 million) despite A-Rod's distraught appeals. With Hicks refusing to compromise any further,[324] Boston had a clear-cut choice: Pony up an extra $15 million over seven years or walk away.

Incredibly, the Red Sox threw in the towel and blamed everyone else. Once word trickled out that talks were suspended through the holidays—translation: A-Rod wasn't coming to Boston—I was doing some Christmas shopping in New Canaan, Connecticut, when a friend called to break the news. I just remember the life seeping from my body. *They did it to us again.* There was Christmas music playing, everyone in the store was in the old holiday spirit…and I just wanted to start ramming my shopping cart into other people. After everything that happened in October, this latest turn of events seemed almost cruel. Only the Red Sox could ruin Christmas.

So the holiday season came and went with no news on the A-Rod front…and then Aaron Boone[325] blew out his knee playing pickup basketball. Suddenly the Yankees needed a third baseman. After scouring rosters for possible alternatives, Yankees GM Brian Cashman ended up sitting next to Rodriguez at the New York Baseball Writer's Dinner—seriously, how the fuck does that happen?—with the lightbulb over Cashman's head flickering even before the salads were served. Within days, the Yankees pounced. Once A-Rod agreed to play third base, he was headed to New York for Alfonso Soriano on Valentine's Day, with Hicks assuming $63 million of A-Rod's contract in the deal.[326] Basically, the Yankees acquired the 2004 MVP in the prime of his career, and they were getting him at market rate ($16 million a year).

Looking back, the Red Sox made four crucial mistakes. First, they didn't close the deal when they could have, leaving the door open for a wildcard scenario like "Boone blows out his knee and the Yankees need to replace him." (Bar Rules should have applied here: If you spend the night hitting on a cute girl, you can't just walk away for an hour and expect

to save enough pennies to make this trade. Here was the reality: Other than the Yankees, the Red Sox were the biggest moneymaking franchise in baseball at the time. Nobody had higher ticket prices. Nobody sold better on the road. Nobody sold more merchandise. And when you throw in all the things that the old owners hadn't tapped—building up NESN (their TV network), making Fenway more profitable (with Monster seats and the like), turning the streets around Fenway into a giant concourse—it's pretty safe to say that A-Rod's contract would have paid for itself. Whatever. By the way, **say what you want about A-Rod**, but you have to hand it to him here: How many professional athletes would have left 15 percent of their contract on the table to play for a winning team?

324 You had to admire Hicks, who was dumb enough to outbid himself for A-Rod by $70 million, then brazen enough to demand money when the Sox were bailing him out of that same franchise-killing contract (and he had no other potential suitors). What a piece of work. It's like somebody heading into a Mercedes dealership, offering $80,000 for a $45,000 car, then trying to decide the terms when someone's doing them a favor by buying out the lease. How do some of these owners get rich in the first place? Have you ever wondered about that?

325 Ahhhhhhhh... the irony...

326 When word leaked that A-Rod could be headed to New York, the Red Sox frantically tried to re-enter the picture, to no avail. You could almost picture Hicks happily sitting in his office, a big smile on his face, as his secretary buzzed him and said, "Tom, the Sox are on the phone again," and Hicks just laughing and saying, "Tell 'em I'm not here," then taking a satisfied victory drag from a cigar.

327 My theory: They believed Hicks' asking price would drop in spring training once A-Rod started butting heads with manager Buck Showalter again, banking on the fact that no other potential suitors would enter the picture. Big mistake.

328 In my magazine column after they finally traded Nomar in August, I compared his reaction to the A-Rod saga to the redheaded guy in *Can't Buy Me Love* after Ronald Miller threw dog poop at his house. Seemed like a reach so I pulled it out of that column. By the way, that redheaded guy also played Malachai in ***Children of the Corn***. Quite a career.

nobody else to step in.)[327] Second, they played the whole "We have to stick to our budget, we can't pony up that extra $15 million" card, which would have been fine except they handed out a two-year, $10 million extension to Byung Hyun Kim that January. (So they weren't willing to risk $15 million for the reigning MVP, but they risked $10 million on an emotionally battered basket case who flipped off Boston fans during the playoffs?) Third, like everyone else (including me), they underestimated the effects of the debilitating saga on Nomar, incorrectly assuming that he could handle being their grudge-free backup plan as the 2004 shortstop.[328] And fourth, they compounded all three mistakes by complaining about the fairness of the Yankee trade after the fact, as if anyone would feel sorry for a team with a $120 million payroll. It just made them look petty and unprofessional.

So when Steinbrenner released that "extra distance" zinger... I mean, he was right. We didn't go the extra distance. We could have acquired a Hall of Famer for $4 million more than we gave Kim, and now we had to watch the American League's best player helping our arch-rivals for the next seven years. If this were the *Shawshank Redemption*, this would be the point where Andy thought his sentence was getting overturned because of Elvis's testimony, followed by Andy getting thrown in the hole and Elvis getting coldly gunned down by the Warden. In other words, back to square one.

Unlike most Red Sox fans, I wasn't willing to concede the 2004 season yet. On the day Alex Rodriguez was introduced to the New York media, I had been living in Southern California for exactly 15 months, a happy, peaceful place where it's 75 degrees every day and nobody cares about anything. It's not that I didn't love the Red Sox as much as everyone back home. But when you're not stuck in New England during the insufferable winters, watching everyone mope around like they just lost their dog, listening to disgruntled radio callers, overhearing people complaining about the team at bars and restaurants, accidentally tuning in to those unhappy sports shows where everyone yells at each other, and so on...well, you tend to be a little more optimistic. Just a little.

And that's where our story continues.

June 2005

THE ELECTRIC FENCE

February 17, 2004

Ever see a dog getting trained with an electric fence? It scampers around the backyard, wearing one of those stupid collars, chasing rabbits and birds, knowing it isn't supposed to pass a certain point in the yard. Only it gets a little carried away, and it can't help itself, and it's running, and it's running, and then...ZAP! Suddenly, it's high-tailing back to the house, its tail tucked firmly between its legs.

For many Red Sox fans, the Yankees are the electric fence. This is how we were raised. That's just the way it is. So when the Evil Empire plucked A-Rod on Valentine's Day, you can imagine what happened. New Englanders simply freaked out. WEEI moved into full-crisis mode. Message-board posters urged everyone else to remain calm, like we were trapped in a well or something. My phone was ringing off the hook. Even my father—a reasonable man, by all accounts—turned into Nancy Kerrigan and did everything but scream, "Why??? Why me???"

My favorite phone call came from my buddy Hench, who was attending a wedding back East. When someone casually broke the news about A-Rod, poor Hench was done for the rest of the reception. His legs buckling under him, he stepped outside for fresh air, pacing in 30-degree weather like a maniac, finally leaving a 90-second message on my machine that featured 20 swears, three tirades, and a climactic 10-letter expletive about Gene Orza. Happy Valentine's Day.

For whatever reason, I didn't flip out. Upon hearing the news that A-Rod had sold his soul, I made the same face that Brett Favre made after Donovan McNabb converted fourth and 26, crossed with Dr. Loomis' goofy smirk after Michael Myers disappeared at the end of *Halloween*. Remember that face? It's the "All right, I should be reeling from this, but I have to admit, that was pretty fucking impressive" Face. That was me. I'm not standing on the ledge. Not even close. I like this stuff. This escalating Red Sox-Yankees feud was already the most compelling storyline in sports. Now it's even better. This baby is *on*.

In fact, just to make Sox fans feel better, I came up with 33 random thoughts about the A-Rod trade, the Yanks, and the upcoming season. [329]

1) Last time I checked, pitchers and catchers haven't even reported yet. We have a full spring training and 162 games to go. Take a breath. Then take a deep breath. Maybe even go for a walk.

2) All right, how can this POSSIBLY turn out well with Jeter playing shortstop and A-Rod playing third? Defensively, Jeter has been a below-average shortstop for years; every possible defensive statistic says so. A-Rod is significantly better. Maybe he isn't Ozzie Smith in his prime, but his defense at a premium position was one of the things that made him special. You're telling me this isn't a little weird? You're telling me the New York press won't make a big deal of this? What happens when Jeter misses a few games (by the way, he missed 43 last season) and A-Rod takes over and shines at shortstop?[330] A-Rod idolized Cal Ripken, even insisting on calling pitches in Texas like Ripken did. Suddenly he's playing out of position next to someone who can't carry his jock? This won't be a big deal? Really?

3) Consider this: No more Grady Little.

4) It's official: America has its greatest sports villain since either the Soviet hockey team in 1980 or the Iron Sheik in the mid-'80s, depending on your perspective. The Yankees are like a cross between Cobra Kai and the Nazis in *Victory*—everyone hates them now, no matter where you live. How is this a bad thing? Isn't it better that we all have something in common now?

5) Nineteen games against the Yanks. Nineteen. With another seven looming in October. Every one of them will feel like a football game. And just wait until A-Rod steps out of the dugout at Fenway for the first time—with 35,000 people booing lustily, with Murph and Sully showering him with obscenities by the on-deck circle. Oh, it's on, baby.

6) For the first time in 16 years, the Red Sox have three prime starters thanks to the addition of Schilling. Isn't this a stronger version of the team that came within one managerial boner of the World Series? Suddenly we're writing them off because a guy who's never even played in a World Series landed on the Yanks?

329 Hold onto your seat—**I'm about to look like a genius** for the next few pages. Doesn't happen often.

330 Torre wisely avoided this by playing Enrique Wilson at short when Jeter went down. He knew.

331 Less than six weeks later, I signed a new three-year deal with ESPN—you'll have to wait until the spring of 2006 for me to start putting up mailbags three at a time. I'm also going to hire a personal trainer and add 20 pounds of muscle, just to complete the effect.

7) Have I mentioned that Pedro is in a contract year? Same with Lowe and Nomar? Except for the occasional Mike Cameron, does anyone ever have a lousy contract year? It's human nature, isn't it? Just wait until I enter my contract year this spring—I'll be putting up mailbags three at a time.[331]

8) During A-Rod's final season in Seattle, the Mariners won 91 games. The following season, they won 116. Look it up.

9) This will make you feel better: When I'm running ESPN6 some day, I'm going to have a show where Susie Essman shows up at Tom Hicks' front door and screams obscenities at him. When he goes to work, we're going to follow him, then she'll scream more obscenities at him. When the courts eventually become involved, she will stand 100 feet away from him with a bullhorn and continue screaming obscenities at him. This will go on for as long as I'm running ESPN6. I promise you that.[332]

10) Wasn't Alfonso Soriano being called The Next Hank Aaron as recently as nine months ago? Wasn't he their only potential franchise player under the age of 26? Was the offensive upgrade from Soriano to A-Rod *that* significant? According to ESPN.com's Jim Baker, A-Rod had 67 win shares over the past two seasons...10 more than Soriano. I don't know what this means, but it makes me feel better. And Soriano hasn't even come close to hitting his ceiling yet—his second and third seasons compare favorably to A-Rod at the same point in his career.[333]

11) You know how we have K-Rod, T-Mac, J-Will, J-Rich, J-Lo and all these other annoying celebrity nicknames? Well, A-Rod started the whole thing. Did we really want a guy on our team who once caused Linda Cohn to say "I-Rod" instead of "Pudge"?[334]

12) Once again: No more Grady Little.

13) Even if the Yankees win the Series, they had to break the $200 million salary mark and destroy the spirit of baseball in order to do it. Warrants mentioning. On the flip side, if the Sox had landed A-Rod—with the assist from Bud Selig allowing them a bargaining window that flagrantly violated the collective bargaining agreement—any championship would have carried a small asterisk with it. Everyone would have said, "You could only end the curse because the Commish bent the rules for

332 Other ESPN6 shows in the works: *Stoned Scrabble; The Jose Canseco Show; Make Mike Tyson Laugh; Gymkata: The Series;* ***Hooker, Stripper or NBA Groupie?***, and *Crossfire with Dikembe Mutombo.*

333 A few weeks after I wrote this, we found out that Soriano was 28, not 26—a little-known tidbit that nearly submarined the A-Rod deal because Cashman forgot to tell the Rangers. For some reason, it's easier to build a jet from scratch than it is to figure out the exact age of Latino baseball players.

334 After his semi-disastrous 2004 season, I wrote that A-Rod needed to take a page from Puff Daddy and change his nickname. **Remember when Puff Daddy changed his nickname** to P. Diddy to distance himself from the shooting incident and some other negative press, in the hopes that his new nickname would give him a new start? After the Varitek fight and the slapping incident in Game Six, I thought A-Rod needs to change his nickname to A-Guez.

you." Who wants that? I would rather win without help. Maybe I'm crazy.

14) Now Dan Shaughnessy can update his *Curse of the Bambino* book for its 162nd printing. Do you think he patented the "Valentine's Day Massacre" phrase on Saturday at 2 p.m.?

15) That reminds me, don't let the national media fool you. This is *not* the second coming of the Ruth sale. For one thing, the Sox didn't screw up by passing on that trade. Nomar and Mags were a wash, offensively. A-Rod was obviously an upgrade from Manny (in terms of defense, reliability, and intangibles, with an advantage in homers but a lower OPS),[335] but the Sox were shelling out significant cash *and* giving up Williamson and blue-chip prospects in the process. From a baseball standpoint, it wasn't a slam-dunk like last week's Yankees trade. I don't care what anyone else says. I wouldn't have made the deal, either.

And then there's this: A-Rod isn't Babe Ruth. He was considered the best player in the American League partly because he played shortstop...and he's not playing there anymore. So calm down. The guy hasn't even played in a World Series. As we witnessed with the careers of Ken Griffey, Frank Thomas, Albert Belle, and others, just because you look like a first-ballot Hall of Famer in your late 20s doesn't mean you're a first-ballot Hall of Famer in your late 30s. Just look at what happened to Kathleen Turner after *Romancing the Stone*.

16) Not only did A-Rod make *People*'s "50 Most Beautiful People" issue, he appeared in one of those Hot Couples photos in *SI*'s Swimsuit Issue last week—just him leaning over his wife in a waterfall. Really, we were throwing Nomar under the bus for *that*?

(And speaking of Nomar . . .)

17) No-mahhhhhhhhhhh! For everyone who doubted him and didn't mind the thought of him playing somewhere else—like me, for instance—isn't there at least a decent chance that he shoves it in everyone's face? Nothing would make me happier, with the possible exception of Julie from the *Real World/Road Rules Challenge* getting arrested for trying to unlock Veronica's safety harness two weeks ago (don't ask).[336]

18) When you think about it, A-Rod selfishly took $252 million from the Rangers, knowing full well that they wouldn't

335 I would like to retract this statement. A-Rod would not have fit into that goofy 2004 Boston clubhouse as well as Manny did. Too much of a prima donna. Schilling even came out and said so.

336 I mean, I could not have been MORE wrong about this one. Totally underestimated **Nomar's lingering bitterness** about being included in the trade. Unfortunately, so did the Sox—they let him mope around for four months and nearly destroy the season before dumping him for Orlando Cabrera. More in a few pages.

have enough money to surround him with comparable talent. After three seasons, he bailed on them and left them for dead. Now he's a good guy because he agreed to play third so he can win a ring? I don't get it.

19) At least one more year of Manny. What can I say? I like watching the guy hit.

20) Another silver lining: This A-Rod fiasco made us realize that Ben Affleck needs to be stopped. I loved *Good Will Hunting* as much as anyone, but did you see him ranting and raving at the Daytona 500? Since when did Ben Affleck become The Voice of Red Sox Fans? Who nominated him? Would a true Sox fan ever propose to a chick with a big ass from the Bronx? In a million years? I really think we should vote on this—let's have an election and everything. Ben Affleck needs to be stopped. I'm not kidding.

(And really, who is Affleck to lecture us about someone ruining the sport of baseball? Isn't this the same guy who sold out with *Reindeer Games*, *Paycheck*, *Pearl Harbor*, *Armageddon*, *Gigli*, and everything else? Has any actor cashed in as gleefully and gratuitously as Ben Affleck? How is this different from A-Rod weaseling his way to New York? And when you think about it, isn't working for the Weinsteins basically the Hollywood equivalent of playing for the Yankees? I thought so.[337])

21) Seriously...no more Grady Little.

22) There isn't any athlete in recent memory—maybe even in the history of team sports—who will have more pressure on him than Alex Rodriguez this season. Everyone will be watching his every move. Every Yankee fan will blame him if things get screwed up. And he just spent the past three years playing in the middle of nowhere, under absolutely no pressure whatsoever. Hmmmmmm.[338]

23) This could be the year that Mariano Rivera's arm comes flying off in a game. Let's face it: He's been on borrowed time for three years. Remember when the Bluesmobile fell apart at the end of *The Blues Brothers*? Exactly.

24) Speaking of breakdowns, when Kevin Brown's body breaks down this season—and he *will* break down—the Yanks won't have enough in their farm system to trade for another

337 All right, I got carried away here—the Weinsteins aren't nearly as bad as Steinbrenner. George never would have had the foresight to back fledgling directors like **Steven Soderbergh and Quentin Tarantino**—he would have bought them a few years later after they were already famous.

338 Actually, there was a precedent: Reggie Jackson's first Yankee season in 1977, which unfolded just like A-Rod's first Yankee season... well, except for his own candy bar (Reggie), a near-brawl in the dugout with manager Billy Martin and infinitely more acrimony with his teammates. Also, **Reggie came through when it mattered** (three home runs in Game Six of the World Series). Other than that, it was exactly the same.

339 You have to admit, points 24 through 27 were pretty good. This column should have been nominated for a Pulitzer.

frontline starter. Does a playoff rotation of Vazquez, Jose Contreras, Mike Mussina and Jon Lieber scare you in October? Me neither. I'll take Pedro, Schilling, Lowe and Wakefield, thanks.

25) Keith Foulke. The first reliable Sox closer in five years. Put it this way: Great closers are like great women—you don't appreciate them until you don't have one.

26) Curt Schilling. Potential Hall of Famer. World Series Champion. Leader in the clubhouse. Could give a crap about curses and panicking fans. I'll go into battle with him any day.

27) The Yanks have the weirdest clubhouse of all-time—they're like a roto team sprung to life, aren't they? Sheffield, Brown, Giambi, Contreras, Matsui, A-Rod...it's like one of those *Saturday Night Live* seasons where Lorne Michaels brought in too many cast members and all hell broke loose. Doesn't clubhouse chemistry count for anything? And will A-Rod's reputation as a prima donna precede him?[339]

28) Along those same lines, you can't buy your way to a championship. Many have tried. Few have succeeded. Last time I checked, you still have to play the whole season. In the words of Adam Carolla, "You can't just go out and buy a championship ring...well, unless Dwight Gooden runs out of coke."

29) Playing second base this season...Enrique Wilson. I don't even have a joke here.

30) At some point during the season, someone will be bright enough to make a "Yankees Most Wanted" deck of playing cards, along the lines of those Iraqi cards last spring. And we can play poker with them and bash the Yankees and stuff. I look forward to it.

31) Just in case you forgot...no more Grady Little.

32) If you're upset because the Yankees ruined the spirit of baseball as we know it, just remember: EVERY business works this way. Monopolies come in and swallow up rivals that can't compete, whether we're talking about the Yankees, Microsoft or Oprah. It's a part of life. Maybe this mess will even inspire things to change some day.

(Nahhhhhhhh . . .)

33) And finally…

I didn't want to head into spring training as the favorite. It's much more enjoyable playing the role of the underdog, hoping to make history, hoping to topple the Evil Empire, hoping this is the year we finally bust through that electric fence. And if it happens—after everything that happened this winter, after Game Seven last October, after nearly nine decades of falling short—I can't imagine anything better as a sports fan.

This is fun. This is going to be fun.

I keep telling myself this.

PINS AND NEEDLES

July 1, 2004

No matter where you are
I can still hear you when you drown
—Billy Corgan

I knew we were in trouble last week. My father and I were having a drink together in Boston. The conversation drifted to the Red Sox, just like it always does. I mentioned that Nomar was moving around at short about as fluidly as Lieutenant Dan at Forrest Gump's wedding. Dad didn't get the reference but shook his head in disgust.

"It all comes back to that A-Rod trade," he said. He was making the Dad Face, the same one as when I used to show him my report card.[340]

"Uh-oh," I said. "Really? You're starting this early?"

At this point, it was June 24th. The team was playing okay. Not great. Okay. It seemed a little early to play the A-Rod card. Not for my dad, of course.

"For an extra $15 million, we could have had the best player in baseball. You have to make that move. You always go the extra mile for a superstar."

"But Dad, that trade wasn't worth it. We had to give up Nomar, Manny, Williamson, prospects, and $15 million just for A-Rod and Magglio Ordonez. That's not a good trade."

"Nomar? He's been awful!"

"Well, they didn't know he was getting hurt at the time."

"They choked," he said, barely even listening to me. "They let him get away. That's the story of this franchise. They let people get away."[341]

After this week's debacle in Yankee Stadium, my father's words kept ringing in my ears. Maybe he's right. This winter, the Sox didn't get it done and the Yankees did. That's been the difference over the years: The Yankees go the extra mile. Of course, they can spend twice as much money as anyone else, and everyone who roots for them is headed to hell some day. But yes, they always go the extra mile. The fact remains, there were two blue-chippers available that both the Red Sox and the

340 Best Dad Face ever: After my freshman year in college, we were eating lunch at the Cape as he perused my report card **(a 2.5 for the first two semesters)**. Finally he looked up, made the Dad Face and said, "What are you DOING?" Complete disgust. And yes, I graduated with a 3.0.

341 Just four months later, Dad was happily saying, "I knew we didn't need A-Rod!"

Yankees wanted—A-Rod and Javy Vazquez—and the Yankees landed them both.

There was a creepy inevitability during these past two nights—the crowd smelling blood, the Sox falling apart in sections, the Yanks going for the kill. They just have a better team. Last year it was debatable; that's what made the ALCS so special. Not this year. These Red Sox give away outs, butcher easy plays, suck the life from their pitchers. Other than Pokey Reese and Varitek, none of their defensive players could even be called "average". It's a talented, expensive softball team, Billy Beane's Moneyball vision sprung to life. Just keep getting guys on base and everything will be fine. Or so they say.

Of course, Beane's Oakland teams haven't won a playoff series yet. And that's the problem: I'm not sure you can win this way. Teams that ignore the Little Things (turning crisp double plays, taking the extra base, cutting off balls in the outfield, getting bunts down in big spots, running the bases without looking like you're drunk) never seem to succeed in October.[342] Eventually, you reach a point where the other team is just as good as you, so you have to roll up your sleeves and beat them by playing some baseball. You know, like the Yankees did in the seventh and eighth innings last night.

It doesn't help that the Sox have been saddled with another shaky manager. Honestly, I'm not sure how this keeps happening. Just in my lifetime, we've had a staggering collection of drunks, butt-kissers, dimwits, village idiots, senior citizens, hotheads and lunatics.[343] This year we have Terry Francona, who looks like Moby and seems like a nice enough guy. Thanks to Francona's lack of aggression—not moving runners over, sticking with starters too long, catering to his stars—the team's passive play is beginning to reflect his personality. And I'm not even sure he's awake half the time.

Believe me, we've been here. The lack of urgency...boy, that reminds me of 2002! The brainfarts...hey, that's just like 2001! The absence of clutch hitting in close games...wow, it's like 2000 all over again! If anything, they seem *too* loose, the kind of team where somebody drops a pop-up and everyone laughs it off like it's the funniest thing that ever happened. It's a season devoid of repercussions. Honestly, I think Nomar could make a costly error in the next 25 games in a row, and Francona would STILL refuse to stick him at DH and put Pokey back where he

342 Not that he read this column, but I think Theo Epstein agreed with me here.

343 The libel laws prevent me from assigning these nouns to each manager, but you can probably figure it out. I only followed four teams in my life that were superbly coached: Carver High in the late '70s (with Kenny Reeves); the Celts in the early-1980s (with Bill Fitch); the Patriots in the mid-'90s (with Parcells); and the Patriots in the 2000s (with Belichick). When your team is running on all cylinders, you know it.

belongs. He's too busy scheming to break the Fewest Sacrifice Bunts in One Season record.[344]

And so they're drowning. Slowly. When your baseball team has "it," you pretty much know. I've written about this before. You start winning games on goofy plays, having those improbable ninth-inning rallies, getting huge hits from the Cesar Crespos of the world...you just kind of know. As sad as this sounds, my favorite moments of this season were Pokey's inside-the-park homer and Kevin Youkilis getting ignored by the dugout after hitting his first major league home run.[345] Nothing else stands out. It's like watching one of those $120 million summer action movies where nothing actually happens.

The injuries haven't helped. Schilling has been pitching with an aching ankle. Pedro's shoulder is like Scott Weiland—it could go at any time. Nomar and Trot missed the first two months. And yes, it's always difficult to evaluate a team that hasn't been healthy yet. At the same time, thanks to all the free agents, this feels like one of those *SNL* seasons where some well-known cast members are leaving for crappy movie careers, only some of the other stars just got here. There's a weird vibe in the air, two eras colliding. Pedro and Nomar are headed for free agency, along with Derek Lowe and the The Derek Lowe Face (back for an unexpected encore), and possibly even Varitek. They're giving way to a new crop of mainstays, with Manny and Ortiz emerging as the dominant figures—always smiling and styling, always the center of attention, almost always ripping the ball. As far as great tag-teams go, they're like Fred Lynn and Jim Rice crossed with Brock Landers and Chest Rockwell. I laugh at least once a day watching these guys. They personify this team more than anyone, two exceedingly likable guys, two of the best hitters in the league...and two guys with no other discernable baseball skills.

Heading into the All-Star Break, the team with the $120 million payroll is headed for around 91 wins. If you watched them every day, you wouldn't be even remotely surprised. You can't build a team around four high-profile starting pitchers, an expensive closer and a crummy defense, paced by an explosive offense that can't create a run from scratch to save its life. Know why? Because you win by scores like 10–3 and lose by scores like 3–2. The pieces don't fit. It's that simple. And yes, maybe the A-Rod saga set the tone for the season. Like my dad

344 If you were charting **my Francona Bitterness Scale** from 1 to 10 throughout the season, I was checking in at a 9.7 for this column.

345 One of my all-time favorite goofy traditions in baseball—the rookie getting snubbed by the dugout after his first career homer. Right up there with hotfoots, shaving cream pies, and pitchers running the bases in oversized warmup jackets.

was complaining last week, the team couldn't get it done when it mattered. And it's been that way ever since. Maybe he's right. Maybe he's right. As Jackie Rogers Jr. once sang, "Damn you, Daddy, sir."[346]

Then again, this has been the happiest Red Sox season of my life. Back at the end of March, while I was stuck reading one of those "Middle-Aged White Guy Sucks the Life Out of Sports" columns in one of the local papers, I had what Mike Tyson once called an "epithany." Did I REALLY need to read this crap? Why was I torturing myself? Couldn't I follow this team without reading any negative columns or sarcastic message board posts? Or hearing four unhappy smug members screaming at one another on the radio? It was possible, right? So I gave it a whirl. It was like quitting smoking or not Googling for Lindsay Lohan websites—it's the right thing to do, you just don't know if it can be done.

As it turned out, going cold turkey wasn't that hard from 3,000 miles away. I still surf the Internet like anyone else, but I won't click on any newspaper links or threads unless its something like Manny's HIV Test Results Are In or Sox Trade For Pujols! Instead, I TiVo every game and come up with my own observations. I examine box scores and team stats like an investor perusing the stocks. And if anything newsworthy happens, I know I'll see it on ESPN.com or find out from friends, readers, the Red Sox announcers, or even NESN's *Post-Game Report* (just in case they have the immortal Sam Horn analyzing the team).[347] Think about it. If the Sox just made the 2004 equivalent of the Scott Sauerbeck trade, or Kevin Millar pulled his bursar sac, do you really need to know right away? What's the difference of a few hours? You're getting the information eventually, right?

This little ploy worked like a charm for nearly three months; it was like getting a baseball colonic. Even my trip home was a roaring success. I can't remember having a better time in Fenway, a place that has simply been transformed by the new ownership. It's like seeing someone turn Michael Myers' old house into a multi-million-dollar mansion—between Monster seats, extra concession stands, the transformation of Lansdowne Street, and everything else, these guys have worked wonders. On Friday night, I tested out the picnic table seats in rightfield. We were looking *down* on the rightfield bullpen, with thou-

346 Totally innocous reason to throw Jackie Rogers Jr. in my column—one of my favorite running *SNL* characters of all time, along with angry poet Tyrone Green (played by Eddie Murphy), the Samurai Guy (John Belushi), the **"Get off the shed!"** guy (Will Ferrell), Trivial Psychic (Chris Walken), Frank Sinatra (Phil Hartman), and Tony Bennett (Alec Baldwin).

347 Poor Sam unleashed so many malapropisms about the "Ressax" during the average show, I still can't believe nobody bothered to write them down and stick them on a website. Isn't that what the Internet is all about?

sands of diehards in the bleachers to our right. And the seats came with $100 of free food and beer, as well as a picnic area behind us. Just an amazing experience. Poppy[348] even slammed one into the bullpen for us.

Here's the point: These things didn't happen before the new owners arrived. Nobody cared about the fans. Nobody looked at Fenway—flawed, ridiculously old Fenway—and said to themselves, "Instead of knocking this baby down, maybe we could breathe some life into it." Hey, even I'm on board at this point, even after sitting through Wednesday's game in a seat that faced right field with my knees hugging someone's back. Whatever. It's been that kind of season for me: no negativity, no sarcasm, just feeling like a fan again. Even with the team treading water, even with my Dad pining for A-Rod, it's been nice to enjoy the summer and the games that came with it.

In fact, everything was going smoothly until Tuesday's visit to the acupuncturist.[349] When I show up for acupuncture, a pleasant German lady with a thick accent gives me a preliminary deep-tissue massage. Then the doctor comes in and sticks tiny needles all over my body. They turn off the lights and play goofy, new age music. I end up going into this weird semi-trance. Sometimes I become so relaxed, I forget to breathe. And it goes that way for about 30 minutes, until they come back and take out the needles, and I walk out of there feeling like I'm stoned. Needless to say, I highly recommend it.

But that's not the point. The German masseuse loves talking to me, asking me all kinds of questions in her halting accent. On Tuesday, when I told her that my back was stiff from the plane ride to Boston, she asked me why I traveled there. I mentioned my Dad, my friends, the Red Sox games...

"The Red Sox—is that the team that hasn't won for many many many many many years?"

(Only with the accent, it sounded like this: "The Red Zox—iz dat de team that hasn't von vor many many many yearz?" I won't use the accent for the rest of this story. Just keep in mind, we're talking about a thick German accent. And keep in mind, the woman grew up in GERMANY. She just moved here, like, five years ago. Still, she managed to say "many" five times. I counted. Back to the story.)

"Yes", I answered. "That's the team."

"How long has it been? A long time, no?"

348 I was still occasionally spelling David Ortiz's nickname incorrectly at this point—it's spelled P.A.P.I. According to ESPN's Dan LeBatard, this is a Latin nickname loosely translated, meaning, **"Big hot Latin lover with the ladies."** Although he may have been screwing with me.

349 Yeah, that's right, **I get acupuncture**. It's saving my back. I tried massages, heating pads, chiropractors, hardcore drugs, self-help books . . . the only thing that worked was acupuncture. So there. Trust me, I would have laid down across Sunset Boulevard and had cars drive over me if it would have helped. You have no idea. I was that desperate.

"Um, 86 years. Yes. That's a very long time."

"What's wrong with them? Why can't they win?"

"I don't know. I don't know why we can't win."

(You would have thought she would stop. Nope. At this point, I was tighter than Melissa Rivers's face. Apparently she didn't notice.)

"Why would you root for a team that can't win?"

"Actually, I grew up there. I didn't have a choice."

"But still, you could pick different team, right?"

"Um...I don't know. I really don't know."

"I don't understand," she said finally. "If it were me, I would just pick different team."

With that, she finished up. Then the doctor came in and stuck needles all over my body. Just another day in the life of a Red Sox fan.

PANIC BUTTON

July 2, 2004

I'm tired of writing about the Red Sox, how they can't stop breaking my heart, how things happen to this team that simply don't happen to other franchises. People in places like Cleveland, Montreal and Kansas City don't want to read these things. The Sox are almost always competitive, which is more than just about anyone else can say. So how can I really complain?

At the same time...

I mean...

NOBODY loses games like this. We're the Frazier to everyone else's Ali. For example, if I told you that some team squandered a game in which they stranded seven runners in the 11th through 13th innings (including an astounding five in scoring position, highlighted by a 5–2 double play with the bases loaded and no outs); weaseled out of three innings where the opposing team had the winning run on third base with less than two outs; lost a potential go-ahead run when the other team's shortstop made a miraculous game-saving catch and nearly broke his face on a seat in the third row; and lost the game when Ruben Sierra, Miguel Cairo, and John Flaherty combined on back-to-back-to-back hits with two outs...you would guess "the Red Sox," right?

Hey, I don't mind the losing. My football team just won two Super Bowls in three years; what goes around comes around. I mind the ups and downs of following this particular team: Dramatic turns, glum phone calls to my Dad, glimmers of hope, senses of doom, and then finally, the stakes to the heart. I'm just worn out. I've been here too many times. I'm getting old. I have long, straggly gray hairs coming from random parts of my head. I blame the Sox.[350]

350 You're reading a man on the edge right now. There's no other way to say it. Word to the wise: Never put anything in writing when **a)** you're coming off **a bad fight with a girlfriend** or a roommate, or **b)** you're a sports columnist upset with your favorite baseball team.

When we're playing the Yankees, I find myself getting the new *Sports Illustrated* in the mail, seeing Manny on the cover, and wanting to perform some sort of Haitian ritual to reverse the bad karma. I find myself muttering loony things, stuff like, "Wouldn't my life be easier if I just rooted for the Pats and the Celtics? Wouldn't I be happier? Would I really be missing out on that much?" I find myself nodding to e-mails like this one, from Mike in Ridgefield Park, New Jersey: "Seriously, if I ever see you, just kill me. Find a nice, big knife, and drive it into my temple. I can't take it. It's just not fair. I hate myself for devoting so much time and effort to the those scumbags who are also known as the Red Sox. Seriously, just kill me."

I find myself darting out of the house after particularly crushing losses, just trying to get as far away from the TV as possible. After last night's heartbreaker, I grabbed the Dooze[351] and walked her all around my neighborhood. Eventually I grabbed a tennis ball and kept bouncing it down the sidewalk like a double into the gap, as she kept chasing it down like Andruw Jones. We did this for a solid hour. I could have kept doing it all night. I just didn't feel like going back inside.[352]

I find myself relying on semi-regular late night phone calls with Hench, which have evolved into impromptu therapy sessions for both of us. Last night, we spent 10 minutes analyzing Francona's decision to pinch-run Kapler for Ortiz in the eleventh inning (with Ortiz on third base, Manny on second, and no outs)—consistently the most inexplicable move in sports. Grady did this all the time; now Francona does it. For every time the Kapler-Ortiz speed difference comes into play, there are 12 other times when it doesn't. Out of those 12 times, there's probably a 50 percent chance that the game will drag on for another couple of innings. In other words, you're six times as likely to see Ortiz's spot come up again as Kapler's speed making a difference.[353] Anyway, the Yankees loaded the bases to pitch to Kevin Millar—a good idea since we're coming up on the one-year anniversary of the death of his career.[354] Millar grounded to A-Rod, who tagged third base, then threw home to get Kapler by 10 feet. If Ortiz was running, he would have gotten him by 12 feet. Either way, Papi was out of the lineup for good. In a game that was going on indefinitely.

Here's my point: Enough with dumb Red Sox managers. Really. I've had it. Hire someone who knows what they're doing, regardless of the sport, like Bill Belichick. So what if he doesn't know baseball? We'll take a few days to explain him the rules—25 guys on a team, nine guys play at once—and he'll figure it out from there. Wouldn't you feel more comfortable with him than someone like Francona? I sure would.[355]

The fact remains that the Sox trail the Yanks by nine in the loss column; from a talent standpoint, it doesn't feel that close.

351 That's the name of **our beloved Golden Retreiver**, one of the great canine athletes of our time. If you're reading in 2006, she may have been cast as the lead in *Air Bud IV* by then.

352 Nobody's better with those plastic Chuck-It throwers than I am — I can wing tennis balls down the sidewalk with control that would make the 1994 Greg Maddux jealous. If this was ever an Olympic event, I would win the gold medal.

353 I love the way I just randomly threw out these numbers with no hardcore evidence to back them up.

354 That throwaway comment singlehandedly turned Millar's season around—he ended up hitting .373 in July with six home runs and 17 RBI. As it turned out, I was just a year early.

Last year's Yankees team had four discernable weaknesses: Their set-up guys, Bernie Williams in center, the David Dellucci-Karim Garcia combo, and Juan Rivera. So what happened? They brought in Gordon, Lofton, and Sheffield. Just for kicks, they upgraded from Boone to the best player in the league. Pretty good winter. And yes, you can do these things when you're allowed to spend between $60 and $120 million more than any other team. Meanwhile, the Sox have declined in a number of categories, including team defense, set-up guys, Millar and Nomar, Walker to Bellhorn, Nixon's back, Nomar's everything, the return of The Derek Lowe Face, even (and I can't believe I'm writing this) Grady Little to Francona. Only Schilling, Pokey, Foulke and Big Papi making The Leap have prevented this from becoming a .500 season. You want to know why the Yankees just swept the Red Sox? That's why. They have a better team.

At the same time, these two franchises bring out the best in each other, and the Sports Fan Side of me appreciates what's happening here (even as I want to slam my TiVo remote against my head). I can't imagine any two teams, in any sport, playing a more competitive game at this point in their respective seasons than the one last night. For God's sake, it's July 1 and Jeter is running full speed into the third-base seats! Any other player in the league pulls up. Jeter keeps going. And sure, he nearly broke his face, and you know A-Rod was standing there thinking to himself, "Cool, now I get to play short!"

But everyone should care as much as Jeter does. That's what made it so shocking when those pinhead Yankee fans booed him in April. Some players should be beyond reproach.**356**

On the other side, we have Nomar Garciaparra, who sulked in Boston's dugout for the entirety of last night's game. You can get away with certain things in Boston, but some sins are unforgivable, no matter how harmless they might seem on the surface. For instance, if everyone else is standing at the top step of Boston's dugout and you're sitting awkwardly on the bench with a "I wish this game would end, I could go for some pizza" face—like Nomar last night—you may as well just start strangling kittens on live TV at that point. I'm not a betting man (okay, that's a lie), but unless Nomar gets traded in the next 48 hours, I would wager that last night's game became one of the defining moments of his career in Boston. And not in a good way.

355 Just once, I want to see a baseball team try this. **Wouldn't you rather see your baseball team hire Belichick** or Phil Jackson than someone who has failed multiple times, like Jim Fregosi?

356 Jeter has always gotten a raw deal from the statheads out there, to the degree that I once wrote a column defending him (and any other player who transcends statistical analysis) on my old website. I use two methods for judging a shortstop. Two and only two. First, when my team hits a grounder at Shortstop X in a big situation, as the ball is skipping along the infield grass, I either think to myself, **a)** "He might mess this up"; **b)** "I hope he messes this up"; or **c)** "Dammit, there's no fucking way he'll mess this up." And second, when Shortstop X comes up in a big situation, I either think to myself, **a)** "We can get this guy out"; **b)** "I hope we can get this guy out"; or **c)** "I'm fucking terrified of this guy." Jeter gets a c on both counts. And you think I'm following that up with an "A-Rod also gets a c but for different reasons" joke, but I'm classier than that.

Looking at the big picture, yesterday was the final chapter of The Tale of Three Great Shortstops, the trio that was supposed to battle for supremacy through the decade. So much for that angle. There was Jeter recklessly crashing into the stands, the ultimate competitor, a franchise player in the truest sense of the word. There was A-Rod greeting Cairo at home plate at the end of the game, a multi-kajillionaire just happy be involved in baseball's version of the Cold War, even if it meant giving up on his dream of becoming the greatest shortstop ever.[357] And there was Nomar, the fading superstar who helped his team blow two games in Yankee Stadium, then showed little interest in even watching the third one. He's been declining steadily for three seasons now—his body breaking down, his defense slipping, his lack of plate discipline a bigger problem than ever. He always seemed to enjoy himself on the field, almost like a little kid, but even that's a distant memory. Maybe his spirit was shattered by the rumored deal to Chicago last winter. Only he knows the answer to that one. For his sake, I hope he's getting traded this month. After last night's display, there's no going back.

Bring on the Pokey Era. Please.[358]

357 I'm pretty sure this was the last nice thing anyone ever wrote about A-Rod.

358 One of the **truly embarrassing moments in this book**. Again, don't put anything in writing when you're pissed off. It never ends well.

THE GREAT DIVORCE

August 1, 2004

In the words of Dr. Loomis at the beginning of *Halloween II*, "He's gone! He's gone from here! The evil is gone!"

All right, maybe it wasn't that bad. Nomar wasn't Michael Myers. From a personality standpoint, they were a wash. Both were consumed with thoughts of escaping. Both had outsiders wasting far too much time trying to figure them out. Both liked to wear masks. Myers was a killing machine; Nomar was a hitting machine. Both slipped as the years went on. By the end, you just wanted them to go away.

It's a little-known sports rule that acrimonious trades get the "ugly divorce" tag, although anyone would rather be traded than divorced. A trade stings for awhile, then you realize you lucked into a clean slate somewhere else. It's like remarrying without going on a single date. An actual divorce is considerably more painful, and there's no standing ovation waiting in a new city 24 hours later. And yet, Nomar's shocking trade from Boston really *did* feel like a divorce. I'm drained, confused, angry, relieved. I keep thinking back and wondering whether this could have been avoided. I want to be happy for him in Chicago, but my spiteful side hopes he hits .220. I've been hissing things like, "We wouldn't have gone after A-Rod if Nomar's freaking agent hadn't demanded a trade" and, "I think Tanner Boyle was a better defensive shortstop at this point."

Wasn't this guy supposed to be the next Bird? I remember a local writer comparing Nomar's first 100 games to the first 100 days of the Kennedy administration. We loved his Springsteen-like work ethic, his quirky OCD routine at the plate, the way he sprayed line drives around like a tennis ball machine. When he strode to the plate at Fenway, he spurred a cacophony of "No-maah's!" We were head over heels, a sea of sycophants in no. 5 jerseys. Here was someone who appreciated the game of baseball and all that went with it. During the 1999 All-Star Game ceremonies at Fenway, he crouched beside Teddy Ballgame's golf cart and grabbed his hand, and you could feel the entire city light up. The torch had been passed. Nomar peaked during those two seasons, hitting .357 and .372 and setting an unofficial record for most frozen ropes in a two-year span. We never imagined that he would be leaving in four years.

In his prime, no. 5 always treated the fans with respect, competed his hardest, played the game the right way (at least until this season). Maybe he didn't enjoy playing in Boston as much as he made it seem—he was too thin-skinned, too removed from his element, genuinely perplexed by the constant negativity of the local media—but I'm not sure *who* would enjoy playing in Boston. The real problem was that he never fully recovered after Al "Burn in Hell!" Reyes plunked him in the wrist. There were disturbing parallels between the downward trend of his stats and Jim Rice's career (when Rice settled into a .300–25–90 guy who could be handled in big spots). Defensively, Nomie was below average and getting worse every season. Other than the bullpen, he was the weak link on a team that came within one run of the 2003 World Series.

And then there was the off-season. Remember in *Death Wish*, when they broke into Charles Bronson's house and violated his family, and his whole demeanor just changed? Forever? That's what happened to Nomar. This thing simply broke him. He couldn't get past it—that they wouldn't pay him, that they moved so quickly in another direction, that he learned about the White Sox trade on his honeymoon, that they left him hanging for six weeks, then showed up for spring training like nothing ever happened. They could have mailed him a horse's head and he wouldn't have been as pissed. Under similar circumstances, I can't imagine how I would react. But the fact remains, *his agent started this whole thing!* This was one of those rare situations where both sides were to blame, with an equal level of incompetence and hypocrisy on both ends.

Anyway, Nomar was done. Shut himself off from the team. Silently seethed. Became a walking black cloud. Took his sweet time (two months) rehabbing an Achilles injury, and when he returned in June his movement in the field (already suspect) was positively glacial. Offensively, he was swinging at every first pitch, almost like he just wanted to get his at-bats over with. I have never followed a more unhappy player on a day-to-day basis. Even when he reached base, you could see him grimacing in disgust on the bag, just a profoundly unhappy guy.[359] By the All-Star Break, it was all you heard in Houston. *You can't believe how miserable this guy is…it honestly looks like he's going*

359 Although could you blame him? If *ESPN The Magazine* tried to trade me to *SI* while I was on my honeymoon, and the deal fell through, **I'd mail them a Polaroid of my middle finger** every couple of weeks.

to go postal in the locker room one of these days...nobody even makes small talk with him anymore. On and on. One person who knows him pretty well told me that the chances of him re-signing with the Red Sox were "considerably less than zero percent." Well, those aren't very good odds.

After the game where Jeter crashed into the stands as Nomar sulked across the field, the Red Sox realized that no. 5 needed to go. Maybe his petulance wasn't responsible for this team playing .500 ball for nearly three months, but the fact remains, they weren't breaking up the '27 Yankees here. This team, as presently structured, wasn't beating anyone in October. They were an *atrocious*, atrocious defensive team. They couldn't win a one-run game to save their lives—you can't beat good teams when you have 27 outs and the other guys have 30. Nomar may have been a productive bat, but his defense was giving up one to two outs every game, and even a genius like Rob Neyer couldn't quantify his effect on the clubhouse from day to day. **360**

More important, the other 29 teams have scouts. They were seeing the same things that Boston fans were seeing: an injured guy missing the exuberance that personified the first four years of his career. It's possible that his trade value wasn't nearly as high as outsiders and casual fans believed.**361** Looking at the deal objectively, the team sacrificed some offense and upgraded defensively from a D-minus (Nomar) and an F-minus-minus-minus (Ortiz) to an A (Orlando Cabrera) and an A-plus-plus (Doug Mientkiewicz). When Pokey Reese returns to play second, you're talking about an infield with three Gold Glovers.**362** That's pretty significant. You're saving an extra two or three outs a game, maybe more. And since sinkerballer Derek Lowe is only as good as the defense behind him, it's like they picked up a brand-new pitcher as well. I don't want to jinx it, but this trade might have included The Derek Lowe Face being shipped out of town. We'll see.

The success of the trade rides with Cabrera, who was trapped in a crummy lineup for a crummy franchise with no hope whatsoever. I always like getting good players from bad teams because it's like dating a girl who was mistreated by her last six boyfriends—they're so happy to be on a good team, they'll do anything to contribute.**363** I'm a little less sold on Mientkiewicz, partly because I don't know how to spell his

360 When this trade happened, probably 75 percent of the writers, radio hosts, fans, and message board posters ended up skewering it. I was in the minority. And yes, I'm telling you this so you will like me more.

361 This happens all the time in sports. It's the That's All We Could Get for him? Syndrome. When the Patriots traded Drew Bledsoe in 2002 for a measly first-rounder, the same thing happened.

362 Wow! **I just turned into Paul Maguire!** "You want to talk about a guy who can't believe he just used the phrase 'you want to talk'? I want you to watch something right now, watch Simmons' reaction as he re-reads this column, watch this, watch this, BAM! Right there!"

363 Not to keep bringing up the Pats, but Bill Belichick is one of the only coaches who has figured this out. The Patriots consistently target competitive veterans stuck on losing teams—most notably Rodney Harrison and Corey Dillon—figuring that a winning atmosphere will push them to another level. As it turned out, this happened with Cabrera, too.

name, partly because he took a giant dump on my AL-only roto team for the past four months. If you want to get technical here, why did the Red Sox include a prize prospect (outfielder Matt Murton)[364] at the last minute? Maybe Nomar didn't have as much trade value as we thought. Maybe the Red Sox were more desperate to dump him than we realized. Maybe it was telling that no teammates defended him on his way out the door.

The bigger question: How will this saga affect Nomar's legacy here? Even though most educated Boston sports fans have trouble trusting the local media—and only because they're so busy slamming everyone that you can't discern the justified attacks from the premeditated, agenda-ridden attacks—I believe more stories are coming and Sox fans will feel different one week from now.[365] If anything, Nomar's relationships with his teammates and bosses were considerably more dysfunctional than we were led to believe. Mistakes were glossed over, stories were covered up, lies were told. Over the last six weeks, nobody wanted to be the one who threw the most popular Red Sox star in 25 years under the bus. Even if he deserved it.

You can't blame Nomar for suffocating under an immense amount of baggage, but you can blame him for not having the balls to ask for a trade, and you can blame his agent for being greedy and unreasonable. By the time the Sox finally pulled the trigger on Nomar—getting maybe 80 cents on the dollar—most fans were relieved and ready to move on. Because this did feel like a divorce. An ugly one. Start with true love, sprinkle in adversity and two sides growing apart…eventually, you pass the point where you can bounce back. Right now, I see a baseball player who asked for too much and couldn't handle the consequences, and I see a baseball team that gambled on a gigantic poker hand and ended up botching it. Yes, I was against the A-Rod trade at the time. And I was wrong. But so were they.

We understand John Henry must be embarrassed, frustrated, and disappointed by his failure in this transaction. Unlike the Yankees, he chose not to go the extra distance for his fans in Boston.

Ouch.

364 If you're reading this in 2020, let's hope the name Matt Murton carries absolutely no significance whatsoever.

365 That turned out to be true. When some former teammates (like Schilling, Millar, and Varitek) threw him under the bus, that didn't help matters. By the way, isn't it time come up with a new term to replace "**throw him under the bus**"? What about "threw him on the train tracks," "pushed him out the window" or even "held his head underwater until he stopped breathing"?

THRILL OF THE CHASE

September 1, 2004

On Friday the 13th, I made a startling confession to my magazine editor: I hadn't given up hope of catching the Yankees. Of course, he cackled in delight. He's a grizzled New Yorker,[366] the type of guy who loves listening to delusional Red Sox fans. Especially when we're talking crazy.

Except for one thing. I wasn't crazy.

"Just wait," I told him. "This Yankees team is dying to be caught. They don't have the pitching this year. They're in the process of blowing out their bullpen."

"Come on, you're nine and a half out!"

"Yeah, but we still play 'em six more times. And we're just coming together after the Nomar trade."

Now he was chortling.

"I love Red Sox fans," he said simply. "You guys are the best."

And that's fine. I'm the first to admit that Sox fans are lunatics. Some find us annoying, others amusing, others exhausting. Thanks to an endless series of books, documentaries and TV features, we're probably in danger of becoming a cliché, if it hasn't happened already.[367] I will grant you all of these things. With that said, on August 13, it wasn't unrealistic to wonder if the Red Sox could catch the Yankees. So when the Good Guys made up seven games in less than three weeks, I can't say that I was shocked. Everyone else had conditioned themselves to focus on the wild card, at least until Cleveland's stunning 22–0 thrashing of the Yanks on Tuesday night. Now all bets are off.

In retrospect, you couldn't blame Sox fans for being pessimistic—after all, WE'RE the Red Sox and THEY'RE the Yankees. The wild card was a safer bet—more easily attainable, less potential for heartache. You know, the old Electric Fence analogy. If the roles were reversed and the Yankees were making a late charge, do you think their fans would complain about things like "We can't catch them, their schedule is too easy in September" (as my dad and others were saying as recently as last weekend)? Of course not. Yankee fans would expect to catch the Sox and act accordingly—sending taunting e-mails,

366 That was Gary Hoenig, the editor of the *ESPN The Magazine*. He's the same guy who secretly believes that **Willie Reed, Dave DeBusschere, Walt Frazier, Earl Monroe, Bradley,** Dick Barnett, Cazzie Russell and John Gianelli all should have made the NBA's Top 50 at 50 list.

367 Actually, it didn't officially happen until April 8, 2005, when *Fever Pitch* was released. By the way, on August 14, the Yanks were 74–41; the Sox were 63–51. When this column was posted 18 days later, the Yanks were 81–50; the Sox were 77–53.

giving co-workers crap, calling Mike and the Mad Dog and making brash predictions. They would be LOVING this. And nobody in New England would be breathing.

So this is about history. As always. For instance, I e-mailed my Uncle Ricky on Monday morning just to ask if he was getting nervous. He replied with one word in block letters: NEVER. When I asked my buddy Jack-O the same question, he sent along the following reply: "I have no reason to be nervous about the Yankees. They're in first place, and their closest competition is the Red Sox. Why would I worry? As Yogi Berra said a few years ago, 'They haven't been able to beat us for 80 years!' 1918, bitch!'"

It's a delighful group. Despite a mystifying sense of superiority, you could see their confidence wavering this season. I think it stems back to October, just before Grady botched Game Seven, when Yankee fans were six outs from pulling a Tyson in Japan, rolling around on the ground, searching for their mouthpiece, wondering what the hell happened. That subtle psychological edge—manifested in the occasional smug chuckle, the condescending slap on the back, even the harmless insult—would have disappeared forever. They may have won the game, but they haven't been quite the same since. Almost like a near-death experience.

Their players tasted that same pressure that night, all of them desperately hoping to avoid becoming That Team That Lost to the Red Sox. After Boone's climactic homer, they reacted with a level of emotion that had only been reached in those post-9/11 games against Arizona (I can still see Rivera slumped by the first base line, completely spent, like he had just escaped from the Nakatomi tower in *Die Hard*). Against the Marlins they looked just as spent, a group of guys who had already played their World Series. You couldn't blame them. We've reached the point where the feud means an equal amount to both sides. Even if the Yankees and their fans don't want to admit it.

This year's Yankee team has overachieved all season. Can you win 100 games without a single 200-inning pitcher? Can you hang on in September when your best current starter (El Duque) has a history of serious arm problems, or with an overworked bullpen revolving around three guys in their mid-30s (Rivera, Gordon and Paul Quantrill). And where's the depth? Can you ever remember a Yankee team trotting out this many crappy pitchers? Tanyon

Sturtze, C.J. Nitkowski, Felix Heredia...I keep waiting for them to sign Brendan Fraser. If it wasn't for Sheffield, they would be 10 games worse right now—he's been hotter than Roy Hobbs after the Chicago trip in *The Natural*. Remember when George overruled Team Cashman and gave Vladimir Guerrero's money to Sheff?[368] That turned out to be the best move of the winter—even when that old bastard screws up, it works out for him. Sheffield's stats (.297, 33 HRs, 98 RBI, .969 OPS) don't capture the 28 homers since June 1, or the incalculable number of clutch hits, or the feeling of dread watching your team pitch to him in late innings. In my lifetime, the Yankees have NEVER had a more terrifying hitter. Gary Sheffield puts the fear of God into me.[369]

Other than Sheff and Jeter (who's scary even when batting .140), the other dangerous Yankee has been Matsui, the Japanese import who seems like a line drive waiting to happen at all times. As for A-Rod, he's having one of those old-school Peyton Manning seasons—solid numbers, always great when they're up by three TDs, not someone you fear in big spots. Imagine if he spent all winter orchestrating this "Boston or New York" move, which worked out thanks to Boone's freak injury, allowing him to finally prove that he was a Hall of Famer on the biggest possible stage...only he was exposed as someone who couldn't come through when it mattered (as well as the 2004 Ewing Theory MVP)? Now that's pressure. The fact that they're still on pace for 100 wins with A-Rod pressing and Giambi battling his mysterious illness that we're not allowed to discuss or even casually mention at cocktail parties. I mean, what does THAT tell you? This team was playing over its head; now it's showing signs of dropping back to the pack. With Sheffield's body slowly breaking down, with the bullpen ready to overheat like a '92 Datsun on the Bruckner Expressway, without a single reliable starter to pick up the slack—I just felt like they could be had.

And I still do. From the championship run, only Rivera, Jeter, Posada and Williams remain (and poor Bernie is running on fumes). For the first time since Morgan Magic, they're battling a Boston team that has better defense and better starting pitching. Boston's top two bats (Ramirez and Ortiz) might be more dangerous than New York's top two bats (Sheffield and Matsui). They play six more times, and it's a different Red Sox team since their last meeting in July, when Varitek planted that

368 The best part of that story: They tentatively agreed to a deal at George's favorite restaurant in Tampa—George, Sheffield, and his uncle Doc Gooden. What would those three possibly talk about during a three-hour dinner? Can there be cameras rolling next time?

369 That's one of my favorite baseball tests: the Fear of God test. In my opinion, this is the best possible way to judge a baseball player and should always be used in Hall of Fame balloting. Like Paul Molitor—**was anyone scarier than Paul Molitor** in a big spot? I would have the media vote on the Fear of God Team and the Suprisingly-Not-Scary Team every year, like they do with the Gold Glove team.

two-hander in A-Rod's mug (after allegedly telling him, "We don't throw at .260 hitters").[370] These Red Sox can win one-run games now (thanks to Mientkiewicz and Cabrera, they don't give away extra outs and unearned runs), and when Youkilis returns this week, they will have the deepest bench in the league. It's a classic playoff team, built around pitching, defense, chemistry and two big boppers. The kind of team the Yankees used to build.

Say what you want about the Nomar trade, but it was like one of those *Real World* situations where the unhappy roommate leaves and everyone is sad to see them go, and then by the end of the episode one of the roommates is shaking their head in the Confessional Room and saying, "It's like a cloud has been lifted."[371] None of his teammates defended him when he left. In the weeks that followed, the players hinted that they haven't missed him, with some even going on the record. You can't blame Nomar for what happened last winter, but you can blame him for exacerbating an already uncomfortable situation. Just look at the way Drew Bledsoe handled a similar plight; it's like night and day.[372] As I wrote at the time, it wasn't like they were breaking up the '27 Yankees by dealing Nomar. They needed to do something.

And they did.

And they're 19–4 in their last 23 games.

If the roles were reversed and this were the Yankees breathing down Boston's neck, and if the Sox were the team with shoddy starting pitching, an overworked bullpen and two banged-up sluggers...well, I think you would be taking this column a lot more seriously.

One last story: When I called my buddy Jack-O during the 22–0 shellacking—you know, just to see if he was nervous yet—he wouldn't admit anything.

"It's still the Red Sox," he explained.

Then he made an analogy. Back in college, I used to routinely destroy our roommate Brendan in Tecmo Bowl. For some reason, Brendan always thought he could beat me, even though I won every game by four or five touchdowns (mainly because he was dumb enough to let me keep playing Bo Jackson and the Raiders).[373] But he kept coming back for more. And when I unleashed the usual round of post-game trash talk, old Brendan

370 That turned out to be incorrect—Varitek even said so. The important thing is that people THOUGHT he said it, and that it's one of the all-time classic sports quotes that somebody didn't actually say.

371 The quintessential example: Frankie's departure during the San Diego season.

372 The similarities didn't stop there. At different times in the '90s, both of them were earmarked for **Larry Legend status** (never happened), and both needed a fresh start somewhere else. Both were overvalued by Boston fans, who conveniently overlooked hardcore evidence that they had peaked as players three to four years before. Both were traded for (what we thought was) 75 cents on the dollar. Both watched their old teams thrive as soon as they were removed from the picture, with both teams eventually winning championships. And somewhere along the line, both of their Boston legacies suffered in the process. Of course, only Bledsoe remained professional until the end.

would come back with things like "Well, I almost had you at third-and-14 that one time!"

"That's what you're like with the Red Sox," Jack-O told me. "You're like Brendan bragging that he almost had you at third-and-14, only every season."

"But we're three and a half back right now. You're not even a little nervous?"

There was a pause on the phone.

"Yeah, I'm a little nervous," he admitted. "But it's still the Red Sox. And this is still third-and-14."

Maybe so. But it's better than fourth-and-20.

373 The original Tecmo Bowl featured only four plays per team, and Bo only had one run play to himself. It was like limiting Will Ferrell to one *SNL* skit per week. Still, you couldn't come close to stopping him—defenders bounced off him like bad guys in a superhero movie. When I mentioned Video Bo's brilliance in an ESPN.com column, the e-mails poured in, with everyone writing in reverential tones as if he were a real person. One reader remembered his buddy ripping off an 85-yard game-winning run, saying he was "helpless as **Bo shed about 874 tackles at once and strolled into the end zone** . . . it took me a long time to get over that one." Another reader wrote, "When I tell my kids about the greatest athletes of my generation, Bo Jackson will be on that list, in large part because of my memories of Tecmo Bo." Everyone has the same highlights: running Bo backward to his own goal line, then turning him around so he could plow through everyone for a 99-yard jaunt. Or watching Bo bust TDs even if the defense called his play (no one else could do that). Or seeing Bo carry defenders like a knapsack for 20 or 30 yards. Video Bo was larger than life.

STILETTO

September 29, 2004

She cuts you once, she cuts you twice
But still you believe
The wound is so fresh you can taste the blood
But you don't have strength to leave
—Billy Joel[374]

374 On the Women Are Purely and Simply Evil Soundtrack, this Billy Joel song ("Stiletto") is right up there with "Hey Hey What Can I Do" by **Led Zeppelin** and "Layla" by Eric Clapton.

You can only feel so involved in a pennant race from 3,000 miles away. Here in Southern California, some Red Sox fans frequent Sonny McLean's, a neighborhood bar in Santa Monica that shows every Boston game. It's the kind of place that makes you feel like you're home again, if only for a few hours, almost like one of those *Total Recall* experiences that Quade had. Maybe I don't stop by Sonny's that often, but I like knowing it's there. You never know when you might need a Boston fix.

Then again, there's a difference between being in a Boston bar in September and actually *being* in Boston. During the tail end of a pennant race, there's an extra surge of energy, a sense of purpose, a common ground. The weather makes you feel like you closed your eyes, spun around a few times, and landed in San Diego. The city crawls with college kids and grad students, all of them hoping to make their mark. The girls look better than ever, squeezing those last few weeks out of summer outfits and tans. On Saturdays, with everyone savoring those last few gorgeous days outdoors, it seems like 20 million people are crammed downtown. And the Red Sox dominate everything. You can't walk 10 feet without seeing a Sox hat, can't step into a bar without seeing baseball players on a TV, can't have a conversation without the topic turning toward the team. The collective mood of the city ebbs and flows with the fortunes of the team, like an oversized college campus, everyone riding the same daily roller coaster. When the Yankees come to town, you can *feel* it. It's like an invasion. *The Yankees are coming.*

Sure, you can follow the Sox on the West Coast. You just miss the little things. Like walking into a bar and knowing that there's a 100 percent chance the game is showing. Seeing Sox hats and jerseys no matter where you are (Store 24, Dunkin'

Donuts, Citizens Bank, wherever). Loitering outside Fenway before game time, sipping on a beer and watching hordes of diehards happily filing through the turnstiles. Singing the "Bah-da-dah!" part of "Sweet Caroline," along with 35,000 other fans as the centerfield speakers blast the song between innings.[375] You can't get these things from DirecTV and message boards. In Boston, it's all Red Sox all the time. Especially this year.

At dinner in Beacon Hill on Sunday, my father mentioned that he liked our chances in October because we had "two aces." I patiently explained to him that Pedro wasn't an ace anymore; Dad vehemently disagreed. That led to this exchange:

Me: When Schilling pitched today, you knew he was going to win, right? And when Pedro pitched on Friday, you didn't know if he would win, right? See, that's why Schilling is the ace.

Dad [thinking about it]: I guess I keep waiting for the old Pedro to come back.

He's not alone. Classic Pedro had another gear on his fastball. Aging Pedro rarely makes guys swing and miss in big spots. Against the Yankees in Game Seven and again last Friday, both nail-in-the-coffin singles happened because Pedro doesn't have that 97-mph heater to save his ass anymore. He's just a different pitcher, a no. 2 starter with a B-plus ceiling. He's certainly no Schilling, whose 20th victory came against Tampa last week (a team we played 78 times this season). Of every development this season, the connection between Schilling and the Fenway fans has been the happiest. He's one of us. There's no other way to say it. If he wasn't a professional athlete, he would be posting on message boards, calling radio stations, and gulping down flat beer at games.[376] For that reason, he resonates with the locals in a "Bird and Neely" kind of way.

All of Schilling's Fenway starts have a certain rhythm: He doesn't waste time between pitches, always throws strikes, saves that extra oomph on his fastball for special at-bats. The crowd supports him from the first strike, lifting him when necessary. And he bristles at departing games, to the never-ending delight of the fans. It feels like a performance from beginning to end. During the Tampa game, the Sox staked him to a 10-run lead before Schilling tired in the eighth. When Francona strode to the mound, the infuriated ace hollered obscenities at himself, ultimately handing the ball to Francona and stomping off as the crowd erupted. These things come across on TV, to an extent,

375 This tradition started a few years ago: The crowd singing "Sweet Caroline before the bottom of the eighth inning. I'm usually against these things, but in this case, it always gets the crowd going. The fans who are against it probably have a grudge against the song, stemming from the scene in *Beautiful Girls* when everyone sings it at the bar. And I really can't blame them.

376 When WEEI's Butch Stearns fanned the flames of a possible Pedro-Schilling feud that month—just another Boston media guy trying to create something from nothing—**someone named Curt From the Car called in** and ripped him a new one. It was Schilling. He had been driving around, stumbled across the show and felt obligated to defend himself. Many have called it the greatest WEEI moment since Rick Pitino's "Larry Bird isn't walking through that door" tirade—Schilling just savaging Stearns and his co-hosts, then hanging up on them like an angry girlfriend. Now *this* was a guy meant to play in Boston.

but nothing like being there, when the noise jolts through you like a stiff breeze. This sounded different from the old Pedro ovations. Not better, just different. At his peak, Pedro made you feel like you were watching an obscenely talented musician who didn't need anyone else; he was simply on a higher plane, so those Pedro ovations always carried a tinge of reverence. Like all great artists, he always remained a little detached, somewhat of an enigma, so you never quite knew if we were getting through. With Schilling, since he's one of us—and more important, since he thinks like a fan—we know we're getting through. So we bring it up a notch.[377]

It's been a wonderful match: right player, right city, right time of his career. You win a title in Arizona, you won a title in Arizona. You win a title in Boston, an entire region remembers you forever. He gets it. He understands. There are a million reasons I would want him pitching the clincher in a World Series, but that's the biggest one. He gets it. Say what you want about Francona, but without Francona, we probably wouldn't have gotten Schilling. It was a package deal, warts and all. And since this team wouldn't have made the playoffs without Schilling—who could have won 25 games with a little luck—you probably take that package. Still, I'm not sure what to make of Francona. He stuck with third-base coach Dale Sveum all season, who was so incompetent that I actually asked a friend this summer if Sveum had a depth-perception problem (like vertigo or something). Francona's Pete Carroll-esque "rah rah" routine grew stale by May;[378] you're almost better off playing dumb in Boston (like Grady or Jimy) than trying that crap. He clearly caters to his stars (especially Schilling and Manny). There just isn't much that seems "managerial" about him. Like everyone else, I often find myself wondering why he's here. Then again, this team has an outside chance to win 100 games. (Confused? Me, too.)

Regardless, I can't imagine anyone forgetting what happened with Tito over three days last week, when he blew the Orioles game by pitching lefty specialist Mike Myers against Baltimore batters who were definitely not left-handed, followed by his incredible decision to willingly recreate one of the most catastrophic innings in baseball history (leaving a cooked Pedro in the game in an eventual loss against the Yankees), followed by his pathetic attempt to get himself thrown out of Saturday's

377 I wrote this paragraph carefully. During those last two months of the season, certain writers and radio hosts were comparing Schilling and Pedro the same way someone would compare an old girlfriend to a new girlfriend—she's not as moody, she puts out more, she lets me hang out with my friends, and so on—deliberately deep-frying Pedro in the process. Not only was that unfair, it belittled everything Pedro had accomplished in Boston.

378 After he bombed in New England to the point that I nicknamed him **Coach Fredo** on my old website, Carroll became the coach of USC and turned into the modern-day Bear Bryant ... and nobody has ever adequately investigated this chain of events.

Yankees game and not being able to do *that*.[379] Examine the wreckage of every Boston playoff collapse and there's always a crappy manager lurking somewhere. I don't see much difference between Francona, Grady, Zim, Mac...in many ways, they're all the same guy, slightly overmatched, face frozen, reacting instead of acting. This doesn't bode well for October.

If the managing situation hasn't changed, at least Fenway feels different. As recently as three years ago, the team's attitude towards season ticketholders could be summed up like this: "Stop complaining, you're lucky to be here."

Here's the team's attitude now: "We're happy you're here, and we're going to do everything possible to make sure you want to come back."

Now we have Green Monster seats. Picnic tables in right field. Special field seats hugging the Sox dugout. A concourse outside where fans can linger before games, maybe even sip a beer and toss down a sausage. There are infinite concession options other than "slippery hot dogs, rubber cheeseburgers and cardboard pizza." The bathrooms are even (somewhat) clean. These owners are like proud neighbors who can't stop working on their house, hoping to preserve Fenway while rebuilding it for the current century (something few of us imagined was possible). And there's no way to measure it, but the atmosphere feels different these days—a little cheerier, a little more festive, just a happier place. In the old days, Fenway was like an aging restaurant surviving on reputation alone; they never changed anything, didn't remember your name and rushed you out of there as soon as you finished eating. Now it's like a place where they call you by your first name, shake your hands, kiss your wife and bring you a free round of appetizers just because they're happy you showed up again.

Does this stuff help you win a World Series? Certainly, every edge counts—especially when Game Seven of the 2004 World Series goes to the American League.[380] But they need to get there first. After Schilling won his 20th, I watched Friday's game at the Red Hat in Beacon Hill,[381] the night at Yankee Stadium when they toppled Rivera on Damon's seeing-eye single. The bar patrons were screaming in delight. Strangers were high-fiving and spilling drinks. My friends and I stayed out until 2 a.m., totally wired from the game. "We have Rivera's number," J-Bug kept saying, eyes bulging, almost like even he

379 If there was ever a time for a shirtless William Ligue Jr. and his son to sprint onto the field and start inexplicably pummeling someone, just to put them out of their misery, this was it. Eventually, the ump tossed Francona out with more than a little disdain, like a neighbor shooing an annoying kid off his property. For some reason, my dad was delighted when this happened, saying, "This is like watching that scene in Hoosiers when Hackman's telling the guy to throw him out, only the guy won't throw him out!"

380 Game Seven of the World Series was scheduled for Halloween night, prompting me to write this paragraph: "I'm not sure what chain of events would need to happen here — it would be extensive — but **the thought of Mike Myers coming out of the Red Sox bullpen, on Halloween night**, to pitch in the deciding game of a World Series at Fenway...I mean... wouldn't that be the most unbelievable scenario in the history of sports? And what if he won the game? Would there be rioting in Boston and Haddonfield? I can't stop thinking about this. Red Sox pitcher Mike Myers enters Game Seven of the World Series at Fenway on Halloween night...this could actually happen. My God."

couldn't believe it. "I'm telling you, he's PSYCHED OUT by us!" Trailing by a game in the loss column, we were all feeling that way. The following morning, the local papers practically awarded the division to the Sox; even Dan Shaughnessy managed to sound somewhat magnanimous.[382] My father was convinced that we were headed for a sweep, and this was a guy who gave up on the season 38 different times already.

Naturally, the Yankees demolished them that afternoon. I caught bits and pieces of the debacle at my friend Richard's wedding reception,[383] sneaking peaks at the television in an outside lounge. With the score 13–0 in the middle innings, I spent a good 10 minutes watching guests squinting in vain for an update, then heading over to the TV for a closer look. Their shoulders sagged every time they saw the score. Every time. Not a good running subplot for a wedding. Finally, they turned the TV off—probably the right move. In Boston, you can't even get away from the Sox when you're getting married.

Sunday was more of the same: Another Yankees blowout, followed by Baltimore squeezing out a win the following night. Everyone in Boston was depressed; it was palpable. We all wanted to catch the Yanks. It felt like climbing a mountain, seeing the top, then losing your footing and tumbling down 200 feet. Of course, the roller-coaster ride was reaching that part where you're suddenly upside down feeling like your lungs might come flying out of your body. There were consecutive walkoff victories over the O's, followed by those aformentioned losses that Francona screwed up, followed by the Sox rallying back for consecutive wins over the Yanks, then two more wins in Tampa (including the wild card clincher). You couldn't ask for a nuttier week. Now they're two and a half behind the Yanks. Who knows?

And yet...

With October looming, I'm just not sure that I'm ready to go through this again.

That's the rub. It's the best Red Sox team of my lifetime, a well-rounded machine with quality pitchers and big bats, a good defensive squad with a deep bench, a likable group of guys who care about one another. They deserve the benefit of the doubt, a clean slate with a fan base that won't panic every time something goes wrong. It's just that we can't help it. During last Friday's Yankee game, you needed Leatherface's chainsaw to cut the tension at Fenway. Ever attended a wedding where the

381 My favorite remaining bar in Boston now that the Brewskeller in Faneuil Hall (in the basement of the Marketplace Café) has been demolished. Warrants mentioning.

382 *Shawshank* alert! *Shawshank* alert!

383 Richard was my old roommate who moved in with me after my buddy Geoff got married in 1997. Ricky had three significant impacts on my life: First, he knew someone named Big Al who sold us an illegal cable box that enabled us to get all the movie/PPV channels. Second, he watched *Boogie Nights* with me at least 25 times during the summer of 1998, to the point that we only communicated with sentences like, "Thank you Eddie" and, "It's a real movie, Jack." And third, his buddy Mark Fanning ended up becoming one of my good friends—we watched the *Larry Sanders Roast* probably 50 times together (with an average THC level of 2.3). I couldn't have been happier—I always had two people to watch TV with at 2:30 in the morning. Then Ricky met this waitress with an annoying laugh who used to maul him while we watched TV—he ended up moving out shortly after. I was happy because a) she was finally out of the apartment and I didn't have to pay ten grand to have her killed, and b) he left the illegal cable box. After he left, Ricky still came back to hang out, only he didn't like that waitress as much (they eventually broke up), so he would sit in his old chair and watch free PPV movies with me, and I could tell that he wished he never moved out. And there's a reason I'm telling you this: If you're living with someone who has an illegal cable box, and you meet a girl that you like, just make sure she's worth it before you move out.

384 Or . . . maybe not.

385 I'm obviously happy that this assessment of Francona's managing skills was wrong—in the 2004 playoffs, he turned out to be more intuitive than Grady, more rational than Jimy, more aggressive than Zimmer, and 20 times more upbeat than McNamara. They wouldn't have won without him. At the same time, if Posada threw out Roberts in Game Four, they would have been swept by the Yankees, and Francona's coming-out party as a manager (those last eight playoff games, when

best man was hammered beyond belief? Remember that peculiar tension after he grabs the microphone and starts rambling, when everyone pretends to enjoy the speech—a seemingly captive audience—but deep down, they're dreading the eventual F-bomb or inappropriate story about the bride, so they're hanging on every word? That was Fenway on Friday night. When Pedro yielded that bullpen shot to Matsui in the eighth, it was like the best man dropping that F-bomb. The place went silent, save for a few brave Yankee fans, everyone else paralyzed by the moment—even the manager, who inexplicably left Pedro out there for a few more batters, losing every Red Sox fan for life.[384]

This wasn't just another loss. People were crushed. Everyone filed out of Fenway like we were leaving a wake, and maybe we were. It was happening again. My Dad and I had tickets for Saturday night's game. I'm ashamed to admit this, but we gave them away. We just weren't ready to go back to Fenway. It was too soon. We ended up seeing *The Shawshank Redemption*, which was playing downtown during its limited two-week re-release, the cinematic equivalent of Keith Richards having his blood changed. Three hours later, Andy and Red were hugging in Mexico and we were ready to continue following the 2004 Red Sox. You know, because hope is a good thing. And no good thing ever dies.

(Well, unless that good thing is being managed by Terry Francona.)[385]

Maybe enough time hasn't passed yet. I still remember everything about last October, 12 playoff games unfolding like rounds in a classic boxing match, so many twists and turns that even Harold Lederman couldn't have scored it.[386] I still remember the minutes and hours after that fateful Game Seven in the Bronx, when I called my father just to make sure he was still breathing. I still remember the following afternoon, when everything hit me at once—the residual emotions of the past three weeks swelling up like a killer wave, knocking me right on my back—and I actually had to leave work early. A few months passed. Last Friday brought everything streaming back. This isn't about a curse, it's about baggage, the way an accumulation of experiences alters your innate reactions. Like every Red Sox fan, I have baggage. Tons of it. Now we're heading into October with another dicey manager. My guard is up. I can't help it. At the same time, I'm going to spend my entire afternoon monitoring that Yankees doubleheader against Minnesota today. Because you never know.

Everything has changed. Nothing has changed. I don't want to go through this again. I can't live without it. I'm not sure I can handle it. I couldn't imagine it any other way.

And if none of this makes sense...well, you obviously aren't a Red Sox fan.

he was totally in The Zone) never would have happened. As always, you need a little luck with these things.

386 You know Lederman as the "official judge" for HBO fights, as well as the man who always confuses my stepdad into thinking that he's actually one of the judges. This has been going on for 20 years. Does Lederman even have a real job? And is there anything better than a fake judge who sounds like Gilbert Gottfried? **I always thought HBO should make him available for bachelor parties.** Imagine heading to a strip joint, sending Lederman to finagle a group rate, then Lederman comes back screaming in his nasal accent, "ALL RIGHT, guys, I worked them down to TWENTY PER PERSON for the cover charge...we have the WHOLE BACK ROOM... we have THREE WAITRESSES...I started a TAB for us, and you can't touch the girls BELOW the waist!"

387 This was written right after Game One of the 2004 ALDS.

388 Before the 2003 playoffs, Hench's wife wanted him to take sedatives before games—like when someone scared of flying pops a pill before getting on an airplane. He actually considered it, too. Anyway, when the Angels took the field before the first inning, I pointed out Schilling as he slowly strolled in from the bullpen, taking his sweet time to walk across the field. So Hench glanced out to Schilling, then inexplicably crouched forward and rocked back and forth a couple of times. He looked like a maniac. It was like he had fought off the pressure of playoff baseball all week, then it quietly snuck up and clubbed him across the head. Fantastic moment. You have to love playoff baseball. Needless to say, Hench didn't handle Schilling's injury very well —we nearly had to carry him out of Angels Stadium.

389 Daniel's other big highlight of the day: The Hooters mini-restaurant just outside Anaheim's stadium features a life-size picture of **two smoking-hot blondes in Hooters outfits**, but has three 70-year-old women working behind the counter. I can't emphasize this strongly enough:

DOWN GOES SCHILLING

October 6, 2004

Final score for Game One: Red Sox 9, Anaheim 3.**387**

So why do I feel like sick? Maybe it's the memory of Curt Schilling sprinting off the mound during an 8–2 game, pulling down a high chopper, awkwardly throwing the ball into right field, then pulling up lame as my buddy Hench shrieked, "He's grabbing his ankle, I think he hurt his ankle!!!"**388**

Or maybe it was the car ride home, when we called a friend at Kimmel's show, put her on speakerphone and heard her say, "Yeah, it looked like Schilling was coming on the show tonight, but he couldn't do it because he had to go to the hospital to get X-rays on his ankle or something."

(Important note: If you're ever talking to diehard Red Sox fans who are driving on a highway after a playoff game and you're about to say the words "He had to go to the hospital to get X-rays on his ankle or something" about the only indispensable player on the team, just give them some kind of a warning first. Unless you want them to careen off the highway to their deaths like *Thelma and Louise*. Which almost happened. And yet I digress.)

When you're a Red Sox fan, even blowouts in the opening playoff game comes with a price. Nothing is easy. Ever. For instance, it was a perfect afternoon for baseball, sunny enough that our friend Daniel ended up spending something like 35 bucks on a two-ounce bottle of sunscreen.**389** We were wearing Red Sox jerseys and T-shirts, standing and high-fiving after big plays, with no real repercussions other than a few flying peanuts. We even had killer seats, close enough to the Angels' on-deck circle that Troy Glaus could hear Hench screaming at him, "Thanks for killing our roto team. Seriously, thanks for the 100-game vacation!!!"**390**

We watched happily as the Sox took the crowd out of the game in the seven-run fourth inning, highlighted by a two-run error by Chone Figgins (who couldn't have looked more uncomfortable at third), followed by the inevitable Manny Ramirez three-run home run (which was so predictable, I even predicted it). I can't remember feeling so at ease during a play-

Unless there's a Hooters with overweight, hairy guys waiting tables in Hooters outfits, this has to be the worst Hooters ever. Hands down. It's like the anti-Hooters. Of course, this didn't stop Daniel from hitting on the ladies behind the counter for a few seconds, just on pure "I'm in Hooters" instinct. He's the best.

390 It's always funny to see a player's face when he's being heckled for killing your fantasy team —they're dying to shout back, "Get a life, get a fucking life!" and they know they can't. In a way, it's better than heckling them about their actual play. And since we're here, here's **my favorite heckling story**:

Back in the late-'80s, when Frank Howard was coaching first base for the Yanks, I was sitting at Yankee Stadium with my friends Bish and Jim. Thanks to Bish's Dad, we were in the first row to the right of the Yankees dugout, maybe 25 feet away from the first-base bag. Three things you should know about Frank Howard at the time: **1)** he was an enormous guy, probably about

off game. Giving Schilling a cushion like that is like stopping at a fancy car wash, the ones where you can sit in the lobby and read magazines while 15 guys who look like Alfredo Amezaga buff and polish your car. You're just in good hands. And we knew it.

There was one moment in the sixth when the Angels loaded the bases with two outs, so the Halo fans started banging those Thunder Stix like trained seals. If the goal of those Stix is to rattle everyone who isn't used to them, mission accomplished. It's like hearing 44,000 snooze alarms going off at the same time—the kind of sound that would eventually cause an ex-con to snap, then spend the next six years driving one of those Buffalo Bill vans on an endless coast-to-coast killing spree. Still, we had Schilling. He stepped behind the mound. Collected his thoughts. Took a deep breath—almost like a guy standing outside his boss's door thinking of the right way to ask for a raise. And he just stood there for a few seconds, soaking in the moment, those ridiculous ThunderStix banging away in the background. Hench thought Schilling was "going to that special place," as he called it. I thought Schilling was just appreciating the moment, maybe even thinking to himself, "God, I'm glad I came to Boston." Maybe it was a little of both.

Regardless, what a scene. You really had to be there. It practically felt like a movie, like the climactic fight in *Karate Kid Part II*, when the Japanese are banging those goofy two-sided drumsticks and Miyagi tells Daniel-San, "For life, not for points." Once Schilling gathered himself, he stepped back on the mound…and immediately retired Dallas McPherson on a grounder to second. One pitch. That's all it took. That's why he's Curt Schilling.

One other Schilling moment: In the previous inning, he was battling Vladimir Guerrero with Darin Erstad on first and two outs. This wasn't vintage Schilling yesterday—he never really got into a groove, although he usually goes into Jack Morris Mode with a big lead (just eating up innings and trying not to mess around).**391** With Vladdy Daddy up, he couldn't mess around. For most of the game, he was throwing 93 and 94. The second strike to Vlad was 95. The third strike? 97. With some SERIOUS zip. Vlad swung right through it. End of the inning. And that's the difference between Schilling and Pedro right now. Pedro doesn't have that fifth gear on his fastball anymore; he's stuck with the four-cylinder engine, opening himself up to

6-foot-7; **2)** his nickname during his playing days was "Hondo"; and **3)** during every at-bat, he would lean forward, stick his hands on his knees and put his butt out. If you were sitting in our section, basically you were looking at Frank's giant ass all game. Not good times. After a few innings and a few beers, we beat every possible Frank joke into the ground but lacked the guts to heckle him (given that he was 6-foot-7 and all). When he jogged out for the eighth (last ups for the Yankees, since they were running away with the game), it was pretty quiet at Yankee Stadium. Quiet enough for a piercing heckle, anyway. So Frank stood in the box, got in position to do whatever first-base coaches do, placed his hands on his knees and stuck his butt out. And he remained like that for a few seconds…at least until I shouted out, "Hey, Hondo…NICE ASS!" Brought the house down. Everyone in our section started giggling and poor Frank jolted up straight as if he'd been shot. You really had to be there. My proudest heckling moment other than yelling **"Magic carried you!"** and "You never won a ring without Magic!" at bloop hits, seeing-eye singles, 10-pitch at-bats and everything else. Schilling has the extra gear. Throw in his impeccable control and his sense of The Moment, and I wouldn't trade him for any other pitcher in baseball if I had to win one game. No way. Not even Johan Santana.

So you can imagine watching Schilling limp off the mound in the seventh, or hearing about his hospital visit later in the afternoon. Supposedly, he's fine. Supposedly. Whether Boston fans will ever be able to fully enjoy a Red Sox playoff win—I guess that remains to be seen.

Pat Riley for four straight quarters of a Heat-Celtics game back in 2000.

391 The biggest reason why pitchers like Schilling, Morris, and Dave Stewart never get their full historic due—there's no statistical formula that can accurately capture **Jack Morris Mode**. How do you quantify a pitcher who can hold a lead, shave 25–30 innings from your bullpen's workload every season, and not care that his ERA goes up a half-point because of it?

ALTERNATE ENDING

October 7, 2004

This was more than a playoff victory. Game Two turned into a template of every painful Red Sox defeat from the past 25 years: scoring chances squandered in the early innings; an agonizing brainfart by Mark Bellhorn on the bases; a defensive lapse on a routine pop-up jumpstarting a rally for the other team; a "Just when I thought I was out, they pull me back in!" homer from Varitek; a go-ahead run against K-Rod just to taunt us; and then the inevitable...

(Wait a second, we aren't collapsing.)

(We just struck out their best three guys with three different relievers.)

(Cabrera just cleared the bases with a double, it's 8–3.)

(Um, the game's ending, everyone's shaking hands...)

It was like watching a movie you've seen a hundred times, only they snuck in an alternate ending. Good teams seize the chance to rip out an opponent's heart *Temple of Doom* style. Good teams take care of business when it matters. Good teams slam the door in dangerous innings, grab that extra insurance run, blow the game open if it's there. Apparently the 2004 Red Sox are a good team. This game was another litmus test, one they failed in late-June during the sweep at Yankee Stadium, then failed again in late-September on Pedro's Friday start at Fenway. This time they passed.

If you're a Red Sox fan, there was a ton of stuff to love. Including...

• The thought of the Angels taking a potential *Dead Man Walking* cross-country flight for Game Three.[392]

• The thought of a potential clincher on Friday afternoon in Boston, in a St. Patrick's Day-level atmosphere (since just about every office downtown is closing early that day).

• The thought of Schilling only having to pitch once this series, meaning he could go 1–4–7 against the Yanks or Twins.

• Pedro pulling a Hulk Hogan in Game Two, lifting his arm and waving his index finger just as the referee (in this case,

392 That's a reference to my "Levels of Losing" column on ESPN.com, where I structured levels for devastating losses, with That Game (Game Six of the '86 World Series) being the highest level, the Stomach Punch being the second level (for anything unexpected that snatched victory from defeat, like Earnest Byner's fumble against the Broncos); the This Can't Be Happening and Broken Axle levels, and so on. Anyway, the *Dead Man Walking* level (Level Five) was named after the 1986 Angels, who collapsed at home in Game Five of the ALCS, then had to fly to Fenway for Games Six and Seven. They couldn't have been more done.

every Boston fan) was counting him out. Not a virtuoso performance, but an effective one: Seven innings, three earned runs, no extra base hits. This wasn't the biggest start of Pedro's career or anything, but it ranks among the most satisfying—the most memorable Red Sox pitcher in 100 years proving that his back remained fork-free, consistently hitting 94 and 95 on the radar gun. Maybe that seven days of rest did him good. When he left the game after the dramatic seventh (after Dave Eckstein and Chone Figgins fouled off a combined 75 pitches), players were hugging him and congratulating him *outside* of the dugout. Hench thought the players were making it clear to Francona that Pedro was done for the night, leading to a series of "Just to be safe, Ortiz and Millar are stripping off Pedro's clothes in the dugout" and "They're sneaking him out of the stadium in a cab before Francona reconsiders" jokes. All warranted, obviously.

• Varitek's shocking two-out homer in the sixth, which quieted the Angels fans, gave the Sox a second life and prevented K-Rod from entering the game with a two-run lead (which would have felt like 12 runs with him). One of those Bernie Carbo/Don Baylor homers (on a much smaller scale, obviously) that slip through the cracks as time passes, but were much bigger at the time.[393]

• The go-ahead run in the seventh came against K-Rod the Invincible, one of those "He's cut! The Russian is cut!" moments. You could literally feel the air go out of the stadium. *Did they just score on K-Rod? What do we do now? Could the scoreboard tell us what to do, please?*

• Francona (?!?!?!) managed a masterful eighth: First, Timlin allowed a leadoff hit to Darin Erstad, then whiffed Vlad on one of those hold-onto-your-seats at-bats (my favorite moment of the game, if only because the sense of doom was so thick, you couldn't breathe). Then, serial killer Mike Myers whiffed Garret Anderson. Then, Keith Foulke struck out the Terrifying Troy Glaus, who was slugging 1.600 in the series (???) when he came up. What an inning. It took about six hours to complete, and I think I stopped breathing at one point, but what an inning.

• Watching those Anaheim fans put away their ThunderStix and quietly skulk out of the park to beat the trafffic... as the

393 If you ever want to determine if someone is a real Red Sox fan, ask them to recount the chain of events in the ninth inning of the Hendu Game. If they don't remember Baylor's homer and they're over 25 years old, you have **a possible bandwagon jumper** on your hands.

394 Not Scioscia's finest series: He also brought Jarrod Washburn in over Percival in Game Three, leading to Ortiz's series-ending homer in the ninth —a move that was so brutal, Hench and I actually high-fived in my apartment when we saw Washburn jogging in from the bullpen. Thanks for the sweep, Mike.

game was still going on, of course. Instead of the Rally Monkey, somebody needs to market the Bandwagon Jump Monkey.

• Everything that happened in the ninth: Angles skipper Mike Scioscia choking and bringing in set-up man Brendan Donnelly over closer Troy Percival.[394] Nixon finally coming through with guys on base. Cabrera with the bases-clearing double to ice the game (his winter price tag keeps rising by the game). And the rest of the Angels fans sprinting out of there like the scoreboard caught on fire.[395]

Here's the thing: Good teams take care of business in unruly settings—in this case, a sold-out stadium in Orange County where Kool-Aid drinkers dutifully bang plastic bats together to make noise whenever they're prompted by the scoreboard. It's like the sports version of a cult. *David Eckstein is coming up…you will bang the ThunderStix for him until his at-bat is over…at the end of the inning, you will give $20 to the usher that comes around, and you will not ask any questions.* Geez, what's going on with them? This is like the Tomahawk Chop crossed with *Night of the Living Dead*. Had the Anaheim scoreboard ever flashed, "If there's a Boston fan in your section, kill them immediately," Hench and I would have been dead in ten seconds.[396]

(The more I'm thinking about it, they're like the Stepford Wives of baseball fans: Everyone wearing red and banging those Stix, few of them knowing anything about the ins and outs of the game. For example, they would chant "Pedro sucks! Pedro sucks!" at odd times, like when there were two outs in the inning and he had just struck someone out. They would stand and cheer when the scoreboard prompted them, but they wouldn't stand with two outs when Colon had two strikes on someone. It was like watching a bunch of foreigners. There was almost something cute about them, like they made you want to say, "Ohhhhhh," like watching a dog wag his tail when he gets a treat.)

The classic Anaheim fan story: Hench and I were walking into the stadium and doing the "Let's go Sox!" routine every time we walked by someone wearing a Sox hat or jersey. I mentioned how there were a surprising number of Boston fans walking around, followed by Hench joking that the number of Angels fans at Friday's game at Fenway would be either zero or zero. So some Stepford fan turns around and sneers, "You gotta get there first!"

395 Ten days later, my father and I did the same thing as the Yankees were creaming the Sox in Game Three. The lesson, as always: I'm an idiot.

396 Do you think it was a coincidence that Reggie Jackson was wearing an Angels uniform when Ricardo Montalban programmed him to kill the Queen in ***The Naked Gun***?

Um...what? Apparently the chip in his skull was malfunctioning.

"We're up 1–0 in a five-game series," Hench said. "I'm pretty sure we're making it to Game Three."[397]

Hey, at least it *felt* like a playoff game last night. The Anaheim fans were fiesty enough that I found myself searching our section for Sox fans, just to see who had our backs in case anything happened. It's almost like being in prison—you're never sure what might transpire, so you want to make sure you know who's on your side just in case there's a riot during lunch. Throw in the inherent drama of the game (four hours, something happening every inning) and Hench and I were luggage leaving the stadium. Happy luggage, but luggage.

Over the years, I have learned never to overeact after one game, especially during the playoffs, when the swings from day to day are so debilitating. But you learn about your team during games like that, much like Yankee fans learned about their team during the grueling 12-inning job with Minnesota. When you prevail in a must-win situation for the opposing team, in a game that you could have easily lost, on the road...that's when you know for sure. For me, the scars from last October fully healed last night. I'm not expecting the other shoe to drop anymore. Some Sox fans reached this point sooner than I did, some fans still aren't there. But it's a nice feeling. Even if our manager continues to scare the hell out of me.

Two more things:

1) There's been a running debate about the question, "Would it be tainted at all if you went to the World Series without going through the Yankees?" People seem pretty split. And I can see both sides. For instance, the '86 Celtics were the best team of the Bird Era, and I always feel cheated that they didn't go through Magic and the Lakers (who they would have swept that year).[398] At the same time, I don't care if the Sox beat the Expos in the World Series with Frank Robinson playing first base. I just want to win one. I'm not looking for a degree of difficulty here.[399]

2) One of my bosses pulled the "This is the year" routine on the phone this morning, asking what would happen to me (and every Boston fan) if we won the World Series. You know, the whole "Wouldn't you lose your identity?" thing. I've gotten this

397 The Stepford fan came back with some, "You guys have been losers for 90 years" and "1918!" material about 20 seconds too late. I think they immediately returned him to the factory for repairs. Reason no. 33,452 why I'm glad the Sox won the 2004 World Series: Not having to deal with losers like that anymore.

398 Everyone forgets this, including the moronic Lakers fans, who love to make the "We beat you two out of three!" argument because the Celts beat them in '84, then the Lakers returned the favor in '85 and '87. Well, the best team of the Bird Era was the '86 team, only the Lakers couldn't get by Sampson, Hakeem, and the Rockets that spring. In my book, that makes it 2–2. Have I mentioned that I hate Lakers fans?

399 In retrospect, **they needed to go through the Yanks** or else Yankee fans could have played the, "You may have won a World Series, but you didn't go through us" card. Now they have to play the, "You may have won one, but you still have 25 to go" card. Big difference. Have I mentioned that I hate Yankee fans?

one a few times over the years, always believing that it was too ludicrous for a column. But since people keep bringing it up, here's the answer: Red Sox fans don't define themselves by the 86-year drought, we're *defined* by the 86-year drought. There's a difference. We hate hearing about the (rhymes with "schmurse"), bristle at every "1918" reference...we just want to reach a point where nobody brings this stuff up anymore. It amazes me how many people don't understand that. All we ever wanted was to be Just Another Team That Won the World Series Recently.

Nine wins to go. And that's that.

POWER OF THE POOP

October 12, 2004

On Saturday night, only hours after the Yankees teamed up with Ron Gardenhire to dispatch the Twins, I was walking to my local Starbucks with the Sports Gal and her brother, Jim. They were talking about music or something. I was lost in thought, trying to come up with ideas for my Sox-Yankees breakdown column.

And then a bird crapped on me.

Right on my shirt, just above the left nipple. A gooey collage of black, white, and green. Almost looked like multi-colored mucus.

Now...

The entire side of my mother's family is Italian. If you didn't know, Italians believe in some crazy things. For instance, my mom is wearing a horn necklace right now that fends off the "malocchio," an Italian phrase for "evil eye," because she's convinced my Aunt Ag gave her the evil eye on her death bed.**400** Keep in mind, my mom has a good job with full benefits. She even manages people and sells stuff. And she's wearing a horn right now. Of course, I'm the guy who wore the same Red Sox T-shirt every day during last October's playoffs. Maybe we're both nuts.

Here's the point: My Mom has always claimed that it's good luck to be pelted by bird crap. It was just one of those things I never questioned, like when she told me how wearing a hat too much would eventually make me go bald. Since a bird had never crapped on me before, I never had an opinion either way. Now, a bird was nailing me right as I was thinking about the Sox-Yanks series. That's just weird.

"When we get to Starbucks, just ask for a napkin and some water to wipe it off," the Sports Gal told me.

"Are you kidding me? This is good luck! I was thinking about the Sox when it happened!"

I explained the Italian Bird Crap theory to them. They seemed confused. And a little bit scared. Maybe they thought the Red Sox had officially driven me bonkers.

"I'm telling you, it's good luck," I maintained.

400 Aunt Ag was furious that I didn't invite her granddaughter to my wedding (in my defense, we only had 122 people), although she was too nice of a person to give my mother the Evil Eye—she even bought me my first Fred Lynn jersey. But my Mom won't be swayed on this one. Of course, she's the same person who believes that ***St. Elmo's Fire*** should have won the 1985 Oscar for "Best Picture."

When we reached Starbucks, I asked for a napkin and water from the guy behind the counter who looked like Ashton Kutcher.[401]

"What is that, coffee?" he asked, studying my shirt.

"Actually, it's bird poop," I told him.

For some reason, this made Ashton take two steps backward behind the counter, like the bird poop was going to jump off my shirt and attack him. Even as he was stepping back, a woman waiting for an iced chai latte whirled around.

"That's good luck," she nodded.

"Are you Italian?

"Yeah. Bird poop, that's definitely good luck."

"I knew it!" I screamed at Ashton. "And I was thinking about the Red Sox when it happened!"

Ashton tentatively handed me the napkin and water, then asked, "Does that mean you still want to wipe it off?" before taking another three steps back.

"I'll wipe it off, but I'm not washing the T-shirt until after the playoffs," I told him.

"Good move," the Italian woman told me. See, she knew.

Now I have the T-shirt hidden away from the Sports Gal, just in case she decides to accidentally wash it with the whites right before Game Seven. Maybe the stain will morph into some crazy Legionnaire's Disease fungus. I don't care. All I know is that I'm saving T-shirts covered in bird poop; the Red Sox are passing around a Dominican dwarf as a good luck charm, Curt Schilling is starting lucky message board threads on the Sons of Sam Horn, Millar, Minky, Nixon, Timlin and others are growing mutant Fu Manchus; and I'm sure there are millions of Sox fans following suit with their own goofy superstitions. For the next 10 days, every little bit helps.[402]

We're playing the Yankees, you know.

Without further ado, let's break this baby down, Dr. Jack style...[403]

LINEUPS

Torre's Yankee teams can't be accurately measured on paper, as evidenced by Jeter's entire career. Take someone like Miguel Cairo, a career .273 hitter with no power who can't get on base. Stick him on the Yankees and suddenly he's belting clutch extra-base hits and grinding out 10-pitch at-bats. It's uncanny. These guys seem to be oozing with confidence right now, as evi-

401 This was the Starbucks on the corner of Beverly and Detroit, one block from La Brea. My first apartment in Los Angeles was on Mansfield Aveue, only three blocks away, and there wasn't another coffee place in the vicinity. Believe me, I hate Starbucks as much as you. But when you don't have any other options, it's almost like how straight guys start having sex with each other in prison—you do what you need to do to survive, and in this case, I can't function without coffee every morning. The real tragedy here is that **Starbucks uses twice as much caffeine** in their coffee as anyone else, so once you start having it, it's almost like crack—you crave it every morning and get headaches if you drink anything else.

402 No, I never washed the shirt.

403 I debated long and hard about including this column in the book, but you know what? It's strangely entertaining after the fact. By the way, I called these Dr. Jack Breakdowns after Dr. Jack Ramsay, who would break things down on ESPN.com in similar fashion.

denced by A-Rod's comments after Game Four in Minnesota: "You should have seen the bench in the eighth when we were behind 5–1. We just knew we were going to win. It was like a college team."

(Well, except for the $200 million payroll.)

As for the Red Sox, they have the 2003 batting champ batting ninth. 'Nuff said. Matching up the offenses, Damon tops Bernie (who somehow remains terrifying in big moments). Jeter gets a sizable edge over Cabrera. Varitek tops Posada (a legendary underachiever in the postseason). Nixon cancels out Matsui.[404] Millar tops John Olerud. Bellhorn and Mueller get a slight edge over Sierra/Lofton and Cairo/Wilson. Ortiz and Manny cancel out A-Rod and Sheffield (although it remains to be seen if Sheffield can climb out of his postseason batting funk—.235, .292, .062, .143 and .222 in his last five playoff series).

So Boston has the edge. But since the Yanks have come through so many times in big spots, especially this season...

Edge: Even.

BENCHES

Not the best year for Yankee benches. It's okay if your top pinch-hitters are Tony Clark and Bubba Crosby, as long as you're managing a team in Japan. Nobody can figure out this Giambi thing—he's like John Travolta in *Boy in the Plastic Bubble* at this point. And is Kenny Lofton really the top speed guy on the bench? Did he win the spring training job over Cool Papa Bell? I'm confused. Things were so bad that Luis Sojo made the 25-man roster of the ALDS, which means he had to quit his 8-to-4 shift at Wal-Mart again.[405]

Meanwhile, Boston has the best bench in baseball; they just don't have a manager who always knows how to use it. Like in Game Three on Friday, with Damon on first and nobody out in the tenth, Francona kept Bellhorn in the game in an obvious bunt situation—which he predictably botched—then pinch-ran for Bellhorn at first with Pokey Reese. Why not insert Pokey or Dave Roberts for the actual bunt? Of course, this is the same guy who removed Bronson Arroyo (throwing a three-hitter) after 91 pitches to bring in Mike Myers against a lefty, when everyone knew that the Angels would immediately pinch-hit a righty bat (so you now had Myers pitching to a righty when he can't get righties out). Don't get me started.

Edge: Red Sox.

404 Not only was that an incorrect statement that ruined the credibility of the column, but Matsui ended up going 25-for-26 in the first three games, with 17 homers.

405 Originally the punchline was Del Taco, but my ESPN.com editors thought it could be perceived as racist and made me change it. Whenever this happens, I always wonder for about 20 seconds if I really AM racist, at least until I remember that it's much funnier to **think of Luis Sojo working in a Del Taco** than a WalMart. He would look funny in the Del Taco hat/uniform combo. Nobody can deny this.

CRAZIEST GUY

The recent *Sports Illustrated* issue vaulted Gary Sheffield into the Crazy Athlete Pantheon.[406] J-Bug said it best: "If Sheffield didn't become a baseball player, he would have been the last face you saw if you owed more than 10 grand to a bookie and didn't have the cash." As for Boston, Manny would have been the representative as recently as two months ago. Then Pedro bought Eriq LaSalle's Jheri-curl Afro from *Coming to America* on eBay, decided that the Yankees were his Daddy and started bringing a 30-inch Dominican midget to the clubhouse after games. Adding his over-the-top dugout antics on non-pitching days, there's at least a 50 percent chance that last year's Game Seven in the Bronx drove him insane. Ladies and gentlemen, our Game Two starter.

Edge: Red Sox.

GUY WITH MOST AT STAKE

Boston has Schilling, who would become a local hero on par with JFK, Sam Adams and Paul Revere if he pitched the Sox to a championship.[407] The Yanks have A-Rod, who offered to give up $15 million out of his own pocket to play for the Red Sox, then gave up his dream of being the best shortstop ever just to prove himself in a series like this one. Who do *you* think has more pressure?

Edge: Yankees[408]

STADIUMS

Going down my "Things that make a stadium great" list, it's dead-even right until Category no. 53: "Meeting point before the game." Fenway has the Beerworks, the Cask and Flagon, the Baseball Tavern, and Copperfields. Yankee Stadium doesn't have any bars that close, so you have to meet at the Babe's bat in front of the stadium, which carried enough homoerotic overtones even before Vito Spatafore was standing out there waiting for Meadow Soprano's boyfriend.[409]

Edge: Red Sox

BASERUNNING

Neither team steals many bases, but Jeter and A-Rod are superior baserunners to anyone on the Red Sox. And don't forget about the Dale Sveum Factor. It's like having Billy Joel as your third-base coach.

Slight Edge: Yankees

406 Some highlights: Sheffield bitching about Barry Bonds like a little kid; the fact that he has a personal chef who travels with him; how he still maintains that **he paid Balco $50,000 for some vitamins** and scar cream; how he punched out the Brewers pitcher for complaining about his error; how he threatened Pedro's life. How this man restrained himself from charging into Fenway's right field stands during that April 2005 game remains the biggest sports upset of the 21st century so far.

407 As it turned out, this didn't quite happen: Ortiz stole half his spot.

408 Hah! I redeemed myself from the Matsui-Nixon paragraph.

409 Tons of Yankee fans took exception to this paragraph, e-mailing me names of various bars within walking distance of the Stadium. But would you go into them if you were a human being? I guess that's the question.

BENCH-CLEARING BRAWLS

These things always come down to the three or four biggest guys on the team, plus two wildcards (the Mickey Rivers types) who sucker-punch guys when they're not looking (everyone else grabs someone their size and hopes they don't get hurt). The Yanks are shorthanded here because a) Brown has a broken hand, and b) everyone will be afraid to go within ten feet of Giambi. Also, they have a number of guys who look like they wouldn't want to get hit because they're heading out to a club that night (including Loaiza, Posada, and Mussina). But since we got a little taste in July during the aborted A-Rod-Varitek brawl, I'd break down the major players like this...

Sox: Ortiz (the biggest guy on the field); Kapler (the strongest); Timlin (the sturdiest); Nixon (even with the ailing back); Cabrera (possible wild card); Varitek and Millar (good tag-team); and Schilling (depending on the ankle).

Yanks: A-Rod (0–1 this season); Bubba Crosby (for his name alone); Tanyon Sturtze (who suddenly throws 96 mph and had the inexplicable meltdown during the July brawl...hmmmmm);[410] Sheffield (if properly angered, he could potentially take out everyone on the Sox like Patrick Swayze at the Double Deuce); Kenny Lofton (possible wild card); Jeter (would always defend his teammates). They clearly miss Don Zimmer here, the only guy with enough testicular fortitude to go after Pedro last October, although he did have a metal plate in his head at the time.

Edge: Red Sox

TEAM CHEMISTRY

This helped the Sox against Anaheim. Won't matter here.

Edge: Even

OFFENSIVE T-SHIRTS IN STANDS

Yankees fans wear harmless stuff like "BOSTON SUCKS" and "WHO'S YOUR DADDY?" Sox fans match those shirts and take it 10 steps further with some truly offensive stuff. During my last trip to Fenway, I saw "JETER HAS AIDS" and "GAY-ROD" shirts. And those were some of the tamer ones. It's a fun rivalry for the whole family.[411]

Edge: Red Sox

FAN IMPACT DURING GAMES

Major weakness for Boston because of our tortured history,

410 I like this line—I did everything but accuse Sturtze of owning Balco stock.

411 My favorite shirt that I wasn't allowed to mention on ESPN.com: The one that says "Yankees suck" on the front and "Jeter swallows" on the back. Now THAT'S comedy.

Fenway turns catatonic whenever something bad happens (like Vlad's four-run hit in Game Three). Yankee fans expect to win at all times. Red Sox fans expect to win as long as something bad doesn't happen. Then we go into the fetal position. Can you blame us?

Say what you want about Yankee fans—and I have—but they're in the game from beginning to end, even chanting every starter's name in the first inning until the player acknowledges them with a token wave (the fan who came up with that idea should win some sort of award). You can take the Fenway fans out of a big game. I wish that wasn't true, but it is. There's just a level of confidence that isn't quite there in Boston (and with reason). Also, because of Pedro's comments last month, he opened himself up to six hours of "Who's Your Daddy?" chants during Games Two and Six. I will now electrocute my nipples.

Edge: Yankees

DEFENSE

Dead-even with two exceptions: Cabrera over Jeter and Olerud over Millar (nullified if the Sox bring Mientkiewicz in with a lead). Also, Damon has more range than Bernie in center. Then again, so do I.

EDGE: Even

STARTING PITCHING

Big break for the Sox with El Duque's tired arm, the exact same injury that sidelined me when I was 14 and we got HBO for the first time. Anyway, it's tough to predict those Yankee starters except for Vazquez, who's one more crummy start from moving into a *Surreal Life* house with Hideki Irabu, Elizabeth Berkeley, Jose Contreras, Mindy Cohn, Ed Whitson, and Meeno Peluce. Brown is hit or miss. Lieber has looked great. And Mussina has a gulp-inducing history against the Sox, including a near-perfect game broken up by the Completely and Utterly Insane Carl Everett.

But they don't have anyone like Schilling—the one guy who terrifies everyone in New York. He isn't just the best big-game pitcher alive; he already has a World Series ring. That changes the equation a little. I wish I felt as strongly about Wakefield, who was inconsistent all season, and Pedro (who has to pitch both games in Daddy Stadium, barring a miracle rain-out on Saturday). But the biggest X-Factor is Arroyo, who pitched a few gems this season and looked superb against the

Angels in Game Three. The night before that game, Schilling posted on the SOSH board, "I take the kid Friday night, he's got nuts the size of Saturn." Now Saturn Balls could potentially be pitching a Game Seven at Yankee Stadium to push the Sox into the World Series. For whatever reason, this doesn't scare the living hell out of me. Mike Myers pitching Game Seven of the World Series at Fenway on Halloween night—now THAT scares the hell out of me.

Slight Edge: Red Sox

OWNERS

As much as I like the Boston guys, George takes just about every sub-category here, including "Overall success as an owner," "Higher payroll," "Unintentional Comedy Rating," "Most likely to cry after a big game," "Worst eyelift," "Most likely to dress like a yacht captain," and "Best sarcastic dig to cut another owner's knees out." Then again, the Boston guys didn't become rich just because their fathers left them money.

Slight Edge: Yankees

BULLPEN

Gordon, Quantrill, Loaiza, Sturtze, Heredia, and Token Crappy Guys no. 1 and no. 2 against Lowe, Embree, Timlin, Leskanic and Myers. Yikes. It's a wash except for Flash, who keeps exceeding every realistic expectation as the season drags into the seventh month—84 games, 93.6 innings pitched, 100 Ks, 0.90 WHIP. Seems perfectly reasonable for a 5-foot-9 curveball pitcher in his late 30s coming off major elbow surgery. Apparently his doctor is Dr. Rudy Wells from the *Six Million Dollar Man*. And yes, I'm well aware that nobody under 30 got that joke. One edge for the Sox here: In extra-inning games, I'd take Lowe and Leskanic over any of the crummy Yankee guys. And you *know* there's going to be one game that goes past midnight. It's Yanks-Sox, for God's sake.[412]

Edge: Yankees

CLOSERS

Say what you want about Foulke, but he saved the Angels series with those consecutive Ks of Anderson and Glaus. I loved how he dusted each of them off the plate, then worked them away. Just flawless. Biggest inning of the year for him. Then again, he's not the greatest closer of all time.

Edge: Yankees

412 As it turned out, there were two.

MANAGER

Joe Torre against Terry Francona. I mean...which guy would *you* rather have? One thing about Torre, and I think it explains why he's so good at his job in a "big picture" sense: When the Yankees rallied back to win that first game in Fenway a few weeks ago—the Pedro-Francona game—Torre knew they clinched the division and went on cruise control (resting Rivera and Gordon in a tight game on Saturday, then giving Brown the rehab start on Sunday). He was toying with the Sox, like an older brother taking an insurmountable lead during a game of one-on-one, then letting his younger bro score a few times to build up his confidence (so he could squash him again the next time).

Here's the point: I think Torre actually thinks of this stuff. I don't know if Francona knows what he's doing five minutes from now.

Major Edge: Yankees

HISTORY OF RIVALRY

Since the end of World War I, the Yankees possess a 26–0 advantage in championships. They've gotten the best of Boston in just about every major encounter, most famously in 1949, 1978, 1999, and 2003. And they bought the most famous baseball player of all time from the Red Sox for $125,000 right as he was entering his prime.

On the flip side, Boston holds an 11–8 advantage in the season series.

Slight Edge: Yankees[413]

BURNING QUESTIONS

How much will Rivera be affected by his family tragedy last weekend? Is Schilling's ankle really okay (as the Red Sox claim)? Will Francona be dumb enough to pitch Schilling on three days' rest? Do the Yanks really have Pedro psyched out? Will it rain on Saturday? Is there a God? And most important, is it really good luck when you get crapped on by a pigeon?

Edge: To be determined

So here's my big prediction...

(Actually, I don't have one. I feel sick.)

413 An alarming (but not surprising) number of readers from the New York area failed to get this joke.

FIRST BLOOD

October 13, 2004

Why didn't I fly back to New York for Games One and Two, you ask? Because Yankee Stadium is like the dentist—you don't want to go there unless you absolutely have to. That's why I stayed home and kept a running diary for Game One of the biggest baseball series in...well, 12 months:

5:01 p.m. PT: Quite an opening from Fox: A confusing *Star Wars* montage punctuated by Jeanne Zelasko barking, "The *Star Wars* trilogy is available on DVD, but this epic battle is coming at you right now on Fox!" I guess America likes this stuff. I guess.

5:13: You know Fox's upcoming medical drama *House*, the one with the scary-looking doctor with the cane who screams, "You're risking a patient's life!" How did Omar Epps get roped into this one? Did he lose a bet? Isn't there a sports movie he should be making? Should I write one during the commercials? Tell me what to do here.[414]

414 Unbelievably, *House* ended up being one of the surprise hits of the 2004–05 season. Go figure.

5:16: Our announcers tonight: Joe Buck, Tim McCarver, and Al Leiter. Buck mentions that Boone's home run happened one year ago tonight—great news—then adds, "For some reason, it seemed predetermined that we'd be right back here later for a rematch of sorts."

(Hey, I can think of a reason. What about the combined $310 million payrolls? Could that be it?)

5:18: The game hasn't even started and we're up to six Babe Ruth sightings, four clips of the A-Rod-Varitek fight, and five clips of Pedro throwing Zimmer down. Fox is doing everything short of simulcasting the game on channel 1918.

5:22: Mussina cruises through the first. Some good news: Fox dumped the radar gun reading that explodes into flames, one of the innovative ideas from this season's executive producer, Satan.

5:29: Schilling starts off throwing in the low-90s, a good sign since Buck casually mentioned that Schilling limped into the Stadium wearing a protective boot on his right ankle. Gulp.

But here's my question: What happens when A-Rod comes to the plate and sees Varitek? You think it's awkward? If you were A-Rod, wouldn't you secretly want to pull a Juan Marichal and smash the bat over his head?[415]

5:33: When it comes right down to it, watching your team pitch to Sheffield is like watching President Bush speak extemporaneously—it's hard to breathe and you just want it to be over as fast as possible. I'm Bill Simmons and I approved that sentence.

5:35: After the inevitable Sheffield double, Manny misplays Matsui's 0–2 single into a double (1–0, Yanks). They should create a stat for poor defensive plays like that one—not quite an error, but something that still led to a run. Call it a Man-Ram.

5:38: Bernie ropes an RBI single (2–0, Yanks). Uncanny. He kills the Sox even when he's decomposing. Meanwhile, the announcers are wondering about Schilling, who hasn't cracked 93 since his 3–2 pitch to A-Rod. Not a good sign.

5:42: Just avoided a phone call from Hench. I'm not saying that the Sox have driven him insane, but he's like the jumpy camp counselor in *Friday the 13th* who keeps screaming, "We're gonna die! We're all gonna die!" for 90 minutes until Jason finally shoves a pitchfork through him. That's not a phone call I need right now.

5:46: After a routine play by Jeter on a ground ball, we just had this exchange:

Buck [joking]: It's good to see Jeter finally not look nervous in the postseason.

Sports Gal [confused]: He normally looks nervous in the postseason?

Me [gritting teeth]: No…no…he was joking…

5:47: Six up, six down for Mussina. He's one of those guys where you can tell right away if he has it. Tonight, he has it. By the way, remember the days when announcers would go out of their way to avoid mentioning a no-hitter? Not Joe Buck. He does everything short of screaming, "HE'S PITCHING A NO-HITTER! HE'S PITCHING A NO-HITTER!" Actually, what am I complaining about? Keep it up, Joe.[416]

5:50: Random question: Does Olerud wear the batting helmet

415 When I'm running ESPN some day, SportsCentury will be devoted to events like **The Marichal-Roseboro Brawl**, The Luke Witte Stomping, Clint Malarhuck's Jugular Vein and even Up Close and Personal with William Ligue Jr.

416 Remind me never to play blackjack with Joe Buck. He's the guy who says stuff like, "Wow, how much are you up? It looks like you're up a lot! What is that, two grand?" and, "How many hands in a row have you won? Like nine? You're unstoppable!"

everywhere, like when he's headed to the grocery store and stuff? I've always wondered about this. What's more likely, standing at first and getting hit by an errant throw, or pulling a box of cereal from a second shelf and having the other boxes fall on top of you? It's a toss-up, right?

5:53: Fantastic exchange as McCarver praises Matsui's bloop double for the fourth time in the past 12 minutes.

McCarver [narrating yet another replay]: ...that's an extraordinary job of hitting by Hideki Matsui.

Leiter [after a beat]: Or just really lucky.

McCarver: Fuck you, Al! Fuck you! Don't pull that shit with me again!

(Actually, McCarver said, "You know what, I think it's more than luck, he hit the ball hard!" But I liked my version better.[417])

6:00: All right, John Henry has more money than God—couldn't he have bribed an airline mechanic in Panama to make up some fake problem with Mo Rivera's chartered plane today? *No puede volar! Un problemo con el avión! Muy malo! Es imposible!*[418]

6:02: Nine up, nine down for Mussina. "I bought some wonderful cheeses today," the Sports Gal tells me.

6:07: Schilling doesn't look like Schilling—high fastballs, wild splitters, barely cracking 90 on the gun. Not good. After singles from Jeter and A-Rod, Sheffield walks to load the bases. Great job by Leiter describing Schilling's mechanics: "Either there's something wrong physically, or he's out of whack mechanically." He's right, Schilling isn't driving off the mound like he usually does. I'd tell you more, but my eyeballs are spurting blood.

6:10: Three-run double by Matsui; 5–0, Yankees. "Bedlam here in the Bronx," McCarver tells us. I mean, those are five words that are NEVER good to hear. Not in any conceivable setting.

6:13: 6–0, Yanks. Hey, at least Mussina isn't pitching a perfect game. We're also minutes away from...

6:15: Yup. There it is. The first "Who's your Daddy?" chant. Speaking of Daddies, my father just turned into Nancy Kerrigan on the phone: "Why does this happen to us? His ankle was fine all season, he was pitching great...then he gets

417 As you probably guessed, this wasn't in the original column since they wouldn't allow it on the website...but I can get away with it in the book. Good times!

418 Rivera was coming back from Panama that night after attending a family funeral. And yes, I took seven years of Spanish and that's like the fifth time it ever paid off.

hurt right before the Yankee series? Right before??? Why does this happen to us? Why?"

6:26: Mussina strikes out the side. He's officially working up the courage to talk to Destiny. Plus, we just had the first super-tight Fox closeup of a depressed player in the dugout (Schilling). Next time, could we see his eye boogers, guys?

6:28: Lemme get this straight: There's *Rebel Billionaire* and there's *My Big Fat Obnoxious Boss*, but *both* are on Fox and *both* are ripping off *The Apprentice*? Has that ever happened before?

6:30: Curt is still pitching for the Sox. Unfortunately, it's Curtis Leskanic. By the way, what about that NLCS Game One matchup of Brandon Backe and Woody Williams? Shouldn't they just move that entire series to FX as a precautionary measure? What ever happened to the days of Orel Hershiser and Mike Scott? Who's pitching Game Two for Houston, Carmen Ronzonni?

6:36: Leskanic allows the first two guys on base, then gets comforted by Kevin Millar, who has a giant Abe Lincoln beard. Somehow this leads to an A-Rod double play.

6:48: But seriously, can you imagine telling your boss, "I need to leave work early today if that's okay, I have to go home and make my giant 10-by-5 MOOSE GOT THE JUICE sign for tonight's Yankees game"?

6:52: After a cartoon baseball named Scooter explains how a curveball works, the Sports Gal happily decides, "I liked Scooter!" I think I'm in hell.[419] Mussina quickly cruises through the fifth.

419 During the 2004 playoffs, Fox used a talking cartoon baseball to explain the ins and outs of the game. Normally these things only happen in France and certain parts of Eastern Europe.

6:58: I agree with Buck and Leiter—if Schilling is throwing 89-mph fastballs, it doesn't make sense to pitch him on three days' rest. McCarver vehemently disagrees. Of course, he just called Bronson Arroyo "Brandon" a few minutes ago.

7:06: I have to say, Leiter has been outstanding. He just pointed out that if Mussina was going for a perfect game, he wouldn't throw a fastball to Cabrera (a dead fastball hitter) on 2–0. As it turned out, he threw the fastball. See, that's all we're looking for. Give me a little inside info. Tell me how a player thinks. Don't flood me with stats, don't babble incessantly, don't make my head hurt, don't tell me things I can see for myself. This isn't rocket science.

7:09: Eighteen up, 18 down for Mussina. Destiny just ordered an apple martini.

7:14: Lofton homers off Wakefield. 7–0, Yanks. Kenny hasn't hit one that far since he was playing for the Birmingham Black Barons in 1939. Where's Derek Lowe in this game, by the way? Are they saving him for Game Eight?

7:19: Cool, I was wondering when they would show the WebMD Injury Report. So let me get this straight, Schilling has a tender right ankle? We're sure?

7:20: Matsui singles in Sheffield from second. 8–0, Yanks. I blame myself for calling the Nixon-Matsui matchup a draw in my Sox-Yanks breakdown. Now he's on pace to go 20-for-26 in the series with 40 RBI. What can I say? The Yankees are my Daddy.

7:22: More from the Sports Gal: "What's the highest score a team's ever gotten in a playoff game?"

7:27: Yesssssssss! Bellhorn doubles off the leftfield wall on an 0–2 pitch in the seventh! So long, Destiny—drive home safely. And just for the record, there's nothing worse than watching a perfect game against your own team—it's like being the only guy at a hot craps table betting the DON'T COME line.

7:32: Following Ortiz's two-out single, McCarver promotes "Brandon Arroyo against Pedro Martinez in Game Two tomorrow night." Holy shit. Poor Buck has to issue the rare *double* correction. Now you know what it would be like if my Mom was a baseball analyst. By the way, since that's two times McCarver called Arroyo "Brandon" tonight, I already awarded Game Three "Keep Until I Delete" TiVo status. McCarver might call him "Charles Bronson" for nine innings. Anything's possible.

7:35: Millar wallops a two-run double off the tip of Matsui's glove. Shhhhhh.

7:34: Nixon strikes an RBI single. *And it's an eight to THREE ballgame!*[420] Mussina leaves to a standing O. Of course, I'm also standing and applauding because Torre inexplicably decided to bring in Tanyon Sturtze. Tanyon Sturtze? Are you kidding me? Do you WANT us to come back?

420 I love this—when the announcer doesn't want to overhype a potential comeback but needs to express that something is happening, so he raises his voice about 10 octaves for the second number in his updated score: "And it's an eight-to-THREE ballgame." I always thought we should incorporate this phrase into everyday life. For instance, say one of your buddies starts hitting on a seemingly unattainable female. At first, you're watching from afar thinking **he's going down in flames like Billy Baldwin in *Backdraft***, but your buddy keeps working it and working it ... suddenly they're heading over to the jukebox together to pick out a few songs. And it's an eight-to-THREE ballgame.

7:37: Kaboom! Varitek slaps an 0–2 pitch into the right-field bleachers! *And it's an eight to FIVE ballgame!* Like the old saying goes, "You can take Tanyon Sturtze out of Tampa Bay, but you can't take the Tampa Bay out of Tanyon Sturtze."

7:48: Grossest moment of the game: A Posada closeup right as he's violently blowing booger spray out of his left nostril. It's *My Big Fat Booger Billionaire*, only on Fox! Meanwhile, Alan Embree retires the Yanks in the seventh. And it looks like Rivera can't pitch tonight. And Flash Gordon has an injured eyeball from an errant champagne cork.

(Okay, I'm sucked in again. You got me.)[421]

7:58: My favorite part of that ubiquitous Cialis commercial: When the announcer quickly voices over near the end, "Erections lasting for more than four hours require immediate medical help." *Nurse, can you get me a billy club please? Thank you.*

7:59: Just in case Dr. House didn't make this clear: "You're risking a patient's life!!!"

(Not quite "His father is the district attorney!"[422]...but it will have to do, I guess.)

8:05: Manny hits a Posada-esque blooper into left. Two on, two out for Ortiz...and they're not bringing in Rivera? Has Joe Torre been accidentally switched with Ron Gardenhire?[423] What's going on this game, Joe? You're risking a patient's life!

8:08: The bad news: Ortiz just came within one foot of tying the game. The good news: Matsui couldn't make the catch, leading to a two-run triple. 8–7, Yanks. What a comeback.

(But geez...how does that ball not go over the wall? And how did Matsui not knock it over the wall? It's uncanny. Could the Yankees catch more breaks?)

8:13: Rivera (after entering to a mammoth ovation) gets Millar for the third out. "The Yankees are holding on by a thread," Buck says. So why do I feel like we missed our big chance?

8:17: More from Buck: "This crowd and this feel here at Yankee Stadium is a feeling of unease." Don't worry, it sounded even worse than it looks. Meanwhile, Timlin brushes back A-Rod, leading to the inevitable A-Rod/Sheffield singles. The Fox guys correctly hammer Francona for not having Mike Myers

421 Notice how we just passed the 150-minute mark for this game and it's not even the eighth inning yet. This all goes back to my 150-Minute Rule: **Nothing should last for more than 150 minutes** unless there's a really good reason. This applies to award shows, movies, sporting events, wrestling pay-per-views, sex, car rides, concerts, even dinners with my stepmom (an impossibly slow eater). Two and a half hours is long enough for just about anything you would ever want to do in life, and if you're passing that mark, you better have an absolutely *fantastic* reason—like Francis Ford Coppola saying, "You know, I can't make any more cuts to *The Godfather*, it's good enough as is, I don't want to ruin it."

422 A reference to Fox's ubiquitous promos from the 2003 playoffs for *Skin*, the show where Ron Silver played a porn czar whose daughter started dating the district attorney's son. It lasted for exactly five episodes before Fox pulled the plug. On the bright side, the girl from *Skin* ended up playing **Marissa's lesbian crush on *The OC*.** So maybe everything happens for a reason.

ready for Matsui. "Right now, Francona is showing that he's not really a matchup guy," Leiter offers.

(Umm...then what is he? Why even have Myers on the roster? Why not have Myers pitch to Matsui, then Foulke to Bernie Williams? This is the way we've done it all season? Why change now? Why? Why?????????)

8:26: Timlin gets Matsui to pop out. Okay. Maybe this is why I wouldn't have made a good manager, along with these three reasons: 1) I don't like sunflower seeds; 2) I would have to wear my baseball hat backwards at some point; 3) I don't look good in baseball jackets because I have a long torso.[424]

8:29: Bernie doubles over Manny's head. 10–7, Yankees. Maybe I *would* have made a good manager. Classic Yankees, by the way. Just when you think you're right there, they get those insurance runs. It's uncanny. I just hate them. I mean, I really, *really* hate them.

8:31: Great, here's Foulke one batter too late—he gets Posada to end the inning. You can actually see the steam coming off my body. "I'm going to take a bath," the Sports Gal says, scurrying out of the room at warp speed.

8:35: Not only did Varitek single with one out in the ninth, he exchanged words with Posada and quietly fired an F-bomb at him. Good times! Let's hope that blows up into a full-scale UFC-style donnybrook later in the series. That's followed by the inevitable Cabrera single, then the inevitable double play. Ballgame.

Yankees 1, Red Sox 0.

(Of course, none of this matters if Pedro slams the door at Daddy Stadium tomorrow night. Stay tuned.)

423 One week before, Gardenhire famously botched his bullpen in Game Four of the ALDS. Hence, the reference. I could never figure out the Gardenhire thing—every time I watch a Twins game, I'm waiting for the dugout shot where Gardenhire is sitting with his shirt off, smoking a Carlton Light, sipping from a can of Miller High Life, and holding on to about 15 Powerball tickets.

424 Three other reasons: **1) I don't feel comfortable sitting in front of my locker naked; 2)** I would absolutely tell reporters to "Fuck off" if I didn't like their questions; **3)** I don't like patting other men on the ass.

DADDY DÉJÀ VU

October 14, 2004

You can drive yourself nuts wondering how Schilling's ankle survived 26 weeks of the regular season, then imploded just one week before the only 10-day stretch that mattered. You can wonder why these things always seem to happen to the Red Sox, never the Yankees. You can question curses and fate and even God. Or you can do what I did before Game Two: Start drinking. Heavily.

Of course, I managed to keep another running diary. Here's what transpired...

5:13 p.m. PT: Three stand-out moments from Fox's pregame show: Jeanne Zelasko breaking the record for "Most hairdos during a sports broadcasting career" (a record previously held by Hannah Storm); tons of talk about Schilling's torn tendon, although we're all waiting on the WebMD Injury Update for the final word; and the Red Sox announcing that Dr. Gregory House will examine Schilling's ankle on Thursday.[425]

5:15: Same announcers tonight: Buck, Leiter and McCarver (celebrating his 63rd birthday on Saturday, making him exactly 10 years younger than Luis Sojo). After some small talk, we see a highlight montage of Game One accompanied by Billy Squier's "Rock Me Tonight." Hey, Fox knows that there's been music released since 1983, right?[426]

5:21: Three up, three down for Jon Lieber in the first. Lemme ask you—why does MLB ban HGH and steroids, but allow cadaver surgeries for blown-out elbow tendons that give pitchers stronger and more durable arms? What's the difference?

5:24: Another question: Can you imagine ever going up to a guy behind a Taco Bell counter and saying, "Is it true your zesty chicken border bowl isn't made until I order it?" Would you even get a response? They'd just stare back at you doing the "Bill Murray in the Cheeseburger Cheeseburger skit" routine, right?

5:27: Pedro's first four pitches to Jeter: 94, 95, 94, 93. All balls. Still, a good sign. Then he makes Fox's radar gun reading

425 In 2036, someone is going to stumble across this book in a yard sale and think to themselves, "Dr. Gregory House... who the hell was that?"

426 Big sporting events are almost always accompanied by music from 20 years ago, and I think I have an explanation for this: TV production higher-ups are in their 40s and 50s for the most part, so when they're thinking, "Hey, I need a song with a hard-rock edge for this spot," instead of taking that 25-year-old PA's advice who says, "Should we use **the Killers or Franz Ferdinand**, or maybe even the White Stripes?" the higher-up says, "Nah, what about Billy Squier or Phil Collins. See if we have it on CD?" And that's how it happens.

flame (96) against A-Rod. Sure, he hit him with the next pitch. But I like the velocity. And yes, even workers at Friendly's haven't grasped for this many straws.[427]

5:32: Sheffield singles home Jeter, with help from Damon's throw that was apparently gunned down by Bernard Goetz in mid-air.[428] 1–0, Yankees.

5:39: With two runners on and the crowd in "Daddy!" mode, Pedro reaches 97 against Matsui, then strikes him out. He hits 96 against Williams, then strikes him out. Then he gets Posada to ground out. Well done. Of course, McCarver can't stop talking about the fact that Varitek and Pedro have huddled four times to discuss signs. Certainly a riveting subplot. I'm 20 seconds away from hitting the SAP button.

5:46: The Sports Gal brightens up noticably during a highlight of Albert Pujols' two-run homer in St. Louis, and only because his name is pronounced *Poo Holes*. I didn't realize I was married to Beavis.

5:48: Lots of talk about Schilling's ankle as Lieber mows down the Sox in the second. Allow me to weigh in: If the Sox were so worried about his ankle, why not pitch Pedro in Game One and Arroyo in Game Two? Was this even explored? Why throw him out to the wolves after a terrible bullpen outing before the game?

5:51: You know, I wasn't going to buy the Schick Quattro, but now that I know Colby from *Survivor* is using it…well…

5:54: Every time they show Francona in the dugout, his arms are crossed and he's rocking back and forth. I think Charlie Babbitt just screamed at him for leaving the toaster oven on again. That's okay, Terry. Three minutes to Wapner. Just hold tight.

6:04: After Cairo walks and Cool Papa Lofton singles, Pedro eventually gets out of a second-inning jam by whiffing A-Rod. Unfortunately, he's on pace for 209 pitches in nine innings. I swear, these Pedro starts at the Stadium are like putting the iPod on "shuffle" and ending up with the same song 20 straight times.

6:07: Buck can't even get out the sentence "Lieber hasn't given up a hit" before Cabrera singles with no outs in the third. Nicely done. Joe Buck *is* the cooler.

427 The very definition of a Rick Reilly joke—I'm leaving it in as a cautionary tale. Of course, he's won like 12 of 13 "Sportswriter of the Year" awards, so maybe he knows something.

428 Goetz was the real-life *Death Wish* vigilante who gunned down four muggers on a New York City subway, then used the "They were asking for it" defense and became a cult hero. Which reminds me, **why hasn't someone re-made *Death Wish***? Isn't the time right? I vote for Sly Stallone as the Bronson character. Then again, I vote for Sly Stallone for anything.

6:11: Mired in a mini-slump, Damon takes a feeble swing on strike one, followed by a broken-bat groundout. "That was a weird at-bat by Johnny Damon," says McCarver, almost derisively. Sounds like Johnny could use some hitting advice from Brandon Arroyo. Meanwhile, Bellhorn lines out to end the inning.

6:12: Boy, you hate to see That Guy from *Total Recall* and *NYPD Blue* making a measly Prestone commercial. I like That Guy.

6:13: Just looked him up on the Internet: Robert Costanzo. You have to love anyone with guest appearances on *The White Shadow*, *90210*, *Charlie's Angels*, *Family Ties*, *We Got It Made*, *Party of Five*, *Growing Pains*, *St. Elsewhere*, *Falcone*, *Charles in Charge*, and *Dream a Little Dream 2* on his résumé. Now that's a career, my friends.[429]

6:15: Cabrera and Manny nearly collide on a popup, followed by Scooter the Cartoon explaining how a changeup works. I've lost the will to live. I'm not kidding. I feel like putting on a wifebeater, eating Hamburger Helper, and buying scratch cards for the rest of my life. I've had it. Find me a trailer.

6:18: Three up, three down for Pedro in the third. He's thrown 370 pitches.

6:20: Turned to the debate just in time to hear this beauty from John Kerry: "Being lectured by the president on fiscal responsibility is a little bit like Tony Soprano talking to me about law and order in this country." That's quickly followed by the Dubya Face—the one where he half smiles and half looks like someone just asked him for the square root of 564,092. Good God. Can we have more options? I feel like Dave Wannstedt trying to decide between A.J. Feeley and Jay Fiedler. I may have to vote for Larry Bird again.[430]

6:22: Lieber gets the Sox on six pitches in the fourth. Way to work the count, guys.

6:26: Wait...

6:26: Hold on a second...

6:26: Here it comes...

6:26: "YOU'RE RISKING A PATIENT'S LIFE!"

6:29: Reason no. 5,437 to hate the Yankees: Their organist

429 My favorite imdb.com page: Randee Heller, who played Gabe Kaplan's wife in *Fast Break*, Ken Reeves' stripper girlfriend in *The White Shadow* and **Daniel-san's Mom in *The Karate Kid***, and then she was never seen again... and I guess my point is this: You don't need to work anymore with a résumé like that.

430 I always hesitate to make any political jokes in my columns, only because people take that stuff way too seriously, and it's a great way to lose readers. But just for the record, I didn't vote for Larry Bird—I voted for Tom Brady.

repeatedly playing the "Let's Go Yankees" song, knowing that everyone will just chant "Who's Your Daddy?" along with it. God, I hate the Yankees.[431]

6:33: Pedro cruises through the fourth. "You rarely hear a raucous crowd in a well-pitched game," McCarver says knowingly.[432]

6:37: I don't think I've ever *not* enjoyed "Sounds of the Game." We can all agree on this, right? More "Sounds of the Game," more Al Leiter? Any dissenters? Any?

6:40: Kenny Albert interviews Jon Lieber's dad in the stands, who's wearing a Yankees jersey with the obligatory idiot behind him doing the "Turn on the game, I'm on TV!" routine on his cell phone. I'm telling you, we need to pass laws. We need to throw these people in jail. We need to pull a *Shawshank* and cast them down with the Sodomites.

6:42: My dad and I just had this exchange on the phone:

Me: If I were a pitcher, would you show up at my home games wearing my jersey?

Dad: Absolutely.

Me: Really?

Dad: Yeah. Unless you were Derek Lowe.[433]

6:47: Celebrities on hand tonight: Jack Nicholson, Lorne Michaels, Conan O'Brien, Matt Damon and Casey Affleck. Makes me want to paraphrase Jeffrey Ross's famous roast joke, "It's an honor to be surrounded by so many talented celebrities [one-second pause]...and Casey Affleck."[434]

Meanwhile, the Sports Gal and I just had this exchange:

Her: Why is A-Rod wearing purple lipstick?

Me: That's not lipstick...his lips are blue from kissing Jeter's ass.

(I'm so bitter right now, I'm just lashing out at everybody.)

6:56: Pedro strikes out Matsui to get out of the fifth. He's throwing a three-hitter. On 430 pitches, but still...it's a three-hitter. And yes, it's starting to dawn on me that this could be Pedro's last start in a Boston uniform.

7:06: Just an unbelievable Johnny Damon at-bat (seven minutes and 16 pitches in all) capped by Fox showing a pitch-by-pitch sequence and somehow missing the final pitch (Damon

431 Here's another good one: When Fox shows their dugout, Torre and Stottlemyre are sitting there motionless, their arms folded, wearing sunglasses, looking like they just dropped dead about 10 minutes ago from the same **batch of bad tapioca**...and for some reason, the cameraman decides that this makes for a fascinating 20-second shot.

432 ESPN won't allow me to openly rip any announcers on competing networks, if only because they would never allow me to rip an ESPN colleague. Which is fair. So I have to come up with creative ways to express my dissatifaction for someone's work, one of which is quoting the announcer and letting them hang themselves. Here's my point: Tim McCarver makes my job very easy sometimes.

433 An especially funny exchange considering how the rest of the 2004 playoffs was about to play out.

lining out to center). Well done. I think I speak for everyone here: We would always rather see live action over any replay or produced piece, even if it's a 45-second highlight montage of Joe Torre picking his nose.

434 The best Jeff Ross joke of all time: When he ripped Sandra Bernhard at the Alan King roast by saying, "I wouldn't fuck her with Bea Arthur's dick," only **Bea Arthur was sitting right there.** Quite possibly the funniest moment in the history of Comedy Central, which is saying something.

7:08: Bellhorn's K ends the sixth. This Sox-Yanks thing has reached the point where I'm not even remotely shocked that Jon Lieber is throwing a one-hitter right now. He could levitate in mid-air like Neo to catch a high chopper and I wouldn't be surprised.

7:12: Well, it's the bottom of the sixth. According to Fox, in his career against the Yankees, Pedro has a 2.12 ERA through the first five innings, 6.33 from the sixth on.

(In other words, "REDRUM! REDRUM! REDRUM!")

7:17: Uh-oh...we're past the 100-pitch count...and there's a guy on first with one out...oh, boy...here we go...

7:18: Olerud homers into the rightfield bleachers on a 1–2 fastball. 3–0, Yanks. I swear on the Dooze's life that I typed the previous paragraph, verbatim, about 30 seconds ago. By the way, Olerud was released by a 63-win team earlier this summer. Classic Yankees. They could pick up a hooker in Times Square, plug her in at second base, and she'd hit .280. It's uncanny.

7:19: "Who's your Daddy?!? Who's your Daddy?!? Who's your Daddy?!? Who's your Daddy?!? Who's your Daddy?!? Who's your Daddy?!? Who's your Daddy?!?"

(Thank God this isn't an NBA game.)

7:25: After escaping the sixth without further damage, we see Pedro shaking hands in the dugout, apparently done for the night. Just to make sure Francona doesn't pull a Grady Little, Ortiz and Millar remove Pedro's clothes, stick a red ball in his mouth and duct tape him to the dugout water fountain.

7:31: Seven shutout innings, two hits allowed, only 79 pitches for Lieber, who looks like Private Pyle without his Yankee hat on. Somehow this will all make sense on my death bed.

7:43: Timlin and Embree combine to get through the seventh. I have to admit, I just spent the last 15 minutes surfing the Internet and checking recent e-mails. A good one from Stephen F. in Boston: "Let me get this straight, Jack Nicholson is a

Laker fan AND a Yankee fan? Can we just paint a mustache on him and call him Hitler?"

7:47: Heading into the eighth, the Sports Gal says, "This is our inning, I can feel it."[435] Nixon immediately singles, prompting a pitching change and a standing O for Lieber. "These fans know how to salute," Buck says. You're right, Joe. Nobody else would have stood and cheered someone who pitched a three-hitter in a playoff game. Man, I hate everybody right now. I feel like Barry Bonds.

7:50: All right, I'll ask: If you were a billionaire, would you waste your time filming a crappy reality show for Fox? Wouldn't you buy a sports team, open your own bar and plow through a neverending assembly line of dumb supermodels? Me, too.

7:51: As Gordon finishes warming up, it's important to note that the Sox went 5-for-10 against Gordon and Rivera last night. Probably not happening again. By the way, do Gordon and Sheffield look like they should be wearing fedora hats and big suits and hanging out together in 1940s jazz clubs? Or am I just hammered right now?

7:54: Double by Varitek! Still no outs as Dale Sveum correctly holds Nixon at third. "That's the difference between scoring a run and not scoring a run," McCarver tells us.

8:01 Ugh. Consecutive grounders by Cabrera and Mueller. Now it's 3–1 with two outs, Varitek on third, and Rivera entering the game to "Enter Sandman." Leave it to the Yankees to steal Sandman's entrance music from ECW. By the way, the odds of the Sox winning this game just dropped from 3-to-1 to 10,000-to-1.[436]

8:05: Coolest moment of the night: The DiamondCam's replay of Damon's bat splitting into 80 pieces. Too bad they can't re-enact that with A-Rod's head. Sadly, Damon strikes out to end the inning. We're running out of time.

8:13: A commercial for the upcoming season of *The OC* causes the Sports Gal to scream "Oh boy!" and sing along to the theme song. I'm questioning my manhood just from being in the same room for that.

8:20: Fox fact: The last 13 teams that fell behind 2–0 in the

435 The Sports Gal had an uncanny ability of being in the room whenever Trot had a big hit, to the point that she would leave the room during big games and say, "I'm going online, tell me when Trot's up again so I can help him get another hit." Bizarre phenomenon that started at the Memorial Day Weekend game in 2000 (the famous Clemens-Pedro duel at Yankee Stadium), when she announced to everyone in our section that Trot was going deep moments before he struck the go-ahead homer. She should be receiving five percent of his paycheck at this point.

436 When I'm the Commish of baseball, only quality closers will be allowed to pick their own entrance music. Everyone else will have to come out to my personal choices, all for comedy's sake. For instance, B.J. Ryan would enter every game to **"The Kid Is Hot Tonight" by Loverboy**. I think this could work.

LCS also lost the LCS. Fantastic news. What about the last 13 teams who fell behind and also lost the only indispensable guy on their team? Can we see those stats? Meanwhile, Foulke loads the bases by walking Jeter, leading to a shot of Derek Lowe warming up and wearing Harrison Ford's beard from *The Fugitive*. Much more fun than The Derek Lowe Face. *I did not kill my wife! You find that man!*

8:28: Foulke gets out of that bases-loaded jam. We'll forget about the fact that he should have started the inning, or that Francona made the same exact mistake in consecutive games. I'm amazed how unterrified I feel when A-Rod's up there. He's just not that scary. There's no other way to say it. Maybe it's the purple lips.

(I don't want to say that the whole season is riding on these next three outs, but...well...)

8:35: Manny cranks a one-out double, shifting everyone at Yankee Stadium into "Uh-oh" mode...until Ortiz and Millar strike out to end the game. Rivera does it again. He's the difference. He's always the difference. And you don't have to worry about him snapping an ankle tendon days before the biggest week of the season, because these things never seem to happen to the Yankees. That's why people root for them. It's the smart move. Like buying a stock that can't lose.[437]

And since I can't come up with an ending, tonight's last word goes to Phil Horning from South Dakota: "As someone who dislikes both teams, I can't believe you compared the Red Sox-Yankees to Ali-Frazier. A more accurate sports rivalry would have been Martina Hingis-Anna Kournikova in the late '90s. Both rivalries were overhyped by the media and the same side always wins."

Actually, that was too depressing. I want to hang myself. Let's give the last word to Tom Loughran from Marshfield: "It's the end of Game Two and the Sox are down two games. I feel like there should still be hope but I just don't know if I have any left. It's like watching *American Chopper*. It might be a different show every time, but you always know how it's gonna end. If you'll excuse me, I'm gonna go boil some water and then dump it down my throat."

Save some for me.

437 At this point, yes—I was FIRMLY convinced that the Red Sox were cooked. I'll admit it.

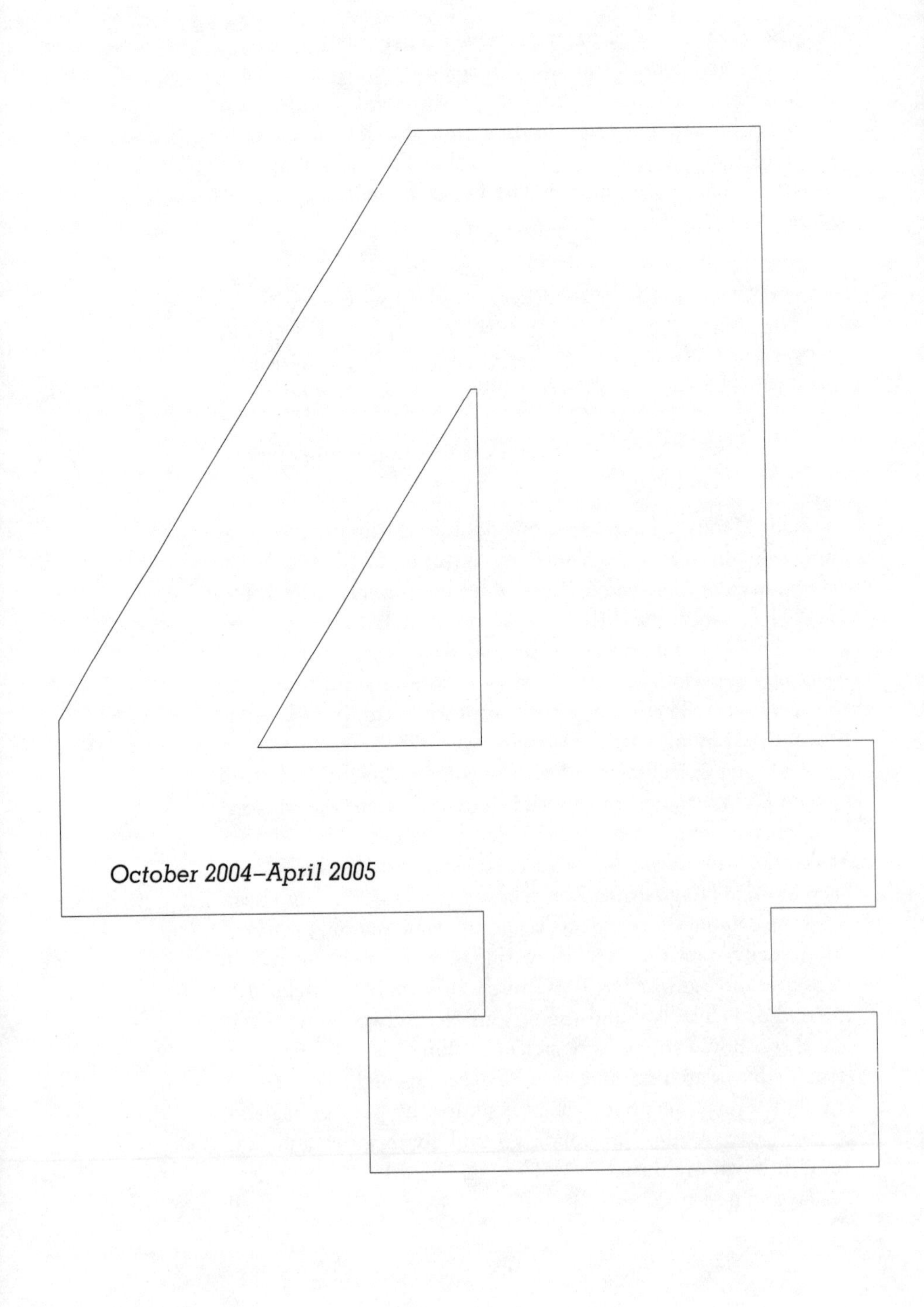
October 2004–April 2005

THE GREAT ESCAPE

SEAT CHANGE

I promised my father that this story would die with me. (Oh, well.)

During Game Four of the 2004 ALCS at Fenway Park, the Red Sox were three outs from getting swept by the Yankees. Up to that point in the series, we had been outscored 35-19. The crowd was frozen and lifeless, rallying only for the token "Even if you guys can't pull off a comeback, we appreciate everything that happened this season" ovation before the bottom of the ninth. The greatest closer of all time had just jogged from the Yankees bullpen like a hired assassin, determined to kill our season. There was nothing that had happened that week—or in the last 86 years, for that matter—to remotely suggest that something special was about to happen. And the following elements were in play:

1) It was 11:58 p.m. on a Sunday night.

2) It was freezing, *freezing* cold.

3) Dad had to wake up at 6:00 a.m. for work.

We were sitting in Section 116. If we wanted to flee the premises right when the game ended, we needed to quickly scamper underneath Fenway to beat the crowd, walk briskly underneath the grandstand to the third base side, navigate a four-block walk to the middle of Kenmore Square, then try to catch a cab—and we would be fighting off 35,000 people trying to do the exact same thing. That was the risk of staying.

"Let's get out of here," Dad said.

"You serious? We can't leave now."

"I'm not saying we have to leave—let's go underneath the grandstand and watch the ninth on the little TV. If anything happens, we'll come back to the seats. If they lose, we'll beat everyone else out of the park."

Now I was bummed. I didn't want to leave. On the other hand, I wasn't the one who had to wake up at six.

"I think it's bad luck if we leave," I said, putting up the good fight.

"We just watched them get killed for two straight games in these seats, what are you talking about? Come on, maybe it will change our luck."

He was full of shit. But whatever.

We left the seats and headed underneath Fenway, settling on the television situated near the entrance behind home plate (the one right in front of the Legal Sea Foods clam chowder stand). If you haven't been underneath Fenway, there isn't a more sinister area in any baseball park—murky, smelly, unhappy, crowded, dank, dungeon-like, you name it. I hate being underneath Fenway for any reason. It certainly wasn't where I wanted to watch the end of the 2004 season.

Along with my father and me, there were maybe 20 other fans standing there, everyone with the same idea: *As soon as the third out happens, we're out of here*. Only none of us were actually leaving. I didn't think of it at the time, but this one moment symbolized my life as a Sox fan more than anything else. After 37 years supporting this team, my father lacked the faith to stick around for three more outs. It had been beaten out of him. On the other hand, he wasn't writing the game off, either. And here's my point: Did any other sports franchise evoke this much pessimism and optimism from its fans at the exact same time? Probably not. Maybe I hadn't reached that point with the team yet, but I understood how he arrived there. Deep down, I was hoping to never end up that way. I thought they could still come back—not for the series, but to avoid the sweep—if only because we had battled Rivera during the season. My father wasn't willing to overlook that possibility, he was just being more realistic. Four decades of heartbreak will do that to a guy.

So Millar comes up. Takes a ball. Takes another ball. And another. We could hear the crowd cheering inside the park, the noise echoing off the walls underneath. Even as the umpire was signalling ball four, I was yanking my father's left arm and dragging him up the runway behind home plate.

"Come on! Come on! Roberts is coming in!"

"All right, all right!"

We found two spots at the top of the runway, right behind home plate between the upper and lower boxes of Section 45. And that's where we watched one of the most famous sequences in Red Sox history—Dave Roberts swiping second base directly in front of us (we had found the perfect angle), followed by Mueller driving him home on a game-tying single. My life as a Red Sox fan would never be the same; I just didn't know it yet. They were about to win eight straight games in 12 days. They were about to change the lives of everyone who cared about them. They were about to perform a region-wide exorcism. But I wasn't thinking about any of those things—I was too busy cheering that tying run, soaking in the pandemonium and sprinting back to our seats at Section 116. We were about to witness the impossible.

The whole sequence probably lasted eight minutes. When the Red Sox failed to win the game and we were headed to the 10th, then—and only then—did I glance at my father in disgust.

"I can't believe you made me leave," I muttered.

"We didn't leave, we saw every pitch!"

"You still wanted to leave."

"I never wanted to leave, I was playing it safe."

"Well, we'll see what my readers think when I put it in my column."

There was a pause.

"Come on, if we hadn't left our seats, maybe they wouldn't have scored."

In retrospect, maybe he was right. Everything worked out for the best. I can't argue that. But I will never forget standing underneath Fenway for that Millar at-bat, chilled to the bone, holding onto the thinnest slice of hope, fully expecting to walk away from another season, standing in the darkest place that a baseball stadium could ever offer, in every respect ... and then Rivera threw those four balls, and even as Millar was tossing down his bat and heading toward first base, I was already pulling my father up that gloomy runway toward the light.

We were alive.

June 2005

THE SURREAL LIFE

October 19, 2004

Wait a second—I'm supposed to write about this???

I don't have a central nervous system left. My head weighs more than Verne Troyer. My heart feels like somebody tried to make meatballs out of it. I can't think straight. I'm a corpse. I'm a walking corpse. For two straight days, I watched my beloved Red Sox stave off elimination against the Yanks, needing 26 innings over 27 hours to stay alive for Game Six in New York. These weren't just baseball games. They were life experiences. They broke you down in sections. They made you question God, the meaning of life, whether sports should possibly mean this much. On Sunday night, I stewed in my seat vowing never to raise my kids as Sox fans.[438] On Monday night, I skipped out of Fenway wondering if any other team could possibly mean this much to a group of people.

438 This was a bigger moment than I let on: My wife was two months pregnant at the time.

The Sox should have lost about 25 different times. The Sox should have won about 25 different times. They rallied to tie consecutive games against the seemingly invincible Yankees bullpen. They stayed alive in extra innings with a never-ending stream of fringe starters and worn-out relievers. Their closer recorded 12 outs on 70-plus pitches in the span of 24 hours. They stranded the winning run on second or third base nearly 200 times. Including Saturday night's game, their three starters recorded 40 outs, leaving another 65 for the bullpen guys. Somehow, none of this was a problem.

Thanks to David Ortiz, Game Four ended a little after 1:30 on Monday morning. Fifteen hours later, I was sitting in the same seats in Section 116 with my father, glancing around and wondering if we ever left. Apparently we did. There was only one major difference between the two nights: In Game Four, the fans were waiting for the Yankees to win the game. In Game Five, the fans were waiting for the Sox to come through. Now everyone in New England is pinning their hopes on the greatest comeback in sports history. It happens that fast.

I arrived at Game Four fresh from the Patriots game, where the defending champs captured their 20th straight win (over Seattle). For most of the game, the fans in Foxboro sat around like spoiled rich kids at a cocktail party, waiting for the shrimp and free booze to arrive. We were like 70,000 Spaulding Smailses. It's not enough for this Patriots team to win anymore. We want them to do it with style. We want to wreck teams. We want to rip their hearts out. When it doesn't happen, we spend the rest of the game secretly hoping the other team tests us, just so we can lay the smack down on them again. The collective arrogance is almost comical.[439]

Sitting in Fenway four hours later, you couldn't help but notice the difference. The fans were supportive. The fans were petrified. We didn't want to get swept. We fully expected to get swept. And everything unfolded like a classic Sox-Yanks game—we took the lead, they battled back thanks to a shaky managing move (Francona taking Lowe out at least three batters too early in the sixth). We were done. You could feel it. When the ninth inning rolled around, we summoned one last ounce of energy for Millar's at-bat against Rivera[440]...and he bled out a walk. Dave Roberts entered as a pinch runner, leading to one of the more underrated moments in baseball: the speedy guy inching off first base, rocking back and forth, absorbing the closer's every move, with everyone in the building knowing that he's taking off for second. Somehow he made it. It was the most exciting stolen base in my lifetime as a Sox fan.[441] Then Mueller singled up the middle—absolute bedlam, great baseball, everything you ever wanted from a game. The Yanks had us 3–0 in the series, 4–3 in the ninth with Rivera on the mound, and we staved them off. At least for a little while.

Now you could see the lightbulb flickering over everyone's heads. *Wait a second. If we can hold on here, we have Pedro and Schilling going in the next two games.* It was like seeing a pair of dirty jeans from the previous weekend, then remembering you may have left $100 in them. So we cheered like crazy. We kept the faith. We didn't care that the clock was inching past 1 a.m. on a Sunday night, or that the game was more excruciating to watch than prostate surgery on the Discovery Channel. Even when we were at the point of the game where Curtis Leskanic needed to pull a Shag Crawford[442] and save the day, somehow it seemed logical he would. And he did.

Everything was leading to Ortiz's game-winning homer in the 12th, which answered a 29-year-old question for me, "What would it have been like to see the Fisk home run in person?"

439 Less than 11 weeks later, the Patriots would win their third Super Bowl.

440 As you now know, this was a white lie. I should have used "they" instead of "we." Thanks, Dad—you made me lie to my readers.

441 And, as it turned out, the most famous stolen base ever. Chico Ruiz stole home to start the collapse of the 1964 Phillies; **Jackie Robinson stole home in the 1955 World Series**; and Babe Ruth was thrown out stealing to end the 1926 World Series. But for sheer excitement, tide-turning importance, and historical significance, I can't imagine anything approached the Roberts steal. He heard about it all winter, he'll hear about it all season, and he'll probably have at least one Red Sox fan mention it to him every day for the rest of his life. If he's a split-second late, the Sox don't win the World Series and you're probably not reading this book right now. I'd say that's a big stolen base.

442 In Game Five of the 1986 ALCS (the Hendu Game), in the ninth inning the Angels loaded the bases against Joe Sambito with the winning run on third. Everyone forgets this now except for Angels

Well, I'll tell you what happens. You scream in disbelief. You jump up and down. You slap hands with complete strangers. You smile like a proud father as the team skips onto the field, some of them racing to home plate, some of them taking time to turn and point at the fans. You want the guy to take 20 minutes rounding the bases, just so you can milk the moment and remember everything about it. And when the hero jumps into the happy pile at home plate, you feel like you're smack dab in the middle. Ortiz may as well have been jumping into 35,000 people. **443**

Needless to say, everyone in New England showed up for work late the following morning. This was bigger than all of us. It wasn't just about avoiding the sweep; it was about an entertaining, charismatic team that could have rolled over and didn't. Those are the teams you end up remembering. We arrived at Fenway on Monday in a different mood, worn out, giddy, appreciative, even a little nostalgic for what was probably Pedro's last Fenway start in a Boston uniform. If this were a Hollywood movie, he would have gone out guns blazing, the old Pedro one last time—cracking 97 on the gun, mixing four unhittable pitches and throwing at people's heads just for sport. But that Pedro has been gone for awhile. The older version creaks along and dances in and out of trouble, a constant tightrope walk, as nothing ever comes easy anymore. Watching him at Fenway, I always find myself glancing at his pitch count on the scoreboard, the same way you keep glancing at an escalating taxicab meter.

Still, it's Pedro. You never know. The Red Sox pulled out all the stops for Game Five—a four-year-old Jimmy Fund patient singing the national anthem, Jim Rice throwing out the first pitch, even Mike Eruzione bringing out the game ball while they showed clips of USA 4–USSR 3 on the scoreboard. **444** The crowd was practically crazed, standing on every two-strike pitch, rejoicing when foul balls ricocheted into the Yankee dugout, cheering when Posada took a foul ball off his right hand, even chanting "Who's your dealer?" at Sheffield. We weren't letting the Sox lose this game. It was like the scene near the end of *Midnight Run* when DeNiro glances at the hovering helicopters and searches for an escape, when he mutters to himself, "Nah, I've come too far, I've come too fucking far...."

Fast-forward to the eighth inning: the Sox trailing by two,

fans. Anyway, Shag came in to get the last two outs; they won the game in the 11th; and Shag got the win, his only appearance of the series. Eighteen years and five days later, Leskanic got the win in Game Four. Should we start calling him Shag Leskanic? Probably not. I just thought it was interesting.

443 Best sports moments I've ever seen in person: **1)** Bird stealing the ball in the '87 Detroit series (only because I was younger and sports meant more to me at the time); **2)** Adam Vinatieri's field goal to beat the Rams (only because Boston hadn't won a title in so long); **3a)** Ortiz's bloop-single to win Game 5; **3b)** Ortiz's homer to win Game Four. But you can't separate those last two, just like you can't separate *The Godfather* and *The Godfather Part II*, or even **the Olsen Twins**. In my book, the combined effect of those two Ortiz hits counts as one.

444 This was a genius move, by the way. I also would have brought out Ric Ocasek, the Cars lead singer who married **Paulina Porizkova** 20 years ago. That's right up there with the 1980 Olympic Team. I mean, have you SEEN Ric Ocasek?

thanks to Jeter's three-run triple in the sixth (set up by a dink hit, a walk, and an HBP), followed by Francona leaving Pedro in as the crowd howled in disgust (get the Other Shoe ready)...followed by Matsui's rocket right to Nixon to end the inning (exhale).[445] Playing with house money, Ortiz launched a Gordon pitch—PLUNK! — off the Volvo sign in left. Chaos. Complete chaos. Senor Octobre did it again; he's like a cross between Dave Henderson, Roy Hobbs, and Ghandi at this point. Then Millar weaseled out a walk,[446] followed by another Dave Roberts appearance and Gordon throwing to first at least 600 times. Maybe Roberts didn't steal second again, but Gordon was sufficiently rattled that he allowed a single to Nixon, followed by Rivera giving up a sacrifice fly to Varitek. [447]

Tie game.

Incredibly, unbelievably, we were just getting started. Over the next six innings, the Sox tried to give away Game Five over and over again—popped-up bunts, botched hit-and-runs, 300-pound DHs trying to steal bases, knuckleballers throwing knuckleballs to guys who can't catch knuckleballs, guys swinging for the fences when they only needed to hit a flyball to win a game—like they broke every rule in the *How to Play Winning Baseball* handbook. I'd tell you more, but I was a carcass by the 11th. Everyone was. I remember telling my dad, "Regardless of how this thing ends, we're going to be oozing out of here after the game."

(Of course, after two straight nights of this, Dad was nearly catatonic. As Mike Myers was warming up in one of the games, I saw my father taking what looked to be Altoids out of a metal case, so I asked him for one. "These are headache pills," he said simply. Oh.)[448]

And yeah...usually we lose this game. Especially to the Yankees. This one seemed destined to show up on ESPN Classic some day, one of those Red Sox losses where you stumble across it and scream "Oh no!" and quickly change channels before your eyeballs start gushing blood. In either the 13th or 14th—God, I can't even remember, it's all a blur—Wakefield struck out Sheffield on a passed ball, followed by another walk and another passed ball. Suddenly they had runners on second and third with two outs, with only a 50 percent chance that Varitek could stop these knuckleballs. Apparently, we got out of this mess. I'm pretty sure I blacked out. I'm not even kidding.

445 You could make an excellent case that, for an entire month, Terry Francona was the luckiest man who ever managed a baseball team. And this move was Exhibit A. Matsui crushed that ball. Crushed it.

446 Two do-or-die games, two huge walks by Millar. Everyone forgets this.

447 One of the all-time most unfair blown saves. Then again, fuck him.

448 My dad was pissed that I mentioned the headache pills—he's a superintendent and wants everyone in his school system to believe that he's superhuman. So when I write about him falling asleep on the sofa every night, or the time I brought a girl over to the house and **he was watching TV in his underwear**, or how his friends called him Suitcase in college, well, he hates this stuff. Hey, he should have steered me toward law school. It's his own fault.

(My last three notes of the game: "13th inning oh my God Varitek and Wakefield"..."Stand up sit down bad back"..."Central nervous system shutting down." If they found me dead outside Fenway after the game, they would have examined this thing and assumed I had died of natural causes.)

By the time we were rallying again in the 14th, Francona needed to go to the bullpen for 35,000 new fans. We were spent. We were cooked. With Johnny D on second and Manny on first, with two outs and Hendu-Hobbs-Ghandi at the plate, we couldn't rise to the moment, not even when Big Papi kept fouling off those nasty pitches from Loaiza. Somewhere along the line, you could see him getting locked in again. He was right there.

"Something's gonna happen here," I remember telling Dad, who couldn't speak at this point.

Something happened.

A bloop hit into center field. The kind the Yankees always get. Johnny D rounded third with the winning run. Half the guys greeted him at home plate, half sprinted toward Ortiz. Then Johnny's group sprinted over to Ortiz for one giant jumpfest. Meanwhile, you could see the Green Monster practically swaying. We were delirious—literally and figuratively—one of the happiest moments in the history of Fenway Park, right up there with Fisk's home run and everything else. The players pointed to us and skipped back into the dugout. Some fans remained at Fenway just to keep cheering. Others streamed out and headed to the nearest bars. Some even stood on Yawkey Way just to cheer the team bus.

My father limped off to find a cab and a heart surgeon. I ended up at the Baseball Tavern, just hoping I would run into somebody I recognized. Wouldn't you know—I wasn't there for 10 seconds before seeing my old college buddy Strollin' Jim Nolan walking toward the entrance. It was that kind of night.[449] We ended up sucking down four Miller Lites in about 10 minutes, shaking our heads and using the same words over and over again ("incredible," "unbelievable," "incredible," "unbelievable," "incredible," "unbelievable"). Basically, Game Five turned us into the Hilton sisters. Then Pedro's favorite little person showed up—Nelson De La Rosa, the 30-inch Dominican—wearing a mini-Red Sox jersey and a cap. People cheered and lined up to take Polaroids with him. Somehow this all made sense.

449 This may have been the biggest surprise. What are the odds that I walk to a bar, hope to randomly meet someone I know there... and run into an old college buddy within 10 seconds? Has to be higher than Rivera blowing consecutive saves, right?

"Maybe he *is* a good-luck charm," I said to Nolan.

"I'd believe anything at this point," he said.

Me, too. There have been 25 other baseball teams that fell behind 3-0 in a series. None of the 25 ever came back. Only two even forced a Game Six. So there's no real precedent for what happened here, and I can't imagine there have been two straight playoff games like that, not with those stakes, not with that much emotion, not after everything that happened last season and the 80-plus seasons before it. For a miracle to happen, you need a shift in momentum that borders on the surreal. Games Four and Five were surreal. There's no other way to say it. Now we have Schilling going in Game Six against a reeling Yankees team that only has five players remaining from its 1996–2000 title run.

"Do we win this series?" Nolan asked me.

"If the New England Patriots can win a Super Bowl," I told him, "anything's possible."

We looked out the window, where fans were lined up on Boylston Street to watch the team buses heading toward the airport. The Yankees entourage went first, greeted by a barrage of jeers and middle fingers. Then the Red Sox buses followed suit, accompanied by screams of encouragement and raised fists.

We were headed back to New York.

LOSING BAGGAGE IN THE BRONX

October 20, 2004

Blank screen.

I'm staring at a blank screen.

(Come on...type something...)[450]

What can you say? What can you say about Curt Schilling? How many words are enough? 500? 2,000? 10,000? This wasn't just an ankle sprain. His right sock was covered in blood, thanks to three sutures (!?!?!?!) holding together his dislocated ankle tendon. In Game One, that same tendon was popping. This time it was leaking blood. He didn't care. The team needed him. So Schilling kept pitching. Put his career on the line. Gritted through the next three hours at Yankee Stadium—seven innings, 25 batters, 99 pitches in all. Won the game. Kept the team alive. Hugged everyone in the dugout when he was cooked. Stuck in a dip, sat back, and waited for the ESPN Classic royalties to start pouring in.

It was that good. Win or lose on Wednesday night, the Schilling Game takes its place alongside the Willis Reed Game, MJ's Flu Game, Bird banging his head against the Pacers, and everything else in the Sheer Guts Pantheon. Sitting in the dugout between innings, he threw a towel over his head and stared at the ground, hands pressed against his ears, looking like someone who just got off a harrowing plane flight. All he needed was a barf bag and the cast of *Lost* standing behind him.

I don't know how he did it. There was nothing different about his situation from Game One, other than the O.J. sock, the sutures and the hands of God (his words, not mine). The Red Sox made a big deal about this "emergency boot" from Reebok, a device that would stabilize Schilling's damaged ankle tendon, but I'm starting to wonder if they bought that device on eBay from Sidd Finch and the Easter Bunny. Schilling didn't even wear it. This was about heart. This was about coming through when it mattered most. This was about choosing to pitch for a tortured franchise, promising things would change, and then perservering only because you gave your word.

Over the next few days, everyone will make a big deal about Schilling's Game Six, only some for the right reasons. We live in

450 I wasn't doing this for dramatic effect—I stared at that blank screen for a good 45 minutes. Out of all the columns during that three-week run, this one was the toughest to write. Emotionally, I was done. Games Four and Five knocked me for a loop; Game Six finished me off. I didn't hand in this column until 5:00 in the morning. For Game Seven, I learned from the experience and stopped by Store 24 for a large **Gatorade, a Red Bull, Sour Patch Kids and a 16-ounce coffee** before starting that column after one in the morning. I think I was wired for four days afterwards—in retrospect, I would have been better off doing an eight-ball of coke.

a sports world where every good moment gets beaten into the ground. It isn't enough for something to happen anymore. You have to vote. You have to watch two guys screaming on a split-screen. You have to read 400 columns about it, then columns by people reviewing those columns. You have to hear sports radio hosts screaming, and once the subject becomes exhausted, one of them takes a crazy angle on the topic just to keep the phone lines ringing for another few hours. It keeps going and going, a vicious little snowball. When it runs out of steam, something else replaces it and the whole cycle starts all over again.

I don't want the Schilling Game to fall into that. I don't want to hear someone claiming that he "wasn't that hurt," or that it "doesn't matter if they don't win Game Seven," or even that Schilling was "milking the moment." You're not taking this away from me. This was even better than Pedro coming out of the bullpen five years ago in Cleveland, and I never thought I would say that about any Red Sox pitcher.

In three decades of following Boston sports, my favorite underrated performance belongs to Kevin McHale, who limped around on a broken foot for two straight months during the 1987 playoffs. The team doctors explained the risks: If he kept playing, there was a chance his foot would never be the same. He would never get the same lift again. That's what they told him. But they were the defending champs and they needed him. So he played, and he was never quite the same. Years later, when he was asked about the decision, McHale explained that you only have so many chances to win a championship, so you do what you have to do. It's that simple.[451]

451 Four months after I wrote this column, I attended a Clippers game where McHale was coaching the visiting Timberwolves. Every time he stood up to bark out orders or challenge a referee, you could see him limping noticably. Basically, **he crippled himself going for that 1987 title**—his foot was never the same, and eventually, his ankles collapsed because they were overcompensating for the bad foot. Watching him limp around, I couldn't help but think about Schilling. Those are the risks.

Even though Schilling was at a different point of his career, the mindset remains the same. After you win one, you just want to get back there...even with a popping ankle tendon, with a suture leaking blood, with 46-degree weather making your legs quiver, with the hopes of an entire region resting on your back. Schilling risked his career and came through. Sometimes in sports, we have a tendency to remember the scarring moments and forget the great ones. I just hope we don't forget this one. Even when people are screaming about it on a split-screen.

So what happens Wednesday night? I'm probably the wrong person to ask. I haven't slept in four days. My back feels like Schilling rammed his protective shoe against it. Even my jaw is sore from chewing gum like a madman during Game Five. The classic move would be for the Sox to win three games in a row, then lose the climactic seventh game. But this isn't a classic Red Sox team. The old Red Sox would have blown Game Four or Game Five, and they definitely would have choked away Game Six. With the old Red Sox, Bellhorn's homer gets ruled a double, A-Rod definitely gets called safe at first base, and Cairo clears the bases for the game winner in the ninth.

Here's the point: Those things haven't been happening. Sometimes you pass a point where history becomes a factor, like with the Patriots three years ago when the diehards kept waiting for The Other Shoe to drop, and we were waiting and waiting, and suddenly Vinatieri's final kick split the uprights, the most liberating feeling you can imagine. That's the thing about baggage as a sports fan—you can shed this stuff. You just need a few breaks. This Boston team is getting them.

I'm not making any predictions. I'm not even trying to be coherent. Just remember these things heading into the game:

1) In less than 24 hours, you could be hearing someone say the following sentence: "So the Red Sox completed the most dramatic comeback in baseball history rallying from three games to zero to defeat the New York Yankees and make the World Series, where they'll be facing off against Roger Clemens and the Houston Astros in Game One."[452]

2) If the roles were reversed, Red Sox Nation would be having a collective coronary right now. Repeat: Coronary. I can't imagine what New York is like. And the thought of Steinbrenner's potential reaction to the biggest choke in sports history…I mean, even if you're NOT a Red Sox fan, you have to be rooting for this, right?[453] Couldn't you see him having Brian Cashman drawn and quartered before the winter meetings?

3) You could make a case that this Yankee team has more pressure on it tonight than any baseball team in recent memory. Not only will they be the guys who finally lost to the Red Sox, they will be the guys who choked away a 3–0 lead. Meanwhile, this Red Sox team is still playing with the house's money. It's an interesting role reversal, although the end result is that I'm peeing blood either way.

4) If the Sox pull this off, for the foreseeable future, every time you're watching a playoff series (in any sport) where

452 In retrospect, even the Baseball Gods decided that would have been too ludicrous.

453 As it turned out, George's reaction was wildly disappointing, and here's why: Suddenly he's really, REALLY old.

someone's up 3–0 and they show the "Teams that have come back from 3–0" graphic, they will feel obliged to mention the 2004 Red Sox. The moment will live on. And on. And on.[454]

5) The Buckner-Armbrister flashback play in Game Six[455] clearly exposed A-Rod as a liar and cheater of the highest order—the kind who would turn over an R in Scrabble and pretend it's a blank letter. Warrants mentioning.

6) If the Red Sox prevail against the Yankees and win the World Series, you will never have to read me whining about the travails of Red Sox fans again.

7) Read that last sentence again.

454 Thanks to one of my ESPN.com editors, Mike Philbrick, for pointing this out to me. It's an unexpected bonus from that 2004 run, one of those gifts that keeps on giving. During the 2005 NBA playoffs, I found myself rooting for teams to take a 3–0 lead just so TNT would show the graphic in Game Four.

455 This was the play where A-Rod tried to knock the ball out of Bronson Arroyo's glove by giving him a pseudo-karate chop. It wasn't the play itself but his reaction afterwards—not only did he lack a sense of humor about it, **A-Rod honestly made it seem like he thought the play was legal**. Biiiiiiig mistake. And yes, in any other year, the ump would have missed the call and the Red Sox would have gotten screwed.

DREAM JOB

October 21, 2004

Honestly, I don't know what to do. I just watched my beloved Red Sox win the American League pennant. That's only happened twice in my lifetime. I watched them rally back from three games down in a playoff series. That's never happened before, not in the history of baseball. I also just watched them beat the Yankees in a deciding playoff game. Not only has that never happened before, it's a possible sign of the apocalypse.

Now get this—all three things happened at the same time.

So what happens now? Where do I go from here? Should I throw myself into politics? Backpack across Europe? Take up gourmet cooking? Learn how to fly airplanes? Should I take the bus to Fort Hancock, cross the border and wander the beaches of Mexico looking for Andy and Red? You tell me. What should I do?

As recently as 75 hours ago, they were dead. Cooked. I still remember standing in Fenway with my father, ready to hustle out of there as soon as the Yankees completed the sweep in the ninth. Dave Roberts changed everything. I started thinking about a comeback that night, about 0.00000003 seconds after Ortiz's walkoff home run landed in the Yankees' bullpen. So did everyone else. We had Pedro going in Game Five, then Schilling in Game Six. That's a puncher's chance. We also had a little momentum. Then Game Five happened, moving us into the "Regardless of what happens, I love this team" stage of things. Then the Schilling Game happened and everyone believed. By the time Game Seven rolled around, October 20th felt like a combination of New Year's Eve and the Fourth of July in Boston. Everyone was headed somewhere, or planning on heading somewhere. Nothing else mattered. Nothing. You couldn't walk five feet without seeing a Sox hat or hearing a conversation about the series. It was physically impossible.

I ended up watching the game in the Financial District, thanks to my buddy Sully's connections at a bar called The Office.[456] We were able to invite 20 guys—closed-off room upstairs, projection TV, pizza and wings, the whole shebang—operating under house rules (only Sox fans) and old-school

456 Some readers were mortified that I didn't watch Game Seven with my father, unaware of what it's like to watch a playoff game in the same room as my stepmother. If you're watching a beauty pageant or an awards show, she's the best—nobody's more entertaining. But Game Seven of a life-or-death baseball series? That's a little different. It could be the eighth inning, bases loaded, two strikes, two outs, Foulke pitching to Sheffield . . . and she would say, "How do you think Sheffield gets his mustache to look like that? Do you think he uses an electric razor?"

country club rules (no chicks). Sometimes, guys just need to be around other guys. This was one of those times. We were 27 outs away from toppling the Yankees. In the words of Clemenza, we were going to the mattresses.[457]

The beers started flowing. Fox kicked off the telecast by using the music from the Rocky-Drago training montage in *Rocky IV*.[458] You can imagine how I felt about that one. *When Nomar died, a part of me died, too. But now you're the one.* Everyone seemed optimistic...right up until Damon was thrown out at home in the first inning, thanks to yet another bone-headed decision from the immortal Dale Sveum. If this guy was a school crossing guard, little kids would be getting pancaked by SUVs like Tony Mandarich in his prime.

We didn't have 10 seconds to bitch before Ortiz crushed a two-run homer to right. Now we were rolling. Derek Lowe pitched the biggest six innings of his life (on two days' rest, no less) and salvaged his dreadful regular season. The Struggling Johnny Damon (his extended name all week) smacked an astounding grand slam, my personal favorite moment of the night, if only because it came from nowhere and sparked a two-minute-long celebration of high-fiving, chest-bumping and general idiocy. Two innings later, Damon came up again and crushed *another* home run, a two-run job into the upper deck. So much for The Struggling Johnny Damon.

8–1, Red Sox. Fifteen outs to go.

We would have felt more confident with that cushion, but the announcers were determined to avoid any Yankees talk and concentrate solely on how the Sox could blow the game. They dragged out every disturbing statistic, every Babe Ruth sign, every negative Boston playoff memory they could find. I'm not positive on this, but I think McCarver and Buck started a "1918!" chant at one point. So yeah, we were a little uneasy. But the Sox kept racking up those outs. Since they had geared their entire broadcast around the inevitable Boston collapse, the announcers didn't know what to do. Forget about the fact that the Yankees had choked in the last two games in Boston, that they lost at home to a 40-year-old guy whose ankle tendon was stapled to his ankle bone, that they had a $180 million payroll, that a Yankee collapse to Boston would be the most devastating moment in franchise history. Forget about showing the stunned fans or Yankee players sitting listlessly in the dugout. None of

457 The amazing thing about this: Nobody brought a girlfriend. Whenever **Country Club Rules are in effect**, someone always blows it by bringing a girl and everyone always reacts the same way—like the guy just squatted and took a dump in the middle of a room. Didn't happen for Game Seven. The stars aligned.

458 *Rocky IV* has a strange way of popping up at significant moments of my life. First of all, it was released in 1986—the same year the Pats lost in the Super Bowl, the Celtics won their 16th title, the Sox blew the World Series, and I crashed my Honda Elite scooter at 40 mph. It's my favorite bad sports movie ever, involving my favorite bad actor ever (Stallone). My buddy Gus and I have joked about it roughly 10 million times over the past 19 years. I've made more jokes about it in columns than any other movie. Not only was it on TV the night I got engaged; but on the day of my wedding, when I woke up at 7 a.m. because of the dreaded nicotine/nerves/ hangover combination, there was a "Rocky Marathon" just starting on TNT. So having a *Rocky IV* song sneak

this mattered to the guys at Fox. As the game dragged on, they started coming around.

"If they hold onto this lead, I'll tell you how big this would be," McCarver said at one point. "This could very well be the biggest win in Red Sox history."

Of course, that's like saying, "If John Kerry wins the election next month, that could very well be the biggest moment of his political career." But it was better than nothing.

When Francona lifted Lowe in the seventh for Pedro Martinez, and Pedro allowed those two rockets to Matsui and Williams...I mean, all those old demons came roaring back. It was the ultimate test. Like a recovering alcoholic opening a hotel mini-bar and seeing those tiny liquor bottles. Our room went silent, save for a few F-bombs and the echoes of the "Who's your Daddy?" chants. Poor Francona had unwittingly plugged Yankee Stadium back into its socket; I kept waiting for him to pull off the Paul Shaffer mask and reveal he was Grady Little.

I can't even describe the things I was thinking about. Terrible, horrible things. Dark things. I just kept remembering the words of my magazine editor, Neil Fine, who called the series "Shakespearean" on Wednesday afternoon. Well, if you were Shakespeare, how would you top last year's collapse if your ultimate goal was for an entire fan base to commit suicide? Wouldn't you have their team roar back from a 3–0 series deficit, then blow an 8-1 lead in the deciding game? Wouldn't that do the trick?[459]

I have never counted down the remaining outs in a game before. Never. Not until last night.

12...11...10...

Here comes Pedro.

(Good God.)

(Come on.)

(Don't do this to me.)

(I will hang myself.)

8...7.

(Exhale.)

6.

Just when the Yanks had some momentum, Bellhorn slammed an insurance homer off Gordon. Can you have insurance homers when the score is 8-3? Apparently so. Timlin made

into the opening montage of the same game in which the Sox were one win away from the greatest comeback in sports history, well, I didn't feel like this was a bad thing.

459 I never allowed myself to wonder about what would have happened here, you know, if Pedro blew a seven-run lead...but thinking about it now, after what happened the previous October, **I honestly think that I would have stopped following baseball.** That would have been it. At some point, you have to draw the line, don't you? I don't know how anyone could have bounced back from that.

it through the eighth unscathed, with a major boost from Mientkiewicz's outrageous scoop on an errant Mueller throw. (Defense, baby!)

5...4...3.

The top of the ninth yielded another insurance run off Gordon, who will be covered in blankets, duct-taped and thrown off one of Steinbrenner's yachts some time this winter. Now Fox was showing the obligatory reaction shots: Yankee fans ready to start sobbing; Cashman frozen in his luxury box; A-Rod's eyes darting around the stadium, trying to figure out a way to cheat to get on base. And that's when it felt real.

That used to be us. Not anymore.

"I almost started crying that inning," Sully said after it was over. "Is this what it feels like to be a girl?"

Seven-run lead. Three outs to go. Timlin got the first two and gave way to Embree, who retired Sierra on a routine grounder to end the game.

(Heeeeeeeeeee-yahhhhhhhhhhhhhhhhhhhhh-hh!!!!!!!!!!!!)

Let the record show that the Yanks went out with a whimper, especially A-Rod (the anti-Babe), Sheffield (disappeared) and Matsui (never the same after Pedro dusted him in Game Four), not to mention Brown, Vazquez, Gordon and even Torre (not his finest series). Only Jeter seemed to care that the Yankees were getting smoked; there was one replay earlier in the game, after his RBI single, when he pumped his fist and shouted at his dugout, "Come on!" He seemed desperate. The Yankees never seem desperate. Now they were headed home for the winter, headed for the no. 1 slot on ESPN50's Biggest Chokes show in 2029.[460]

Meanwhile, the Red Sox were celebrating at Yankee Stadium. Have I mentioned that yet? We were doing our own celebrating at The Office, reacting like college kids in Cancun who just found out that Lindsay Lohan was entering a wet T-shirt contest.[461] Exchanging high-fives and heterosexual man-hugs, I couldn't stop glancing at the TV. *It's official, right? We definitely beat them, right?*

"What's wrong with you?" Sully asked.

"Honestly? I keep waiting for them to announce that there's a Game Eight."

Well, there wasn't. I said my goodbyes, headed out the

460 By the way, if I'm one of the commentators on this show, riddle me with bullets like Sonny Corleone. I'm begging you.

461 Sadly, that joke was written before Lindsay became a charter member of **the Jennifer Connelly All-Star Team**—reserved for Hollywood hotties who lost too much weight and lost their best feature in the process. The rest of the starting-five: Traci Lords, Jennifer Aniston and Rachel Bilson.

door and walked around Faneuil Hall and Beacon Hill for the next 45 minutes, soaking in a scene I never thought I would see. Fans wearing Sox hats and T-shirts, everyone whooping and hollering. Car horns honking. A steady rumble of distant cheers coming from every direction—Kenmore, Copley, BC, BU, Charlestown, you name it. If there's a better sound in life, I haven't heard one. Even greater than I imagined. Looking back, I probably had that same dumb smile walking around that Andy Dufresne gets when they're working on the roof and everyone is drinking his beer.[462]

To recap: Greatest comeback in sports history. First trip to the World Series in 18 years. First meaningful victory over the Yankees. All at the same time.

You have to be a Red Sox fan to understand. You just do. It wasn't just that the Yankees always win. It was everything else that came with it—the petty barbs, the condescending remarks, the general sense of superiority from a fan base that derives a disproportionate amount of self-esteem from the success of their baseball team. I didn't care that they kept winning as much as that they were assholes about it. Not all of them. Some of them. In 96 hours, everything was erased. Everything. It was like pressing the reset button on a video game.

And yeah, I know. We need to win the World Series to complete the dream. But you can win the World Series any year; you only have one chance to destroy the Yanks. As my friend Mike (a Tigers fan) wrote me last night, "Everyone outside of Yankee brats are celebrating quietly with you guys. It's like you killed Michael Myers, Jason, Freddie Krueger and Hannibal Lecter in one night."

It was the choke of chokes, an unprecedented gag job. For once, finally, the Yankees have some baggage. Just like every other baseball team.

One last story: I rolled into my father's house at 1:30 a.m., only to find him sound asleep in the living room, holding the TV remote in his hand like he'd been cryogenically frozen. On the television in front of him, Fox25 was showing live footage from Kenmore Square, as thousands and thousands of Boston fans were celebrating the impossible. After I muttered "Dad!" a few times, he finally jolted awake, glanced at me, then glanced at the TV.

"I can't believe it," he mumbled. "We beat the Yankees."

And it wasn't a dream.

462 This was one of the defining walks of my career—not just because they had won, but because I was gearing up to write such an important column. At a bar called The Four's on Canal Street, they have a framed photo of Bob Ryan's column after the Celtics won the 1981 Finals. I read it every time I'm in there. The point is, you never know when someone is going to frame one of your columns. When I'm writing about something big like this—and it's only happened six times in my life: Pats-Rams; Games Five and Seven of the Yankees series; Game Seven of the 2003 Yankees series; Game Four of the 2004 World Series; and *Celebrity Boxing I* on Fox—I actually get butterflies in my stomach before sitting down in front of the computer, almost like a boxer before a big fight. It's hard to explain. But it's absolutely the best and (most terrifying) part about doing this for a living. And since James Lipton won't return my calls, I'm telling you.

HEY, WHY NOT US?

October 25, 2004

Regardless of how the 2004 World Series ends up, I can't remember another moment in Red Sox history like the sixth inning in Game Two.

Curt Schilling was working on a four-hitter with the aid of painkillers, sutures, staples, rubber bands, Krazy Glue and everything else you can imagine...only his defense had been betraying him all game. His pitch count was swelling toward the 90s. The pain in his bum ankle actually brought him to his knees at one point. And the weather was so chilly at Fenway, people were practically clotheslining the hot chocolate guy. This wasn't a playoff game, it was an endurance contest. For everyone.

Especially Schilling. With two outs in the sixth and the Sox leading by three, Bill Mueller booted a routine grounder. That was followed by Bellhorn improbably booting *another* grounder, Boston's fourth error of the game. Suddenly the Cards had the tying run (Reggie Sanders) coming up. This one had all the makings of an old-school Red Sox inning, one of those sequences that comes on ESPN Classic at 2:30 a.m. and causes any Boston fan to avert his eyes in horror, then frantically start pressing buttons until the channel changes.

Except for one thing: The fans didn't quit this time.

Normally when these "Uh-oh" scenarios happen at Fenway, you hear people groan in disgust, and then everyone tightens and awaits the inevitable kick to the groin. That's the history of this team: *Expect the worst, get the worst.* But after the Yankees series, we believe in these guys, just like we believe Brady and the Patriots will make one or two plays when it matters most. The Red Sox earned that faith against the Yankees last week. The hard way.[463]

463 Another valid Patriots-Sox comparison. The more I read these chapters, the more I'm convinced that there's no way the Sox could have won a World Series without "Pats 20, Rams 17" happening.

So we cheered. Banged our mittens and gloves together. Hooted and hollered. Tried to carry Schilling one more time, like we spent the afternoon sitting next to Stuart Smalley and staring into his full-length mirror. Sitting in Section 9, I remember thinking to myself, "My God, I really think he can get through this." And he did. Hard grounder to third for the force. End of the threat. Schilling waited for Mueller to gather his hat from the ground, shouted words of encouragement as Mueller jogged by him, then limped toward the dugout. He was finished. Totally spent. Eighteen outs, 94 pitches, another unforgettable performance.

Yeah, the Red Sox won. 6–2. And they're headed back to St. Louis with a 2–0 lead, just two wins away from...well, you know. Heading into Game Three, the Cards still haven't gotten a decent pitching performance, haven't gotten their 2–3–4–5 clicking, haven't had a chance to play La Russa Ball with a lead. Throw in a terrific group of fans and things should be different on Tuesday for them. You would think.[464]

But Game Two belonged to Schilling. The night started with Schilling ambling to the bullpen, soaking in the cheers and doffing his cap to the bleachers. We watched him jog around the outfield, awkwardly loosening up his legs like a 40-year-old guy preparing to play pickup hoops at the Y. We held our collective breath for his warmup pitches, reassured ourselves that he looked okay. We watched him standing proudly in the bullpen, holding his cap to his chest, soaking in James Taylor's spinetingling version of the National Anthem. When he limped toward the dugout at 8:09, we cheered him every step of the way. I'm not sure if he's larger than life, but he's headed that way. [465]

He's a strange guy to figure. Schilling chose Boston partly because of the passion of the fans (the emotional), partly because he understood his legacy could be transformed with a Red Sox championship (the rational).[466] He spent the first few weeks of the season answering questions on the Sons of Sam Horn message board, shutting things down after a few local writers raised a predictable (and embarrassing) stink. If he's driving around and hears something inflammatory on WEEI, he calls in and argues with the hosts. He broke the unofficial record for Most Local Commercials Filmed in a Single Season.[467] Even his wife has become recognizable in town, giving more interviews than some guys on the team. Clearly, Schilling loves being the center of attention. This rubs some the wrong way; personally, I wish every athlete was more like him. But watching him carry this team throughout the season—saving his best for big games, eating up those Jack Morris innings to save his bullpen, then risking his ravaged ankle (and the twilight of his career) over these past few weeks—even his biggest detractors couldn't deny that something special happened here. No Boston fan will forget no. 38.

464 Honestly? This was a bold-faced lie. I never wrote this (and only because I was petrified of jinxing the team), but I knew we were going to win the World Series after Game Two. The Cards should have taken Game One—a choppy, poorly played, topsy-turvy game that has a weird tendency of going to the road team early in a World Series—and Schilling shouldn't have given the Sox anything in Game Two. The Cards needed to split and they didn't, and **there was absolutely no way Suppan was beating Pedro** in Game Three. Again, I didn't write any of this. But any Sox fan who claims they weren't thinking about these things is lying.

465 Okay, so it's corny and I don't usually write things like that. Then again, I started this column at something like 1:00 a.m., and handed it in at 5:00 a.m., plus I was working on about nine Red Bulls. So there you go.

466 At the time, I didn't know about the $15 million bonus he had coming if the Sox won the World Series (the financial).

The night ended with Schilling grimacing his way towards the dugout, yet another historic night in the books. With an elusive championship only two victories away, I'm surprised how much I'm thinking about the end of the road—not the possible end of the (rhymes with "Schmurse") and all that media-driven crap, but how much I'm going to miss watching this team. It's almost over; I can't stop thinking about it. Baseball teams resonate more than teams in any other sport, only because of the frequency of the games, the up-and-down nature of the season, the endless array of characters. For better or worse, 25 to 30 strangers affect your life for six straight months. Day in, day out. Only rarely is it worth it.

This season was worth it. My generation grew up with stoic heroes like Yaz and Rice, burdened by an invisible ownership that didn't care about the park or the fans. Many of our favorite players ended up skipping town for reasons that never really made sense. And a legacy of misfortune hung over everything. The 2004 Red Sox made up for everything, a good group of guys who bring out the best in one another. The kind of team you dream about following.

However this turns out, the month of November will feel remarkably ordinary. No more Schilling limping out of a phone booth, wearing a Superman cape, ready to go to work again. No more Ortiz at-bats with guys on base, the ones where Papi goes into that mini-crouch, looking like a cobra ready to strike. No more Foulke jogging in from the bullpen with Danzig blasting from the speakers. No more sparkling plays from Cabrera at short, the ball of energy who turned the season around in August. No more random Varitek at-bats where he looks like the black sheep Molina brother for seven innings, then inexplicably cranks a 450-foot homer when it counts. No more goofy Manny moments when he careens around the outfield like a drunk guy running from the police, then crushes a frozen rope five minutes later.**468**

I could go on and on. Just a wonderful season. And sure, they screw up from time to time—like those eight errors in the first two games—and I wish the manager was a little more, umm, consistent. But they believe in themselves. More importantly, we believe in them. That became abundantly clear in the sixth inning of Game Two, one of those moments that normally brings Red Sox Nation to its collective knees. Not this time.

467 Just spent the last 10 minutes trying to figure out who previously held the record in Boston—**I'd have to go with Drew Bledsoe.** After his breakout season in '94, he would have sold used razors in your basement if you asked him.

468 Interesting note about this paragraph: I picked six guys who summed up the greatness of that 2004 championship team, and for whatever reason, the Red Sox only decided to bring back five of them. Why they spent an extra $10 million on Edgar Renteria, when Cabrera won them the World Series, is something I will never fully understand. Sometimes you can get too cute. And yes, if Renteria ends up winning three World Series MVPs or something, this section will look ridiculous.

Three words sum everything up. Inside Fenway this weekend, they were selling blue T-shirts for $25 that simply said, "WHY NOT US?" They were selling like hot cakes.

Why not us?

Of course, Schilling started that bandwagon. He kept repeating that phrase over and over before the playoffs, and now we're here—two wins away from that giant group hug—and I'm kicking myself for not buying one of those T-shirts last night. Sometimes in life, you just have to believe.

THE BRINK OF THE GROUP HUG

October 27, 2004

"How will your life change if the Red Sox win the World Series?"

My wife asked me that question last night, minutes before Foulke clinched Boston's third straight win over the Cardinals. Let's just say that it's a best-of-seven series and Game Four happens tonight. Seemed like a relevant question.

"That's easy," I told her. "Everything would get wiped away. No more baggage. No more Babe Ruth pictures, Buckner highlights, fans walking around with Curse signs, 1918 chants, announcers hinting at doom around every corner. Everyone would just leave us alone. We'd be just another baseball team."

That was the simple answer.

Here's the complicated answer:

This is about life and death. And not in the traditional sense. A Red Sox championship always felt like a race against time. When journalist Marty Nolan wrote, "The Red Sox killed my father and now they're coming after me," he wasn't kidding. I keep thinking about my dad, and my friend Walsh, and my buddy Geoff's mother-in-law, Neets, and every other over-50 person in my life who happens to follow this team. Those are the people who passed a certain point in life and started wondering, "Wait a second, is this thing EVER going to happen?" Obviously, I'm not quite there yet, but after three decades of following this team, I could feel the guillotine inching closer and closer. That's what it's like to be a Red Sox fan.

On the Sons of Sam Horn message board, there's a terrific thread started by an eloquent poster named jacklamabe65,[469] who went online before Game Seven of the Yankees series and listed all the people the Red Sox needed to Win It For. That was the name of the thread. Here was the last paragraph:

"Most of all, win it for James Lawrence Kelly, 1913–1986. This one's for you, Daddy. You always told me that loyalty and perseverance go hand in hand. Thanks for sharing the best part of you with me."

The lurkers were touched. Within six days, there were 32 pages of posts (and counting) from SOSH members, some of

469 Real name: Shaun Kelly, a longtime teacher at the Greenwich Country Day School (my old school) who took over Mr. Ramsey's classroom (my favorite teacher). Somehow, I didn't find this out until three months after writing this particular column. As always, small world.

470 Uncle Ricky once bought me **an autographed Mookie-Buckner baseball**, as well as a framed Curse of the Bambino montage with pictures of the Babe, Buckner and Aaron Boone. After the World Series ended, when I was getting revenge for 35 years of ridicule, he sent me the following email: "26 vs 6 and if you include the Boston Braves, and you probably would because you need all you can get, it's 7…26 to 7…SPARE ME…the curse will never die because once the Sox fail, and they will, to get into the ALDS, ALCS and the WORLD SERIES the CURSE will come back like flies to poop. Don't get too far over your skis, it's a tough fall." Yankee fans are the best.

the most heartwarming stuff you can imagine. It's an amazing thread. Plow through the posts and it's like plowing through the history of the franchise—just about every memorable player is mentioned at some point—as well as the basic themes that encompass the human experiences. Life and death. Love and family. Friendship and loss.

"Win it for my grandfather (1917–2004), who never got to see the Red Sox win it all but always believed. And for my dad who watches each and every game wishing his dad was there to watch with him."

"Win it for my 10-year-old son Charlie who fell asleep listening to Game Seven of the 2003 ALCS assuming the Sox would win. When he woke the next morning, he asked me, eagerly, "Did we win, Dad?" When I told him, gently, no, we did not win, his anguished moan startled me. I knew I had raised him as a Red Sox fan and I began to question whether that was a good thing."

"Win it for my grandfather, who succumbed to Alzheimer's in 2002. In one of my last conversations with him, he asked me how Ted Williams was doing. During Game Seven on October 20, his birthday, he was smiling down on the Red Sox."

"Win it for my boss, a dear friend who lost his dad unexpectedly in March of this year. More than once this season, I've seen him glance at the phone after a game, half expecting his father to call to commiserate, rejoice, or just shoot the breeze—I've also seen the sadness in his eyes as he realizes that the call isn't coming. Win it for his dad, a lifelong fan who never had the opportunity to witness his beloved team taking it all."

There are hundreds of posts like those. And since I never took the time to post my own thoughts, I'm doing it now. If you don't mind.

Here we go…

Win it for Buckner. He deserves to live a normal life again. Always did. Same with Grady Little. And Bob Stanley. Basically, everyone who ever played for the team, except that traitor, Clemens.

Win it for Dave Cirilli, the creator of the Ewing Theory. If the Red Sox won the World Series after trading Nomar, that would be just another notch in his belt. We're talking *SportsCentury and Beyond* material at this point.

Win it for Teddy Ballgame, whose dastardly son humiliated

and degraded him in the final years of his life (and then even after he died). Not the way he should have gone out.

Win it for my mom, who dressed me up in a Freddie Lynn jersey for two straight Halloweens; drove my shell of a body home from Tom Demas' house after Game Six in '86; and learned not to ask "What's the score?" when I was sitting in front of the TV with a frown on my face. Last weekend, she wore a Sox jersey into a French restaurant just to taunt her brother, my Uncle Ricky, a trash-talking Yankees fan in deep denial right now. Everyone thought she would take it off during dinner. She kept it on the whole time. Now that's a Mom.[470]

Win it for Theo Epstein—30 years old and living the dream. The Nomar-Cabrera trade remains the second-gutsiest move in the history of Boston sports, right behind Belichick benching Bledsoe for Brady.

Win it for the guys at Sonny McLean's, the guys at SOSH, the guys at Sullivan's Pub in Charlestown and the guys from the Baseball Tavern (where I have never ordered an appletini in my life, contrary to published reports).[471]

Win it for my friends who love the team and have no problem talking with me about inane things like "Do you think Dale Sveum has a depth-perception problem?" and "Doesn't Rich Garces seem like the type of guy who could clear out the bullpen with one good fart?" for hours on end.

Win it for all the non-Boston readers who didn't mind that I spent the last three weeks writing the same things about the same baseball team. Thanks for the free pass.

Win it for the Sports Gal, who's giving serious consideration to naming our first kid Papi Orlando Johnny Martinez Simmons some day.[472]

Win it for the bird who crapped on my shirt two weeks ago. Sure, I have Legionnaire's Disease now. But it was worth it.

Most of all, win it for my Dad, who carried me into Fenway when I was little and kept carrying me as a Sox fan ever since. I hope he does the same for Papi Orlando Johnny Martinez Simmons some day, right after he bounces the little kid on his lap and tells the story of the time the 2004 Red Sox won the World Series.

(You know…if it ends up happening and all…)

(I'll shut up now...)

Leftover thoughts from the first three games:

471 On Boston.com, they had a Celebrity Sightings page where readers posted celebs they ran into during the home playoff games. **Some jokester claimed they saw me drinking an appeltini at the Baseball Tavern**, which was funny for two reasons—first, if you ordered a drink like that in the Tavern, you would get beaten up; and second, I've never had an appletini in my life. Although I can neither confirm nor deny rumors about my dad.

472 A little foreshadowing—I couldn't help it.

473 When the Red Sox acquired him for the 2003 stretch run, after watching a few Suppan starts, I called my buddy Gus (a producer for *Baseball Tonight*) and asked him, "Why didn't you tell me that Jeff Suppan sucks this much?" Without missing a beat, Gus responded, "I thought you knew!"

• If you had told me 12 months ago that...

1) The Red Sox would be leading a World Series two games to none

2) Pedro Martinez would be pitching against Jeff Suppan in Game Three

...I would have started doing backflips. I'm not kidding. Backflips. Suppan stunk out the joint in Boston last year. Now the Cardinals were trusting him to save their season? Please. If I hear one more person call Suppan a "great big-game pitcher" this week, I'm going to throw up. He's Jeff Suppan, for God's sake.[473]

Only one person was deciding Game Three: Pedro. You knew the Sox would scratch four or five runs off Suppan before LaRussa brought out Ray King's gravity-defying head and the rest of the Cards bullpen. Could Pedro hold the lead? It turned out to be one of the defining moments of his Boston career: A fitting farewell (barring a Game Seven) to Sox fans. Let the record show that he received a healthy dose of luck in the first (Manny throwing out Larry Walker) and third inning (Suppan's five-second aneuryism at third base, prompting the first moment in baseball history where a third base coach walked away from a baserunner in disgust *during the play*). But this was someone who had been decidedly *un*lucky all season; nobody was victimized by more bloop hits and slow rollers than Pedro. So maybe he was overdue for some good fortune. Although the Cards were flailing away like Leatherface in those final four innings, he still engineered a masterful stretch over those last 14 batters—changing speeds, mixing pitches, and working fast enough that it brought back fleeting memories of the old days. When it came time to pull him after seven innings and 98 pitches, we reaped the benefits of that agonizing Yankee game in late September. Maybe everything happens for a reason.

• On that Suppan play: Yet another sequence in the 2004 playoffs that always happened TO the Red Sox in the past, much like A-Rod's karate chop on Arroyo, Tony Clark's ground rule double, Bellhorn's homer in Game Six getting changed from a double, the three Wakefield passed balls in Game Five not amounting to anything, and everything else. It's the Bizarro Red Sox Month.

(Maybe I should change the subject before I anger the Baseball Gods. Um...)

• Hey, there can't be anything dumber than MLB and this DH/No DH thing for the World Series—it's like playing someone for money in bar pool, only on one of those unfamiliar tables where the other guy knows all the angles and dead spots. Can you imagine if the NBA suddenly decided that the Western Conference wouldn't have a three-point line anymore and all Western home games would be played without threes? Would this EVER happen?

• Here's a joke from Greg T. in San Diego:
Q: What do you call 25 guys watching the World Series?
A: The Yankees.

• I totally forgot how much I enjoy the Tony La Russa Era. For one thing, he's one of those guys who always looks the same—like David Robinson and Dick Clark[474]—and there's at least an 80-percent chance that he's completely bald and staples his hat to a Dennis Eckersley wig. His press conferences are phenomenal, just a superior mix of sarcasm and condescension (he makes Bill Parcells look like Pete Carroll). And he's firmly entrenched in that Brett Favre Zone, where the announcers are so busy paying homage to him for three hours, they never notice when he screws up (like bringing in Cal Eldred—his worst reliever—in a must-win Game Three). My favorite La Russa quirk: when something bad happens, then he stares out onto the field like someone who just realized that their car was being towed. Just an entertaining package all around.

• Weird fact in case you missed it: The Celtics won their first championship against St. Louis (1957); the Bruins broke a 29-year Stanley Cup drought against St. Louis (1970); and the Patriots won their first Super Bowl against St. Louis (2002). Hey, I'm just the messenger.

• Cards fans last night: a solid D-minus. I know it was raining, and I know the Suppan blunder was a killer...but c'mon. That was like a Braves crowd without the tomahawk chop chant. Not an impressive night for the alleged best fans in the National League. They know they're still allowed to make noise when their team falls behind, right?[475]

• Someone asked me what was my favorite random thing about the 2004 Sox. At gunpoint, I think it's Foulke emerging from the Fenway bullpen to "Mother" by Danzig, such an

474 Other members on this list: Bono, Chris Rock, Gary Payton, Scottie Pippen (although the hair always changes), **Jeff Goldblum; Junior Griffey, Jeff Bridges,** Bernard Hopkins, Grace Jones, and Sheryl Crow.

475 The St. Louis fans had a great argument for this one: The Suppan play was one of those "Oh my God, we're doomed" moments... looking back, you can't really blame them.

arcane choice that I've been dying to find out how this happened. I'm not killing the song, believe me. It's a classic. You just wouldn't expect to hear it at a baseball game; it's the kind of song that's the theme for one of those HBO documentaries about siblings in a Wisconsin trailer park who were wrongly accused of killing their mother. Was Foulke inspired by a *Beavis and Butthead* re-run? Did he attend high school with Danzig? Is he still coming to grips with his relationship with his mom? Does the song get him fired up? Is it some sort of elaborate pratical joke? I'm brimming with questions here. Again...I'm not arguing. Fantastic song, Hall of Fame video, definitely gets you fired up. Just not something you would expect to hear at a baseball game. Nothing personifies this goofy 2004 Sox team quite like the closer running out to the musical stylings of Mr. Glen Danzig.[476]

476 Here's what happened: Apparently Gabe Kapler and Bronson Arroyo decided that Foulke needed an entrance song because every good closer had one, so they made a concerted effort to find him a kick-ass song, ultimately selling him on "Mother." If this information wasn't enough for the team to match Kapler's Japan offer that winter, I don't know what was.

• For Yankee fans, it's Day Seven of "Operation Spin Control. My favorite excuses so far include:

"You still need to win the World Series or it means nothing."

"This wasn't that big of a deal—I was much more upset when we lost to the Diamondbacks."

"Don't tell me we choked. Three of those games came down to the last at-bat."

And, "I was 10 times more upset when the wispy mustache fell out of style."

(All right, I made the last one up. But if the Sox end up winning the title, I'm looking forward to hearing, "Congratulations, now you only have 19 to go before you catch us.")

• Reason no. 435 why I wouldn't make a good manager: I would have benched Mark Bellhorn before Game Five. Now he's a possible candidate for World Series MVP.

• You need a little luck to get this far. Consider the things that *didn't* happen for the Sox in the past 24 months: 1) the A-Rod deal fell through; 2) Millar's Japan deal fell through; 3) Montreal told them that they didn't have enough to get Vazquez, so they turned to Plan B (Schilling); 4) the Yankees trumped them for Contreras; 5) Nomar turned down two different extensions in 2003; 6) anyone could have claimed Manny off waivers this winter; 7) they almost traded Lowe for Loiaza before the Yankees trumped their bid; and 8) they wouldn't have gotten Cabrera if Nomar hadn't sulked throughout that 13-inning game at Yankee Stadium, turning public sentiment against him just enough that they could trade him without causing a riot downtown.

• My only pet peeve about having a Boston team in a championship: When the Boston mayor makes the stupid bet with the other team's mayor. Drives me crazy. For instance, before the World Series, Mayor Menino of Boston wagered a bunch of Boston beer and food products (Legal Seafood's clam chowder, a case of Sam Adams beer, 11 pounds of Dunkin' Donuts coffee and a bunch of other Boston-related stuff) in exchange for Anheuser-Busch products, Toasted Ravioli, Bissinger chocolate and some other St. Louis goodies from Mayor Clark Griswold.

Um...that's a bet? Those are high stakes? *Oh, no, we lost... darn, we're never gonna replace all that clam chowder. I never should have let him sucker me into that.* Please. Just one of these times, I want one of the mayors to throw something out there like, "If you guys win, I'll sleep with a tranvestite...if we win, you have to try heroin and speed at the same time." Now THAT would get people talking.

• Strangest subplot in the history of sports: A possible lunar eclipse for Game Four which could coincide with a possible Red Sox World Series sw-

(Whoops. I almost wrote the S-word.)

DESTINATION: DESTINY

October 28, 2004

I woke up thinking about the Red Sox. Answered e-mails, read the paper, showered, shaved, never stopped thinking about the Sox. Found that I was so excited, I could barely keep a thought in my head. Cruised through the day doing ordinary things, thinking the entire time, "Holy crap, my life could be completely different in eight hours."

Is this how parents feel when they're about to have a baby? Like nothing has changed, but everything's about to change? That's how I felt yesterday. The Sox were about to win the World Series. And I was about to become Just Another Baseball Fan again. That's all we ever wanted. Outsiders made up fake curses, called us losers, pointed to a legacy of failure, questioned our sanity. We kept hoping. We kept the faith. We kept passing this team down from generation to generation, hoping it would be worth it. And it was. The last eleven days were the greatest sports ride of our lives: eight games, eight wins, one championship, a boatload of memories. We crawled through 500 yards of shit-smelling foulness and came out smelling like roses on the other side. **477**

477 Two *Shawshank* references in the first two paragraphs. I'm on pace for 76 in the column right now.

Anyway, I have very few rules in life, but here's one of them: Any time the Red Sox can win a World Series on the same night as a lunar eclipse, I keep a running diary. I'm not doing this for you. I'm doing it for me. I want to read it in fifty years, show my kids, frame this baby and stick it on a wall. *Here's how Dad was feeling on the night the Red Sox won the championship.* I like that idea.

Of course, the Red Sox had to come through. Here's what transpired.

5:15 p.m PST: We're coming to you live from the Sports Guy Mansion! I'm sitting here with the Dooze, the Sports Gal and a bottle of Veuve Clicquot on ice. We just endured Fox showing a sequence of Sox-related breaks over the past two weeks, followed by the obligatory Curse of the Bambino montage with 348 photos and video images of Babe Ruth. Thanks, guys. You've made this a blast from start to finish.

478 Back in March, I joked in a column that, "If the Sox lose out on another World Series with Christ playing center field, it's clearly not happening in my lifetime."

479 I'm pretty sure that McCarver meant that Marquis usually throws groundballs—he just said it wrong. Wait, why the hell am I defending Tim McCarver?

5:20: Tonight's announcers: Buck (son of the famous Cards announcer) and McCarver (longtime Cardinals catcher). Why not just go the whole way and have Ozzie Smith, Whitey Herzog and Dizzy Dean as sideline reporters? And where's Al Leiter tonight? Did McCarver have him liquidated?

5:25: Sideline reporter Chris Myers: "For the Sox fans who travelled here, they're still kinda numb, they don't know how to act." Yup. That's us.

5:27: According to Buck, we have two groundball pitchers tonight: Derek Lowe and Jason Biggs-lookalike Jason Marquis. Nobody epitomizes the Sox experience like D-Lowe, who wore every hat possible during the Pedro Era—superb set-up man, quality closer, embattled closer, creator of the The Derek Lowe Face, 20-game winner, guy who threw a no-hitter, major disappointment, hero of the Oakland series, head case who tanked his contract year, money pitcher who came through against the Yankees. I can't accentuate this strongly enough—I gave up on this guy at least 15 times over the past six years. You never knew what to expect with him. Just like rooting for the Red Sox.

5:28: Leadoff home run, Johnny D! *The power of Christ compels you! The power of Christ compels you!*[478] Boston is 9–0 when scoring first in the 2004 playoffs. That leads to this exchange:

McCarver: One thing about groundballs, they don't go out of the ballpark.

Sports Gal [after a beat]: I don't get it.[479]

5:32: Following a walk to Manny, we get our first prolonged closeup of a homicidal Tony La Russa. My mother called La Russa "brooding and VERY sexy" this week, but added that he looks just enough like Robert Evans where she could never be "totally attracted" to him. And you wonder why I'm a lunatic. Meanwhile, Marquis gets out of the first.

5:40: After Tony Womack's leadoff hit over Cabrera's head, McCarver claims that Cabrera "jumped too soon," was subsequently proven wrong by the replay, then continued to discuss the dangers of "jumping too soon." I love when announcers refuse to admit they were wrong despite overwhelming evidence to the contrary. This is exactly how I would announce games. You can't let little things like facts and indisputable evidence get in the way of your points. You just can't.[480]

5:45: Thank God for Scott Rolen. He strands Womack on third to end the first. Even Ben Affleck isn't in this big of a slump.

5:58: The Sox strand two in the second. Marquis looks shakier than a barrel of monkeys.

6:03: Inspired by a Hank Aaron sighting, McCarver tells a story about Hammerin' Hank's 756th home run that didn't count. Curt Simmons was pitching, Chris Pelekoudas was the home plate umpire, and I can't believe I'm writing this down. Meanwhile, three up, three down for D-Lowe in the second.

6:06: All right, I'll ask: Is *Nanny 911* premiering on Fox or the Spice Channel?[481]

6:10: Following a Ramirez single, Fox shows Jimmy Fallon and Drew Barrymore wearing Red Sox sweatshirts and clapping excitedly. I wish I was actually driving the Red Sox Bandwagon right now, just so I could screech to a halt, whirl around, point to them and scream, "Get off! RIGHT NOW! I mean it! Get off! Move it! Gather your things and GET THE HELL OFF!"[482]

6:15: Ortiz doubles, then Manny gets thrown out at home on a Varitek grounder. Third and first with two outs, as Buck and McCarver effusively praise Pujols for throwing out Manny on a routine play (he was out by 10 feet). Go Cardinals! Come on, guys, it's been 10 minutes, show us another Babe Ruth photo.

6:18: Mueller walks on four pitches. Bases loaded for Trot. "This is an accident waiting to happen," McCarver says. "You wonder how long Marquis can keep walking through the raindrops." Actually, I wasn't wondering that. But Trot ends up CRUSHING a 3–0 pitch to deep center, just missing a grand slam by about five feet. 3–0, Red Sox.

(Note: Nothing sums up this Sox team like Trot getting the green light on 3-0. Get busy living, or get busy dying.)

6:20: The Sports Gal sums up everyone else's feelings: "Why the hell are they showing Red Sox fans celebrating at a bar in New York City????"

480 The master of this is ESPN's Paul Maguire, who actually starts arguments with himself during NFL games: "I'm gonna tell you what, that was roughing the passer right there! I want you to **watch this replay, watch how late Junior Seau hits Manning**, watch this… nope, that was a perfect timing! That was NOT roughing the passer!"

481 My favorite part of re-reading these running diaries—the promos for shows that have long-since failed. For instance, I have a March Madness diary from my old website that features roughly 6,000 *Falcone* jokes. Gets better with age. Like a fine wine.

482 They were filming scenes for the excruciating *Fever Pitch*. I will never forgive Lucchino, Werner and Henry for allowing them on the field, especially after Fallon revealed in an ESPN.com interview that he was a Yankees fan, then a Mets fan, and now, he's kind of a Red Sox fan, but he likes all three. Ugh. Thankfully, the movie bombed.

6:38: After a hurried trip to Starbucks,[483] we make it back for the top of the fourth—nobody scored or anything—just in time to see Manny argue with the black sheep Molina brother, Francona running out to cool things down...and then the game continuing like nothing ever happened. See, this is where my idea for networks hiring lip readers during games would come in handy. *Let's go to Marlee Matlin, who knows exactly what the argument was about.*

6:42: What's sadder, that Fox keeps showing these *House MD* promos, or that I was just bummed out that "You're risking a patient's life!" wasn't included in the last one?

6:44: Myers reports that La Russa argued with the home plate ump between innings, complaining that Marquis wasn't getting the same calls as D-Lowe. *We don't like our hotel room in Boston, we don't like the food at the hotel, we aren't getting the same calls.* Hey Tony, you want some cheese with that whine? Get a haircut.

(Sorry I just turned into my stepfather there...my apologies.)[484]

6:47: After Womack's leadoff single, D-Lowe has retired 12 straight guys, as well as any chance of The Derek Lowe Face for the night. When that sinker starts cutting away from lefthanded hitters, you know he's got it going. I'm officially counting outs. Fifteen to go.

6:49: Well, we had the lunar eclipse. I think this is a good sign. More importantly, Bonnie Tyler gets to fill out a 1090-form this year—Fox just replayed the moon with "Total Eclipse of the Heart" playing in the background. Plus, the Red Sox are trying to complete a World Series sweep. This is officially the weirdest night of all time. I keep expecting Dooze to ask, "Hey, who's winning?"

6:58: Marquis becomes the first Cards starter to get through the fifth inning this week. Of course, it took him 106 pitches. But he did it. This Cards rotation reminds me of the SNL cast this year—seems nice enough on paper, but nobody can carry the show when it matters. Basically, they have five Chris Parnells.

Time for a quick story: I didn't dress warmly enough for the Pats game two weeks ago, so I bought a hooded Pats sweatshirt

483 This provoked more sarcastic e-mails than any throwaway line I've ever written. **People were OUTRAGED that I went to Starbucks during Game Four**, even though it was the closest coffee place to my house and I needed a caffeine boost (because I was headed for a 3 a.m. night writing the column). My readers never cease to amaze me. But here's the funny thing—there was NEVER a Starbucks trip during the game. I swear on Larry Bird's life, I went before the game but needed a filler line because nothing interesting happened from 6:20 to 6:38—seriously, you can watch the tape—so I messed with the facts and moved the Starbucks trip to 6:38. Big mistake. It turned out to be like one of those early *Saved by the Bell* episodes in which Zack tells a white lie, then comes up with a much bigger lie covering up that lie that makes it 10 times worse.

484 Somehow I made it through this entire book without mentioning my stepdad, Don Corbo, who taught me the two most important lessons I ever learned in life: "The only thing you have is your word" and "The only person you can count on is yourself." Good guy. Although I will never totally forgive him for taking me to Madison Square

and matching old-school ski cap (with Pat Patriot on it) at the Pro Shop, which I wore at Game Four against the Yanks later that night. Needless to say, the combo returned for Game Five...and nine days later, I'm still wearing the sweatshirt (with the cap as a late-inning closer). Also, I still have a T-shirt covered in bird poop hidden in my bedroom. Other than that, I'm *totally* normal about this Red Sox thing. Just wanted to get that on the record.[485]

7:04: One-out double for Renteria, one of those Latin guys who's listed at 29 but probably went to high school with Roberto Clemente. That's followed by a wild pitch from Lowe. "If you're looking for the local and you get the express, you're in trouble," McCarver explains, inadvertently quoting Jenna Jameson.

7:07: Mabry strikes out, followed by Black Sheep Molina grounding out to end the inning. You know what? It's not happening for the Cards. It's just not. They should just put on Finland's 1980 hockey uniforms and get it over with. At the rate they're going, they may not get 10 minutes in the Red Sox World Series DVD.

7:14: Just called my dad: "Twelve outs to go."

7:16: Desperate to jinx the Sox, Fox has Chris Myers interviewing Boston fans, including a 12-year-old kid who says, "I can't wait to come back and brag that I got to see the Red Sox win the World Series."

(You know, in the old days, I'd be cringing right now and awaiting the inevitable Pujols grand slam. Not anymore. Okay, maybe a little.)

7:18: Top three places where I wish Fox had planted cameras tonight: 3) Steinbrenner's house; 2) Buckner's house; 1) Nomar's house. I just picture a sullen Nomar watching the game in the dark, as Mia brings him a glass of water and he mutters, "Thanks, beautiful."[486]

7:19: After a Damon two-out triple, Cabrera strands him at third. Marquis has gotten out of more trouble tonight than Bobby Brown. By the way, you know when you spend a weekend in Vegas drinking and smoking and playing cards, then you come home and there's that weird Sunday night where you feel disoriented, your head hurts and your heart is pounding from

Garden to see a WWF card in 1982, but deliberately overpaying for great seats within 10 rows of the ring so I could see firsthand that pro wrestling was fake. Seeing **Greg "The Hammer" Valentine** fall backwards after Pedro Morales missed him with a punch by three feet may have been the most traumatic moment of my youth that didn't involve the Red Sox.

485 You can see the Pats sweatshirt/cap combo on page 353, an action shot from my running diary of Game Four of the 2005 World Series. (And, yes, it was like 85 degrees in L.A. that day.) After the Series, I broke out that ski cap for seven more Patriots games—including the three playoff wins—and went 7–0. That cap still hasn't lost. I'm thinking about putting it in a safety deposit box so it doesn't get stolen.

486 Totally unprovoked dig at Nomar's Nike commercial congratulating **Mia Hamm** after her retirement. Couldn't resist.

the nicotine/liquor withdrawal? That's how I'm starting to feel. I think this is fun. I think.

7:26: Good question from the Sports Gal: "Why wouldn't the Red Sox want to keep this team together if they win?" Because we're not the ones who would have to pay Lowe and Pedro a combined $90 million over the next four years. That's why.[487]

7:31: With Walker on first, D-Lowe gets a Pujols pop-out to end the sixth. After he got squeezed on a 2–2 pitch, the self-destructive hanging sinker was looming. Didn't happen. And yes, I went to the lucky ski cap for that one.

7:36: Just went online to find D-Lowe's pitch count (71). Normally, the network provides these things, but...well...

7:38: Boston goes quietly in the seventh, leading to That Guy from Creed singing "God Bless America" between innings. Somehow, they found the one singer who sucks more than the Cardinals' offense.

7:44: Classic shot of the nervous Red Sox owners, including Tom Werner looking like he's about to start puking up pea soup like Linda Blair in *The Exorcist*. Sadly, they don't show bachelor GM Theo Epstein, who could become the next JFK Jr. in Boston with tonight's potential win.[488]

7:47: Fox runs the always-entertaining "How life was different the last time the Sox won the World Series" graphic. Not only had penicillin not been discovered in 1918, but the NBA didn't exist yet. I think there's a VD joke here somewhere. Whatever.

7:49: D-Lowe strikes out Mabry to end the seventh. At the rate we're going, I'll be driving down Derek Lowe Avenue in Back Bay in five years. Six outs to go.

(Final line on Lowe: seven innings, no runs, three hits. A win gives him the decision in all three clinchers this month. Not a bad month. All he's missing is Billy Zabka handing him a trophy and crying, "You're alright, Lowe, you're alright.")

7:51: My favorite part of the *My Big Fat Obnoxious Boss* promo: When the contestant realizes it's a hoax and screams, "We just took six weeks out of our life to make jackasses out of

487 As it turned out, I nailed that number exactly—Pedro received $54 million from the Mets, Lowe got $36 million from the Dodgers. That's creepy.

488 After the Series, a reader named Jeremy from Boston e-mailed this question: "Would you agree that **a gay porn film starring Tom Brady and Theo Epstein** would be the highest-selling gay porn film OF ALL TIME?" Top-five strangest mailbag questions I've ever received.

ourselves?" I mean, if you can't trust the producers of a reality TV show, who CAN you trust?

7:53: Just got an e-mail from my buddy Chipper in Milwaukee: "Just in case, I'm moving the family down into the basement for the next few hours." Probably the right move.

7:54: Nixon doubles, Mueller singles. Second and third, nobody out. Trot's third double of the night, by the way. Has there ever been a World Series team that juggled more heroes from game to game? Meanwhile, La Russa puts down his *Wall Street Journal*, takes off his smoking jacket, puts down his pipe, and tabs his closer (Jason Isringhausen). The right move. For once.

8:04: Isringhausen gets out of the jam: Strikeout, groundout, strikeout. Still 3–0, Sox. Notice the complete lack of panic on my part. It's by design.

8:11: You know, Francona has been so on fire this series, I'm not even questioning Bronson Arroyo pitching the eighth. It's like playing blackjack with someone who wins 15 grand in chips, then inexplicably wants to split 10s against a 9. *Whatever, dude. Do what you need to do.* If you want to bring in a white guy with cornrows to get two of the last six outs, by all means, do it.

8:17: Arroyo gets Cedeno, then walks Sanders (33 BBs all year) on a full count. Terrific. Now they're bringing in Embree. That leads to the classic La Russa over-managing move: pinch-hitting young Hector Luna for Womack (one of the few Cards who seems to be aware that it's the World Series). Of course, Luna strikes out. It was a Luna eclipse. Thank you, thank you very much. By the way, I'm starting to see three laptop screens right now.

8:21: Just had this exchange with the Sports Gal:

Me: If I have a heart attack and die, copy the text in this document, paste it into an e-mail, and send it to Kevin Jackson at ESPN.

Her: You serious?

Me: Actually, yeah.

8:22: Embree gets a pop-up from Walker to end the eighth. Exhale. I immediately call my Dad, who beats me to my first sentence: "Three outs to go!"

8:28: Boston's at-bats are starting to take on a "The sooner we get this over, the sooner we can start pouring champagne on each other" vibe. Meanwhile, having run out of Babe Ruth pictures, Fox skips the middleman and shows Dan Shaughnessy—who's feverishly shoving pins into a Foulke voodoo doll in the Busch Stadium press box. Then Fox shows the Buckner-Mookie clip, followed by the clip of the Boone homer. Keep trying, guys. You're not getting us this time.[489]

8:31: To the bottom of the ninth.

(Things I won't be doing right now: Calling my Mom and telling her to press record on the VCR because I want to have it on tape when the Red Sox win the World Series. That happened in '86. Went poorly. That was the one time in my life as a sports fan where I never saw it coming—like Joe Pesci getting made at the end of *Goodfellas*, then taking that bullet to the back of the head. Won't happen again. Why are we talking about this?)

8:33: Here comes Foulke, who's been lights-out all month, prompting McCarver to gush, "It has been a post-season...where ordinary Foulke...has become *extraordinary* Foulke." Somewhere, Jim Nantz is nodding in approval.

8:36: Pujols singles up the middle. One on, no outs. Just put the lucky ski cap back on.

8:38: Rolen flies out to right, then gets escorted in a hearse to the local morgue. One out. I'm having trouble typing.

8:39: Jim Edmonds strikes out. Two outs. "Should I get the bottle of champagne?" my wife asks. Um, no. Let's hold that thought.

8:40: I'm staring at Edgar Renteria right now wondering, "Does this look like the guy who will make the last out when the Red Sox win the World Series?"

(You know what? Yes. Yes he does.)

8:41: One-hopper back to Foulke, underhand scoop to first...

HEE-YAHHHHHHHHHHHHHHHHHHHHHHHHH-HHHHHH!!!!!!!!!!!!!!!!!!!!!

8:41: HOLY $%#%@%@ #^%#$@#$@!!!!!!

8:42: All right...

489 This seems like a good place to say that I will never, ever, EVER forgive Fox for pulling this crap—especially Buck, a solid announcer who should have known better than to exploit the emotions of fans like that. There's a difference between building up drama and torturing an entire fan base. And by the way, Buck was the same guy who flipped out like the dad from *Footloose* when **Randy Moss did the fake moon** in the NFL playoffs two months later, calling it "disgusting" and refusing to allow them to replay Moss' TD celebration. So Joe, you care about protecting your viewers from a fake moon, but it's okay to torture Red Sox fans with 10,000 Babe Ruth references when they're trying to enjoy the World Series, and throwing it to commercials for Cialis with "Who's your Daddy?" is perfectly acceptable? Interesting.

Forget about ending the curse and having 86 years of baggage erased in one fell swoop. If you don't get emotional watching a group of guys celebrating and hugging when you feel like you know them, when you suffered all the same highs and lows, when you spent the last seven months with them...I mean, why even follow sports at all?

(Translation: It's getting a little dusty in here.)[490]

8:43: Best glass of champagne in my life.

8:44: Just called Dad. Been waiting to make that call my whole life. "It happened in my lifetime!" he keeps saying. Plus, the apocalypse didn't happen.

8:47: Standing on a podium, Bud Selig announces Manny as MVP while Manny makes exaggerated pointing gestures at his teammates. Couldn't be more fitting. They placed him on waivers, tried to trade him to Texas for A-Rod...and he ends up winning the World Series MVP 10 months later. Just like Theo drew it up. Plus, Manny gave us this exchange:

Jeanne Zelasko: Do you believe in curses?

Manny: I don't believe in curse, I believe you make your own destination.

(Not only a strangely appropriate response for the moment, but Mike Tyson must have been delighted.)

8:50: Time for the round of phone calls with my Sox fan friends. My favorite reaction comes from a stunned J-Bug, who says, "I'm in shock, I'm just in shock...I feel like this won't hit me until March, then I'll be walking down the street and start doing the Fred Flintstone skip out of nowhere."

That's a little how I feel. Reminds me of a story. Sometimes we bring home doggie bags for the Dooze. This one time, we brought her home a pork chop, which she picked up and slinked over to the living room before dropping it on the ground. Then she kept glancing at the pork chop and back at us. Really? *This is for me? You serious?* That's how I feel right now. Like Dooze staring at that pork chop. *A World Series championship? Red Sox players celebrating? Really? For me?*

8:56: Highlights from the past five minutes: every replay of the celebration; poor John Henry rushing through his interview (he's not exactly an extrovert); Pedro stealing the trophy from Henry, then standing in front of the camera with a huge smile

490 When writing this column, I debated whether to include Fox's closeup shot of **Barrymore and Fallon hugging and kissing on the field**—which happened within a minute of the final out, to everyone's ultimate dismay—but decided I didn't want to taint everything else that was happening. But as a footnote, it's okay. Let the record show that Barrymore and Fallon tainted the greatest sports moment of my life by 0.000000001 percent. It was like cutting the umbilical cord of your first baby while Fallon and Barrymore were inexplicably making out five feet away.

on his face; Theo pouring champagne on Lucchino (who pretended to be cool but was fighting off the urge to scream, "You're messing up my hair!"); a fan holding a sign that said "86 YEARS SWEPT AWAY"; and Fox heading to commercial as Schilling (how have I not mentioned Schilling in this column yet?) gave a toast to a huddled group of teammates—"To the best Red Sox team ever assembled!"—followed by everyone lifting champagne bottles and screaming "Yeah!"[491]

(I'm not sure if that was the best 15 minutes of my life, but it's definitely up there.)

9:03: One more phone call to Dad. "We must have watched thousands of games together over the years," he says. "I never knew if it would happen. Plus, we were there for the Yankee games! We were a part of this!" He's babbling. I'm babbling. Everyone's babbling. You tend to babble after the impossible happens.

9:33: I'd like to announce that Game Four just received coveted Save Until I Delete status on my TiVo, joining *Fast Break* and the first episode of *Battle of the Network Stars*.[492] Lofty company. I just watched the Red Sox win the World Series. It happened. I have proof.

10:15: After an hour of phone calls and e-mails, my friends Hench and Dave show up with a bottle of champagne. We spend the next 90 minutes in my kitchen, drinking bubbly and talking about the season.[493] Everyone agrees that our lives have somehow been changed by this, as crazy as that sounds. It's like removing a decaying tooth that pained you every time you ate something. The curse? That was the tooth. Just a nagging, annoying thing that never went away.

Now the 1918 jokes are done. Now TV networks can't ruin our playoff games anymore. Now we can watch Red Sox games without waiting for the Other Shoe. Now we don't have to deal with manipulative books and documentaries, or hear about Buckner, Zimmer, Grady, Pesky, Torrez, Stanley and Schiraldi ever again. It's a clean slate. We're like those ugly contestants who show up on *The Swan*, get 50 grand worth of plastic surgery, then start sobbing in front of a full-length mirror when they see themselves. That's every Red Sox fan right now.

Eighty-six years wiped away. Just like that. It was destination.

(And destiny, too.)

491 That's right up there with **"For Granny, for Nate... for Caretaker,"** "You're the best ballplayer I ever had, and you're the best goddamn hitter I've ever seen" and "I love you guys" in my book. What a moment.

492 Just a few weeks later, the Pistons-Pacers melee would join that elite group.

493 This was fun, but it wasn't nearly as good as what was happening in the Red Sox locker room. If someone released a Best Champagne Celebrations DVD, wouldn't you buy it? I think this is the real reason we're all so jealous of athletes—no other walk of life offers the chance to prevail in something, then spend the next hour with your buddies spraying champagne on each other and acting like idiots. We should be able to bid on this on eBay.

ZIHUATANEJO

April 12, 2005

When my friend Sully[494] came up with two extra tickets for Opening Day, I called my father to break the good news. We were headed to Fenway.

"It's April 11th," I told him. "Take the day o–"

"I know," he interrupted. "I already took it off."

"You did? You didn't even know if we had tickets yet."

"I was going to watch it at home. I mean, they're handing out World Series rings at Fenway. It's not exactly something that happens every year."

Looking back, the moment wasn't nearly as inspiring as the chef's speech about Pele before Louden Swain's final match in *Vision Quest*...but the fact remains, my father doesn't take days off unless he's battling Montezuma's Revenge or something. He's one of those guys who leaves 15 to 20 vacation days unused every year. On Monday, April 11, 2005, he would be skipping work. Happily. And all for a baseball team.[495]

You can't overstate how the 2004 Red Sox affected everyone in New England, as well as Boston fans across the country and around the world. Now we had a chance to thank them. Leading up to Opening Day, this was a hotter ticket than either World Series game. Everyone wanted to pay their respects. Everyone wanted to be there for the impossible. Until last October, I can remember attending games at Fenway and glancing at the championship flags on the first-base side, which went **1918–1916–1915 –1912–1903** on the green balcony (going from left to right). There was an empty space to the left of the 1918 banner, with more than enough room for another flag. Fat chance. I would stare at that space and think about things like, "I hope I'm not still staring at that space 50 years from now."

That's what it was like to be a Red Sox fan.

I know, I know, it's all been written. For much of the country, the Sox transformed from "lovable and tragic" to "oversaturated and annoying" in a scant six months, culminating in a morass of lame documentaries, gratuitous TV appearances, exploitative books and the indefensible *Fever Pitch* (which played into every outsider's stereotype of Sox fans and even

494 Ironically, my friend Sully is just like Red in *Shawshank*—he's the man who knows how to get things. Plus, he actually made it on the outside without having to break his parole.

495 Count me among the Sox fans who weren't quite ready to start the 2005 baseball season. How could anything top what happened last October? As one of my buddies (who shall remain nameless) joked, "I feel like I woke up after having **a threesome with Natalie Portman and Scarlett Johansson**, only they're still asleep and I'm pounding the snooze alarm every nine minutes."

invented a few new ones). By the end of March, even I was tired of hearing about the Sox. Okay, that's a lie.[496] But it was pretty bad. For the most part, the owners and players were eating up the attention, failing the "act like you've been there before" test about as badly as it's ever been failed. On Sunday afternoon, my father and I were watching a feature where UPN's *Red Sox Report* followed C-list celebrity and author Johnny Damon around for the day. As Johnny traded barbs with Regis and Kelly, Dad suddenly piped, "Oh, God, we don't have a *chance* this season."

But did it matter? For instance, the front office made the precarious decision to tinker with a championship team, revamping the starting rotation, changing shortstops, overhauling the bench, and threatening last year's unique chemistry.[497] Like many Sox fans, I swallowed hard after some of the more questionable moves, reminding myself that they could go 0–162 for the next 10 years and it wouldn't change what happened last October.

At the same time, I *loved* last year's team. I wanted to see those same players (as many as possible) defend their title. Isn't that part of being a champion? During the first six games of the season—all on the road, with a whopping 10 newcomers on the Opening Day roster—you couldn't help but feel a wee bit detached. These weren't The Champs. These were Most of the Champs. There's a difference.

On Monday afternoon, we finally had the chance to pay our respects to last year's team. Walking around the city that morning, there was a giddy vibe in the air, like a crowd of people getting ready for a fireworks show (only for blocks on end). The number of Red Sox shirts and caps was simply staggering. And it wasn't limited to the fans. When I met some friends at a bar called Dillon's on Boylston Street, both bartenders were wearing Red Sox gear and the waitress was sporting an "I BELIEVE" shirt. These are the things that happen when your team wins the World Series. We headed to the park at 1:30, found our seats by 2:00 — my father was already there—and watched the Yankees finish batting practice. Once they cleared the field, members of the Boston Pops took their places behind second base, and then one of the announcers said a sentence that finished with the words, "...your defending world champion Boston Red Sox!" as everyone went bonkers.

496 A quick recap: Schilling and his family appeared on Barbara Walters' year-end special (complete with Schilling hobbling around on crutches in Fenway with sappy music playing in the background); Damon hit the talk-show circuit and wrote a book; Schilling appeared on *Celebrity Poker*; five Sox players appeared on *Queer Eye*; the owners paraded the championship trophy around like hunters showing off a deer's head; various Sox players posed for about a combined 1,700 magazine covers; and roughly 500 Sox books were released. On the bright side: nobody "accidentally" leaked an amateur porn of themselves; nobody was arrested or incarcerated; nobody showed up for spring training grotesquely overweight; Schilling and Damon did turn down appearances on *Extreme Makeover: Home Edition*, HBO's *Taxicab Confessions* and Playboy's *Totally Busted*; and every Sox fan took a vote and decided to agree that **the *Queer Eye* thing never happened**. You hear me? It NEVER happened. So on the aforementioned scale, if the '85 Bears were a 10 out of 10 and the '97 Marlins a 1 out of 10, I'd rank the Sox a solid 6 1/2.

497 Even though we're in Year One of a 500-year grace period, I thought

Here's what I wrote in my notebook to cover the next 10 minutes: "Pops play *2001 Space Odyssey*—banners dropping from Wall—WHOA!! 2004 COVERING WHOLE WALL! HOLY SHIT! OH MY GOD!"

This was our Zihuatanejo moment. People were hugging and high-fiving. People were fighting off tears. People were staring at the Wall in disbelief, like they were watching the spaceship land in *Close Encounters*. I was so overwhelmed, I can't even remember what song James Taylor performed next, or the names of every Red Sox legend on the field (Yaz, Rice, Fisk, Evans ...). Then the owners handed out the rings, our first chance to cheer last year's winning manager (Francona, recovering from a scary viral infection); last year's Superman (Big Papi, who should just change his last name to Kennedy at this point); one returning hero (Lowe, who seemed genuinely touched by the huge ovation); one surprise returning hero (the immortal Dave Roberts, who nearly brought the house down); every key player from last year's team with the exception of Cabrera (stuck in Anaheim) and Pedro (stuck in New York); one savior (Schilling, the last player introduced); and one walking reminder of everything that happened since 1918 (Johnny Pesky, the loudest ovation of them all).

I was doing fine until Pesky. Really, I was. For the next seven seconds, I made the Tom Cruise Memorial "I can't believe Goose is dead" Face before fighting it off. Others were less successful. On April 11, 2005, let the record show that it was extremely dusty in Fenway Park.

We watched everyone move to centerfield, the conquering brigade, with Ortiz and Pesky walking arm in arm. They raised the 2004 flag together, a red triangle whipping happily in the wind.**498** And just when the day couldn't get any better, the Sox made the ball-busting decision to introduce the entire Yankees lineup—BOOOOOOOOOOOOOOO!!!!!!!!!!!—highlighted by the glorious (and spontaneous) decision to *cheer* Rivera. You know, just to thank him for all the blown saves.**499** It was so funny, even Rivera started laughing and raising his arms in mock celebration, the best random moment of the day—at least until a moment of silence for Dick Radatz was cut short because someone screamed out, "A-ROD, YOU SUCK!"

See, that's the thing—we didn't just raise the banner, the Yankees had to stand there and watch. From my perch in Section 22, I snapped a digital photo of them lined up along the

they made two off-season moves too many. The first: Instead of spending $30 million to bring back Cabrera, they spent an extra $10 million for Edgar Renteria, which was somewhat confusing—like *Curb Your Enthusiasm* replacing Jeff Garlin after the first season with John Goodman because he's a slightly bigger name. Why even bother? The second: After Dave Roberts gently requested a trade because he wanted to play every day, the team sent him to San Diego, robbing the Sox of a proven fourth outfielder/late-inning baserunner/good clubhouse guy, as well as a walking reminder of the most important moment in Red Sox history and someone who would have been A GUARANTEED STANDING FUCKING OVATION EVERY TIME HE CAME TO FENWAY! **How could they trade Dave Roberts?** Why not just throw in the Bunker Hill Monument and the set from *Cheers* while you're at it? Strangely, I was ten times more upset about losing Roberts than losing Pedro (who received a ridiculous amount of money from the Mets, and that was fine, because it's all about beating the Yankees now and Pedro couldn't beat them).

third-base line, with the WORLD SERIES 2004 CHAMPIONS banner behind them. I'm going to blow it up, frame that sucker and hang it in my office like a deer's head. For my entire life, the Yankees kept getting the better of the Red Sox. Last October, everything changed. Yesterday, the moment was immortalized. And no matter what transpires this season, the Red Sox beat the Yankees, and the Red Sox won the World Series, and it happened, and we celebrated, and that's that.

Well, except for one thing.

Last September, I found out that I was going to be a father. Eventually, my wife and I learned that we were having a baby girl—I know, the irony—but during Game Three of the Yankee series, I didn't know what we were having. I just knew that I already felt terrible for Baby X. As the Yankees slugged their way to 19 runs and a potential sweep, I was slumped in my seat in Section 116, debating the merits of bringing another Red Sox fan into the world. Why do something so cruel to a little kid? Why dump nine decades of baggage on them? It seemed like an inherently selfish act, almost as if I were trying to drag them down with me. I kept imagining a little kid sobbing after their first October heartbreak—like me after the Bucky Dent game—knowing that the kid belonged to me, that I did it to them, that I could have saved them.

After the game, I asked my father about it: "Dad, if you had to do it over again, would you have raised me as a Red Sox fan?"

He thought about it for a few seconds.

"Yeah, probably. We were living here, who else would we have rooted for?"

Excellent point. Either you were born into the Red Sox, you were swept up by them, or you inherited them the same way people inherit baldness and high blood pressure. Inevitably, you passed them down to the next generation. You hoped everything would be worth it some day...even if all evidence pointed to the contrary. You hoped. You hoped. You hoped.

(Yes, I would be raising my child as a Red Sox fan.)[500]

Just 24 hours later, Roberts stole second base. Within 12 days, 86 years of baggage was swept away. I'm not claiming that I helped spawn The Miracle Fetus or anything, but our doctor determined that the baby was conceived shortly after the Cabrera trade. Maybe she didn't do as much as Schilling or Big Papi, but she definitely did more than Byung-Hyun Kim.

498 Since this was a feel-good column, I decided to ignore the wildly untalented Terry Cashman (that "Willie, Mickey and the Duke" singer) belting out that putrid Red Sox song as they raised the 2004 flag, which I think he wrote in a taxi on the way to the ballpark. **"This is for Lynn, and Rice, and Yaz..."** That's the song he came up with, a roll call with bad background music? I kept waiting for him to sing, "This is for my mortgage, now I get to pay it...this is for groceries, now I get to buy them..." Here's what really gets me: James Taylor was there! You're telling me that JT couldn't have sung something relevant or written something for the occasion? Do you think we'll ever have another situation in life where Terry Cashman gets the nod over James Taylor?

499 Including consecutive blown saves against Boston during the first week of the season.

Regardless, she's entering a world where the Red Sox aren't considered lovable losers, where we can watch playoff games without enduring dozens upon dozens of Babe Ruth references, where 35,000 people aren't secretly expecting the worst possible outcome in every big game. And when I carry her into Fenway some day, I'm pointing to the 2004 banner and telling her, "That was the team that changed everything."

Maybe she'll care, maybe she won't. But I have a feeling she will.

500 She was born on May 2, 2005, at 6:25p.m. We named her Zoe (although I did think about giving her a Muslim name) and by the time she was four weeks old, little Zoe owned approximately 235 pink Red Sox outfits. I think this is going to work.

ACKNOWLEDGMENTS

My wife looked over my shoulder when I was writing this and asked, "What are you doing?"

"I'm writing the acknowledgements for my book."

"Is that the thing in the back where the writer thanks everyone who helped out?"

"Yeah."

"Well, you better thank me and Zoe—you were an absolute pain in the ass when you were writing this book. In fact, put that in the book. Say that you work too hard and you don't know how your wife and daughter put up with you. And put us first. We deserve to be first. And put the dogs in, too. I think you walked them like three times in April and May."

Actually, she's right. So thanks to Kari, thanks to Zoe, and thanks to Rufus and the Dooze. I couldn't have written this book without them. Obviously.

And while we're here...

Thanks to my parents and steparents—some people are lucky to have one parent who believes in them. I have four.

Thanks to five teachers who made me believe that I could write for a living: Wally Ramsey, John Van Atta, Jim Brann, Mark Kramer, and the late Maurizio Vannicelli.

Thanks to Ray Fitzgerald, Leigh Montville, Peter Gammons, Bob Ryan, Norman Chad, Nick Hornby, the late Hunter S. Thompson, Mike Lupica, and (especially) William Goldman, all of whom made me believe that I could write from a fan's perspective and get away with it.

Thanks to everyone who gave me a chance on the way up: Gary Sulentic; David Lennon; Bob Holmes; Bob Sales; Vicki Kennedy; and especially John Wilpers.

Thanks to Mark Torpey, my old sports editor of the Boston Herald—if he had ever given me a chance, maybe I wouldn't have ended up starting the Sports Guy column and landing at ESPN. So thanks, Torps. I'm autographing a copy of this book and sending it to you with some sort of Lou Gorman/Jeff Bagwell joke.

Thanks to Kevin Jackson, Jay Lovinger, Michael Philbrick, and Michael Knisley from ESPN.com, who edited many of these columns from the past four years and always allowed me to write about whatever I wanted. Special thanks to KJ for imploring me to post a column on the morning after the Pats-Rams game—I will always be grateful for that kick in the ass.

Thanks to John Papanek for pumping me up during the 2004 Playoffs when I was impossibly burned out and dreading yet another 4 a.m. in front of the laptop.

Thanks to Jimmy Kimmel for his friendship and advice over the last three years, as well as teaching me that it's okay to bring your laptop into the bathroom if you're taking a dump. I never would have thought of that on my own.

Thanks to Gary Hoenig, Neil Fine, and Michael Solomon, all of whom couldn't have been more helpful while I was writing this book. Every single suggestion made sense.

Thanks to Jay Mandel and Cara Stein from William Morris, two of maybe 10 agents on the planet with whom I would ever feel comfortable. Somehow I found them both in a three-year span.

Thanks to Mark Shapiro, John Skipper, John Kosner, and Geoff Reiss for believing in me (both aesthetically and financially). Special thanks to Skipper for letting me pursue Kimmel's show and always making me feel like I have a home with ESPN.

Thanks to the great John Walsh, who rolled the dice with me in the spring of 2001 and evolved into a true friend and a mentor. I owe him at least 45 lunches and dinners. And counting.

Thanks to Jason Buggy, Joe House, Gus Ramsey, Kevin Hench, John O'Connell and Shawn Sullivan, six great friends who made their presence felt in this book at various points. While we're here, thanks to Geoff Gallo, Rob Stone, Chip Keane, Kurt Sanger, Steve Bishop, Jim Grady, John Hopp, John Richard, Mike Mendleson, Mark Dursin, Richard Gerardi, Mark Fanning, Nick Aieta, and Sal Iacono, all of whom allowed themselves to become characters in my columns at various points over the years. I don't think anyone has a funnier group of friends than I do. With the possible exception of Michael Jackson.

Thanks to the loyal readers back in the old BSG days for spreading the word. Out of everyone, I hope you enjoyed this book.

Most of all, thanks to Dave Roberts. We never should have traded you.

Bill Simmons
July 2005

ABOUT THE AUTHOR

Bill Simmons writes the popular Sports Guy column for ESPN.com's Page 2 and *ESPN The Magazine*. A former sports reporter for the *Boston Herald*, he founded the award-winning bostonsportsguy.com website in 1997 and was a writer for *Jimmy Kimmel Live*. He commutes between his home in Los Angeles and Fenway Park.